THE EARLY FURNITURE
OF FRENCH CANADA

JEAN PALARDY

the early furniture
OF FRENCH CANADA

TRANSLATED FROM THE FRENCH BY ERIC McLEAN

MACMILLAN OF CANADA
TORONTO

REPRINTED 1965
PAPERBACK EDITION FIRST PUBLISHED 1971
PRINTED IN CANADA BY ALGER PRESS LTD.
FOR THE MACMILLAN COMPANY OF CANADA LTD., 70 BOND STREET, TORONTO 2

I DEDICATE THIS BOOK
TO

THE MINISTRY OF CULTURAL AFFAIRS

OF THE

PROVINCE OF QUEBEC

AND TO

THE CANADA COUNCIL

with whose support this history of the early
furniture of French Canada has been published.

*

The second edition has been made possible by further
grants from the Ministry of Cultural Affairs of the Province
of Quebec and the Canada Council and by individual
donations.

CONTENTS

LIST OF SPECIAL PLATES

LATE EIGHTEENTH-CENTURY BEDROOM.

Original beams, roughcast wall, pinewood floor. Poster bed dating from late 18th c. or early 19th c., with *tour de lit*. Coffer, of English influence, with bracket base. Small chair *à la capucine*, multi-coloured *catalogne* carpet and sheepskin.

(House of Mr and Mrs Roger Burger, Belle-Rivière, St Scholastique, P.Q.).

COVER

EARLY NINETEENTH-CENTURY LOZENGE-DESIGN CHEST, IN ITS ORIGINAL COLOURS.

Chest, decorated with lozenges and with its original colour preserved. In the background : the reverse of a door with shaped panel. Pinewood floor and hooked rug.

w. 3' 6''	H. 2' 2½''	D. 1' 8''
107 cm	67 cm	51 cm

WOOD : pine

PROVENANCE : Saint-Gervais de Bellechasse, P.Q.

(Coll. Mrs Nettie Sharpe, St Lambert, P.Q.).

PAGE 34

MID EIGHTEENTH-CENTURY ARMOIRE, WITH VARIE-GATED DIAMOND POINT CARVINGS. ORIGINAL COLOURS.

Armoire, having two doors with prominent mould-ings and variegated diamond-point carvings. An undulating strip runs around the framing and panels. Original fische hinges and escutcheons. The cor-nice, base and feet were restored or replaced. There are traces of the original blue-green paint. Mid 18th c.

w. 4' 4¾''	H. 6' 3½''	D. 1' 9''
134 cm	192 cm	54 cm

WOOD : pine

(Coll. Mr and Mrs Paul Hawkins, Chambly, P.Q.).

PAGE 58

LATE EIGHTEENTH-CENTURY ARMOIRE, WITH SHAPED UPPER PANELS, IN ITS ORIGINAL COLOURS.

Armoire with two doors, each having three panels. The upper ones are shaped in the Louis XV manner. Original fische hinges. Original colours. Late 18th c.

w. 4' 3¼''	H. 6' 3¼''	D. 1' 7¾''
130 cm	191 cm	50 cm

(Coll. Mr and Mrs Stanley Cosgrove, Montreal).

PAGE 106

EIGHTEENTH-CENTURY LOW BUFFET, WITH TWO DOORS CARVED WITH THE CROSS OF ST ANDREW, IN THE MAN-NER OF THE SOUTHERN LOIRE VALLEY. 18th C.

A low buffet, reminiscent of those of the Southern Loire Valley and of the Guérande region. Original fische hinges. Top replaced. Original colours. Of Louis XIII derivation. 18th c.

w. 4' 2''	H. 3' 2½''	D. 1' 7¾''
127 cm	97 cm	50 cm

(Coll. Mr and Mrs H.C. Flood, St Sauveur des Monts, P.Q.).

PAGE 144

LATE EIGHTEENTH-CENTURY BEDROOM.

Room in a house built in 1775. Original tongue-and-groove pinewood floor. Furniture : bedstead with four turned posts (19th c.); low buffet, having two drawers and panels carved with diamond points (original colour); peasant armchair, with cham-fered legs and elm-bark seat; small chair *à la capu-cine;* doll's cradle, carved with geometric designs. On the low buffet : pine casket, with lock; small wooden horse; tin candlestick.

(House of Mrs Nettie Sharpe, St Lambert, P.Q.).

PAGE 184

LIVING-ROOM OF A MODERN HOUSE WITH TRADITIONAL FURNITURE.

Living-room of a modern house, inspired by an old interior. The woodwork and beams come from an old house. All the furniture was stripped, including the corner cabinet, originating from the old Presbytery of St Louis de Lotbinière. Furni-ture : *os de mouton* armchair, with padded armrests; armchair, from the old church of Louiseville, Maskinongé; tables with curved legs. Hooked rugs. On the wall : a rug with *appliqué* and naive designs.

(House of Miss Barbara Richardson, St Agathe des Monts, P.Q.).

PAGE 228

EARLY NINETEENTH-CENTURY ARMOIRE, DECORATED WITH VARIEGATED GEOMETRIC DESIGNS.

Marriage armoire, in folk-art style, with door panels in the Adam manner. Numerous *appliqué* hearts decorate its surface. Rosettes, sinusoids, gouge inci-sions, grooves, festoons in the cornice, thumb-nail and *dents de loup* carvings profusely decorate this piece. Parallel grooves recall those found on some Bresse armoires and even on Huron or Iroquois ceramics. One of the most interesting Canadian armoires. Original hinges. Early 19th c.

W. 4' 3¼"   H. 6' ¼"   D. 1' 7"
130 cm   184 cm   48 cm

WOOD : pine

PROVENANCE : Sainte-Geneviève de Pierrefonds, P.Q.

(Coll. Mr and Mrs Peter Laing, Montreal).

PAGE 268

DOORS FROM A LATE EIGHTEENTH-CENTURY ARMOIRE, IN THE LOUIS XV MANNER. ORIGINAL COLOURS.

Doors taken from an armoire, with shaped panels, in the Louis XV manner. Although deteriorated, the original colours have been preserved and the panels are decorated with flowers and a heart pierced by an arrow.

WOOD : pine

(Coll. Mr and Mrs A.F. Culver, Pointe au Pic, P.Q.).

PAGE 330

COMMON ROOM.

Common room of the old Marcil house, built in 1775 and formerly belonging to the parish of Lon-gueuil. Furniture : original built-in armoire, with shaped panels. *Habitant* armchair, children's chairs; salt-box; lanterns; Betty lamps; *catalogne* carpet and hooked rugs. The original colour of every piece of furniture has been preserved.

(House of Mrs Nettie Sharpe, St Lambert, P.Q.).

PAGE 362

EIGHTEENTH-CENTURY KITCHEN.

Eighteenth-century kitchen, Montreal. Fireplace and accessories : fire-dogs, fire-tongs, a pair of bellows, iron kettle, iron grills, tripods, roasting spit activated by a dog placed in cylinder fixed to the wall (reconstruction). Bucket-benches; spinning-wheel; butter-churn; cauldrons; kettle; salt-box; lanterns. Furniture : two-tiered buffet, carved with diamond points; chair-table or hutch-table; armchair, with turned feet and baluster-back, in the Louis XIII manner; chair with spindle-back; chair of *Ile d'Orléans* type. *Catalognes* and hooked rugs.

(Reconstruction of the kitchen, Château de Rame-zay, Montreal).

PAGE 380

PREFACE BY MARIUS BARBEAU

Jean Palardy's survey of French Canadian furniture, the masterly quality of which I should like to acknowledge here, is the first complete study published on the subject. As such, it constitutes a valuable addition to the existing literature dealing with the arts and crafts of French Canada.

An artist in his earlier days, Jean Palardy used to paint during the summers in the region of Baie Saint-Paul, on the north shore of the St Lawrence, sixty miles below Quebec. I first met him in 1932 when I was collecting folksongs and tales, being engaged in research for the National Museum on the folklore of the very picturesque region of Charlevoix county. I was so impressed by his intelligence and powers of observation that I invited him to become my assistant in the study of the arts and crafts of the district.

Together we went through every village from door to door, attic to attic, barn to barn, examining all the old things which had been stored away — spinning wheels, skein-winders, warping-frames, looms, commodes, chairs, benches, chests, hooked rugs, tufted bedspreads (*boutonnues*), *catalogne*, flax combs, old homespun garments, bonnets, toys, and rustic pottery. In the stables and out-buildings, we found wooden ploughs, field rollers, harrows, sleighs, carts, and those special Canadian conveyances, the *carriole* and *cabarouet*. Here and there a few windmills and watermills were still to be seen, and also those huge sloping-disc treadmills for driving threshing machines.

In a country where novelties take precedence over the things from the past, the need for research was most urgent, especially since widespread demolition and fire continue their destructive work.

When our survey was completed, Jean Palardy continued to study the things around him with a heightened sensibility and began to collect the best pieces he could find for furnishing his house at Petite Rivière Saint-François. He went on to become a real collector of French Canadian antiques and introduced many of his friends to the pleasure of owning armoires, chairs, commodes and wood carvings. He developed his wide interests in French Canadian art and produced many documentary films during and after the Second World War.

The vogue of collecting exquisite regional pieces has spread rapidly. Today it is fashionable to search for old furniture in every nook, and dealers scour the countryside on both sides of the St Lawrence for the booty coveted by their customers.

Fortunately for us, Jean Palardy on his own initiative undertook this study of the finest examples of French Canadian furniture, with the help of the Canada Council and the Ministry of Cultural Affairs for the Province of Quebec.

He was not content to let these works remain anonymous but had the enterprise to seek out the regional origins and the names of craftsmen, and to identify the woods used. He searched through the French provinces from which the early French Canadians had come and discovered here and there resemblances between the French prototypes and the furniture of the St Lawrence Valley. In France he consulted folklore specialists and experts including Monsieur Rivière, Director, and Mlle Suzanne Tardieu, both of the Museum of Folk Arts and Traditions, Monsieur Delafosse, Director of the Archives of the Department of the " Charente-Maritime " at La Rochelle, and many others who all welcomed and helped him.

This book is the fruit of the author's intensive research and admirable effort. I wish it the great success it deserves, in France as well as in Canada. It will contribute to the restoration of a healthy appreciation of these arts and crafts, which together with the folksongs, folktales, and legends of Canada have been neglected until recently.

I hope we may soon see an official body established at both Quebec and Ottawa for the preservation of these incomparable cultural resources which have been passed on to us by " La France Royale ". In collaboration with the National Museum and the Museum of the Province of Quebec, researchers like Jean Palardy, with their extensive knowledge, could make a valuable contribution to such a useful national agency, giving it a genuine impetus, under the aegis of the Fleur de Lys.

MARIUS BARBEAU
D. LITT. (HON.) OXON., F.R.S.C.

PREFACE BY GEORGES HENRI RIVIÈRE

My old friend Marius Barbeau has drawn attention to the merits of this important, long-awaited book by Jean Palardy. I, for my part, should like to expand upon the features common to both Canadian and French traditional furniture, which the author has demonstrated resemble one another almost fraternally, excepting, of course, the specifically Canadian variations.

Traditional furniture " was at its height between 1785 and 1820 " in Canada — almost at the same time as in France. It is touching to think that the Canadian branch produced its finest French flower after being lopped from the tree.

Peace brought to both countries a prosperity that included the peasants, and with peace came a development of the finest styles. Prosperity brought the peasants closer to the bourgeoisie in Canada than it did in France. Evidence of this can be seen in Canadian traditional furniture, particularly in the rapid adoption by the Canadian peasant of the typically bourgeois chair and commode and even the corner cabinet.

The open-hearth fire was quickly replaced by the stove in Canada as the winters were so much more severe. The violin-shaped clock, which was popular among French peasants, was unknown by the Canadian peasant, but this was simply because it was introduced only at the end of the eighteenth century in France. The repertory of Canadian peasant furniture is the same as its French counterpart, except for a few differences that I have briefly indicated.

The old-fashioned chest was placed for a time at the foot of the bed. The armoire had pride of place in the bedroom and formed part of the dowry — its shape remained more or less the same as that found in the west of France, notably the Nantes-Bordeaux region from which a great many early settlers came. The built-in armoire appeared in both countries. The two-tiered buffet was as widespread in Canada as in France — it was equally familiar in both lands in its mature form but the glazed form was influenced in Canada by English and Dutch styles, and was not found in the homes of French peasants. The dresser, as in France, was the show-case for the finest household china. It is interesting that the folding table as found in several French provinces, especially Burgundy, was preferred in Canada to the long table, which better suited the traditional eating customs of the French family. High stools and benches had their place but the four-poster bed and the master's armchair were the prominent pieces. Dough-boxes were to be found everywhere, as in France, indicating that bread was made at home. Spinning-wheels developed along similar lines in both countries — both the large, hand-operated wheel worked while standing, and the small pedal-operated one worked while seated. Hearth accessories and utensils were the same in both France and Canada.

13

The similarity in the sequence of styles in France and Canada is most striking — Louis XIII with its diamond points, the *Régence* and Louis XV styles with their *rocailles* and shaped lines, fashions which appeared in Canada some time after the French prototypes were introduced, and mixed styles which left room for creativity. There were two slight differences however — at the beginning of the colony, there was less emphasis on the popular geometric designs (although as Jean Palardy points out they were occasionally used on homemade cradles and caskets); later, English styles had a strong influence in Canada.

Oak was preferred at first for fine pieces in Canada, as it understandably was in France for a much longer period. However, the light indigenous woods soon became fashionable in Canada, but in France such woods were used only in the later periods.

The traditional furniture of both France and Canada was made by joiners working in solid wood. In Canada the woodworkers continued French traditions and techniques. In both countries there were itinerant woodworkers. Trade guilds and journeymen's associations were not formed in Canada, largely because of the more liberal social structure, although craftsmen's fraternities existed (*La Confrérie de Sainte-Anne*), evidence of the Christian faith as also found in the craftsmen's associations of the *ancien régime*.

There are also parallel attitudes to be found in the period of the decline of traditional furniture in both countries. In France as in Canada, there is evidence of indifference, vandalism, pseudo-rustic styles in bad taste; but also there are efforts by enthusiastic collectors to study the history and evolution of furniture and to win respect for the heritage of each country. There is also the ever increasing need to preserve the best specimens in central museums.

Some time ago, Marius Barbeau rescued from oblivion the wonderful treasury of folk songs of French Canada. Now, Jean Palardy has done the same for another part of Canada's heritage, and this deserves to be equally known and appreciated. They both illustrate a glorious culture common to our two countries.

GEORGES HENRI RIVIÈRE

CHIEF CURATOR, MUSEUM OF THE FOLK ARTS AND TRADITIONS OF FRANCE.
DIRECTOR, INTERNATIONAL COUNCIL OF MUSEUMS.

FOREWORD

Until now, no serious study has been undertaken on the regional or traditional furniture of French Canada. With the exception of some brief observations in the accounts of early travellers and a few recent magazine articles, no one seems to have taken the trouble to describe the style of this furniture or to publicize its merits.

Marius Barbeau was the first to begin to study, classify, and collect the furniture of French Canadian churches in 1925. At the same time, a small number of American and English Canadian collectors began to be interested in this furniture and started to collect it.

It is sad that no one from the Province of Quebec was interested in our national heritage at an earlier time and that this French Canadian craft was completely ignored until 1925. However, there were extenuating circumstances for this ignorance or lack of interest, in that four-fifths of the furniture of our ancestors was destroyed by fire or vandalism. Therefore, when I began this work there were neither textbooks nor monographs on the subject that I could consult. Everything had to be created.

Four methods of observation for the analysis of traditional furniture have been outlined by Mr Georges Henri Rivière, Curator of the Museum of Folk Arts and Traditions of France.

The first is the direct method : a study of furniture in its actual state, wherever it might be found. This is primarily a descriptive study and an analysis of the shapes, a study of finishing techniques and ornamentation.

The second could be called socio-ethnographic. It consists of studying the furniture in its social milieu. The rural society, more than any other, has survived the great changes which have marked the evolution of French Canada.

The third is the technological method, which consists of observing the craftsmen who still possess the traditional techniques and skills in the making of furniture — methods often passed on by their fathers. I have found such observations invaluable because these woodworkers, whose craft is transmitted through several generations, explained why furniture was made in one way rather than another at a particular time, and why certain Canadian woods were used in preference to others.

Finally, there is the historical method, which consists of searching archives, inventories of estates drawn up upon the owner's death, marriage contracts, apprenticeship papers, building contracts, parish account books, craftsmen's account books, monastery ledgers and records, seminary registers and *Intendants*' memoranda and correspondence.

The study of furniture in its rural setting is very valuable despite frequent modifications and changes in location. The examination of each piece in detail — its structure, style, and method of making — is also extremely useful, but it is the historical method which is fundamental and which complements the other three. In spite of all research and observations, our knowledge in this field is limited, and there are many questions which cannot be answered with absolute certainty. One of the reasons for this is that the evolution of our traditional furniture has been very slow, and there has been an enormous number of styles and variants which appeared in the Canadian rural communities sometimes after a time lapse of as much as a century after their creation in the mother country. Often a village craftsman would see an early piece of furniture from France in the *seigneur's* manor-house, and would then try to reproduce the proportions and the details from memory.

In most cases, it is difficult, if not impossible, to fix the date of origin exactly for the furniture illustrated in this book. I have been careful to avoid any false precision, especially as

Canadian woodworkers did not sign their pieces, unlike the Parisian cabinet-makers and some of the provincial woodworkers. In a few exceptional cases, however, both the name of the Canadian woodworker and the date of payment for the piece made are recorded. It is therefore difficult to be absolutely certain about precise dates, and so after going into the matter as thoroughly as possible, I have decided to use approximate dates — late 17th c., early 18th c., mid 18th c...

In this book I have tried to introduce some order into this part of our inheritance. The work is limited to Canadian furniture in French traditional manner, from the seventeenth century to the first part of the nineteenth century, when it ceased to exist.

It has been my aim to gather together the most representative types of French Canadian furniture as evidence of our ancestors' way of life. I have chosen photographs illustrating the most characteristic examples which have escaped wanton destruction and the ravages of fire, but I have also included a number of curious pieces which represent an unusual combination of different styles. These items were influenced by English, Dutch, New England and American styles at different times. There are also other more recent pieces whose forms and naive design have a touching appeal.

I have not mentioned Nova Scotia, which must have exercised some influence on French Canada, simply because I have not been able to make a distinction between the furniture of Nova Scotia and that of England or New England, their characteristics being almost identical. I have not included certain pieces of furniture of the seventeenth and eighteenth centuries, such as special types of food-lockers, *tombeau* beds, folding beds and chairs, children's bedsteads, gossip chairs *(caqueteuses)* and the *bergère* armchairs, as I have been able to find no trace of them except in the records which indicate that they existed.

A description and a comparative study of each piece of furniture will be found in the *Catalogue Raisonné*. It includes details of ornamentation, the provincial origins of the designs in France, styles which have been borrowed, and foreign influences including those of England, America, Holland, and even of the Canadian Indians. It gives the characteristics, transpositions, and Canadian versions of imported designs, as well as a number of historical details about furniture mentioned in archives, or having a family history transmitted through several generations. The source of the piece and the exact place in which it was found often provide precious information on certain regional characteristics, even though it may have been moved so often that it is found far from its point of origin. The period in which the piece of furniture was made is given together with its present condition, any restoration which may have been done, the wood of which it was made, its dimensions, and the name of the present owner. I have also given, in footnotes, the original French quotations and their sources from records of the seventeenth and eighteenth centuries.

I have spent a great deal of time on the preparation of this book, in order to place my researches at the disposal of all who love the folk traditions of our country, whether connoisseur or amateur. I know how fascinating it is, when one is about to acquire a piece of furniture which will become a part of one's daily life, to learn its origin and history and the process of evolution which led to its particular form. I hope that this work will meet the needs of all those who seek information on the subject, although I do not claim to provide an answer to all their questions.

It is also my hope that the book will enlighten those who are beginning to take an interest in our heritage and in the Canadian civilization of the past, of which we have reason to be proud. A people which neglects its heritage loses its individuality. It will also lose its dignity and its will to survive as a people. The great nations throughout history have been those that nourish their traditions, take pride in their past, and are capable of enjoying in the present the glory and beauty of an earlier age.

J. P.

ACKNOWLEDGEMENTS

I wish first of all to thank the Ministry of Cultural Affairs of the Province of Quebec and the Canada Council whose generous support has made this book possible. I am profoundly grateful to the many people who have contributed in various ways to the preparation of this book, especially to M. Marius Barbeau, the well-known ethnologist and folklore scholar, long associated with the National Museum of Canada, and a pioneer in the study of the folk arts and traditions of French Canadians and Canadian Indians. It was M. Barbeau who made me aware of the richness of Canada's past. For two years I had the privilege of working with him, collecting folk songs and tales, oral evidence of traditional crafts, ritual customs and popular culture. My subsequent contacts with M. Barbeau have always been rewarding experiences.

I am particularly honoured by the keen interest which His Excellency, Major-General Georges P. Vanier, Governor General of Canada, has shown in this project.

M. Georges-Émile Lapalme, the first to hold the office of Minister of Cultural Affairs of the Province of Quebec, fully understood the need for a study on this aspect of Canadian culture — a need evident not only in Canada but also abroad. I am grateful for his support.

I am deeply indebted to Mrs Richard R. Costello, Mrs Howard W. Pillow and Mr Charles W. Palmer for their constant encouragement and friendship and their very real help.

I was also encouraged by Guy Frégault, Deputy Minister of Cultural Affairs of the Province of Quebec; Jean Octeau, Executive Secretary attached to the Ministry of Cultural Affairs of the Province of Quebec; the Very Reverend Father Georges-Henri Lévesque, O.P., and Eugène Bussière, respectively Vice-President and Associate Director of the Canada Council; René Arthur, Chief Assistant to the Prime Minister of the Province of Quebec; Robert Élie, Cultural Counsellor to the Delegation of Quebec in Paris; the late Cleveland Morgan, Honorary President of the Museum of Fine Arts of Montreal; René Garneau, Minister-Counsellor to the Canadian Embassy in Paris; Gérard Morisset, Curator of the Quebec Provincial Museum; Luc Lacourcière, Director of the Archives of Folklore, Laval University; Jacques Rousseau, Professor at Laval University and Associate Professor at the Sorbonne; the late F. St. George Spendlove, former Curator of the Canadiana Collection of the Royal Ontario Museum, Toronto; the late Louis Carrier, former Curator of the Château de Ramezay, Montreal; E.P. Richardson, sometime Director of the Art Institute of Detroit and now Director of the Henry Francis Du Pont Winterthur Museum; the painter Jean-Paul Lemieux, and the author Hugh MacLennan.

My sincere thanks are due to the talented photographer, Évariste Desparois, who interpreted my exacting requirements with great patience and skill; to Eric McLean, music critic of the " Montreal Star ", a fervent amateur of French Canadian culture, who collaborated closely with me in translating the text into English; and to Mr F.J.B. Watson, Director of the Wallace Collection, London, for his valuable comments on the English text.

Many people supplied me with miscellaneous information, placed archives, documents and collections at my disposal and showed a lively interest in my work. I am especially grateful to Mrs May Cole, Mme Claude Bertrand, Mme Colette P. Loranger, Miss Barbara Richardson and Dr Herbert Schwarz, who are all enthusiastic collectors; Mrs George V. Ferguson; Mme Constance Garneau; Gerald Budner; Antoine Roy, archivist of the Province of Quebec; Robert-Lionel Séguin, archivist attached to the Inventory of Works of Art of the Province of Quebec; Mlle Marie Baboyant, librarian at the Gagnon Collection of the City of Montreal; Olivier le Fuel, *Expert,* Paris; Henri Paul and Louis Jaques, photographers; the archivists of many convents of Quebec; Hubert Plomer, cabinet-maker; Georges Dionne, chief foreman of E.J. Maxwell and Company, Montreal; and several antique dealers, Mrs Nettie Sharpe, Bertrand Baron, Roger Burger, Nathan Davies, Antoine Prévost and John L. Russell.

I am also indebted to S. Breitman and M. E. Booth, antique dealers of Montreal, for their interest and expert help in determining the provenance of a large number of the pieces of furniture illustrated in this book. I would like to express my gratitude to the museums, religious orders and collectors who gave me every possible facility in my research.

I remember with great pleasure the welcome I received in France from the curators of the provincial museums, and in particular from M. Stany Gauthier, Curator of the Musée d'Art Populaire, Nantes; from M. Pierre Quarré, Curator of the Musée des Beaux-Arts, Dijon; and from M. Jean Lapeyre, Curator of the Dieppe and Fécamp Museums.

My special thanks are due to M. Georges Henri Rivière, Chief Curator of the Musée des Arts et Traditions Populaires de France and Director of the International Council of Museums, as well as to his assistant, Mlle Suzanne Tardieu who was kind enough to give the manuscript its preliminary reading. They devoted much time to extending my knowledge of the regional furniture of France and showed a keen interest in this study of the furniture of a distant French province, silent evidence of the traditional crafts inherited from the mother country long ago.

This revised second edition, supplemented by an index, has been made possible by further grants from the Ministry of Cultural Affairs of the Province of Quebec and the Canada Council, and by generous donations from Mr John McConnell, Mr Bartlett Morgan, Mr G. Hamilton Southam, Mr D.R. McMaster, M. Paul Bienvenu and Mr Charles S. Band.

I would like to pay tribute to the Prime Minister of the Province of Quebec, M. Jean Lesage, and to the Minister of Cultural Affairs, M. Pierre Laporte, who both encouraged and facilitated the appearance of a second edition aimed at the wider dissemination and study of an aspect of our national heritage and the preservation of Canadian traditions.

May I express my sincere thanks to all those who have taken an interest in this book.

INTRODUCTION

THE GREAT ADVENTURE

The first French colonists arrived in Canada at the beginning of the seventeenth century. These pioneers came with the intention of settling permanently in New France and always brought a few craftsmen with them.

Marc Lescarbot, lawyer, poet and colonist, who arrived in 1606 with the expedition of De Monts, Champlain and Poutrincourt, recorded the need of artisans which the new colony had. " It was enough that we had a number of joiners, carpenters, masons, stone-cutters, locksmiths, tool-makers, plank sawyers, seamen ... who carried on with their occupations, for which they were greatly esteemed and rewarded. "[1] These craftsmen built the first *habitations* in Canada at Ile Sainte-Croix and Port Royal.

Two years later, in 1608, Champlain landed at Quebec and built the first *habitation* on the shores of " the Great River of St Lawrence. " The description he left of that first house at the foot of Cape Diamond is accurate enough, but he made no mention of how the rooms were furnished. No one seems to have attached much importance to furniture, which was very rudimentary and functional in that age of discovery, benches, tables, and chests being made on the spot as required.

The first concern of the early French settlers in Canada was to cope with the natural dangers which the new country presented — the cold and the possibility of an attack by Indians. A fort with dry ditches and a drawbridge, and good warm houses had to be built with the least possible delay.

French colonists arrived in small numbers at first, and although France and England were at peace, the Kirke brothers besieged Quebec, taking advantage of the French preoccupation with the crushing of the last Huguenot stronghold at La Rochelle. The capture of Quebec by the Kirkes in 1629 interrupted the flow of immigrants from France until the Treaty of St Germain-en-Laye in 1632. Champlain then returned to Canada with permanent settlers and advised

(1) Lescarbot, Marc. *Histoire de la Nouvelle-France.* Paris, 1618, p 546.

Louis XIII of the new colony's need for a wide variety of settlers to develop the land rather than to engage exclusively in the fur trade. French settlers continued to arrive from 1632 to 1759, despite the numerous conflicts with the fur-trading companies.

The early colonists sailed from the ports of Honfleur, Rouen, Dieppe, La Rochelle and Bordeaux in ships hardly larger than present-day St Lawrence schooners. These ships were heavily laden with cargo and passengers — churchmen, soldiers, and civil servants in the cabins on the upper deck; colonists in the hold, surrounded by tools, farming implements, ironware, casks, sacks and luggage, food supplies and livestock. They brought with them only one chest containing their clothing, along with a palliasse, a few personal belongings, and bags containing their tools, a few kitchen utensils and some seed.

The crossing lasted from two to three months. Often, after sailing for a month, the colonists would be forced back to the Spanish coast by a storm. Sometimes the ship would be wrecked and all lives lost. If they succeeded in making the crossing they still had to face the fog, icebergs and floes of the Grand Banks of Newfoundland and the Gulf of St Lawrence. They were never sure of reaching the new colony and prayed at all times that God would protect them from the dangers which arose each day. Once the vessel reached Tadoussac, the travellers sometimes had to wait two to three weeks for a north-east wind which would allow them to continue to Quebec. For these brave pioneers, the journey across the Atlantic was an adventure and an ordeal, it was inevitably hazardous, full of danger and incident, and always involved a large element of risk.

The new arrivals thought of the colony as a great land of dark and threatening forests where savages hid ready to massacre them in their fields by day, or in their homes by night. These brave settlers seeking their livelihood in the great forests of New France were certainly strong and sturdy, having survived wars, famines and epidemics in the old world before undertaking the hardships of the voyage. The men were qualified carpenters, smiths, masons and farmers, and the women sufficiently strong to raise large families and help their husbands to work the land. They left behind them a temperate climate and had to adapt themselves to a country in which the winter was very long and extremely cold, where spring was often little more than a prolongation of winter, where summer, although limited to two months, was almost tropical, and where an unseasonable frost in autumn could destroy the work of a year in one night. They came from many different provinces of France, being recruited by the *seigneurs* to whom the king had granted domains in New France. The *seigneur* apportioned his settlers a section of his land in tenure, and in exchange, they had certain obligations — seigneurial rents, tithes on the grain which was ground at the seigneurial mill, and military service in time of war. However, in Canada there was a much more flexible social organization than in France.

A short time ago I met three families who lived like their ancestors of the seventeenth and eighteenth centuries. These families were related and each had more than ten children. They all lived on a small " concession " in the mountains of Charlevoix county. They fed themselves on dairy products, curds, salted pork, fish and game, cucumbers and pumpkins. They grew their own wheat and rye which they had ground at the grist mill, and baked their own bread in their outdoor ovens. They carried no money in their pockets, and lived by barter, exchanging cords of wood or spruce gum for tea, sugar, salt, molasses, and spices, the only provisions which they did not produce themselves. The women spun the wool of their sheep and wove flannel for their clothes and blankets. They also fashioned shoes and " Canadian boots " from the leather of their own animals. Their houses were remarkably clean. The wooden floors were painted orange and covered with *catalogne* or home-made rag carpets with multi-coloured streaks, or hooked rugs with original patterns and subjects. Their traditional furniture was perhaps rustic, but it was solid, functional, and beautiful. These families were simple, honest, and God-fearing, and sang all day as they worked. Their daily life followed the exact pattern of their ancestors.

The first pioneers brought only a chest containing their clothes as it was impossible to bring their furniture from France. However, the governors, high church dignitaries, government officials, and ladies who came to found hospitals and convents, brought some pieces including dome-topped chests and church furniture that the small number of local woodworkers could not make, having neither the ability nor the time as they were too busy building houses.

Some of the first pieces of furniture were sent from La Rochelle on the ship *Le Saint Jean* in 1634, but water entered the hold in a bad storm and the ship was forced to return to La Rochelle. The first reference to furniture destined for Canada is found in an inventory of the " state of the merchandise " on board the *Saint-Jean*, dated January 1635.

> " Item 51 containing two shipments of dome-topped chests, covered with red leather and painted, in two bales which have not come unwrapped and which can be assumed not to have been damaged in the least — these cost 46 livres. " " Item 61, containing a tabernacle and six chandeliers with a box to hold them, which are to be found undamaged and set at cost price, 33 livres 12 sols. "[1]

The cargo also contained a large number of farming implements. Other furniture was brought from France in 1639 by the first nursing sisters who founded the *Hôtel-Dieu* in Quebec, Mother Marie de Saint Ignace, Mother Anne de Saint Bernard, and Mother Marie de Saint Bonaventure. They had to travel upstream from Tadoussac to Quebec in a barque while their belongings stayed on board the ship, " ...we found four beautiful rooms and two smaller ones, but the only furniture was a kind of table, or rather a plank supported by four sticks, and two benches of the same sort, but we thought highly of them ... nor were we better supplied with beds, having left all our equipment on the ship. So we begged a kindly priest to have the goodness to send us a few tree branches on which to sleep, which he did willingly, but they were so infested by caterpillars that we were completely covered by them. "[2]

In 1639 Mme de la Peltrie, foundress of the Ursulines of Quebec, embarked at Dieppe for New France, accompanied by Mother Marie de l'Incarnation, Mother Marie de Saint-Joseph, Mother Sainte-Croix and Mlle Charlotte Barré, her servant and " ...not being able to find space for the baggage of her little colony on the ships which were to leave in the spring, because she had spoken about it too late, she had a ship fitted out at her own expense, and filled it with provisions, furniture and other necessities, to the sum of 8 000 livres. "[3]

In 1644-5 *Messieurs les Associés de Montréal* helped Mlle Jeanne Mance to obtain furniture for the chapel of the *Hôtel-Dieu* of Montreal which she had founded.

Later, on the death of Mlle Jeanne Mance, furniture from France was included in the inventory of her belongings, "...a cabinet of ebony with two drawers, an upper drawer and a lid that could be locked... "[4] and in another inventory " ...in the room of the said widow St Helaine... a cabinet of ebony valued at 58 livres... "[5] These were the small cabinets designed in the Italian Renaissance style which were no doubt brought from France.

A few other inventories mention French furniture, " ... an armoire with four doors, made of walnut from France... ".[6] There is also the example of the furniture belonging to M. de Lamothe-Cadillac, founder of the city of Detroit, which was probably brought to Detroit by canoe from Montreal. " Two little credence tables made of walnut from France closing with

(1) B5654 No. 102. Archives of La Charente Maritime, communicated by Mr Marcel Delafosse, archivist.
(2) Juchereau de Saint-Ignace, Mère. *Les Annales de l'Hôtel-Dieu de Québec*, Quebec, 1939, p. 19.
(3) *Les Ursulines de Québec depuis leur établissement jusqu'à nos jours*. Vol. I, Quebec, 1878.
(4) A J M, I O A. Inventaire des biens meubles, tiltres et Enseignemens de deffunte Damoiselle Jeanne Mance vivante administratrice de l'hospital de Montréal, le 19ᵉ Juin 1673. Greffe Basset.
(5) A J M, I O A. Inventaire des biens de la succession de feu Jacques Le Moyne, Escuyer Sieur de Ste Helene, 1691. Greffe Basset.
(6) A J M, I O A. Inventaire à la Requeste de jacque Millet des biens de Feu Charles Rinville et De Louise Lesueur Sa femme, le 22ᵉ 9bre 1757, à Chambly. Greffe Grisé.

a swivel ...an altar made of walnut from France, with its platforms, two steps, and a tabernacle with its lock. ''[1] Towards the end of the seventeenth century, there was no longer any need to import such furniture as French artisans had arrived in sufficient numbers to supply the demand and the colonists were sufficiently established to free the woodworkers from the task of building houses.

THE FRENCH CANADIAN HOUSE

The very first houses built by the settlers in the heart of the forest were only rudimentary, temporary shelters. They were constructed in a few days from spruce or cedar logs squared with an axe and laid one on top of the other, and were replaced, as soon as the forest was cleared, by much more spacious solid houses built of local stone.

The houses were usually built near one another. A system of dividing the land settled by the *habitants* had been adopted from the beginning of the colony. Concessions were generally made measuring 3 *arpents* in width, most often along the banks of the St Lawrence River, and 60 to 90 *arpents* in length, stretching back from the river. In this country of wide, open spaces, the settlers felt themselves less isolated living near one another. They could quickly band together when attacked by their great enemies, the Iroquois, who repeatedly raided the settlements for more than sixty years. Cedarwood fences separating each field prevented the snow from being blown away and kept it in the fields until the spring thaw when it formed excellent nourishment for the land. They also prevented the farm animals from wandering onto neighbours' land and ruining the growing crops.

The Venerable Mother Marie de l'Incarnation described the houses around Quebec in 1644 when the population was not more than 200 " ... those of the *habitants* except two or three, are half-timber and stone buildings. ''[2] These houses were in the Norman style, decorated with sections of exposed timbers filled in with rubble and lime-mortar similar to those still preserved in the older part of Rouen. This type of house apparently enjoyed only a brief popularity in Canada as the extreme climate of autumn rain, winter frost and spring thaw accelerated the disintegration of the exterior lime-mortar which involved too frequent repairs, as the early settlers soon discovered.

The French Canadian house had walls two to four feet thick. They were really double walls made of outcrop stone from their fields or beaches, held together with a generous amount of mortar, and covered on the outside with roughcast, which was white-washed twice a year. The space between the double walls was filled with rubble and mortar. The gables were very steep and suggest those of the houses in Brittany, Normandy and the western provinces of France. The main entrance door was rarely centred, and there were many windows including one or two side windows on the ground floor and two smaller ones in the attic.

When the colony began, the roofs were generally made of vertically overlapping planks or thatch, but these soon gave way to cedarwood shingles. These houses had either a double chimney in the centre, or a single chimney at each end. The windows were framed externally with dressed stone or wood embedded in the masonry.

The front door led straight into a large common room, the walls and chimney of which were covered with roughcast. The floor was made of wide spruce or pine planks and the bedroom of vertical tongue-and-groove boards. A panelled or half-glazed door opened into these rooms. The ceiling, *le plancher d'haut* as it was called in French Canada, was supported by rough-hewn beams. A small narrow stairway without a rail was placed against one wall. This led to the attic which was always closed by a trap-door.

(1) B R H. Inventaire des meubles et immeubles et autres effaits appartenant à M. de Lamothe Cadillac, gouverneur de la Louisianne, laissés entre les mains du Sr Pierre Roy, habitant de Détroit. (25 aoust 1711), 1918, p. 24.
(2) *Lettres historiques de la Vénérable Mère Marie de l'Incarnation*. Paris, 1681, p. 384.

Quebec region. 17th c.

Quebec region. Hipped roof. 17th c.

Montreal region. Lower pitched roof. 18th c.

Quebec region. Two-storied house with verandas. Late 18th *and* 19th c.

Fig. 1 - *FOUR TYPES OF FRENCH CANADIAN HOUSES.* - *All the family activities took place in the common room, which in the early days of the colony occupied the whole of the ground floor. Bedrooms were made by the construction of pine-wood partitions at the end of the seventeenth century, and the parlour (shown on the left, below) was partitioned off from the common room at the end of the eighteenth and during the nineteenth century.*

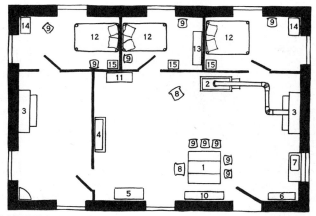

Fig. 2 - *THE COMMON ROOM AND OTHER ROOMS.* MID 18th c. - 19th c. - *1. Folding table; 2. Stove; 3. Chimneys; 4. Two-tiered buffet; 5. Low buffet; 6. Bucket bench; 7. Sink; 8. Armchairs; 9. Chairs; 10. Bench; 11. Coffer; 12. Beds; 13. Armoire; 14. Commodes; 15. Wash-stands.*

THE PATTERN OF DAILY LIFE

Once established, the colonists began to think of re-creating the daily life which they had known in France, for although they had arrived with only bare necessities and their courage, the strong traditions of the mother country were still a part of their make-up. The everyday objects they made resembled those which they remembered using in France. Inspired by the designs and styles of the French provinces in which they were born, they succeeded in creating a type of architecture peculiar to Canada, adapted to the climate and the available materials; their conception of furniture was equally striking.

The majority of early colonists of New France came from Normandy, Picardy, Perche, the Ile de France, Gascony, the Massif Central, Burgundy, and particularly from the western provinces — Haute-Bretagne, the region of Rennes and Nantes, Vendée, Touraine, Anjou, Beauce, Poitou, Saintonge, and Aunis. They were inspired by the distinctive styles of their home provinces, which accounts for the strong influence of these regions wherever the French established their settlements — in Acadia, on both shores of the St Lawrence, in Detroit, Illinois, and the valley of the Mississippi as far as Louisiana.

Their furniture gives the impression of massive architecture, especially the low buffets with lozenge or diamond-point motifs, the armoires with scrollwork panels and projecting or

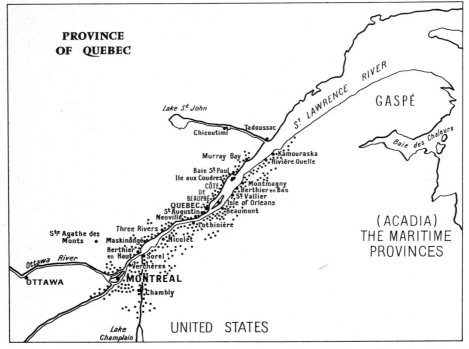

Fig. 3 - *THE ST LAWRENCE VALLEY. - The places of origin of most of the furniture illustrated are indicated by the smaller dots.*

domed cornices, the tables with turned legs and stretchers, and the rustic armchairs. The construction of these pieces, shaped and ornamented from solid wood, is extremely robust. In New France, there was no need to economize with wood, as there had been in France. A peculiarly Canadian accent is found in the details rather than in the structure of the early colonial furniture.

In France, there is a great deal of early furniture with characteristics from Normandy, Brittany and other provinces, and this is much sought after by enthusiastic collectors. In Canada, the same designs are to be found, but they are generally much simpler. For example, the basket of flowers in high relief, which is nearly always found as a decoration on the upper cross-pieces of wedding armoires in Normandy, was never popular in Canada.

There are many characteristics which link French Canadian furniture with that of other French provinces, and it is a delight to study the similarity of line, to trace the transpositions, the interpretations and the simplifications which distinguish Canadian from French furniture in a Louis XIII table, a peasant arm-chair, or a Louis XV commode. They were rarely exact reproductions.

Some specialists regard certain designs as " bastard " styles, but personally I prefer to think that, although some designs are rather awkward, they possess a charming naivety which gives them their Canadian character and in no way detracts from their French qualities. It seems to me that the Canadian woodworker, with his particularly personal approach, used his ingenuity and imagination to produce simple pieces, sometimes awkward in proportions, but always pleasing in appearance.

These are the things which give the furniture its essentially Canadian character. Influences other than that of France helped to form these new styles, for instance, those of England and the United States at the end of the eighteenth and the beginning of the nineteenth century.

TRADITIONAL FURNITURE

It would be as well to define here what we mean by traditional or regional furniture, because it is with this furniture that we are concerned. The research for this work was directed towards discovering the origin of different types of furniture to be found in French Canadian houses, most particularly in rural houses. The early pieces which are now being discovered in Canada were originally everyday furniture. They present none of the air of refined elegance or luxury that one looks for in Paris or Versailles in the furniture of the aristocracy or the rich bourgeoisie of the seventeenth and eighteenth centuries. There is no exotic wood, no marble, no ormolu, no finely chiseled bronze — inconceivable decorations in the primitive cottages of the first settlers of the great Canadian forests. Canadian traditional furniture was merely from yet another province of France, perhaps more rustic but having equal charm.

This book is concerned with furniture made with local wood by country carpenters who expressed the character, taste, and aspirations of the peasant class.

Traditional furniture is quite distinct from furniture in the grand style, but it is related, and in many instances borrowed technical and artistic innovations from the more refined pieces, without giving up its peasant character. It is the work of a skilled carpenter or joiner and is made of solid wood, as opposed to the veneer and inlay work of the cabinet maker.

This book deals only with furniture made by joiners or woodworkers. The furniture of Canada, as in other French provinces, was the work of joiners or woodworkers who were known as *menuisiers* as opposed to *ébénistes* (cabinet-makers).

Diderot and D'Alembert in their *Grande Encyclopédie* defined a rough carpenter *(charpentier)* as the man who frames a house; the building carpenter *(menuisier en bâtiments)* as the man who makes panelling, ceilings, window casements, doors, skirting boards, etc.; the furniture woodworker *(menuisier en meubles)* as the man who makes furniture only from solid jointed wood; and the cabinet-maker *(ébéniste)* as the man who specializes in marquetry or veneered furniture.

I have seen only three or four examples of Canadian woodworkers' furniture in which a touch of marquetry had been added, and these had been made towards the end of the eighteenth or at the beginning of the nineteenth century. In the little museum of the *Hôpital-Général* of the Grey Nuns in Montreal, there is an arbalète-fronted commode whose sides are embellished with Union Jacks in marquetry.

Our woodworkers were obliged to acquire all the skills defined by Diderot except the refinements of the cabinet-maker, and they even turned their hands to carving in order to meet the ever increasing demands of the rapidly growing colony for more churches. In the rest of the book I shall use only the term woodworker.

French provincial furniture was decorated with geometrical designs which originated in folk drawings which are common to most European countries. These designs are to be found all the way from the Mediterranean to Scandinavia and were taken to Canada by the early colonists. They included stylized patterns of flowers, leaves, trees, stars, crosses of all shapes, roses, roundels, chip-carved circles, lozenges, discs, shells, hearts, and human figures — some of which are generally held to have been created fortuitously with a pair of compasses.

These widespread designs were also used on Canadian furniture although the variety was not quite as rich and they generally had a more naive form than in Europe. This same process of simplification also affected the classical ornamentation at the end of the eighteenth century. Sometimes the metamorphosis of the design was so great that it is difficult to relate it to the European original, and in some cases the Canadian designs were completely indigenous.

In classifying traditional French Canadian furniture I have employed the morphological functional classification of French furniture developed by M. Georges Henri Rivière, beginning with the principle " that each piece of furniture corresponds to a need and that no piece of furniture is superfluous. " I have omitted the furniture which did not find a use in Canada but have complemented the list by adding such interesting pieces as bucket-benches, rocking chairs, console tables, wash-stands, doors, armoire doors, built-in cupboard doors, spinning-wheels, chandeliers, functional and decorative objects, and mantelpieces.

1. FURNITURE FOR HOLDING LINEN, CLOTHES, AND PRECIOUS OBJECTS

Chests, coffers and dome-topped chests or trunks *(bahuts)*
Armoires, with one door
Armoires, with two doors
Armoires, with four doors

2. FURNITURE FOR STORING DISHES, FOOD OR PROVISIONS.

High buffets or two-tiered buffets
High buffets,
    with four doors, without a drawer
              with one drawer
              with two drawers

Low buffets,
    with two doors, without a drawer
              with two drawers
              with three drawers

Dressers *(vaisseliers)*
    The lower part being a low buffet, the upper part open shelves
Hanging shelves
Bucket-benches
Buffets with glass doors, or glazed buffets

3. FURNITURE USED IN THE PREPARATION AND PRESERVATION OF FOOD

Dough-boxes, kneading-troughs, food-lockers

4. BEDS

Canadian closed-beds *(cabanes)*

Cradles

5. SEATS

Stools, high stools

Benches

Chairs

Armchairs

Rocking chairs

6. TABLES

Wash-stands

Console tables

7. DESKS

8. COMMODES

9. DOORS, ARMOIRE DOORS AND BUILT-IN CUPBOARD DOORS

10. SPINNING-WHEELS, CHANDELIERS, CLOCKS

11. FUNCTIONAL AND DECORATIVE HOUSEHOLD OBJECTS, AND MANTELPIECES

DOCUMENTARY SOURCES

I have often been asked what furniture would be found in the country house of French Canada in the 17th and 18th centuries. Furniture of the 17th century is extremely rare, but a few pieces have survived the numerous fires and acts of vandalism (which could be justifiably called old Canadian customs), — a study of the fires and the wilful destruction of furniture from the beginning of the colony until today would make sad and voluminous reading. It is not generally known that only one seventeenth-century building has escaped fire in the whole of Quebec City, and even this has been so transformed that its period characteristics are no longer recognizable.

From the founding of Quebec, Three Rivers and Montreal up to the present day, there has been an endless number of fires, often separated by only a few months or years, in which whole towns have been razed, and in the countryside an astronomical number of houses, colleges, convents and churches have been burnt down. Fortunately, the account books of the parishes, convents and seminaries, and the judicial archives were usually saved. The notarial records have been invaluable in this research and constitute a mine of information for any study aimed at re-creating the material domestic world of the early French Canadian *habitant*.

According to French custom, immediately following a death, the notary proceeded to draw up an itemized inventory of the goods and furniture of the deceased in order to divide them between the heirs. In many cases, the inventory was made while the corpse was still in the house. These inventories were so precise and detailed that the meanest objects were listed — " a wretched rickety chest..., " "... a miserable chair missing one leg and the back... "

In many cases, the description of the piece and the date of the inventory are sufficient to identify its form and style — " six chairs in birch wood with turned legs, upholstered with *point de Hongrie* and having green fringes... ", " ... a buffet of butternut wood in two sections, with four doors and its two drawers, fische hinges and iron fittings. "

The woodworker never signed his work, but he might be mentioned by name in a contract or an account book, the usual form of entry being — " paid to the woodworker a certain sum for a particular piece of furniture. "

Entries for church furniture in parish account books often mention the name of the craftsman, describe the piece and give the cost of altars, retables, pulpits, silverwork, etc.

The early furniture made for convents was not very elaborate as there was little spare money at the time, so when food-lockers or tables were needed they were made by the convent woodworker. Most of the elegant furniture now found in monasteries and convents (and more recently in their museums as they are just beginning to take an interest in their historical pieces), was left by patrons, usually bishops or governors who had often stayed in the house, by priests who had retired there in their old age, or by lady boarders, who were generally widows of the gentry in the colony and had moved into the convent to spend their last days, bringing with them their favourite pieces of furniture.

An oral account of colonial days is still to be found in religious houses and among country folk, but such accounts should be accepted with caution, although occasionally the information is reliable and can be verified. A clock which had once belonged to Mme de la Peltrie was found a few years ago in the original house of a direct descendant of the settlers at Cap Rouge. It was later confirmed that one of his early ancestors had acquired it from Mme de la Peltrie in exchange for a steer to feed the Ursuline nuns and their pupils during a famine.

In the country districts around Quebec City, the present owner is often a direct descendant of the original seventeenth-century settler, and a great deal of tradition and legend has been passed down by word of mouth through succeeding generations. Unfortunately most of this information is rather vague and skimpy and much of it cannot be accepted as authentic.

QUESTIONS OF STYLE

The inventories and account books of the early period are much more reliable, and from the information they contain we can state positively that the furniture in French Canada from 1650 to 1750 was inspired largely by the Louis XIII style which had a great influence on provincial furniture. The main characteristics of the style were straight lines, large surfaces, pediments, armoire doors, chests with multiple panels, lozenges, flat or relief diamond points and wood-turnings. The Louis XIII style continued to be popular in Canada until the beginning of the nineteenth century. However, after 1750 the *Régence* and Louis XV styles became widespread. English and American styles were introduced after 1780 and had a marked influence on French Canadian traditional furniture which resulted in an original blending of characteristics and motifs of each style. This combination of styles is seen most clearly in armoires, commodes and chairs.

Designs evolved very slowly in rural Canada, as in other French provinces, and there was always a certain interval before external influences made themselves felt. Today, by contrast, a style becomes old-fashioned almost as soon as it is presented. Everything now ages so rapidly that it is hard to believe that the things which aroused our enthusiasm only a short time ago should already be out of fashion; this, apparently, applies equally to our architecture and our furniture. However, many of the early designs have survived in spite of their age and have been preserved in museums and private homes where they still arouse the admiration of connoisseurs and cultivated amateurs.

In both France and Canada, some styles had a greater influence on traditional furniture in rural areas than others. The Louis XIV designs had very little effect in country districts, perhaps because they were too elaborate, too heavily ornamented, and consequently, difficult to make, whereas in Paris and Versailles these designs harmonized with the ostentation and luxury of the aristocracy, and their brilliant but over-lush architecture. But the two great styles which succeeded the Louis XIV period exercised a much greater influence on the provinces, after the usual time lag. By the end of the Louis XIV period, ornamentation was already losing its symmetry. The rectilinear structure of earlier styles disappeared and acanthus leaves and shells were given greater emphasis, leading to the *Régence* style in which the lines became less severe, shaped ornamentation more profuse, and in which the curve presaged the exuberance of the serpentine forms of the Louis XV style.

The *Rocaille* style began around 1725, being suggested by the grottoes, rocks and shell arrangements so popular in the gardens of the period. Its principal motif was an arrangement of branches and foliage in crosier form, permitting great freedom of imagination and fantasy. It flourished under Louis XV and reached its highest point around 1750, influencing all Europe.

However, the Louis XV style exerted the most lasting influence on French and Canadian regional furniture, but not until the end of the eighteenth and the beginning of the nineteenth centuries. In French Canada the influence of these styles is to be found on a simpler level and the exuberance is of a more rustic nature.

All commercial and cultural ties with France were broken after the English conquest. In spite of this break, which lasted several years, a few Canadian craftsmen travelled to France at the end of the eighteenth century. François Baillairgé, the carver and woodworker, studied in Paris for three years — painting and architecture at the Royal Academy, sculpture in the studio of Jean Baptiste Stouf — and returned to Canada in 1781[1]. François Malépart de Beaucourt, the painter, and Laurent Amiot, the silversmith, also studied in France for some time and brought back to Canada pattern-books and note-books filled with observations on the styles of the period.

The influence of English styles began to be felt at this time in Quebec and Montreal where the recently arrived English and Scottish woodworkers and cabinet-makers settled. Their names and advertisements are to be found in news sheets, almanacs, and trade year-books from 1780. These cabinet-makers were the first in Canada to use exotic woods, one being mahogany, which the French Canadians called by its English name. They introduced Queen Anne, Chippendale, and later, Adam and Sheraton styles, and began to advertise furniture made of mahogany, walnut, rosewood " in the latest mode. " They immediately captivated the French Canadian élite — the *seigneurs*, army officers, government officials, and all who easily adapted themselves to the new regime. These " modernistic " designs quickly replaced the French designs, with the exception of a few *Directoire* and *Empire* borrowings.

In 1787, English chair-makers in Montreal and Quebec were making chairs and arm-chairs of yellow birch in the style of English Windsor chairs which they painted pale green[2]. This colour became a standard one and is still used today.

By 1806, many mahogany pieces were mentioned in inventories of well-to-do French Cana-dian families, such as those described in the inventory of the estate of the Baroness of Longueuil and her late husband, David Alexander Grant, which was drawn up at their manor house on St Helen's Island. In the inventory of the Hertel de Rouville family at their manor at Cham-bly, many such pieces were divided between the Hertel de Rouvilles and the Salaberrys, their cousins. The most popular English styles were Queen Anne, Chippendale, Adam and Regency. This new furniture in the recently introduced wood was not popular in the country districts, although the new English styles had a great influence on the French Canadian woodworkers. Commodes, armoires, and chairs took on an English look while retaining certain French char-acteristics.

American influences were introduced to Canada from New England. A few low buffets and commodes were inspired by the special design of the Dunlaps, a family of New Hampshire woodworkers, canopied or hooded cradles by the Mennonites of Pennsylvania and New Jersey, and chair-tables (or hutch-tables) by Pennsylvanian designs. The influence of American Hep-plewhite became quite widespread in the nineteenth century, as did Regency and Hitchcock chairs which were popular in the United States around 1835.

The popularity of English and American furniture spread throughout French Canada in the first half of the nineteenth century. One antique dealer told me that before French Cana-dian traditional furniture became known, he used to come to Quebec only to buy Chippendale and Sheraton style armchairs and chairs, or Duncan Phyfe tables for his customers in Boston.

(1) Morisset, Gérard. *Coup d'œil sur les arts en Nouvelle-France*, Québec, 1941, p. 29.
(2) Lambert, John. *Travels through Canada and the United States of North America in the years* 1806, 1807 *and* 1808. London, 1814, vol. I, pp. 316-17.

In the single county of Montmagny, nearly all the houses contained such furniture, and most of it had been made by Canadian or American woodworkers.

Native characteristics, borrowed features, and adaptations of different styles can be seen in the different pieces listed in the *Catalogue Raisonné*. A comparative table of French, English, and American styles is given below. It should be noted that successive styles overlap and influence one another.

FRENCH, ENGLISH AND AMERICAN STYLES - 1500 - 1860

| | FRANCE | | ENGLAND | | AMERICA |
YEARS	REIGN	STYLE	REIGN	STYLE	STYLE
1500	Louis XII-Henri III 1498-1589	RENAISSANCE	Henri VII-Elizabeth Ist 1485-1603	TUDOR ELIZABETHAN	
1600 1625	Henri IV 1589-1610	LOUIS XIII	The Stuarts & Commonwealth 1603-1688	JACOBEAN CROMWELLIAN CHARLES II	
1650	Louis XIII 1610-1643				
1675	Louis XIV 1643-1715	LOUIS XIV	William & Mary 1689-1702	WILLIAM & MARY	WILLIAM & MARY 1700-1725
1700 1725	Regency 1715-1722	RÉGENCE	Anne 1702-1714	QUEEN ANNE	QUEEN ANNE 1725-1750
1730 1750	Louis XV 1722-1774	LOUIS XV	Early Georgian 1714-1760	CHIPPENDALE c. 1749-1779	CHIPPENDALE 1760-1790
1775	Louis XVI 1774-1792	LOUIS XVI	Late Georgian 1760-1830	ADAM c. 1760-1792	HEPPLEWHITE 1790-1810
	Directory 1795-1799	DIRECTOIRE		HEPPLEWHITE c. 1785-1790	
1800	Consulate & 1st Empire 1799-1814	FIRST EMPIRE		SHERATON c. 1785-1806	SHERATON 1790-1818
1825	Louis XVIII 1815-1824 Charles X 1824-1830	RESTAURATION		REGENCY 1795-1837	REGENCY 1820-1840
	Louis-Philippe 1830-1848	LOUIS-PHILIPPE	Victoria 1837-1901	EARLY VICTORIAN c. 1837	
1850	Napoleon III 1852-1870	SECOND EMPIRE		LATE VICTORIAN c. 1851	

HISTORY
AND CATALOGUE RAISONNÉ
OF THE EARLY FURNITURE

CHESTS, COFFERS AND DOME-TOPPED CHESTS

European furniture was extremely simple, even in the magnificent feudal castles, before the sixteenth century. It was limited to solid coffers, tables, dressers, benches, stools, and beds. Rich people stored their clothes, silver and jewels in chests, which they took with them when making a journey. The peasants also stored their clothes and food in chests, which naturally were the first pieces of furniture to reach New France with the settlers. There were two main types of these chests, the flat-topped *(coffre)* and the dome-topped *(bahut)*; the latter were also used on journeys and were the precursors of the later convex-topped travelling trunks. These chests were to be found in every house, being as common as tables and benches.

The first references to chests that I found in archives read " an old wooden chest with several garments 13 livres, 10 sols "[1] and " a dome-topped chest covered in red Levant morocco, locking with a key of medium size "[2]. Without question these two articles were brought from France by their owners.

In the seventeenth century, the bride took a chest to her new home as part of her trousseau. In it she stored linen, clothing, lace, and jewellery, " ... add to this a chest which Marie-Yvonne Couillard claims to be the one which her father Pierre Couillard gave her when she married, and in which is the clothing that her father gave her at the time of her marriage to David... "[3] In the eighteenth century, as part of her dowry, the bride took an armoire with her, in the nineteenth century a bed, and today she takes a bedroom suite.

The chests which are to be found today in the attics of French Canada are generally very simple but sturdy. They were made with tongue-and-groove pine planks held together with dowels, and mortise-and-tenon joints. The lid was generally attached by strong hinges and closed at the front with a heavy lock, as everything was kept under lock and key.

A few of these chests were held together with forged nails or by dove-tail joints, " two large old chests, one with dove-tail joints, and the other nailed, with an iron lock and key. "[4] Some had several panels separated by stiles and others were made to be placed on a special table which sometimes had spiralled or twisted legs in Louis XIII style, " a chest with its pedestal,

(1) A J M, I O A. Inventaire de ventes des Meubles de Deffunt Jean Boudeau du 14e May 1651. Greffe de Sainct-Père.
(2) A J M, I O A. Inventaire des biens de defft le Sr Lambert Closse, 8 février 1662. Greffe Basset.
(3) A J M. Inventaire des biens de feu Claude David, 20e et 22e Xbre 1684, de la Rivière Saint-Michel. Greffe Adhémar.
(4) A J M, I O A. Invantaire à La Requeste de françois Et Julien Rochon du 3e mars 1727. Greffe Coron.

locking with a key. ''[1] Madame d'Youville, foundress of the Grey Nuns had, according to oral tradition, such a chest which contained her documents and account books and which she would take with her when making a journey, replacing it on its pedestal upon her return. A number of chests were ornamented with geometric designs — lozenges, diamond points, or hearts, symbolizing love or marriage; or the Canadian adaptation of the linen-fold pattern, a vestige of the Middle Ages.

A few Canadian chests had the shaped panels of the Louis XV style but this type was rare even in France. There was also the round travelling chest *(bahut rond)*, " a little round chest, locking with a key ...a round chest, sound and complete, two livres...''[2] Many flat-topped and dome-topped chests were covered in calf-skin or porpoise skin and fur, but while many inventories mention these, the few that have survived are found only in convents.

Chests were generally placed at the side or at the foot of the bed. They not only held linen, but were also used as a step when climbing into bed. Sometimes they were placed against the wall of the common room and served as a seat for social evenings during the winter, as in the old song " *La Destinée, la Rose au bois...* "

> " *Les garçons en visite,*
> *assis sur le coffre comme c'est bien la façon*
> *pour jouer de la musique*
> *et aussi du violon...* "

(" The boys when paying a visit, would sit on the chest as was the custom and play the harmonica and also the violin. ")

After the first quarter of the eighteenth century, the term *coffre* replaced *bahut* in mid-18th century inventories. The Canadian chest was then influenced by the Louis XV style, but had shaped panels and cabriole legs. Some had bracket feet in the English style and others had a drawer in the lower part of the façade, being the forerunners of the commode.

---

1. PANELLED CHEST, WITH SIMPLIFIED LINEN-FOLD PATTERN. 17th C.

Eight-panelled chest, derived from the medieval linen-fold pattern, but interpreted in a more naive manner. The feet are a later addition. One of the finest Canadian chests.

W. 4' 1"	H. 2' 1¾"	D. 1' 10¼"
124 cm	65 cm	57 cm

WOOD : pine

PROVENANCE : Saint-Grégoire de Nicolet, P.Q.

(Coll. of the author, Montreal).

2. PANELLED CHEST, IN THE LOUIS XIII MANNER. 18th C.

Chest, with eleven panels, the central one being carved with a lozenge. The lid and the base mouldings are later additions.

W. 3' 7¼"	H. 1' 5"	D. 1' 7¼"
95 cm	43 cm	49 cm

WOOD : pine   PROVENANCE : Quebec

(Coll. Musée du Monastère des Ursulines, Quebec).

3. DOME-TOP CHEST, IN LATE 16th C. STYLE. LATE 17th C.

Dome-top chest *(bahut)*, in the late sixteenth-century style. A typical example of the dome-top chests of this period, which the first settlers brought from France. This particular one is constructed with dove-tail joints, and preserves its original green colouring.

W. 1' 11¼"	H. 1' 11¾"	D. 1' 2½"
59 cm	60 cm	37 cm

WOOD : pine   PROVENANCE : Beauport, P.Q.

(Coll. Mr and Mrs Jean-Paul Lemieux, Sillery, P.Q.).

4. ROUND-TOP CHEST. 17th C.

Seventeenth-century round-top chest, which is frequently mentioned in inventories of the time. This kind of chest was carried under the arm during journeys.

W. 2'	H. 11"
61 cm	29 cm

WOOD : butternut PROVENANCE : Lotbinière, P.Q.

(Coll. Mr and Mrs Georges-Étienne Gagné, Neuville, P.Q.).

---

(1) A J M, I O A. Inventaire des biens et meubles de deffunt Jacques Testard Sr de la forest 18 juin 1663. Greffe Basset.

(2) A J M, I O A. Inventaire des biens meubles de la communauté d'entre Mathurin Langevin et Deffunt Marie Regnaud sa feme, 27 octobre 1673. Greffe Basset.

5. CHEST, WITH EIGHT PANELS. EARLY 19th C.

Eight-panelled chest, closely similar to a chest in the Quebec Provincial Museum. The location of the keyhole, in the centre of asymmetrical panels, should be noted. The back bears an inscription, painted in black, which reads " 1806 *le 2 Octobre* ". The one in the Provincial Museum also carries an inscription, " 1805 *appartient à Pierre...* ", (the surname being illegible). The colour, red ochre, is original.

w. 3' 4"	H. 2' 2"	D. 1' 8¾"
102 cm	66 cm	53 cm

WOOD : pine   PROVENANCE : Sainte-Foye, P.Q.

(Coll. of the author, Montreal).

6. CHEST, WITH DIAMOND-POINT CARVING. 18th C.

Four-panelled chest, carved with diamond points, in the Louis XIII manner.

w. 3' 9½"	H. 1' 10¼"	D. 1' 7½"
116 cm	57 cm	50 cm

WOOD : pine

(Coll. Museum of Fine Arts, Montreal).

7. CHEST, CARVED WITH GEOMETRIC DESIGNS. 18th C.

Four-panelled chest, carved with primitive geometric designs.

w. 3' 5"	H. 1' 7¾"	D. 1' 6½"
104 cm	50 cm	47 cm

WOOD : pine   PROVENANCE : Isle of Orleans, P.Q.

(Coll. Mr and Mrs F.M. Hutchins, Pembroke, Ont.).

8. DOWER CHEST. LATE 17th C.

Dower chest, mounted on a table with spirally turned legs, and having two drawers. A rare piece of furniture, this particular one was formerly owned by Madame Marguerite d'Youville, foundress of the Grey Nuns. She used it for her documents and silverware. Inside there is a written inscription :
" 15 forks...
16 spoons...
a large silver écuelle...
11 small spoons... "
The small dome-top chest with dove-tail joints is placed on the table top, fitting in a frame. The little chest is easy to carry. See page 32.

w. 2' 2¾"	H. 2' 8½"	D. 1' 4¼"
68 cm	82 cm	42 cm

WOOD : pine   TABLE : birch

PROVENANCE : Montreal

(Coll. Hôpital-Général of the Grey Nuns, Montreal).

9. CHEST, DECORATED WITH THE CROSS OF ST ANDREW. 18th C.

Panelled chest, carved with the cross of St Andrew, or *pointes de gâteaux*, on both the front and sides. A peasant product.

w. 4' 2¾"	H. 2'	D. 2' 1"
129 cm	61 cm	64 cm

WOOD : pine

(Coll. Detroit Institute of Arts, Detroit, Mich. U.S.A.).

10. CHEST, CARVED WITH LOZENGES. 18th C.

Chest, with front and side panels carved with lozenges. The stiles and rails are chamfered. Derived from the Louis XIII style.

w. 2' 8¾"	H. 1' 9½"	D. 1' 5¾"
83 cm	55 cm	45 cm

WOOD : pine

(Coll. Miss Karen Bulow, Préville, P.Q.).

11. CHEST, WITH SMALL PANELS. 18th C.

Chest, with ten panels on the façade, and four on each side. The latter form compartments *(caissons)*, in the Louis XIII manner.

w. 3' 8"	H. 2' 1¾"	D. 1' 9½"
112 cm	65 cm	55 cm

WOOD : pine

(Coll. Musée Provencher, Cap Rouge, P.Q.).

12. CHEST, WITH TWO PANELS. 18th C.

Chest, with two front and two side panels, in the Louis XIII manner.

w. 1' 2"	H. 1' 8½"	D. 1' 9"
36 cm	52 cm	53 cm

WOOD : pine

PROVENANCE : Les Éboulements, P.Q.

(Coll. Mr and Mrs J.N. Cole, Montreal).

13. SMALL RUSTIC CHEST, CARVED WITH GEOMETRIC DESIGNS. 18th C.

Small rustic chest, in its original colouring of blue-green, and carved with geometric designs. It was probably made by an unskilled hand, although it is of attractive proportions.

w. 1' 5"	H. 1' 2"	D. 10"
43 cm	36 cm	25 cm

WOOD : pine

(Coll. Mr and Mrs J.N. Cole, Montreal).

14. SMALL RUSTIC CHEST, CARVED WITH GEOMETRIC DESIGNS. EARLY 19th C.

Small rustic chest, carved with primitive geometric designs reminiscent of shells and a violin.

w. 2' 2¼"	H. 1' 7¼"	D. 1' 4¼"
67 cm	49 cm	42 cm

WOOD : pine

(Coll. Mrs E. Thornley-Hart, Sainte-Agathe des Monts, P.Q.).

15. SMALL MARRIAGE COFFER, WITH SHAPED BASE. EARLY 19th C.

Small marriage coffer, the lower structure of which, with its bracket feet of English or American derivation, is shaped and decorated with spirals and hearts.

| w. 2' | H. 1' 6'' | D. 1' |
| 61 cm | 46 cm | 31 cm |

WOOD : pine

PROVENANCE : Saint-Augustin de Portneuf, P.Q.

(Coll. Dr and Mrs Herbert T. Schwarz, Montreal).

16. CHEST WITH SHAPED PANÉLS, IN THE LOUIS XV STYLE. 18th C.

Chest, with a structure derived from the Louis XIII manner, but with shaped panels in the Louis XV manner. This is rare both in Canada and in France.

| w. 3' 6'' | H. 2' | D. 1' 10'' |
| 107 cm | 61 cm | 56 cm |

WOOD : pine

PROVENANCE : Cap Saint-Ignace, P.Q.

(Coll. Mr and Mrs Hugh McMillan, Jr., Salisbury, Conn. U.S.A.).

17. CHEST, WITH CURVED FEET. LATE 18th C.

Chest with rustic curved *pieds de biche*. Very rare.

| w. 3' 2'' | H. 1' 11'' | D. 1' 7'' |
| 97 cm | 58 cm | 48 cm |

WOOD : pine UPRIGHTS : birch

(Coll. Provincial Museum, Quebec).

18. SMALL CHEST, WITH CARVED FAÇADE. 19th C.

Small chest, having a façade ornamented with a carved medallion containing hearts and a shell. Undoubtedly a small marriage chest, as the hearts suggest.

| w. 2' 2'' | H. 1' 3½'' | D. 1' 1'' |
| 66 cm | 39 cm | 33 cm |

WOOD : pine

PROVENANCE : St Charles-sur-Richelieu, P.Q.

(Coll. Mrs Nettie Sharpe, Saint-Lambert, P.Q.).

19. SMALL CHEST, IN A VERY OLD STYLE. LATE 17th C.

Small chest, with a flat lid, resembling a dome-top chest, in the late 16th c. manner (cf. n° 3).

| w. 1' 11½'' | H. 1' 4¼'' | D. 1' 2¾'' |
| 60 cm | 42 cm | 37 cm |

WOOD : pine PROVENANCE : Quebec district

(Coll. Mr and Mrs J.N. Cole, Montreal).

20. PANELLED CHEST. LATE 18th C.

Chest, decorated with one front panel, carved with geometric designs and two side panels.

| w. 3' 5½'' | H. 1' 11¼'' | D. 1' 10½'' |
| 105 cm | 59 cm | 57 cm |

WOOD : pine PANELS : ash

(Coll. Mrs Richard R. Costello, Sainte-Agathe des Monts, P.Q.).

21. CHEST, IN THE REGENCY MANNER. 19th C.

Chest, with seventeen panels. The front stiles are ornamented at the corners with a fluted motif, reminiscent of the stiles on Regency clocks.

| w. 3' 10'' | H. 2' 2½'' | D. 1' 10'' |
| 117 cm | 67 cm | 56 cm |

WOOD : pine PROVENANCE : Charlesbourg, P.Q.

(Coll. Miss Barbara Richardson, Sainte-Agathe des Monts, P.Q.).

22. DOME-TOP CHEST, WITH FOUR FALSE DRAWERS. EARLY 19th C.

Dome-top chest, with seven drawers, the upper four being false. The lower portion forms a commode with bracket feet showing English or American influence. A combination of a dower chest and a commode.

| w. 4' 1'' | H. 4' ¾'' | D. 1' 10½'' |
| 125 cm | 124 cm | 57 cm |

WOOD : pine PROVENANCE : Beaumont, P.Q.

(Coll. Mr Paul Gouin, Montreal).

23. CHEST, WITH TWO DRAWERS IN THE BASE. EARLY 19th C.

Chest, constructed with dove-tail joints, with two drawers in the base and handles on the sides, reminiscent of those that army officers carried with them. Of English derivation.

| w. 2' 7½'' | H. 2' 5'' | D. 1' 10½'' |
| 80 cm | 74 cm | 57 cm |

WOOD : pine

(Coll. Brigadier and Mrs G.V. Whitehead, Dorval, P.Q.).

EARLY NINETEENTH-CENTURY LOZENGE-DESIGN CHEST, IN ITS ORIGINAL COLOURS.

1. COFFRE A PANNEAUX INSPIRÉS DES PLIS DE SERVIETTE. XVIIᵉ S.
PANELLED CHEST, WITH SIMPLIFIED LINEN-FOLD PATTERN. 17th C.

2. COFFRE A PANNEAUX, D'ES-
PRIT LOUIS XIII. XVIIIᵉ S.
PANELLED CHEST, IN THE
LOUIS XIII MANNER. 18th c.

3. COFFRE-BAHUT, DANS L'ES-
PRIT DE LA FIN DU XVIᵉ SIÈCLE.
FIN XVIIᵉ S.
DOME-TOP CHEST, IN LATE
16th c. STYLE. LATE 17th c.

7. COFFRE ORNÉ DE DESSINS GÉOMÉTRIQUES.
XVIIIe S.
CHEST, CARVED WITH GEOMETRIC DESIGNS.
18th C.

BAHUT DE MARIAGE. FIN XVIIe S.

VER CHEST. LATE 17th C.

COFFRE A PANNEAUX ORNÉS DE
DIX DE SAINT-ANDRÉ. XVIIIe S.
EST, DECORATED WITH THE CROSS
ST ANDREW. 18th C.

COFFRE A DEUX PANNEAUX. XVIIIe S.
EST, WITH TWO PANELS. 18th C.

PETIT COFFRE RUSTIQUE ORNÉ DE DESSINS
OMÉTRIQUES. XVIIIe S.

SMALL RUSTIC CHEST, CARVED WITH GEO-
METRIC DESIGNS. 18th C.

18. PETIT COFFRE A FA-
ÇADE SCULPTÉE. XIXᵉ S.
SMALL CHEST, WITH CAR-
VED FAÇADE. 19th C.

19. PETIT COFFRE A L'AN-
CIENNE. FIN XVIIᵉ S.
SMALL CHEST, IN A VERY
OLD STYLE. LATE 17th C.

COFFRE A PANNEAUX.
XVIIIe S.
ELLED CHEST. LATE
h C.

COFFRE D'ESPRIT RE-
CY. XIXe S.
ST, IN THE REGENCY
NNER. 19th C.

22. COFFRE-BAHUT A SEPT TIROIRS, DONT QUATRE NE SONT
QU'APPARENTS. DÉBUT XIXe S.
DOME-TOP CHEST, WITH FOUR FALSE DRAWERS.   EARLY 19th C.

23. COFFRE ORNÉ DE DEUX TIROIRS A LA BASE. DÉBUT XIXe S.
CHEST, WITH TWO DRAWERS IN THE BASE.   EARLY 19th C.

ARMOIRES, TWO-TIERED BUFFETS, LOW BUFFETS

These are the most interesting and elaborate of the rural pieces which, because of their large surfaces, enjoyed a great variety of structural transformation and richness of design throughout the eighteenth and at the beginning of the nineteenth century.

From 1650 to 1750, Canadian woodworkers were inspired by Renaissance and Louis XIII styles which were also in vogue in the other French provinces. Later they began to interpret, in a primitive and intuitive way, the designs which succeeded the Louis XIII style.

ARMOIRES

Buffets and armoires were derived from the chest, the façade of which was increased in height by additional vertical panels and surmounted by a cornice.

The armoire was constructed as a single piece, as opposed to sectional furniture. It had either a single door (hat-cupboards or wardrobes), or two doors, " an armoire in pine, with two doors closing with a key "[1], " ... a very old, large armoire, with two doors of yellow birch, with hinges, lock and the rest in pine... "[2] or sometimes four doors *(armoire à l'ancienne)*.

The most common sort of armoire has two doors. The earliest armoires had doors with simple or square panels, or panels carved with lozenges inside a double frame of projecting moulding. This was succeeded by the multiform diamond-point motif in high relief.

Antique dealers and collectors often confuse lozenges and diamond points. Lozenges do not project. Their apparent relief is caused by a groove cut in the panel. Diamond points, on the other hand, are carved out of a thicker panel in higher relief suggesting the facets of a cut diamond. The lozenge made its appearance on armoire doors in the seventeenth century, and it was not until the eighteenth century that it was transformed into the diamond point. The evolution of the diamond-point design began when the groove outlining the lozenge became deeper, and the sides were bevelled. Soon after, diamond points in high relief began to appear. This transformation took place first in France and was later copied in Canada.

Throughout the eighteenth century, a wide variety of these pieces made their appearance. There was a range of design and themes including *galettes* (pancakes), or disc shapes with multiple crowns, an idea which originated on the west coast of France from Haute-Bretagne down to the Basque region. They were finished with diamond points decorated with geometrical designs, in some cases diamond points were combined with discs. Other armoires of the transitional period were those with shaped mouldings, in the Louis XV style, which framed diamond-point panels.

The fantasy period of the Canadian armoire was a development which coincided with the era of prosperity following the Seven Years War. It brought with it a whole abundance of ornamentation in the spirit of Louis XV, interpreted in a Canadian fashion — centre posts carved with foliated scroll-work, shaped doors, panels and bottom rails ornamented with multiple

(1) A J M, I O A. Inventaire des Biens Meubles et Immeubles dellaissez après le Decedz de Deffunte Marie Remy Jadis femme de Pierre Desautels 25e novembre 1676. Greffe Basset.
(2) A J M, I O A. Inventaire des biens de Pierre Buisson et de Françoise Levasseur, sa femme, 30 septembre 1732. Greffe Saint-Romain.

spirals, rosettes, and shells. Later, the panels, centre-posts, stiles and rails overflowed with foliage, sea-weed, hearts, suns, ribbons, fluting, reeding and fine zig-zag incisions, the last suggesting Iroquois and Huron ceramic motifs and resembling the designs found on certain armoires from the Bresse region of Burgundy.

Elegant armoires combining the spirit of both Louis XVI and English Adam styles also began to make their appearance. The Adam brothers of London, according to some experts, were the first to return to Classical designs and their style seems to have had more influence on the Canadian craftsman. Some of these armoires and rare two-tiered buffets with a dome top and bulging front and sides, very similar to Dutch or Austrian baroque designs, have fortunately been preserved. A notable example of this style is attributed to François Baillairgé.

There were also armoires and commodes in the *Canadian Rococo* style, derived after an interval from Louis XV *Rocaille*, which began to appear in the late eighteenth and early nineteenth centuries. They were made in the Montreal region in the workshops of church carvers and woodworkers such as the Liéberts, the Quévillons, the Pepins and their apprentices.

A characteristic often found in Canadian armoires is a certain lack of balance in the design, caused by the bulkiness of the top and bottom rails — in France this rarely appears except in a few Lorraine armoires.

Other characteristics to be noted on Canadian armoires and two-tiered buffets are the cornices, rails and uprights of the doors. Cornices usually projected, and were decorated with multiple mouldings and *bandelets*, often with an assortment of ornamentation. The doors, although derived from the current French models, had some curious combinations of mouldings. In spite of these awkward touches, Canadian armoires have an appealing, though slightly primitive air about them.

M. Stany Gauthier, Curator of the Museum of Folk Arts, Nantes (housed in the medieval château of the dukes of Brittany), who is a great expert on the traditional furniture of the French provinces, in the course of one of many interesting conversations summed up the situation: "The general forms, framework and structure of Canadian armoires are very French ... that is indisputable. It is the style which predominates between Nantes and Bordeaux which has most influenced Canadian craftsmen; but it is in the details that one detects the stamp of a separate province of France."

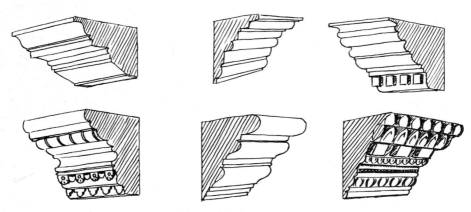

Fig. 4 - *Profiles of armoire cornices.*

Of all the early French Canadian furniture, the armoire is the most monumental and the most interesting. But in spite of its size, it was held together like smaller pieces, with mortise-and-tenon joints and pegs, and was not glued. If an armoire were too large to pass up a narrow stairway or a turn in the stairs, it could easily be dismantled simply by removing the pegs and taking each piece apart.

In 1740, the woodworker Jean Gagnée was paid eight pounds " for dismantling the armoires in the Bishop's palace and putting them together again in his room at the Seminary. "[1]

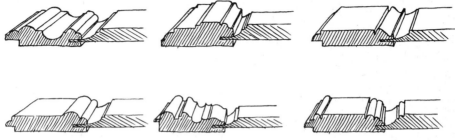

Fig. 5 - *Mouldings of armoire doors.*

24. ARMOIRE " A L'ANCIENNE ", IN THE LOUIS XIII MANNER. LATE 17th C.

Armoire *à l'ancienne*, in the Louis XIII manner, having four doors, carved with lozenges and surrounded by heavy mouldings as on some two-tiered buffets. Its framework is in one piece (unlike the two-tiered buffet) which gave it the name " *à l'ancienne* " (often found in late 17th c. inventories). A transitional piece, between the coffer and armoire proper. In structure it appears as several chests placed one upon another, with doors let into the façade and the lid replaced by a solid top. The wooden latches were added later to replace the broken locks. Authentic ironwork.

w. 4' 4"   H. 6' 7½"   D. 1' 9"
   132 cm   202 cm   53 cm

WOOD : pine   PROVENANCE : Quebec

(Coll. Museum of Fine Arts, Montreal).

25. DETAIL.

26. DETAIL.

27. TWO-DOOR ARMOIRE, CARVED WITH MULTIPLE SPIRALS AND SHELLS. LATE 18th C.

Two-door armoire, with shaped panels carved with multiple spirals. The shaped lower rail is carved with spirals, flowers and shells. The cornice cabling and fluting are derived from Adam or Louis XVI styles. This is a very Canadian armoire, on account of the profusion of contours and spirals, characteristics not found in French armoires. The design of the shells on the lower rail is also typically Canadian. Original fische hinges and colouring of deep green and blue. One of the most interesting pieces of furniture in the Canadian repertoire.

w. 4' 9¾"   H. 6' 6¾"   D. 1' 6½"
   147 cm   200 cm   47 cm

WOOD : pine   PROVENANCE : Quebec district

(Coll. Detroit Institute of Arts, Detroit, Mich. U.S.A.).

28. ARMOIRE, WITH MULTIPLE PANELS, IN THE ADAM STYLE. LATE 18th C.

Armoire, with twenty-six panels in the façade. The panels, the centre post and top rail are decorated with grooves, in the Adam manner, but the general appearance of the armoire remains French. One of the most beautiful Canadian armoires. Another, almost identical, made by the same craftsman, is in the Quebec Provincial Museum.

w. 4' 3⅜"   H. 6'   D. 1' 3¾"
   131 cm   183 cm   40 cm

WOOD : pine   PROVENANCE : Sorel, P.Q.

(Coll. Canada Steamship Lines, Tadoussac, P.Q.).

(1) Quinsonas, Comte de. *Monseigneur de Laubérivière* 1711-40, Paris, 1936, p. 175.

29. ARMOIRE, FROM RIVIÈRE OUELLE, CARVED WITH VARIOUS MOTIFS. LATE 18th C.

Armoire, from Rivière Ouelle, carved with various motifs, having shaped panels of Louis XV derivation. The centre post is decorated with water leaves, and seaweed coming out of a vase. The upper rail has naively carved rosettes, fish, water leaves, a caribou, a siren and a cock on top of a balsam tree or a *mai*. The side panels are inspired by Adam or Louis XVI styles. Period rat-tail fische hinges. The shaped lower rail and thick cordon are typically Canadian. The combination of anthropomorphic, zoomorphic and phytomorphic designs makes this armoire a most enchanting piece of furniture. Another armoire made by the same woodworker, and also from the Rivière Ouelle district, is in the National Museum in Ottawa, but only the centre post is ornamented.

| w. 4' 2" | H. 6' 8¾" | D. 1' 3" |
| 127 cm | 205 cm | 38 cm |

WOOD : pine   PROVENANCE : Rivière Ouelle, P.Q.

(Coll. Mr and Mrs Edgar Davidson, Montreal).

30. DETAIL.

31. DETAIL.

32. ARMOIRE, DERIVING FROM THE LOUIS XVI AND ADAM STYLES. LATE 18th C.

Armoire, derived from the Louis XVI and Adam styles. The panels, centre post, stiles and rails have fluting, wolf's teeth, stylized foliage, *rais de cœur*, and geometric ornamentation. The cornice has cabling and dentils, together with *rais de cœur* and gouge-work, while the lower rail, of English derivation, is festooned and decorated with a central motif of grooves. The escutcheons are missing, but the rat-tail fische hinges are the originals. An exceptional and well proportioned Canadian armoire.

| w. 5' ½" | H. 6' 10½" | D. 1' 9" |
| 154 cm | 210 cm | 53 cm |

WOOD : pine

PROVENANCE : Berthier-en-Haut, P.Q.

(Coll. Canada Steamship Lines, Tadoussac, P.Q.).

33. DETAIL

34. SMALL RUSTIC ARMOIRE, WITH ONE DOOR. LATE 18th C.

Small rustic armoire, with one shaped panel decorated with spirals and a shell. The knob has been added and the cornice has been restored. Original rat-tail fische hinges. Small armoire-foodlocker with pleasant proportions.

| w. 2' 3½" | H. 4' 11½" | D. 1' 3½" |
| 70 cm | 151 cm | 39 cm |

WOOD : pine   PROVENANCE : Vaudreuil, P.Q.

(Coll. National Museum of Canada, Ottawa, Ont.).

35. ARMOIRE, WITH MOTIFS DERIVING FROM BOTH LOUIS XIII AND LOUIS XV STYLES. MID 18th C.

Armoire, with motifs deriving from both the Louis XIII and the Louis XV styles. A transitional armoire, having shaped panels, carved with diamond points in the Louis XIII manner and framed with Louis XV-style shaped moulding. The geometric design may well be a debased variation of a shell motif. It was probably made by a craftsman who was not very familiar with the new *Régence* and Louis XV styles which appeared towards the middle of the eighteenth century. The cornice and base are later additions, but the fische hinges are authentic.

| w. 4' 5¼" | H. 6' 6¼" | D. 1' 5¼" |
| 136 cm | 199 cm | 44 cm |

WOOD : pine

(Coll. Mr and Mrs Pierre Gouin, St Sulpice, P.Q.).

36. SMALL RUSTIC ARMOIRE, WITH ONE DOOR. EARLY 19th C.

Small rustic armoire designed as a food-locker, having one door, with panels carved with fluting and fans or bat-wings in the Adam manner. There is a naive shaped lower rail, decorated with spirals and a simplified shell. The form is reminiscent of certain small armoires from the Massif Central. Peasant workmanship.

| w. 3' | H. 5' | D. 1' 4¾" |
| 91 cm | 152 cm | 42 cm |

WOOD : pine

PROVENANCE : Saint-Barthélémy, P.Q.

(Coll. Canada Steamship Lines, Tadoussac, P.Q.).

37. SMALL RUSTIC ARMOIRE, DERIVED FROM THE ADAM STYLE. EARLY 19th C.

Small rustic armoire, derived from the Adam style. The dentil cornice, shaped lower rail and door decorated with fan or bat-wing motifs, derive from the Adam style. Original slide bolts and rat-tail fische hinges. The lower rail has been renovated. A small, peasant piece.

| w. 3' 6¾" | H. 4' 8¾" | D. 1' 5⅝" |
| 108 cm | 144 cm | 45 cm |

WOOD : pine

(Coll. Mr and Mrs J.W. McConnell, Saint-Sauveur des Monts, P.Q.).

38. ARMOIRE FROM BERTHIER-EN-HAUT, IN THE LOUIS XV AND LOUIS XVI STYLES. LATE 18th C.

Armoire from Berthier-en-Haut. Both the shaped panels and the lower rails are decorated with spirals, rosettes and shells, the cornice and upper rail with fretwork and festoons, the lower rail with Louis XVI *entrelacs*. The feet suggest a cabriole curve. Original fische hinges and keyhole escutcheons. The proportions, and the shell and rosette decoration make it a very pleasing piece.

w. 4' 5⅝"   H. 5' 6¼"   D. 1' 6"
136 cm   168 cm   46 cm

WOOD : pine
PROVENANCE : Berthier-en-Haut, P.Q.
(Coll. Mr Gilles Corbeil, Saint-Hilaire, P.Q.).

39. ARMOIRE, CARVED WITH DISCS OR " GALETTES ". MID 18th C.

Armoire, having two doors carved with discs *(galettes)*, with many crowns. The lateral panels and the centre post, with its narrow rectangular panels, have disc carvings. This type of armoire is widely distributed along the west coast of France, from Brittany to the Pyrenees (from where many of the ancestors of the Canadians came). Usually the discs are intermingled with lozenges or diamond points. Note the enormous stiles and the moulding enclosing the frame, and also the absence of a cornice. It shows French provincial influences, but is very Canadian in the design of the *galettes*. Rare and interesting.

w. 5' 1¼"   H. 6' 5"   D. 1' 10"
156 cm   196 cm   56 cm

WOOD : pine   PROVENANCE : Beaumont, P.Q.
(Coll. Canada Steamship Lines, Tadoussac, P.Q.).

40. ARMOIRE, CARVED WITH DIAMOND POINTS, IN LOUIS XIII STYLE. MID 18th C.

Armoire, having two doors with prominent double mouldings and decorated with small lozenges and rectangles shaped like diamond points. The side panels also have small lozenges. A very prominent cornice. Original fische hinges and keyhole escutcheon. A massive but finely proportioned armoire.

w. 4' 6"   H. 6' 6½"   D. 1' 9½"
137 cm   199 cm   55 cm

WOOD : pine   PROVENANCE : Montreal district
(Coll. Mr L.V. Randall, Montreal).

41. SMALL ARMOIRE, WITH DIAMOND-POINT CARVING, IN THE LOUIS XIII STYLE. MID 18th C.

Small armoire, having two doors carved with diamond points framed by heavy mouldings. Shaped lower rail. Original fische hinges, but the wooden latch is a later addition.

w. 3' 2"   H. 2' 9"   D. 1' 5¾"
97 cm   84 cm   45 cm

WOOD : pine   PROVENANCE : Montreal district
(Coll. Mr and Mrs A.F. Culver, Montreal).

42. TWO-DOOR ARMOIRE, DECORATED WITH LOZENGES AND DISCS OR " GALETTES ". MID 18th C.

Two-door armoire, decorated with lozenges and discs or *galettes*. Lozenges also garnish the side panels. This type of armoire is found between Nantes and Bordeaux, and even as far as the Basque country. Note the protruding moulding on the door-frame. Original fische hinges and keyhole escutcheons. The armoire is mutilated and misshapen because of loose joints, and the wooden latch spoils it. It should be restored. Part of the base moulding and the feet are missing.

w. 4' 11"   H. 6' 8¾"   D. 1' 11"
150 cm   205 cm   58 cm

WOOD : pine
(Coll. Provincial Museum, Quebec).

43. ARMOIRE, CARVED WITH DIAMOND POINTS, IN THE LOUIS XIII MANNER. LATE 18th C.

Armoire, with panels decorated with small diamond points added at a more recent date. The moulding which surrounds the frame is reminiscent of certain kinds of French armoires. Period fische hinges, latch added. Heavy centre post, rails and stiles. An attractive piece.

w. 4' 3¼"   H. 5' 2½"   D. 1' 4½"
130 cm   159 cm   42 cm

WOOD : pine   PROVENANCE : Montreal district
(Coll. Mr and Mrs Jean Raymond, Westmount, P.Q.).

44. ARMOIRE, CARVED WITH LOZENGES, WITH TWO DRAWERS IN THE CORNICE. EARLY 19th C.

Armoire, having two doors carved with lozenges, and two drawers in the cornice, surmounted by a double row of dentils. This type of curved cornice does not exist in France, but is found on English furniture of the William and Mary style. An interesting piece. The wooden latch is a later addition.

w. 4' 7⅝"   H. 5' 6½"   D. 1' 8"
141 cm   169 cm   51 cm

WOOD : pine
PROVENANCE : Saint-Cyrille de l'Islet, P.Q.
(Coll. Canada Steamship Lines, Tadoussac, P.Q.).

45. ARMOIRE, CARVED WITH LOZENGES, UNDER HAUTE-BRETAGNE INFLUENCE. 18th C.

Armoire, carved with bevelled lozenges, a dentil cornice, and a naively shaped lower rail. This type is very frequently found in Haute-Bretagne, particularly in Guérande. The design of the bevelled lozenges of the panels is typical of this area.

w. 4' 11"   H. 5' 1¼"   D. 1' 4"
150 cm   156 cm   41 cm

WOOD : pine   PROVENANCE : Montreal district
(Coll. Provincial Museum, Quebec).

46. ARMOIRE, CARVED WITH DIAMOND POINTS DECORATED WITH GEOMETRIC DESIGNS. 18th C.

Small armoire, in the Louis XIII manner, having two doors carved with diamond-point panels decorated with geometric designs. It is extremely rare to find geometric designs on the diamond points themselves, either in France or Canada. The lateral panels have simplified linen folds, while the upper panel bears an enormous petalled rosette in the centre of a geometric design. Period fische hinges and keyhole escutcheons. A sober and well-made armoire. Photo : Canada Steamship Lines.

WOOD : pine   PROVENANCE : Yamachiche, P.Q.

(Coll. Canada Steamship Lines, Tadoussac, P.Q.).

47. TRANSITIONAL ARMOIRE, WITH DIAMOND-POINT CARVING. MID 18th C.

Armoire with two doors and a single drawer, ornamented with double mouldings, lozenge and St Andrew's-cross panels, in diamond-point form. The mouldings on the two upper panels are in the Louis XIV, the rest in Louis XIII style. Transitional piece. One of the rare Canadian armoires with a false centre post. In structure it is akin to the diamond-point armoires of the Jura and the Franche-Comté. Original handles, fische hinges and keyhole escutcheons. An imposing and excellently constructed piece.

w. 4' 4''	h. 7' 4½''	d. 1' 9⅝''
132 cm	225 cm	55 cm

WOOD : pine   PROVENANCE : Verchères, P.Q.

(Coll. Canada Steamship Lines, Tadoussac, P.Q.).

48. DETAIL.

49. TRANSITIONAL ARMOIRE, CARVED WITH LOZENGES. LATE 18th C.

Armoire, with two arched doors, the panels of which are decorated with lozenges. The two upper panels are shaped in the Louis XV manner. The arched doors are in the Louis XIV manner. This is known as a transitional armoire on account of the break with rectilinear lines and the introduction of incurved lines. The cornice is a later addition.

w. 4' 4''	h. 6' 8½''	d. 1' 7''
132 cm	203 cm	48 cm

WOOD : pine   PROVENANCE : Quebec district

(Coll. Donnacona Paper Co. Ltd, lent to the Provincial Museum, Quebec).

50. ARMOIRE, WITH SIMPLIFIED LINEN-FOLD ORNAMENTATION. LATE 17th C.

Armoire, with two doors, probably the lower stage of a two-tiered buffet, as the festooned border on the top would suggest. This illustrates the transition of the chest into a buffet. The panels are decorated with simplified medieval linen folds. The rat-tail fische hinges are substitutes for the original fische hinges. The keyhole escutcheon is missing and a wooden latch has been added later. An appealing piece, having a Gothic look.

w. 4'	h. 4' 6½''	d. 1' 11¼''
122 cm	138 cm	59 cm

WOOD : pine

PROVENANCE : Saint-Louis de Lotbinière, P.Q.

(Coll. Mr L.V. Randall, Montreal).

51. RUSTIC ARMOIRE, WITH REEDED DESIGNS. EARLY 19th C.

Rustic armoire having two doors and panels carved with simplified linen folds and reeding over the whole façade. Period hinges. Of peasant make, an attractive piece, having a local tang.

w. 4'	h. 5' 8½''	d. 1' 5½''
122 cm	174 cm	44 cm

WOOD : pine   PROVENANCE : Saint-Romuald, P.Q.

(Coll. Provincial Museum, Quebec).

52. RUSTIC ARMOIRETTE, WITH ONE DOOR. LATE 18th C.

Rustic armoirette, with one door and two shaped panels. Wrought-iron period hinges. The wooden latch is a later addition. A small peasant piece.

w. 2' 10¼''	h. 3' 3¼''	d. 1' 7¾''
87 cm	100 cm	50 cm

WOOD : pine

PROVENANCE : Château-Richer, P.Q.

(Coll. Canada Steamship Lines, Tadoussac, P.Q.).

53. CHILD'S ARMOIRETTE, WITH TWO DOORS. LATE 18th C.

Child's armoirette, having two doors with plain panels and bracket feet. Period rat-tail fische hinges.

w. 1' 6¾''	h. 1' 7''	d. 6¼''
47 cm	48 cm	16 cm

WOOD : butternut

(Coll. Mr Jean Dubuc, Quebec).

54. ARMOIRETTE, WITH ONE DOOR. MID 18th C.

Armoirette, with one plain panel. Probably a small bedside piece. Original fische hinges and keyhole escutcheons.

w. 1' 3½''	h. 1' 8½''	d. 8½''
39 cm	52 cm	22 cm

WOOD : pine

(Coll. Miss Barbara Richardson, Sainte-Agathe des Monts, P.Q.).

55. ARMOIRETTE, WITH TWO DOORS. MID 18th C.

Small armoire, with two doors. The frames of the panels are chamfered. The panels are decorated with a small motif in arch form in the Louis XIII manner. Original fische hinges. The dowels are a later addition. Worn feet. A handsome food-locker.

| w. 1' 7¼" | H. 2' 3¼" | D. 9¾" |
| 49 cm | 69 cm | 25 cm |

WOOD : pine   PROVENANCE : L'Assomption, P.Q.

(Coll. Mr Léonard Larin, Montreal).

56. RUSTIC ARMOIRE, WITH TWO DOORS. MID 18th C.

Rustic armoire, with two doors. The panels are shaped and have small shell and simplified linen-fold decoration. The lower rail is ornamented with a small shell. Both lower and upper rails are heavy. Original fische hinges. The wooden latch is a later addition. A rustic piece with naive proportions.

| w. 4' 1" | H. 5' 1" | D. 1' 4½" |
| 124 cm | 155 cm | 42 cm |

WOOD : pine
PROVENANCE : Saint-Augustin de Portneuf, P.Q.

(Coll. Canada Steamship Lines, Tadoussac, P.Q.).

57. MULTI-PANELLED ARMOIRE, UNDER LOUIS XIII AND LOUIS XV INFLUENCE. LATE 18th C.

Armoire, having two doors, with shaped upper panels. The other panels are square or rectangular. The centre post has rectangular panels, and the cornice is decorated with ovolos and naive *rais de cœur*. The cornice has been restored. The wooden latches are a later addition. A robust armoire.

| w. 4' 8" | H. 6' 4¼" | D. 1' 7" |
| 142 cm | 194 cm | 48 cm |

WOOD : pine

(Coll. Canada Steamship Lines, Tadoussac, P.Q.).

58. ARMOIRE WITH ARCHED DOORS, IN THE LOUIS XIV MANNER. MID 18th C.

Armoire, with two arched doors and six panels in the Louis XIV manner. The angles of the panels are timid imitations of simplified linen folds. The lower rail and bracket base are in an unusual style, and may possibly have been modified. Massive stiles. The base mouldings have been renovated. Period fische hinges and keyhole escutcheons.

| w. 4' 5" | H. 6' 11⅝" | D. 1' 7" |
| 135 cm | 212 cm | 48 cm |

WOOD : pine   PROVENANCE : Quebec district

(Coll. Dr and Mrs Wilfrid Caron, Cap Rouge, P.Q.).

59. SERPENTINE-SHAPED ARMOIRE, FROM ST LOUIS, MISSOURI, IN THE LOUIS XIV MANNER. LATE 18th C.

Serpentine-shaped armoire (known as the Chouteau armoire from St Louis, Missouri, U.S.A.), with two arched doors. The panels and upper rail are decorated with *fleurs de lys* and stylized flowers. The shaped lower rail has a shell carving and the stiles are carved with stars. The feet are in the claw-and-ball manner, of American Chippendale derivation. To my knowledge this is the only specimen of an armoire with claw-and-ball feet (generally found on certain Canadian commodes). Period fische hinges and keyhole escutcheons. One of the rare pieces of French inspiration from the Mississippi Valley. According to oral tradition it was made towards the end of the eighteenth century by a woodworker of Canadian origin for the Chouteau family of St Louis. The cornice is a later addition. An interesting Mississippi armoire.

| w. 5' 3" | H. 8' | D. 1' 1" |
| 160 cm | 244 cm | 33 cm |

WOOD : Mississippi walnut

PROVENANCE : Saint Louis, Missouri, U.S.A.

(Coll. Missouri Historical Society, Saint Louis, Missouri, U.S.A.).

60. ARMOIRE, DECORATED IN A RUSTIC MANNER. LATE 18th C.

Armoire, with two doors. The panels and friezes of the upper rail have *guilloché* motifs. The upper rails of the doors and the bottom rail are carved with tiny shells. Wolf's teeth run along the angles of the stiles, and the feet suggest a cabriole curve. Original fische hinges. The cornice is a later addition.

| w. 4' 5" | H. 6' 8" | D. 1' 4" |
| 135 cm | 203 cm | 41 cm |

WOOD : butternut and pine

(Coll. Canadair Limited, Saint-Laurent, Montreal).

61. SMALL RUSTIC ARMOIRE, CARVED WITH MULTIPLE SPIRALS. LATE 18th C.

Small rustic armoire, having shaped doors decorated with multiple spirals. The mouldings of the centre post are prolonged inside the rails. This is a Canadian characteristic. Massive rails and stiles. The small cornice is ornamented with dentils. Original fische hinges and keyhole escutcheons. A naive and distinctly Canadian piece.

| w. 4' | H. 5' 1" | D. 1' 4" |
| 122 cm | 155 cm | .41 cm |

WOOD : pine   PROVENANCE : Saint-Hilaire, P.Q.

(Coll. Mr and Mrs Jean Raymond, Westmount, P.Q.).

62. ARMOIRE, DECORATED WITH FOLIATED SCROLLS, IN THE LOUIS XV MANNER. LATE 18th C.

Armoire with two doors. The panels are shaped

and carved with foliated scrolls (derived from crosiers and foliage) in the *rocaille* manner and interpreted in a rustic fashion. The centre post is decorated with an acanthus leaf, surmounted by a *palmette*. The cornice has a projecting profile and is profusely moulded. The carving recalls that of the workshops of Liébert, Pépin and Quevillon. The feet are missing and the bracket base, added later, does not harmonize with the armoire.

w. 3' 11"	h. 6' 8¼"	d. 1' 4¾"
119 cm	204 cm	42 cm

WOOD : pine   PROVENANCE : Montreal district

(Coll. Mr and Mrs A.F. Murphy, Westmount, P.Q.).

63. CANADIAN ARMOIRE " A LA BOURGUIGNONNE ". LATE 18th OR EARLY 19th C.

Armoire, having two doors, shaped panels with simplified linen-fold carving, and a cornice and horizontal frieze on the upper rail. The base has moulding in the Renaissance tradition. This is a typical Burgundian-type armoire, and the craftsman who made it no doubt made a faithful copy of either an actual Burgundian armoire or an engraving of one. In Burgundy the flattened baluster feet are called *miches* or *flamusses*. Original fische hinges and keyhole escutcheons. A fine example of an armoire executed by a skilled hand, probably the work of a church master-carver and wood-worker. The spirals decorated with foliage recall the work of the Liéberts or the Quevillons.

w. 4' 9½"	h. 7' 3½"	d. 1' 7¾"
146 cm	222 cm	50 cm

WOOD : pine

(Coll. Royal Ontario Museum, Toronto, Ont.).

64. ARMOIRE, CARVED WITH FLORAL MOTIFS. LATE 18th C.

Armoire, with two doors and shaped panels. The rails and centre posts are decorated with floral motifs, vases, and shells of *Régence* and Louis XV derivation. The stylized flowers are those found in all provincial furniture, especially in Haute-Bretagne, Touraine and Lorraine. The flower with a double row of petals which occurs on the panels is similar to a zinnia. Dentil cornice. The feet suggest a curve. Original flame-shaped keyhole escutcheon and rat-tail fische hinges. A very Canadian piece, perhaps overladen with ornamentation, but still very attractive.

w. 4' 3"	h. 6' 10¼"	d. 1' 6½"
130 cm	209 cm	47 cm

WOOD : pine
PROVENANCE : Saint-Jean-Baptiste de Rouville, P.Q.

(Coll. Mrs Nettie Sharpe, Saint-Lambert, P.Q.).

65. DETAIL.

66. DETAIL.

67. UNUSUAL ARMOIRE, FROM BATISCAN. LATE 18th C.

Unusual armoire, from Batiscan, with shaped panels carved with spirals. The bottom rail has an *appliqué os de mouton* motif carved with geometric roundels and foliage. The shaped *appliqué* top rail also suggests *os de mouton* curves and has foliage carving with, in the centre, a heart containing three geometrical roundels. The stiles are also carved with foliated scrolls arising from vases. Original fische hinges and keyhole escutcheons. One of the finest of Canadian armoires with its handsome proportions and profusion of spirals.

w. 4' 9"	h. 7' 8½"	d. 1' 9½"
145 cm	235 cm	55 cm

WOOD : pine   PROVENANCE : Batiscan, P.Q.

(Coll. Canada Steamship Lines, Tadoussac, P.Q.).

68. SMALL RUSTIC ARMOIRE, WITH ONE ARCHED DOOR. LATE 18th C.

Small rustic armoire, with one arched door and rectangular side panels. The bracket base is a later addition.

w. 1' 10"	h. 2' 9"	d. 1' 10"
56 cm	84 cm	56 cm

WOOD : pine

(Coll. Canadair Limited, Saint-Laurent, Montreal).

69. SMALL RUSTIC ARMOIRE, WITH ONE DOOR. LATE 18th C.

Small rustic armoire, with one door. The panels and lower rails are shaped. The keyhole escutcheon is missing. The wooden latch was undoubtedly added when the lock was broken. Original rat-tail fische hinges.

w. 1' 11¼"	h. 2' 6½"	d. 1' 4½"
59 cm	77 cm	42 cm

WOOD : pine   PROVENANCE : Quebec district

(Coll. Mr L.V. Randall, Montreal).

70. SMALL SERPENTINE-SHAPED ARMOIRE, WITH ONE DOOR, IN THE LOUIS XV MANNER. LATE 18th C.

Small serpentine-shaped armoire, with one door, in the Louis XV manner. The panel is shaped and carved with spirals. The bottom rail is decorated with an upturned shell, flowers, foliage, spirals and a small *palmette*. The double-scroll curved feet are ornamented with acanthus leaves. There is a slight serpentine curve on the sides. Original keyhole escutcheons and fische hinges. Some details of the carving are similar to that on certain commodes, see no. 477, 503, 504. The volutes of the feet have been restored. A small, attractive piece.

w. front 2' 4"	h. 3' 3⅜"	d. 1' 6¾"
71 cm	100 cm	47 cm
w. rear 2' 10¾"		
88 cm		

WOOD : butternut

PROVENANCE : L'Acadie, P.Q.

(Coll. Mr and Mrs David G. McConnell, Dorval, P.Q.).

71. SMALL SERPENTINE-SHAPED ARMOIRE, WITH ONE DOOR. LATE 18th C.

Small serpentine-shaped armoire, with one shaped panel carved with spirals. A shell decorates the shaped bottom rail, and the double scrolls of the feet are surmounted by an acanthus leaf. The sides are slightly serpentine-shaped. The keyhole escutcheon is missing and a wooden latch has been added. Original rat-tail fische hinges. The door is off-joint, mutilated and poorly restored. (Canadian museums hardly seem to care about the presentation of their own furniture. These precious pieces at least deserve to be kept decently and in good order.) These small pieces of furniture are very rare and therefore are very much sought after by collectors. This example is one of a pair; the other has been found, but is even more damaged.

w. 2' 4''	H. 3' 1½''	D. 1' 6½''
71 cm	95 cm	47 cm

WOOD : pine

PROVENANCE : Ancienne Lorette, P.Q.

(Coll. Museum of Fine Arts, Montreal).

72. RUSTIC ARMOIRE, IN THE LOUIS XV MANNER. LATE 18th C.

Rustic armoire, having shaped panels, with similarities to the Louis XV style. The bottom rail and the suggestion of a cabriole curve in the feet reveal a certain naivety of interpretation, as does the heaviness of the upper rail with its curious horizontal friezes. The cornice is heavily moulded. Original fische hinges and keyhole escutcheons. A Canadian armoire with high feet and attractive proportions.

w. 4' 2⅝''	H. 6' 10''	D. 1' 6½''
129 cm	208 cm	47 cm

WOOD : pine PROVENANCE : Saint-Jude, P.Q.

(Coll. Mr and Mrs Fred Mulligan, Pleasant Valley, Henrysburg, P.Q.).

73. RUSTIC ARMOIRE, FROM LONGUEUIL. LATE 18th C.

Rustic armoire, with two doors. The shaped panels and the doors are carved from a single plank. The proportions and workmanship are primitive. Massive rails, centre post, and stiles. The wooden latch is a later addition. Original rat-rail fische hinges. A rare example of carved doors made from one plank. Heavy armoire made by an unskilled hand, but not without some appeal.

w. 3' 6''	H. 5' 5''	D. 1' 5''
107 cm	165 cm	43 cm

WOOD : pine PROVENANCE : Longueuil, P.Q.

(Coll. Mr and Mrs F.M. Hutchins, Pembroke, Ont.).

74. DETAIL.

75. DETAIL.

76. TWO-DOOR ARMOIRE, PROFUSELY DECORATED WITH GEOMETRIC DESIGNS. EARLY 19th C.

Two-door armoire. The doors are decorated with zig-zag incisions, parallel and opposed grooves, roundels, chip-carved circles, wolf's teeth, lozenges, grooves, daisies, St Andrew's crosses, stars, and gouge-work, etc. The mouldings on the panels are *appliqué*. A very rare kind of Canadian armoire; its decoration recalls the geometric designs found all over Europe, as well as the carved grooves on some furniture from the Bresse region of Burgundy, and even the designs found on Huron and Iroquois ceramics. A prestigious Canadian armoire. Original fische hinges and keyhole escutcheons.

w. 4' 1''	H. 5' 6''	D. 1' 4''
124 cm	168 cm	41 cm

WOOD : pine PROVENANCE : Montreal district

(Coll. Mr L.V. Randall, Montreal).

77. SMALL ARMOIRE, CARVED WITH LOZENGES ON THE DRAWERS. LATE 18th C.

Small armoire, with two doors and shaped panels and bottom rail, in the Louis XV manner. The two drawers are decorated with lozenges of Louis XIII derivation. There are friezes and carved discs on the stiles, and a suggestion of a cabriole curve to the feet. Original fische hinges, slide bolts and hinged rings. An agreeable piece which combines two styles.

w. 4' ⅝''	H. 4' 1''	D. 1' 6¼''
123 cm	124 cm	47 cm

WOOD : butternut

PROVENANCE : Montreal district

(Coll. Mr and Mrs Thomas Caverhill, Montreal).

78. ARMOIRE, CARVED WITH MULTIPLE SPIRALS, IN THE LOUIS XV MANNER. LATE 18th C.

Armoire, with two doors and shaped rails carved with multiple spirals. The bottom rail with its elegant shaping would benefit from restoration, as one spiral is missing. Note the prolongation of the panel on the centre post inside the rails, which is a Canadian characteristic. Original fische hinges and keyhole escutcheons. A very Canadian piece.

w. 4' 4''	H. 6'	D. 1' 6¾''
132 cm	183 cm	48 cm

WOOD : pine

PROVENANCE : Sainte-Marie-Salomé, P.Q.

(Coll. Mr and Mrs Pierre Gouin, Saint-Sulpice, P.Q.).

79. SMALL ARMOIRE, IN THE LOUIS XIII AND LOUIS XV MANNERS. MID 18th C.

Small armoire, with panels shaped in the Louis XV manner. The framework is inspired by the rectilinear forms of the Louis XIII style. Original fische hinges.

w. 3' 5⅜"	H. 4' ½"	D. 1' 1½"
105 cm	123 cm	34 cm

WOOD : pine   PROVENANCE : Saint-Vallier, P.Q.

(Coll. Miss Barbara Richardson, Sainte-Agathe des Monts, P.Q.).

80. ARMOIRE, IN THE LOUIS XV MANNER. LATE 18th C.

Armoire, with shaped panels carved with shells and fine moulding in the *Régence* and Louis XV manner. Spirals on the bottom rail have been broken off. The rounded corners of the stiles are interrupted in the centre and suggest chamfering. The prominent cornice, carved with *rais de cœur* and dentils, has been restored at the extreme left. Original fische hinges. The keyhole escutcheon is missing and a wooden latch has been added. Painted with grey aluminium paint. A classical piece.

w. 4' 2¼"	H. 6' 2¾"	D. 1' 5"
128 cm	190 cm	43 cm

WOOD : pine   PROVENANCE : Sainte-Adèle, P.Q.

(Coll. Mr and Mrs Victor M. Drury, Lake Anne, P.Q.).

81. DETAIL.

82. DETAIL.

83. RICHLY DECORATED ARMOIRE. LATE 18th C.

Armoire, having a façade profusely carved with floral and vegetal motifs. In France, panels are not generally decorated except in Haute-Bretagne, the Rennes district and Lorraine. This armoire was made by the woodworker who made no. 64 but it has a greater amount of ornamentation covering the whole façade. It also has shaped panels carved with spirals, and olive or willow leaves. Interlaced foliated scrolls, as on the panels, run up the centre post. Foliated, scrollwork and stylized flowers appear on the rails and stiles, with cabling, *rais de cœur*, dentils, pearls and ovolos on the cornice. Original fische hinges. The Louis XV keyhole escutcheons are later additions. There is an astonishing exuberance in the decoration, which is almost superabundant, although it is none the less an interesting armoire.

w. 4' 8½"	H. 7'	D. 1' 7"
144 cm	213 cm	48 cm

WOOD : pine   PROVENANCE : Châteauguay, P.Q.

(Coll. Canadair Limited, Saint Laurent, Montreal).

84. DETAIL.

85. ARMOIRE, WITH PANELS DECORATED WITH FOLIATED SCROLLS. LATE 18th C.

Armoire, with shaped panels decorated with foliated scrollwork. A massive shaped rail carved with a small stylized flower in the centre. The leaves and flowers are carved inside a kind of cartouche, which is also garnished with a background of punchwork. The armoire has been stripped of all paint except on the foliated scrolls. Although showing French influence, this armoire is typically Canadian in its proportions and details. An attractive piece.

w. 5' 1"	H. 6' 9½"	D. 1' 3¾"
155 cm	207 cm	40 cm

WOOD : pine   PROVENANCE : Saint-Lin, P.Q.

(Coll. Canada Steamship Lines, Tadoussac, P.Q.).

86. DETAIL.

87. ARMOIRE, DECORATED WITH APPLIQUÉ " ROCAILLE ". LATE 18th C.

Armoire, with two shaped panels. The upper panels are naively decorated with daisies, vine leaves, bunches of grapes and motifs in the *rocaille* manner. All these motifs are carved and *appliqué* with hand-forged nails. The framework is in the Louis XIII tradition and the feet are in the form of torches. Original rat-tail hinges and keyhole escutcheons. An unusual piece of furniture which is very definitely Canadian in manner.

w. 4' 3¼"	H. 6' 2⅝"	D. 1' 5½"
130 cm	189 cm	45 cm

WOOD : pine

(Coll. Miss Barbara Richardson, Sainte-Agathe des Monts, P.Q.).

88. SMALL RUSTIC ARMOIRE, WITH A SHALLOW BOW FRONT. MID 18th C.

Small rustic armoire, with a shallow bow front. It has two doors with shaped panels, a drawer and a festooned bottom rail. The rounded corners of the stiles recall those of a commode. The drawer and bottom rail have been restored. Original fische hinges.

w. 2' 8¾"	H. 2' 7¾"	D. 1' 6⅝"
83 cm	80 cm	47 cm

WOOD : pine

PROVENANCE : Laprairie de la Madeleine, P.Q.

(Coll. Miss Barbara Richardson, Sainte-Agathe des Monts, P.Q.).

89. ARMOIRE, WITH PANELS IN THE FLEMISH MANNER. LATE 18th C.

Armoire, with panels reminiscent of those on Flemish and Dutch furniture. The bracket base shows English influence. Period fische hinges and keyhole escutcheons.

w. 4' 8''	H. 4' 5¼''	D. 1' 8''
142 cm	136 cm	51 cm

WOOD : pine

PROVENANCE : Hôpital-Général, Quebec

(Coll. Mr and Mrs J.N. Cole, Montreal).

90. ARMOIRE, DECORATED WITH FOLIATED SCROLLS, FROM ST-HILAIRE. LATE 18th C.

Armoire, with shaped upper panels in the Louis XV manner. The centre post and the bottom rail are carved with foliated scrollwork and stylized flowers, and are comparable to the carving found on armoires from the Rennes district. This armoire, although showing the influence of Haute-Bretagne, is very Canadian. Dentil cornice, original fische hinges. One of the finest and most charming Canadian armoires.

w. 4' 4¼''	H. 5' 7¼''	D. 1' 8''
133 cm	171 cm	51 cm

WOOD : pine   PROVENANCE : Saint-Hilaire, P.Q.

(Coll. Mr and Mrs Jean Raymond, Westmount, P.Q.).

91. ARMOIRE, CARVED WITH FOLIATED SCROLLS, FROM L'ASSOMPTION. LATE 18th C.

Armoire, having shaped panels and carved with spirals and foliated scrollwork. The foliated scrolls on the centre post consist of a succession of small crosiers interlaced with foliage derived from *rocaille*. The rectilinear structure of this armoire is inspired by the Louis XIII style. Original fische hinges and keyhole escutcheons. A small and attractive Canadian armoire.

w. 4' 3¾''	H. 6' 3¾''	D. 1' 7''
131 cm	192 cm	48 cm

WOOD : pine   PROVENANCE : l'Assomption, P.Q.

(Coll. Mr and Mrs A.M. Laurie, Longueuil, P.Q.).

92. BONNETIÈRE, FORMERLY IN THE POSSESSION OF MADAME D'YOUVILLE. LATE 18th C.

Bonnetière or bonnet-cupboard, a form of wardrobe which comes from the bedroom of Madame d'Youville, the foundress of the Grey Nuns. This armoire, with only one door, was used as a wardrobe and also as a wash-stand. A basin, soap dish and other toilet requisites were placed on an inner shelf and it bore a mirror on the inside of the door. This austere piece (like certain convent furniture) has been piously preserved by the nuns to whom it was left by Madame d'Youville. In Canada this model was nearly always used as a wardrobe, and rarely as a bonnet-cupboard as in France. It has a projecting cornice, together with original rat-tail hinges and keyhole escutcheons. The wooden latch was added later, but the dark brown colouring is the original.

w. 2' 3''	H. 6' 6''	D. 1' 2¾''
69 cm	198 cm	37 cm

WOOD : pine   PROVENANCE : Montreal

(Coll. Hôpital-Général of the Grey Nuns, Montreal).

93. BONNETIÈRE OR WARDROBE, DECORATED WITH RENAISSANCE MOTIFS. EARLY 19th C.

Bonnet-cupboard or wardrobe, having one door and two panels carved with Renaissance motifs. The wrought-iron hinges are ornamented with *fleurs de lys*, and the slide bolt is original. The left-hand upright of the door has been replaced. This piece is rather unusual.

w. 1' 11¾''	H. 4' 3⅝''	D. 1' 7½''
60 cm	131 cm	50 cm

WOOD : pine

(Coll. Mr and Mrs Dean P. Stockwell, Town of Mount Royal, P.Q.).

94. ARMOIRE, IN THE ADAM MANNER. LATE 18th C.

Armoire, with *appliqué* ornaments on the panels, in the Adam manner. The prominent moulding on the bottom rail is derived from the Louis XIII style. The suggestion of a cabriole curve on the feet is inspired by Louis XV models. Two festooned ribbons surround the cornice, which is also decorated with cabling. Original fische hinges. The cornice and base mouldings have been restored. A finely proportioned Canadian armoire.

w. 4' 2''	H. 6' ¾''	D. 1' 5½''
127 cm	185 cm	44 cm

WOOD : pine

(Coll. Royal Ontario Museum, Toronto, Ontario).

95. DETAIL.

96. ARMOIRE, DECORATED WITH SHELLS AND SPIRALS. LATE 18th C.

Armoire, with panels and bottom rail, abundantly carved with shells and spirals. The cornice has a double ribbon of gouge-work. The profusion of shells and spirals give it a very Canadian look.

w. 4' 4''	H. 6' 4''	D. 1' 5''
132 cm	193 cm	43 cm

WOOD : pine

PROVENANCE : Saint-Barthélémy, P.Q.

(Coll. Mr and Mrs Edgar Davidson, Montreal).

97. ARMOIRE WITH SHAPED PANELS, IN THE LOUIS XV MANNER. LATE 18th C.

Armoire, having shaped panels and bottom rails reminiscent of certain armoires from Bresse and Vendée. The three rectangular panels in the centre post are carved with a geometric roundel, two anchors and a crosier with foliage. The upper rail, divided into two rectangular friezes in guilloché groundwork, has a disc in the centre. The stiles have rounded corners. The cornice is missing. Original fische hinges and keyhole escutcheons. Robust armoire with very French lines.

w. 4' 6''   H. 6' 7¼''   D. 1' 9½''
137 cm   202 cm   55 cm
WOOD : pine
PROVENANCE : Saint-Marc-sur-Richelieu, P.Q.
(Coll. Mr and Mrs Antoine Dubuc, Chicoutimi, P.Q.).

98. ARMOIRE, FROM ST MARC-SUR-RICHELIEU. LATE 18th C.

Armoire, with shaped panels. The cut of the bottom rail is reminiscent of armoires from Vendée and Bresse armoires (cf. no. 97). It was found in the same village as no. 97 and presumably was made by the same craftsman. Planing marks can be seen on the surface of the panels. Original fische hinges, keyhole escutcheons, and red ochre colouring.

w. 4' 11''   H. 7' 5''   D. 1' 7''
150 cm   226 cm   48 cm
WOOD : pine
PROVENANCE : Saint-Marc-sur-Richelieu, P.Q.
(Coll. Miss Barbara Richardson, Sainte-Agathe des Monts, P.Q.).

99. ARMOIRE, IN THE " ROCAILLE " MANNER, DECORATED WITH MARQUETRY. EARLY 19th C.

Armoire, with shaped panels carved with foliated scrollwork, flowers and *rocaille* motifs. Interlaced marquetry work runs all along the centre post. The stiles and doors are also inlaid with marquetry. The shaped, openwork bottom rail is ornamented with foliage and crosiers derived from *rocaille*. Squat, curved feet. The doors, at one time overlapping, are now flush with the stiles and rails. Screw hinges have been substituted for the original fische hinges. The dentils of the cornice are missing. A very well executed piece, constructed by a Master church-carver and woodworker of the School of Liébert or Quevillon. The carving recalls work of Amable Gauthier who left several pieces in the early nineteenth-century Church of St Isidore de Laprairie. This armoire was found in the same village. A rare piece of Canadian marquetry furniture. It is typical of the *Canadian rococo* style.

w. 4' 2½''   H. 7' 9½''   D. 1' 7''
128 cm   237 cm   49 cm

WOOD : butternut
PROVENANCE : Saint-Isidore de Laprairie, P.Q.
(Coll. Dr and Mrs Herbert T. Schwarz, Montreal).

100. ARMOIRE, IN THE ADAM AND LOUIS XVI MANNERS. EARLY 19th C.

Two-door armoire, with six panels decorated with *appliqué* mouldings, carved suns and fluting in the Adam and Louis XVI manners. The doors are flush with the stiles and rails. The stiles are decorated with parallel reeding, with cabling on the corners. On the base the reeding takes the form of chevrons. A festooned bandelet is topped by a moulded cornice carved with cabling, vertical and parallel reeding and small suns incised with a burin. The plain bottom rail spoils the general effect. The Adam style is the dominant influence on this delicate and soberly decorated piece. Original hinges and keyhole escutcheon.

w. 4' 8''   H. 6' 6½''   D. 1' 7''
142 cm   199 cm   48 cm
WOOD : pine
(Coll. Institute of Applied Arts, Montreal).

101. ARMOIRE, WITH DRAWER, IN THE LOUIS XV MANNER. LATE 18th C.

Armoire, with shaped panels in the Louis XV manner. The drawers and base mouldings are of Louis XIII derivation. Robust stiles decorated with *caissons*, and a prominent cornice. The panels and base are unbalanced. Massive lower rails. The petal-shaped hinged rings, keyhole escutcheons and fische hinges are all original. An unusually proportioned but interesting armoire.

w. 4' 5⅝''   H. 7' 7¾''   D. 1' 9⅜''
136 cm   233 cm   54 cm
WOOD : pine   PROVENANCE : Quebec district
(Coll. Miss Barbara Richardson, Sainte-Agathe des Monts, P.Q.).

102. MULTI-PANELLED ARMOIRE. 19th C.

Armoire, with twenty-two panels of varying sizes. Fluted centre post. Undulating bandelet on the cornice. Bracket base showing English influence.

w. 4' 9''   H. 6' 9¼''   D. 1' 6''
145 cm   207 cm   46 cm
WOOD : pine   PROVENANCE : Sherbrooke district
(Coll. Mr and Mrs Eric Reford, Magog, P.Q.).

MID EIGHTEENTH-CENTURY ARMOIRE, WITH VARIEGATED DIAMOND POINT CARVINGS.
ORIGINAL COLOURS.

24. ARMOIRE « A L'ANCIENNE », D'ESPRIT LOUIS XIII. FIN XVIIᵉ S.
ARMOIRE " A L'ANCIENNE ", IN THE LOUIS XIII MANNER.   LATE
17th C.

25-26. DÉTAIL.
DETAIL.

27. ARMOIRE, ORNÉE DE MULTIPLES SPIRALES ET DE CO-
QUILLES. FIN XVIIIe S.
TWO-DOOR ARMOIRE, CARVED WITH MULTIPLE SPIRALS
AND SHELLS. LATE 18th C.

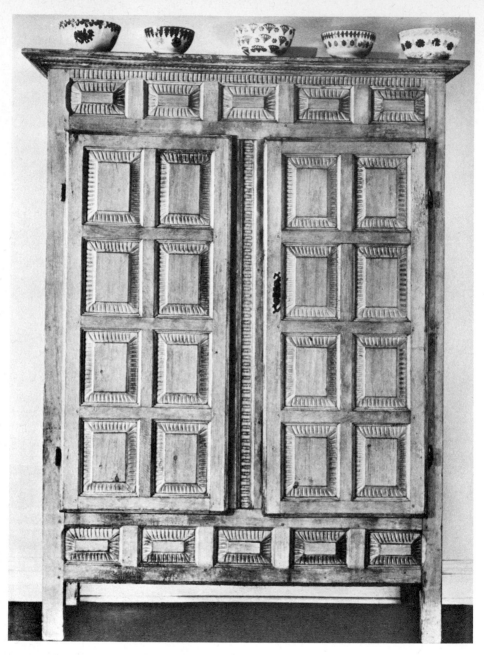

28. ARMOIRE A MULTIPLES PANNEAUX, D'ESPRIT ADAM.
FIN XVIIIᵉ S.
ARMOIRE, WITH MULTIPLE PANELS, IN THE ADAM STYLE.
LATE 18th C.

29. ARMOIRE DE LA RIVIÈRE OUELLE, A MULTIPLES
DÉCORS. FIN XVIIIᵉ S.
ARMOIRE FROM RIVIÈRE OUELLE, CARVED WITH VARIOUS
MOTIFS. LATE 18th C.

30-31. DÉTAIL.
DETAIL.

32. ARMOIRE, D'INSPIRATION LOUIS XVI ET ADAM. FIN XVIIIᵉ S.
ARMOIRE, DERIVING FROM THE LOUIS XVI AND ADAM STYLES. LATE 18th C.

33. DÉTAIL.
DETAIL.

34. PETITE ARMOIRE RUSTIQUE A UN VAN-
TAIL. FIN XVIIIᵉ S.
SMALL RUSTIC ARMOIRE, WITH ONE DOOR.
LATE 18th C.

35. ARMOIRE DE TRANSITION, D'INSPIRATION LOUIS XIII
ET LOUIS XV. MILIEU XVIIIᵉ S.
ARMOIRE, WITH MOTIFS DERIVING FROM BOTH LOUIS XIII
AND LOUIS XV STYLES.   MID 18th C.

36. PETITE ARMOIRE RUSTIQUE A UN VANTAIL. DÉBUT XIXᵉ S.
SMALL RUSTIC ARMOIRE, WITH ONE DOOR. EARLY 19th C.

37. PETITE ARMOIRE RUSTIQUE, D'INSPIRATION ADAM. DÉBUT XIXᵉ S.
SMALL RUSTIC ARMOIRE, DERIVED FROM THE ADAM STYLE. EARLY 19th C.

38. ARMOIRE DE BERTHIER-EN-HAUT, D'INSPIRATION
LOUIS XV ET LOUIS XVI. FIN XVIIIe S.
ARMOIRE FROM BERTHIER-EN-HAUT, IN THE LOUIS XV
AND LOUIS XVI STYLES. LATE 18th C.

39. ARMOIRE DÉCORÉE DE DISQUES OU DE « GALETTES ».
MILIEU XVIIIᵉ S.
ARMOIRE, CARVED WITH DISCS OR "GALETTES". MID
18th C.

40. ARMOIRE A POINTES DE DIAMANT, D'ESPRIT LOUIS XIII.
MILIEU XVIIIe S.
ARMOIRE, CARVED WITH DIAMOND-POINTS, IN LOUIS XIII
STYLE.   MID 18th C.

41. PETITE ARMOIRE A POINTES DE DIA
MANT, D'ESPRIT LOUIS XIII. MILIEU XVIIIᵉ 9
SMALL ARMOIRE, WITH DIAMOND POIN
CARVING, IN THE LOUIS XIII STYLE. MI
18th C.

42. ARMOIRE DÉCORÉE DE LOSANGES ET DE « GALETTES ».
MILIEU XVIIIᵉ S.
TWO-DOOR ARMOIRE, DECORATED WITH LOZENGES AND
DISCS OR " GALETTES ". MID 18th C.

43. ARMOIRE A POINTES DE DIAMANT, D'ESPRIT LOUIS
XIII. FIN XVIIIᵉ S.
ARMOIRE, CARVED WITH DIAMOND POINTS, IN THE LOUIS
XIII MANNER. LATE 18th C.

44. ARMOIRE A LOSANGES, A CORNICHE ORNÉE
DE DEUX TIROIRS. DÉBUT XIXᵉ S.
ARMOIRE, CARVED WITH LOZENGES, WITH TWO
DRAWERS IN THE CORNICE. EARLY 19th C.

45. ARMOIRE A LOSANGES, D'INFLUEN-
CE HAUTE-BRETAGNE. XVIIIᵉ S.
ARMOIRE, CARVED WITH LOZENGES,
UNDER HAUTE-BRETAGNE INFLUENCE.
18th c.

46. ARMOIRE A POINTES DE DIAMANT
ORNÉES DE DESSINS GÉOMÉTRIQUES.
XVIIIᵉ S.
ARMOIRE, CARVED WITH DIAMOND
POINTS DECORATED WITH GEOMETRIC
DESIGNS. 18th c.

47. ARMOIRE DE TRANSITION, A POIN-
TES DE DIAMANT. MILIEU XVIIIe S.
TRANSITIONAL ARMOIRE, WITH DIA-
MOND-POINT CARVING. MID 18th C.

48. DÉTAIL.
DETAIL.

49. ARMOIRE DE TRANSITION, A LOSANGES. FIN XVIIIe S.
TRANSITIONAL ARMOIRE, CARVED WITH LOZENGES. LATE 18th C.

50. ARMOIRE ORNÉE DE PLIS DE SERVIETTE SIMPLIFIES. FIN XVIIe S.
ARMOIRE, WITH SIMPLIFIED LINEN-FOLD ORNAMENTATION. LATE 17th C.

51. ARMOIRE RUSTIQUE, A DÉCOR DE STRIES. DÉBUT
XIXᵉ S.
RUSTIC ARMOIRE, WITH REEDED DESIGNS. EARLY 19th C.

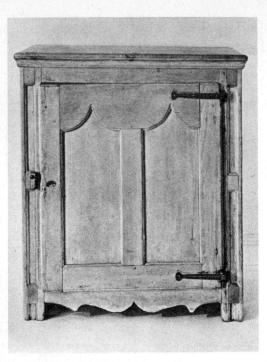

52. ARMOIRETTE RUSTIQUE A UN VANTAIL. FIN XVIIIᵉ S.
RUSTIC ARMOIRETTE, WITH ONE DOOR. LATE 18th C.

53. ARMOIRETTE D'ENFANT A DEUX VANTAUX. FIN XVIIIᵉ S.
CHILD'S ARMOIRETTE, WITH TWO DOORS. LATE 18th C.

54. ARMOIRETTE A UN VANTAIL. MILIEU XVIIIᵉ S.
ARMOIRETTE, WITH ONE DOOR. MID 18th C.

55. ARMOIRETTE A DEUX VANTAUX. MILIEU XVIIIᵉ S.
ARMOIRETTE, WITH TWO DOORS. MID 18th C.

56. ARMOIRE RUSTIQUE A DEUX PORTES. MILIEU XVIIIᵉ S.
RUSTIC ARMOIRE, WITH TWO DOORS. MID 18th C.

57. ARMOIRE A MULTIPLES PANNEAUX, D'INFLUENCE
LOUIS XIII ET LOUIS XV. FIN XVIIIᵉ S.
MULTI-PANELLED ARMOIRE, UNDER LOUIS XIII AND
LOUIS XV INFLUENCE. LATE 18th C

58. ARMOIRE A DEUX PORTES CINTRÉES, D'ESPRIT
LOUIS XIV. MILIEU XVIIIe S.
ARMOIRE WITH ARCHED DOORS, IN THE LOUIS XIV
MANNER. MID 18th C.

59. ARMOIRE GALBEE DE SAINT-LOUIS, MISSOURI,
D'ESPRIT LOUIS XIV. FIN XVIIIe S.
SERPENTINE-SHAPED ARMOIRE, FROM ST LOUIS,
MISSOURI, IN THE LOUIS XIV MANNER. LATE 18th C.

60. ARMOIRE A DÉCORS RUSTIQUES. FIN XVIIIe S.
ARMOIRE, DECORATED IN A RUSTIC MANNER.
LATE 18th C.

61. PETITE ARMOIRE RUSTIQUE A MULTIPLES SPI-
RALES. FIN XVIIIe S.
SMALL RUSTIC ARMOIRE, CARVED WITH MULTIPLE
SPIRALS. LATE 18th C.

62. ARMOIRE ORNÉE DE RINCEAUX, D'ESPRIT LOUIS XV.
FIN XVIIIe S.
ARMOIRE, DECORATED WITH FOLIATED SCROLLS, IN THE
LOUIS XV MANNER. LATE 18th C.

63. ARMOIRE CANADIENNE « A LA BOURGUIGNONNE ».
FIN XVIIIe OU DÉBUT XIXe S.
CANADIAN ARMOIRE " A LA BOURGUIGNONNE ". LATE
18th OR EARLY 19th C.

64. ARMOIRE DÉCORÉE DE MOTIFS FLORAUX. FIN XVIIIᵉ S.
ARMOIRE, CARVED WITH FLORAL MOTIFS.   LATE 18th C.

65-66. DÉTAIL.
DETAIL.

67. ARMOIRE EXCEPTIONNELLE DE BATISCAN. FIN XVIIIᵉ S.
UNUSUAL ARMOIRE, FROM BATISCAN. LATE 18th C.

68. PETITE ARMOIRE RUSTIQUE A UN VANTAIL CINTRÉ. FIN XVIIIᵉ S.
SMALL RUSTIC ARMOIRE, WITH ONE ARCHED DOOR. LATE 18th C.

69. PETITE ARMOIRE RUSTIQUE A UN VANTAIL. FIN XVIIIᵉ S.
SMALL RUSTIC ARMOIRE, WITH ONE DOOR. LATE 18th C.

70. PETITE ARMOIRE GALBÉE A UN VANTAIL, D'ESPRIT LOUIS XV.
FIN XVIIIᵉ S.
SMALL SERPENTINE-SHAPED ARMOIRE WITH ONE DOOR, IN THE
LOUIS XV MANNER. LATE 18th C.

71. PETITE ARMOIRE GALBÉE A UN VANTAIL. FIN XVIIIᵉ S.
SMALL SERPENTINE-SHAPED ARMOIRE, WITH ONE DOOR. LATE
18th C.

72. ARMOIRE RUSTIQUE, D'ESPRIT LOUIS XV. FIN XVIIIᵉ S.
RUSTIC ARMOIRE, IN THE LOUIS XV MANNER. LATE 18th C.

73. ARMOIRE RUSTIQUE DE LONGUEUIL. FIN XVIIIᵉ S.
RUSTIC ARMOIRE, FROM LONGUEUIL. LATE 18th C.

74-75. DÉTAIL.
DETAIL.

76. ARMOIRE DÉCORÉE DE DESSINS GÉOMÉTRIQUES.
DÉBUT XIXᵉ S.
TWO-DOOR ARMOIRE, PROFUSELY DECORATED WITH
GEOMETRIC DESIGNS. EARLY 19th C.

77. PETITE ARMOIRE A TIROIRS ORNÉS DE LOSANGES. FIN XVIIIe S.
SMALL ARMOIRE, CARVED WITH LOZENGES ON THE DRAWERS. LATE 18th C.

78. ARMOIRE DÉCORÉE DE MULTIPLES SPIRALES, D'ESPRIT LOUIS XV. FIN XVIIIe S.
ARMOIRE, CARVED WITH MULTIPLE SPIRALS, IN THE LOUIS XV MANNER. LATE 18th C.

79. PETITE ARMOIRE, D'ESPRIT LOUIS XIII ET LOUIS XV. MILIEU
XVIIIe S.
SMALL ARMOIRE, IN THE LOUIS XIII AND LOUIS XV MANNERS. MID
18th C.

80. ARMOIRE D'ESPRIT LOUIS XV. FIN XVIIIe S.
ARMOIRE, IN THE LOUIS XV MANNER. LATE
18th C.

81-82. DÉTAIL.
DETAIL.

83. ARMOIRE TRÈS ORNEMENTÉE. FIN XVIIIᵉ S.
RICHLY DECORATED ARMOIRE. LATE 18th C.

84. DÉTAIL.
DETAIL.

85. ARMOIRE A PANNEAUX ORNÉS DE RINCEAUX.
FIN XVIIIᵉ S.
ARMOIRE, WITH PANELS DECORATED WITH
FOLIATED SCROLLS. LATE 18th C.

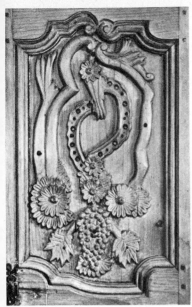

86. DÉTAIL.
DETAIL.

87. ARMOIRE A DÉCOR DE ROCAILLE. FIN
XVIIIᵉ S.
ARMOIRE, DECORATED WITH APPLIQUÉ " RO-
CAILLE ". LATE 18th C.

88. PETITE ARMOIRE RUSTIQUE LÉGÈREMENT CINTRÉE. MILIEU XVIIIe S.
SMALL RUSTIC ARMOIRE, WITH A SHALLOW BOW FRONT. MID 18th C.

89. ARMOIRE A PANNEAUX D'INSPIRATION FLAMANDE. FIN XVIIIe S.
ARMOIRE, WITH PANELS IN THE FLEMISH MANNER. LATE 18th C.

90. ARMOIRE DECORÉE DE RINCEAUX, DE SAINT-HILAIRE.
FIN XVIII⁰ S.
ARMOIRE, DECORATED WITH FOLIATED SCROLLS, FROM
ST HILAIRE. LATE 18th C.

91. ARMOIRE ORNÉE DE RINCEAUX, DE L'ASSOMPTION.
FIN XVIIIe S.
ARMOIRE, CARVED WITH FOLIATED SCROLLS, FROM
L'ASSOMPTION. LATE 18th C.

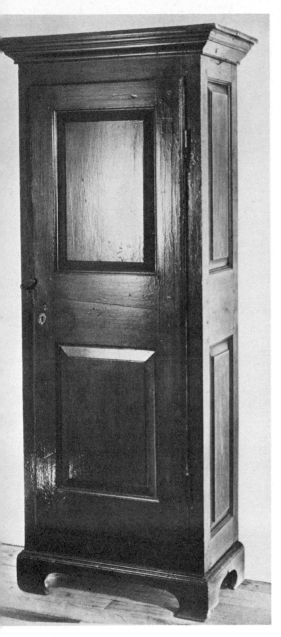

92. BONNETIÈRE AYANT APPARTENÙ A MADAME D'YOU-
VILLE. FIN XVIIIᵉ S.
BONNETIÈRE, FORMERLY IN THE POSSESSION OF MADAME
D'YOUVILLE. LATE 18th C.

93. BONNETIÈRE OU GARDE-ROBE A DÉCOR RENAIS-
SANCE. XIXᵉ S.
BONNETIÈRE OR WARDROBE, DECORATED WITH RENAIS-
SANCE MOTIFS. 19th C.

94. ARMOIRE A DEUX PORTES, INSPIRÉE DU STYLE ADAM.
FIN XVIIIᵉ S.
ARMOIRE, IN THE ADAM MANNER. LATE 18th C.

95. DÉTAIL.
DETAIL.

96. ARMOIRE DÉCORÉE DE COQUILLES
ET DE SPIRALES. FIN XVIIIᵉ S.
ARMOIRE, DECORATED WITH SHELLS
AND SPIRALS. LATE 18th C.

97. ARMOIRE A PANNEAUX CHANTOURNÉS, D'ESPRIT
LOUIS XV. FIN XVIIIe S.
ARMOIRE WITH SHAPED PANELS, IN THE LOUIS XV
MANNER. LATE 18th C.

98. ARMOIRE DE SAINT-MARC-SUR-RICHELIEU. FIN XVIIIe S.
ARMOIRE, FROM ST-MARC-SUR-RICHELIEU. LATE 18th C.

99. ARMOIRE ORNÉE DE MARQUETERIE ET DE MOTIFS
ROCAILLE. DÉBUT XIXᵉ S.
ARMOIRE, IN THE "ROCAILLE" MANNER, DECORATED
WITH MARQUETRY. EARLY 19th C.

100. ARMOIRE, D'INSPIRATION ADAM ET LOUIS XVI.
DÉBUT XIXᵉ S.
ARMOIRE, IN THE ADAM AND LOUIS XVI MANNERS.
EARLY 19th C.

101. ARMOIRE, ORNÉE D'UN TIROIR, D'INSPIRATION
LOUIS XV. FIN XVIIIᵉ S.
ARMOIRE, WITH DRAWER, IN THE LOUIS XV MANNER.
LATE 18th C.

102. ARMOIRE A MULTIPLES PANNEAUX. XIXᵉ S.
MULTI-PANELLED ARMOIRE. 19th C.

LATE EIGHTEENTH-CENTURY ARMOIRE, WITH SHAPED UPPER PANELS, IN ITS ORIGINAL COLOURS.

TWO-TIERED BUFFETS

In the seventeenth and eighteenth centuries the two-tiered buffet *(buffet deux-corps)* was in very wide use. It is found in inventories under many names — a pair of armoires, an armoire, or a buffet, " a pair of armoires in butternut, in two tiers, with four doors and two drawers locking with a key estimated at 80 livres " [1] ... " an armoire of pine wood in two tiers with four doors and four shelves, the armoire being fitted with hinges, locks and keys, the whole being six feet high by about four feet long, priced and assessed at the sum of ten livres " [2] ... "two buffets placed one on top of the other. " [3]

This two-tiered furniture was made of yellow birch, pine, or butternut, but very few of these large pieces have come down to us. The doors of these buffets have a projecting double moulding and the panels are decorated with low-relief lozenges, the precursors of the diamond point. Sometimes the cornice, always jutting out and rich with mouldings, was embellished with a pediment in the Italian Renaissance style.

The Canadian two-tiered buffet is one of the most beautiful pieces of the seventeenth and early eighteenth centuries and differs only in detail from the traditional French model. It was used for storing linen, dishes, etc., and in most country houses was placed in the common room.

A description of a two-tiered buffet and its contents is found in the inventory, dated 1673, of the goods and chattels of Jeanne Mance of Montreal : " A buffet of jointed birch with four doors, having two drawers locked with two keys. The opening of the buffet with the keys having been entrusted to us by the said Damoiselle Dupuy and the said Bailly, we found the following articles :

First : Ten pairs of unbleached linen sheets for what they are worth.
Item : Twenty-six shirts, new and old.
Item : A chrisom-cloth in *Couppé* stitch.
Item : Six dozen embroidered napkins, and eight linen napkins.
Item : Eight table-cloths of coarse linen.
Item : Three large embroidered table-cloths.
Item : A camisole of *Bazin*.
Item : In the upper part of the buffet, four salt-cellars, an ewer, four plates, a ladle, two candle-sticks and the base of another, all of pewter.
Item : In a napkin, about a pound and a half of brown sugar.
Item : In a little linen bag about half a pound of starch. A pound and a half of rice and about half a pound of peppercorns in wooden boxes. " [4]

103. TWO-TIERED BUFFET, CARVED WITH LOZENGES, OF THE RENAISSANCE TYPE. LATE 17th C.

Two-tiered buffet, with two drawers and four doors carved with lozenges and having prominent double moulding. Plain lateral panels and flattened bun feet. The moulding in the base is missing. Original hinged rings, keyhole escutcheons and fische hinges. This type was widely distributed during the seventeenth century. This piece is similar to no. 104, except for several small variations.

(1) A J M, A P Q. Inventaire des biens de la Com^te du s^r Martel & boucher sa femme 3e & 4 may 1703. Greffe Adhémar.
(2) A J Q, A P Q. Inventaire de Feue Damoiselle Pinault, Québec 1746.
(3) A J M, I O A. Inventaire et Description des Effets de la Communauté dentre Joseph Duquet d. Desrochers et Deffunte françoise bourdeaux sa seconde femme, 22e février 1754, Montréal. Greffe Desmarest.
(4) A J M. Inventaire des biens meubles, tiltres et Enseignemens de deffunte Damoiselle Jeanne Mance vivante administratrice de l'hospital de Montréal 19e juin 1673. Greffe Basset.

w. 5' 4"   H. 7' ½"   D. 2' ½"
   163 cm   215 cm   62 cm
4' 10½"   1' 9¾"
   149 cm   54 cm
WOOD : birch

PROVENANCE : Hôpital-Général, Quebec

(Coll. Detroit Institute of Arts, Detroit, Mich. U.S.A.).

104. TWO-TIERED BUFFET, CARVED WITH LOZENGES, OF THE RENAISSANCE TYPE. LATE 17th C.

Two-tiered buffet, with two drawers and four doors, carved with lozenges, and framed with double mouldings. The side panels are decorated with the cross of St Andrew, and the cornice with dentils. The hinged rings and fische hinges are original, but the wooden latches were added much later, no doubt when the locks failed. The base moulding is missing. This is a robust and massive piece derived from Italian Renaissance and Louis XIII styles. It is the oldest type of Canadian two-tiered buffet. It should be remembered that lozenges were the forerunners of diamond points.

w. 4' 7½"   H. 6' 4"   D. 1' 10¼"
   141 cm   193 cm   56 cm
4' 3¼"   1' 8"
   130 cm   51 cm
WOOD : birch   PROVENANCE : Yamachiche, P.Q.

(Coll. Canada Steamship Lines, Tadoussac, P.Q.).

105. BUFFET, APPARENTLY IN TWO TIERS, BUT IN FACT CONSTRUCTED AS A SINGLE UNIT, IN THE LOUIS XIII MANNER. EARLY 18th C.

Buffet, made as an armoire in one piece but having the appearance of a two-tiered buffet. It has two drawers and four doors with prominent mouldings and undulating band. The upper panels are carved with lozenges, the lower panels with the cross of St Andrew *(pointes de gâteaux)*. The prominent pediment is ornamented with an undulating band. Very robust stiles. Original hinged rings, keyhole escutcheons and fische hinges. The wooden latch is a later addition.

w. 4' 7½"   H. 6' 7"   D. 2'
   141 cm   201 cm   61 cm
WOOD : birch   PROVENANCE : Baie Saint-Paul, P.Q.

(Coll. Museum of Fine Arts, Montreal).

106. TWO-TIERED BUFFET, CARVED WITH DIAMOND POINTS. EARLY 18th C.

Two-tiered buffet, having two drawers and four doors with double moulding, and panels carved with diamond points. The small rectangular panels have an undulating band, as in the preceding two-tiered buffet, and probably was made by the same craftsman, as both pieces come from the same district. The upper stage should have been set further back, since it is not fixed to the lower stage (cf. no. 105). A very prominent cornice, typical of certain Canadian armoires. This buffet, of Louis XIII derivation, is later than buffets with lozenges. (Relief diamond points appeared at the beginning of the eighteenth century.) The side mouldings, which should surround the lower stage under the drawers, are missing. Original fische hinges, hinged rings, and keyhole escutcheons in the form of a flame.

w. 4' 2⅝"   H. 6' 8¾"   D. 1' 9"
   129 cm   206 cm   54 cm
WOOD : birch   PROVENANCE : Baie Saint-Paul, P.Q.

(Coll. Mr Jean Dubuc, Quebec).

107. TWO-TIERED BUFFET, WITH BROKEN PEDIMENT, IN THE RENAISSANCE TRADITION. LATE 17th-EARLY 18th C.

Two-tiered buffet, having four doors carved with lozenges and prominent double mouldings. There are two drawers in the lower stage. The lozenges carved in the upper stage are the tentative beginnings of diamond-point decoration. The broken pediment above the cornice is definitely in the Renaissance manner. Original hinged rings, keyhole escutcheons and fische hinges. Robust and well-proportioned two-tiered buffet.

w. 4' 2⅜"   H. 6' 10⅜"   D. 1' 8"
   128 cm   209 cm   51 cm
3' 8⅝"   1' 5"
   113 cm   43 cm
WOOD : butternut

DRAWER MOULDINGS : pine

PROVENANCE : Saint-Nicolas, P.Q.

(Coll. Mr and Mrs Cleveland Morgan, Senneville, P.Q.).

108. TWO-TIERED BUFFET, WITH BROKEN PEDIMENT, IN THE RENAISSANCE AND LOUIS XIII TRADITIONS. EARLY 18th C.

Two-tiered buffet, having two drawers, four doors with double mouldings and panels carved with diamond points. The broken pediment shows Renaissance and Louis XIII influence. The two large side panels are carved with lozenges. Original hinged rings and fische hinges. A well-proportioned piece of furniture.

w. 4' 8"   H. 7' 1"   D. 1' 10¼"
   142 cm   216 cm   57 cm
4' 3"   1' 8½"
   130 cm   52 cm
WOOD : pine   PROVENANCE : Deschambeault, P.Q.

(Coll. Museum of Fine Arts, Montreal).

109. ARMOIRE, IN THE FORM OF A TWO-TIERED BUFFET. LATE 18th C.

Armoire, having two drawers and four doors with

shaped panels in the Louis XV manner. The rectangular friezes on the upper rail have *guilloché* ornamentation. The feet are missing. Original fische hinges, iron knobs and slide bolts. The upper panels show Queen Anne influence. The curious combination of shapings makes this an interesting piece.

| w. 4' 4¾'' | H. 6' 3¼'' | D. 1' 8'' |
| 134 cm | 191 cm | 51 cm |

WOOD : pine

PROVENANCE : Saint-Rémi de Napierville, P.Q.

(Coll. Mrs Richard R. Costello, Sainte-Agathe des Monts, P.Q.).

110. THREE-TIERED BUFFET. EARLY 18th C.

Three-tiered buffet, having two drawers and six doors with plain panels. The top stage is probably a later addition. Original hinged rings, fische hinges and keyhole escutcheons. A rustic buffet with simple lines.

w. 4' 1⅜''	H. 7' 4¾''	D. 1' 8¼''
125 cm	225 cm	52 cm
3' 8⅝''		1' 6½''
113 cm		47 cm
3' 5''		1' 4¾''
104 cm		43 cm

WOOD : pine   PROVENANCE : Batiscan, P.Q.

(Coll. Canada Steamship Lines, Tadoussac, P.Q.).

111. TWO-TIERED BUFFET, WITH SERPENTINE PEDIMENT, EMBELLISHED WITH FRUIT MOTIFS. LATE 18th C.

Two-tiered buffet having a serpentine pediment, two drawers and four doors with shaped panels. The fruit-basket motif, on two of the door panels, is the only Canadian example known (it is very frequent in France). The heart carved on the basket suggests that it was a marriage piece. Well-executed, multiple mouldings. It was made by a skilled craftsman and came from the same dictrict as no. 112. The two pieces are closely related, especially the moulded centre posts and the wooden knobs within a gouged circle. Original keyhole escutcheons and fische hinges. A very attractive piece.

w. 4' 9''	H. 8' 3''	D. 2' 1''
145 cm	251 cm	64 cm
5'		
152 cm		

WOOD : pine   PROVENANCE : Lotbinière, P.Q.

(Coll. Museum of Fine Arts, Montreal).

112. TWO-TIERED BUFFET, IN THE LOUIS XV MANNER. LATE 18th C.

Two-tiered buffet, having two drawers and four doors with shaped panels, carved with a rosette in the middle of a wreath. The lateral panels have gouged lozenges, each with a circle in the middle. Moulded centre post. Original wooden knobs, fische hinges and keyhole escutcheons. The feet and lower rails have been restored. The cornice bears dentils. Inside one door is the carved inscription "I. FÉRÉ". This is the name of a family who lived at St Croix de Lotbinière towards the end of the eighteenth century, and included a notary and a woodworker called Jean Baptiste. An interesting regional piece.

| w. 4' 8'' | H. 7' 7¾'' | D. 1' 9½'' |
| 142 cm | 233 cm | 55 cm |

WOOD : pine   STILES : mountain ash (maskobina)

PROVENANCE : Sainte-Croix de Lotbinière, P.Q.

(Coll. of the author, Montreal).

113. TWO-TIERED BUFFET, WITH SERPENTINE PEDIMENT AND FLORAL MOTIFS, IN LOUIS XV MANNER. LATE 18th C.

Two-tiered buffet, with serpentine pediment and four doors with shaped panels, two of which are carved with floral motifs. The centre posts and the upper rail of the lower stage are carved with foliated scrolls (crosiers interlaced with foliage). The arches on the doors and the shaping on the panels are much closer to Louis XIV than to Louis XV, although the pediment is definitely in the Louis XV manner. This two-tiered buffet has certain similarities with nos. 111 and 112. Original fische hinges and keyhole escutcheons.

w. 5' 7''	H. 7' 8''	D. 2' 1¼''
172 cm	234 cm	64 cm
		1' 7¼''
		49 cm

WOOD : pine   PROVENANCE : Quebec

(Coll. Mr and Mrs Leslie W. Haslett, Sainte-Marguerite, P.Q.).

114. TWO-TIERED BUFFET, IN THE LOUIS XV MANNER. LATE 18th C.

Two-tiered buffet, with four doors and shaped panels in the Louis XV manner. The side panels and the lower rail are shaped. Double volute feet. The upper stage is set much further back than in most two-tiered buffets. A very French cornice, with rounded corners. Original fische hinges and keyhole escutcheons. A traditional, refined model, painted in white.

w. 4' 3''	H. 6' 4''	D. 1' 9½''
130 cm	193 cm	55 cm
3' 3½''		1' 4''
100 cm		41 cm

WOOD : pine

PROVENANCE : Saint-Pascal de Kamouraska, P.Q.

(Coll. Museum of Fine Arts, Montreal).

115. TWO-TIERED BUFFET, IN A SOMEWHAT BAROQUE INTERPRETATION OF THE LOUIS XV STYLE. LATE 18th C.

Two-tiered buffet, with four doors, the upper ones being arched. The shaped panels are carved with foliated scrolls, garlands and spirals. The cornice and the bracket feet show the influence of Chippendale and Dutch baroque. This piece of *Canadian rococo* furniture comes from the sacristy of the old church at Three Rivers. The original colouring of dark green and gold leaf remains.

w. 4' 8¼"   H. 8' 2¼"   D. 2' 1"
143 cm   250 cm   64 cm

WOOD : butternut

PROVENANCE : Three Rivers, P.Q.

(Coll. Château de Ramezay, Montreal).

116. TWO-TIERED BUFFET, WITH A SWELLING BASE, IN THE BAROQUE MANNER, SUPPOSEDLY THE WORK OF FRANÇOIS BAILLAIRGÉ. LATE 18th C.

Two-tiered buffet, with a swelling base in the Baroque manner. The lower stage has two drawers, two doors and a sliding writing-board covered with green baize. The upper stage, with its two doors, has six serpentine-shaped panels and Baroque cornice. The side panels are also shaped, but only the lower ones are serpentine-fronted. This two-tiered buffet recalls Dutch and Austrian *tombeau* buffets. Until recently it was the property of the Baillairgé family and supposedly had been made in Quebec by François Baillairgé, the celebrated woodworker and carver. I think that Baillairgé must have drawn his inspiration from an engraving of a Dutch or Austrian two-tiered baroque buffet. It is a rare specimen of baroque furniture made in Canada.

w. 4' 6½"   H. 6' 8¾"   D. 1' 11¼"
138 cm   204 cm   59 cm
3' 11½"   1' 9"
121 cm   53 cm

WOOD : butternut

PROVENANCE : Les Cèdres, P.Q.

(Coll. Mr and Mrs J.W. McConnell, Dorval, P.Q.).

117. TWO-TIERED SERPENTINE-SHAPED BUFFET, IN THE LOUIS XV MANNER. 18th C.

Two-tiered serpentine-shaped buffet in the Louis XV manner, with four doors and shaped panels carved with spirals. The shaped lower rail has spiral decoration with a fine shell in the centre. Serpentine-shaped lateral panels. This two-tiered buffet is said to have come from the old presbytery of Quebec Cathedral. Original keyhole escutcheons and fische hinges. One of the finest Canadian two-tiered buffets, derived from French models.

w. 4'   H. 8' 11⅝"   D. 1' 6½"
122 cm   273 cm   47 cm
4' 4½"   1' 2⅝"
133 cm   37 cm

WOOD : pine   PROVENANCE : Quebec

(Coll. Mr and Mrs J.W. McConnell, Montreal).

118. DETAIL.

119. TWO-TIERED BUFFET, IN THE LOUIS XIV MANNER. MID 18th C.

Two-tiered buffet, with four doors. The upper doors are arched in the Louis XIV manner. The shaping of the panels and lower rail are of Louis XV derivation.

w. 4' 5"   H. 6' 8½"   D. 1' 9"
135 cm   204 cm   53 cm
                                   1' 3¾"
                                   40 cm

WOOD : pine   PROVENANCE : Quebec district

(Coll. Donnacona Paper Company Ltd, lent to the Provincial Museum, Quebec).

120. TWO-TIERED BUFFET, IN THE LOUIS XV MANNER. EARLY 19th C.

Two-tiered buffet, with four panelled doors in the Louis XV manner. Two of the doors are arched. Shaped lower rail. Dentils on the pediment. Original hinges. The lower rail has been damaged.

w. 4'   H. 7' 1"   D. 1' 8"
122 cm   216 cm   51 cm
3' 7"   1' 10"
109 cm   56 cm

WOOD : pine   PROVENANCE : Rivière Ouelle, P.Q.

(Coll. Canada Steamship Lines, Tadoussac, P.Q.).

121. TWO-TIERED BUFFET-DRESSER. 18th C.

Two-tiered buffet-dresser having four doors with shaped panels of Louis XV derivation. The shallow upper stage was used for storing dishes. Original ironwork. The cornice is damaged and the feet have been cut. There exist several two-tiered buffet-dressers with doors in the upper stage.

w. 4' 5½"   H. 7' ¾"   D. 1' 5¾"
136 cm   216 cm   45 cm
                                  8¼"
                                  21 cm

WOOD : pine

(Coll. Provincial Museum, Quebec).

122. TWO-TIERED BUFFET, WITH FOLIATED SCROLLS, IN THE ADAM MANNER. EARLY 19th C.

Two-tiered buffet, with four doors. The lower doors are carved with branches and foliage. The stiles are fluted in the Adam manner. The bracket base is carved with geometric designs. The lower part of the upper centre post has a carving of a plant in a small basket. The stiles and top rail are decorated with foliated scrolls and Adam-style fans. Interesting asymmetry in the decoration of the panels.

w. 4' 6"   H. 6' 11¾"   D. 1' 3"
137 cm   213 cm   39 cm
3' 10¾"
117 cm

WOOD : pine   PROVENANCE : Lachute, P.Q.

(Coll. Canada Steamship Lines, Tadoussac, P.Q.).

123. TWO-TIERED BUFFET, IN THE REGENCY MANNER. EARLY 19th C.

Two-tiered buffet, with *appliqué* moulding on the panels, in the Regency manner. Bracket feet. Original hinges.

w. 4' ⅜"   H. 7' 1¼"   D. 1' 6"
122 cm   217 cm   46 cm
                               1' 4"
                               41 cm

WOOD : pine   PROVENANCE : Varennes, P.Q.

(Coll. Mr and Mrs John A. Reilly, Longueuil, P.Q.).

124. TWO-TIERED BUFFET, CARVED WITH REEDED CHEVRONS. EARLY 19th C.

Two-tiered buffet, with two drawers and four doors. The door panels are carved with a double groove. The stiles and centre posts have parallel grooves in chevron form, inspired by Indian arrowheads. Pearls embellish the corners of the stiles, the prominent cornice is decorated with an undulating band, *dents de loup* pattern and parallel fluting. Bracket feet. An original model.

w. 4' 3"   H. 6' 1"   D. 1' 5¼"
130 cm   185 cm   44 cm
3' 6"   1' 1¼"
107 cm   34 cm

WOOD : pine

(Coll. Mr and Mrs F.M. Hutchins, Pembroke, Ont.).

125. RUSTIC TWO-TIERED BUFFET. EARLY 19th C.

Rustic two-tiered buffet, with four doors, resembling room doors. The understructure has colossal bracket feet. The cornice is decorated with festoons and parallel and vertical reeding. The hinges, although original, do not suit the overlapping doors, and fische hinges would have been better. The rails and massive centre posts make it a naive yet charming piece of furniture.

w. 4' 9"   H. 6' 8½"   D. 1' 8"
145 cm   205 cm   51 cm
4' 4"   1' 3"
132 cm   38 cm

WOOD : pine   PROVENANCE : Isle of Orleans, P.Q.

(Coll. Canada Steamship Lines, Tadoussac, P.Q.).

126. LARGE TWO-TIERED BUFFET, WITH MULTIPLE DECORATIONS. EARLY 19th C.

Large two-tiered buffet with two drawers and four doors. The door panels have *appliqué* mouldings. The small lower panels suggest shaping and foliated scrolls in the Louis XV manner. The cornice is carved with cabling and primitive arabesques. Tiny diamond points and stylized flowers frame the panels. This example combines many influences, but is predominantly Regency.

w. 6' 2"   H. 6' 5"   D. 2' 3¼"
188 cm   196 cm   69 cm
5' 1½"   1' 8"
156 cm   51 cm

WOOD : pine

PROVENANCE : Laprairie de la Madeleine, P.Q.

(Coll. Museum of Fine Arts, Montreal).

103. BUFFET DEUX-ÇORPS A LOSANGES, D'INSPIRATION
RENAISSANCE. FIN XVIIe S.
TWO-TIERED BUFFET, CARVED WITH LOZENGES, OF THE
RENAISSANCE TYPE.   LATE 17th C.

104. BUFFET DEUX-CORPS A LOSANGES, D'INSPIRATION
RENAISSANCE. FIN XVIIe S.
TWO-TIERED BUFFET, CARVED WITH LOZENGES, OF
THE RENAISSANCE TYPE. LATE 17th C.

105. BUFFET A DEUX CORPS APPARENTS, MAIS BATI D'UNE SEULE PIÈCE, D'ESPRIT LOUIS XIII. DÉBUT XVIIIᵉ S. BUFFET, APPARENTLY IN TWO TIERS, BUT IN FACT CONSTRUCTED AS A SINGLE UNIT, IN THE LOUIS XIII MANNER. EARLY 18th C.

106. BUFFET DEUX-CORPS ORNÉ DE POINTES DE DIAMANT. DÉBUT XVIIIᵉ S.
TWO-TIERED BUFFET, CARVED WITH DIAMOND POINTS. EARLY 18th C.

107. BUFFET DEUX-CORPS A FRONTON BRISÉ, D'INSPI-
RATION RENAISSANCE. FIN XVIIᵉ - DÉBUT XVIIIᵉ S.
TWO-TIERED BUFFET, WITH BROKEN PEDIMENT, IN THE
RENAISSANCE TRADITION. LATE 17th-EARLY 18th C.

108. BUFFET DEUX-CORPS A FRONTON BRISÉ, D'ESPRIT
RENAISSANCE ET LOUIS XIII. DÉBUT XVIIIe S.
TWO-TIERED BUFFET, WITH BROKEN PEDIMENT, IN
THE RENAISSANCE AND LOUIS XIII TRADITIONS. EARLY
18th C.

109. ARMOIRE IMITANT UN BUFFET DEUX-CORPS.
FIN XVIIIᵉ S.
ARMOIRE, IN THE FORM OF A TWO-TIERED BUFFET.
LATE 18th C.

110. BUFFET TROIS-CORPS. DÉBUT XVIIIᵉ S.
THREE-TIERED BUFFET.   EARLY 18th C.

111. BUFFET DEUX-CORPS A FRONTON CINTRÉ ET A
DÉCORATION FRUITIÈRE. FIN XVIIIe S.
TWO-TIERED BUFFET WITH SERPENTINE PEDIMENT,
EMBELLISHED WITH FRUIT MOTIFS. LATE 18th C.

112. BUFFET DEUX-CORPS, D'ESPRIT LOUIS XV. FIN
XVIIIe S.
TWO-TIERED BUFFET, IN THE LOUIS XV MANNER. LATE
18th C.

113. BUFFET DEUX-CORPS A FRONTON CINTRÉ, ORNÉ DE MOTIFS FLORAUX, D'ESPRIT LOUIS XV. FIN XVIII⁰ S.
TWO-TIERED BUFFET. WITH SERPENTINE PEDIMENT AND FLORAL MOTIFS, IN LOUIS XV MANNER. LATE 18th C.

114. BUFFET DEUX-CORPS, D'ESPRIT LOUIS XV. FIN XVIII⁰ S.
TWO-TIERED BUFFET, IN THE LOUIS XV MANNER. LATE 18th C.

115. BUFFET DEUX-CORPS, D'ESPRIT LOUIS XV, MAIS
BAROQUE. FIN XVIIIᵉ S.
TWO-TIERED BUFFET, IN A SOMEWHAT BAROQUE INTER-
PRETATION OF THE LOUIS XV STYLE. LATE 18th C.

116. BUFFET DEUX-CORPS VENTRU, D'ESPRIT BAROQUE,
DIT DE FRANÇOIS BAILLAIRGÉ. FIN XVIIIe S.
TWO-TIERED BUFFET, WITH A SWELLING BASE, IN THE
BAROQUE MANNER, SUPPOSEDLY THE WORK OF FRANÇOIS
BAILLAIRGÉ.   LATE 18th c.

119. BUFFET DEUX-CORPS, D'INSPIRATION LOUIS X[
MILIEU XVIIIe S.
TWO-TIERED BUFFET, IN THE LOUIS XIV MANNER. [
18th C.

117. BUFFET DEUX-CORPS GALBÉ, D'INS-
PIRATION LOUIS XV. XVIIIe S.
TWO-TIERED SERPENTINE-SHAPED BUFFET,
IN THE LOUIS XV MANNER. 18th C.

118. DÉTAIL.
DETAIL.

120. BUFFET DEUX-CORPS, D'ESPRIT LOUIS XV. DÉBUT XIXᵉ S.
TWO-TIERED BUFFET, IN THE LOUIS XV MANNER.   EARLY 19th C.

121. BUFFET DEUX-CORPS-VAISSELIER. XVIIIᵉ S.
TWO-TIERED BUFFET-DRESSER.   18th C.

122. BUFFET DEUX-CORPS DÉCORÉ DE FEUILLAGE, D'ESPRIT ADAM. DÉBUT XIXe S.
TWO-TIERED BUFFET, WITH FOLIATED SCROLLS, IN THE ADAM MANNER. EARLY 19th C.

123. BUFFET DEUX-CORPS, D'INSPIRATION REGENCY. DÉBUT XIXe S.
TWO-TIERED BUFFET, IN THE "REGENCY" MANNER. EARLY 19th C.

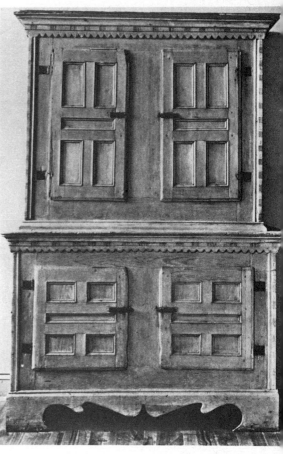

124. BUFFET DEUX-CORPS, ORNÉ DE CHEVRONS STRIÉS.
DÉBUT XIXᵉ S.
TWO-TIERED BUFFET CARVED WITH REEDED CHEVRONS.
EARLY 19th C.

125. BUFFET DEUX-CORPS RUSTIQUE. DÉBUT XIXᵉ S.
RUSTIC TWO-TIERED BUFFET. EARLY 19th C.

126. GRAND BUFFET DEUX-CORPS A MULTIPLES ORNE-
MENTS. DÉBUT XIXe S.
LARGE TWO-TIERED BUFFET, WITH MULTIPLE DECOR-
ATIONS. EARLY 19th C.

LOW BUFFETS

Among the pieces of furniture of the same family, the low buffet *(buffet bas*, mistakenly called " *bahut* " in French Canada today) was to be found in a great many houses, being used for storing food and dishes and also as a serving-table. It appears in inventories after 1700, " a buffet of pine, with two closing doors and two drawers, furnished with hinges, key and ironwork " [1] ... " a pine buffet with its fische hinges and locks. " [2]

The low buffet is almost identical with the lower part of the two-tiered buffet, and where there were drawers they were put immediately above the doors. Low buffets were decorated with lozenge panels, or panels with a simplified linen-fold pattern, and later with diamond points. After a time however the panels of the façade, sides, and lower rails became shaped, influenced by the Louis XV style. A few of these pieces had a bow or serpentine front. In certain very rare cases, the doors had an accentuated bulge in the baroque style.

127. LOW BUFFET, IN THE LOUIS XV MANNER. LATE 18th C.

Low buffet, with shaped doors and side panels, in the Louis XV manner. The shaping on the lower rail is often found on late-eighteenth-century French furniture.

w. 5' 4"   H. 3' 5½"   D. 1' 6½"
163 cm   105 cm   47 cm
WOOD : pine
PROVENANCE : Sainte-Madeleine de Rouville, P.Q.
(Coll. Mrs Nettie Sharpe, Saint-Lambert, P.Q.).

128. TWO-DOOR LOW BUFFET. LATE 18th C.

Two-door low buffet, with shaped panels and lower rails. It greatly resembles some French provincial low buffets, and may even be a copy. The keyhole escutcheons are in the form of a flame. The top is a later addition.

w. 4' 8"   H. 2' 10½"   D. 1' 7½"
142 cm   88 cm   50 cm
WOOD : pine and butternut
PROVENANCE : Quebec district
(Coll. Dr and Mrs Claude Bertrand, Outremont, P.Q.).

129. LOW BUFFET, CARVED WITH DIAMOND POINTS, FROM SAINT-VALLIER. 18th C.

Low buffet, with two drawers and panels carved with diamond points. This kind of furniture was widely distributed throughout French Canada, and was generally used as a food-locker. The wooden latch was added when the lock was broken. The bottom moulding is a very recent addition. The door knob has a petal-shaped forged-iron plate.

w. 4' 3¾"   H. 4' 1⅜"   D. 1' 9"
131 cm   125 cm   53 cm

WOOD : pine   PROVENANCE : Saint-Vallier, P.Q.
(Coll. Canada Steamship Lines, Tadoussac, P.Q.).

130. LOW BUFFET, WITH THREE DOORS AND THREE DRAWERS. LATE 17th C.

Low buffet, with three doors and three drawers. Original petal-shaped plates, hinged rings and fische hinges. A rare Canadian three-door low buffet, possibly inspired by the *traite Picarde* type. The feet are missing.

w. 5' 2¼"   H. 2' 1⅜"   D. 1' 9¾"
158 cm   64 cm   55 cm
WOOD : pine   PROVENANCE : Quebec
(Coll. Musée de l'Hôtel-Dieu, Quebec).

131. LOW BUFFET, IN THE LOUIS XIII MANNER. 18th C.

Two-door low buffet, with panels decorated with a motif reminiscent of the simplified linen-fold pattern, but with a disc in the centre. The same ornamentation is to be found in Norman traditional furniture. The upper stage and the feet are missing. The side panels are shaped in the Louis XV manner.

w. 4' 2"   H. 3' 7"   D. 1' 9¼"
127 cm   109 cm   54 cm
WOOD : pine
PROVENANCE : Saint-Michel de Bellechasse, P.Q.
(Coll. Canada Steamship Lines, Tadoussac, P.Q.).

132. LOW BUFFET, WITH SHAPED DOORS. LATE 18th C.

Low buffet, with two drawers and shaped doors framed with attractive mouldings. The lower rail is festooned and carved with a shell. The centrepost is embellished with a rectangular panel. The

---

(1) A J M, I O A. Invantaire de Jacques Cusson et Michelle Cholecq sa femme auparavant Veuve de françois Viger, le 20 décembre 1729. Greffe Chaumont.

(2) A J M, I O A. Inventaire d'André Demers, le 19e février 1732. Greffe Chaumont.

stiles have rounded corners. This piece would have been excellent if the panels had been carved with flat mouldings. Original knobs and ironwork.

w. 3' 6"   H. 3'   D. 1' 4½"
107 cm   91 cm   42 cm

WOOD : pine   PANELS : poplar

(Coll. Dr and Mrs Herbert T. Schwarz, Montreal).

133. LOW BUFFET. 18th C.

Low buffet, of exceptional height, with two doors and two drawers. The hinged rings and fische hinges are recent. The numerous vertical and horizontal panels on the stiles and rails are typical of the Lotbinière district.

w. 3' 10½"   H. 4' 10"   D. 1' 7¼"
118 cm   147 cm   49 cm

WOOD : pine   PROVENANCE : South Shore

(Coll. Provincial Museum (Hôtel Chevalier), Quebec).

134. LOW BUFFET, WITH BOTTOM RAIL UNDER AMERICAN INFLUENCE. LATE 18th C.

Low buffet, with stiles and shaped panels in the Louis XV manner. The bottom rail is of a definitely American inspiration, copied from Dunlap furniture, produced by a famous New Hampshire family. Note the details of the shaping in the bottom rail (this book contains several specimens derived from Dunlap furniture).

w. 3' 3¼"   H. 2' 8¾"   D. 1' 7"
100 cm   83 cm   48 cm

WOOD : birch and elm core

PROVENANCE : Parisville, P.Q.

(Coll. Canada Steamship Lines, Tadoussac, P.Q.).

135. LOW BUFFET, WITH HEART-EMBELLISHED DOORS. LATE 18th C.

Low buffet, with doors having hearts carved in relief. The top is inclined like a slant-top desk. It is both a low buffet and an upright desk, used for keeping papers and letters. It was probably part of a dowry.

w. 4' 10¼"   H. 4' 6"   D. 1' 11"
148 cm   137 cm   58 cm

WOOD : pine

(Coll. Provincial Museum, Quebec).

136. LOW BUFFET, WITH TWO DOORS AND ONE DRAWER. LATE 18th C.

Low buffet, with one drawer and two doors with shaped panels. The feet are simplified pieds de biche. All the ironwork is original.

w. 3' 7¾"   H. 3' 2¼"   D. 1' 11"
111 cm   97 cm   58 cm

WOOD : butternut

(Coll. Mr and Mrs Gordon Reed, Saint-Sauveur des Monts, P.Q.).

137. SMALL LOW BUFFET, FOUND PARTICULARLY IN CONVENTS. LATE 17th C.

Small low buffet, with one drawer and a door decorated with a lozenge. This is typical convent furniture, and was used as a small armoire in the cells of the Augustinian nuns of the Hôpital-Général, Quebec, from the seventeenth century.

w. 3' 6"   H. 3' 11"   D. 1' 9"
107 cm   119 cm   54 cm

WOOD : pine   PROVENANCE : Quebec

(Coll. Musée de l'Hôpital-Général, Quebec).

138. TWO-DOOR BUFFET. LATE 18th C.

Low buffet, with two doors and shaped panels. The moulding in the base has retained the rectilinear characteristics of the Louis XIII style. The fische hinges are a later addition.

w. 4' 7"   H. 3' 9"   D. 1' 11"
140 cm   114 cm   58 cm

WOOD : pine   PROVENANCE : Saint-Vallier, P.Q.

(Coll. Canada Steamship Lines, Tadoussac, P.Q.).

139. LOW BUFFET, WITH SERPENTINE FRONT. LATE 18th C.

Low buffet, with serpentine façade, two doors and two drawers. The bottom rail is heavily proportioned. Squat feet of English influence. Original handles, keyhole escutcheons and fische hinges.

w. 3' 6"   H. 3' 1¾"   D. 1' 9½"
107 cm   96 cm   55 cm

WOOD : pine

(Coll. Mrs Richard R. Costello, Sainte-Agathe des Monts, P.Q.).

140. LOW BUFFET, WITH ARBALÈTE FRONT, IN THE BAROQUE MANNER. EARLY 19th C.

Low buffet, with arbalète front and shaped sides. Fluting in the Adam or Louis XVI manner. The motifs on the lower rails and the acanthus leaves on the feet are derived from Louis XV and Baroque. Typical of the work of the Quevillon School. The upper tier is missing. The work of an ébéniste rather than of a menuisier. Canadian rococo.

w. 4' 9¼"   H. 3' 5¾"   D. 1' 9"
145 cm   106 cm   53 cm

WOOD : pine   PROVENANCE : Maskinongé, P.Q.

(Coll. Mr and Mrs F.M. Hutchins, Pembroke, Ont.).

141. LOW BUFFET, PARTICULARLY USED IN CONVENTS. 18th C.

Low buffet, with two doors, one drawer and shaped panels. A piece of furniture from the cells of the Augustinians of the Hôtel-Dieu, Quebec. Unfortunately the lower rail has been mutilated. Generally these jointed pieces are of very careful workmanship, and were executed by excellent woodworkers. The deep red colouring is original, as is the ironwork.

| w. 3' 5" | H. 3' 10" | D. 1' 10" |
| 104 cm | 117 cm | 56 cm |

WOOD : pine   PROVENANCE : Quebec

(Coll. Musée de l'Hôtel-Dieu, Quebec).

142. TWO-DOOR LOW BUFFET, DECORATED WITH LOZENGE-CARVING. LATE 18th C.

Low buffet, with two doors and panels decorated with lozenge carving. The angles of the panels are simplified versions of the linen-fold motif. The fluting, reeding and thumb-nail impressions (or gouge decorations) on the stiles are in the Louis XVI manner. A well-made piece of furniture.

| w. 4' 3½" | H. 4' 3½" | D. 1' 9¾" |
| 131 cm | 131 cm | 55 cm |

WOOD : butternut

PROVENANCE : Quebec district

(Coll. Dr and Mrs Claude Bertrand, Outremont, P.Q.).

143. LOW BUFFET, DECORATED WITH FOLIATED SCROLLS. LATE 18th C.

Low buffet, with two doors, two drawers and panels decorated with incised or scratch carving. The delicate engraving of trees and foliage was executed with a burin. A curious combination of Louis XV shaping, geometric designs, the cross of St Andrew and Louis XIII rectilinear uprights and mouldings.

| w. 4' 5⅜" | H. 5' 3⅜" | D. 1' 7¼" |
| 136 cm | 161 cm | 49 cm |

WOOD : pine

(Coll. Mrs L.S. Bloom, Westmount, P.Q.).

144. RUSTIC LOW BUFFET, WITH BOW FRONT AND SIDES. LATE 18th C.

Rustic low buffet, with shallow bow front and sides. The shaping of the lower rail is primitive. Both the rat-tail fische hinges and the keyhole escutcheons are original. A piece of furniture which is charming in its simplicity.

| w. 4' | H. 3' 3" | D. 1' 11" |
| 122 cm | 99 cm | 58 cm |

WOOD : pine

(Coll. Mr and Mrs Scott Symons, Toronto, Ont.).

145. LOW BUFFET, WITH SHAPED PANELS, CARVED WITH THE CROSS OF ST ANDREW. LATE 18th C.

Two-door low buffet, with shaped panels, carved with the cross of St Andrew. It is a transitional piece combining both the Louis XIII and the Louis XV styles.

| w. 4' | H. 3' 6¼" | D. 1' 7⅜" |
| 122 cm | 107 cm | 49 cm |

WOOD : pine   PROVENANCE : Beaumont, P.Q.

(Coll. Canada Steamship Lines, Tadoussac, P.Q.).

146. LOW BUFFET, FOUND PARTICULARLY IN CONVENTS. LATE 18th C.

Low buffet, with two doors and one drawer. The rail is carved with a shell and a spiral, and the lateral panels are shaped. The fische hinges and petal-shaped plates of the hinged rings are original. This is another well-made piece, particularly found in nuns' cells.

| w. 2' 10" | H. 3' 2" | D. 1' 7½" |
| 86 cm | 97 cm | 50 cm |

WOOD : pine   PROVENANCE : Quebec.

(Coll. Musée de l'Hôtel-Dieu, Quebec).

147. LOW BUFFET, WITH TWO ARCHED DOORS. 18th C.

Low buffet, with two drawers and two arched and shaped doors. The fische hinges, keyhole escutcheons, and petal-shaped plates of the knobs are made of contemporary forged iron. Note the small rosettes carved on each side of the middle rail.

| w. 3' 9" | H. 4' 3" | D. 1' 9" |
| 114 cm | 130 cm | 54 cm |

WOOD : pine   PROVENANCE : L'Islet, P.Q.

(Coll. Dr and Mrs Wilfrid Caron, Cap Rouge, P.Q.).

148. LOW BUFFET, WITH DOORS DECORATED WITH LOZENGES. LATE 17th C.

Low buffet, with two doors carved with lozenges, and two drawers, all with rich mouldings. The knobs and keyhole escutcheons are made of contemporary forged iron. The great majority of these buffets date from the end of the seventeenth century and from the beginning of the eighteenth century. This is a fine example.

| w. 4' 2¼" | H. 4' | D. 1' 10¼" |
| 128 cm | 122 cm | 56 cm |

WOOD : pine   PROVENANCE : Quebec district

(Coll. Mrs George McCullagh, Sainte-Agathe des Monts, P.Q.).

127. BUFFET BAS, D'ESPRIT LOUIS XV. FIN XVIIIᵉ S.
LOW BUFFET, IN THE LOUIS XV MANNER. LATE 18th C.

128. BUFFET BAS A DEUX VANTAUX. FIN XVIIIᵉ S.
TWO-DOOR LOW BUFFET. LATE 18th C.

129. BUFFET BAS A POINT
DE DIAMANT, DE SAINT-VAN
LIER. XVIIIe S.
LOW BUFFET, CARVED WIT
DIAMOND POINTS, FROM S
VALLIER. 18th c.

130. BUFFET BAS A TRO
VANTAUX ET TROIS TIROIRS
FIN XVIIe S.
LOW BUFFET, WITH THRE
DOORS AND THREE DRAW
ERS. LATE 17th c.

131. BUFFET BAS, D'ESPRIT LOUIS XIII. XVIIIᵉ S.
LOW BUFFET, IN THE LOUIS XIII MANNER. 18th C.

132. BUFFET BAS A VANTAUX CHANTOURNÉS.
FIN XVIIIᵉ S.
LOW BUFFET, WITH SHAPED DOORS.   LATE
18th C.

133. BUFFET BAS. XVIIIᵉ S.
LOW BUFFET.   18th C.

134. BUFFET BAS, A TRAVERSE INFÉRIEURE D'INFLUENCE
AMÉRICAINE. FIN XVIIIᵉ S.
LOW BUFFET, WITH BOTTOM RAIL UNDER AMERICAN
INFLUENCE. LATE 18th C.

135. BUFFET BAS A VANTAUX ORNÉS DE CŒURS. FIN
XVIIIᵉ S.
LOW BUFFET, WITH HEART-EMBELLISHED DOORS. LATE
18th C.

137. PETIT BUFFET BAS, A L'USAGE DES
RELIGIEUSES. FIN XVIIᵉ S.
SMALL LOW BUFFET, FOUND PARTICU-
LARLY IN CONVENTS.   LATE 17th C.

136. BUFFET BAS A DEUX VANTAUX ET
UN TIROIR. FIN XVIIIᵉ S.
LOW BUFFET, WITH TWO DOORS AND
ONE DRAWER.   LATE 18th C.

138. BUFFET BAS A DEUX VANTAUX. FIN XVIIIᵉ S.
TWO-DOOR LOW BUFFET.   LATE 18th C.

139. BUFFET BAS, A FAÇADE GALBÉE. FIN XVIIIe S.
LOW BUFFET, WITH SERPENTINE FRONT. LATE 18th C.

140. BUFFET BAS EN FORME D'ARBALÈTE, D'ESPRIT
BAROQUE. DÉBUT XIXe S.
LOW BUFFET, WITH ARBALÈTE FRONT, IN THE
BAROQUE MANNER. EARLY 19th C.

141. BUFFET BAS, PARTICULIER AUX COU-
VENTS. XVIIIᵉ S.
LOW BUFFET, USED PARTICULARLY IN
CONVENTS. 18th C.

142. BUFFET BAS, A DEUX PORTES ORNÉES DE
LOSANGES. FIN XVIIIᵉ S.
TWO-DOOR LOW BUFFET, DECORATED WITH
LOZENGE CARVING. LATE 18th C.

143. BUFFET BAS ORNÉ DE FEUILLAGE. FIN XVIIIᵉ S.
LOW BUFFET, DECORATED WITH FOLIATED SCROLLS.
LATE 18th c.

144. BUFFET BAS RUSTIQUE A FAÇADE ET COTÉS CINTRÉS.
FIN XVIIIᵉ S.
RUSTIC LOW BUFFET, WITH BOW FRONT AND SIDES.   LATE
18th C.

145. BUFFET BAS A PANNEAUX CHANTOURNÉS ET ORNÉS
DE CROIX DE SAINT-ANDRÉ. FIN XVIIIᵉ S.
LOW BUFFET, WITH SHAPED PANELS, CARVED WITH
THE CROSS OF ST ANDREW. LATE 18th C.

146. BUFFET BAS, PARTICULIER AUX COU-
VENTS. FIN XVIIIᵉ S.
LOW BUFFET, FOUND PARTICULARLY IN
CONVENTS. LATE 18th C.

147. BUFFET BAS A DEUX PORTES CINTRÉES.
XVIIIᵉ S.
LOW BUFFET, WITH TWO ARCHED DOORS.
18th C.

148. BUFFET BAS A VANTAUX ORNÉS DE LOSANGES ET A
DEUX TIROIRS. FIN XVIIᵉ S.
LOW BUFFET, WITH DOORS DECORATED WITH LOZENGES.
LATE 17th C.

EIGHTEENTH-CENTURY LOW BUFFET, WITH TWO DOORS CARVED WITH THE CROSS OF ST. ANDREW.
IN THE MANNER OF THE SOUTHERN LOIRE VALLEY.

ARMOIRE DOORS, BUILT-IN CUPBOARDS

Built-in cupboards were to be found in convents, hospitals, public institutions, church vestries, and in many country homes. When a house was built, a recess was left in the stone wall or interior cross-wall for shelves. The woodworker would then frame the recess and make doors, either on the spot or in his workshop. These cupboards were used for food or dishes in the home, or candlesticks, censers, etc., in the sacristy.

In country houses, the doors generally had square or shaped panels. Some of them were topped with a type of console cornice, such as the one still to be seen at the *Hôtel-Dieu*, Quebec. This wall-cupboard was built around 1755 after a fire had destroyed the first hospital. Other examples of built-in cupboards with shaped panels in the Louis XV manner are those made for Monseigneur Jean Olivier Briand, seventh bishop of Quebec, when he retired to the Seminary, by Pierre Émond, the woodworker-carver who had built the bishop's private chapel. In this chapel Émond had created one of the most charming ensembles of panelling to be found in Canada. The retable is admired by all connoisseurs. Between 1770 and 1780 he also designed for the Augustinian nuns, the built-in pharmacy cupboard and the panelling and mantel of the dispensary fireplace at the *Hôpital-Général*, Quebec.

A large number of very beautiful doors were ripped from old armoires and used on built-in cupboards or made into screens, at a time when armoires fetched poor prices. It is one of the greatest disappointments for a collector today to find one of these old armoires which has been mutilated by having its doors torn off.

149. DOORS OF BUILT-IN CUPBOARD IN THE LOUIS XV MANNER. LATE 18th C.
Doors of built-in cupboard, with panels shaped and carved with spirals of Louis XV derivation. The doors were made about 1775, at the time of the construction of the *maison du Sieur Marcile, habitant de Longueuil*.
w. 4' 2''   H. 6' 2''
127 cm   188 cm
WOOD : pine   PROVENANCE : Saint-Lambert, P.Q.
(Coll. Mrs Nettie Sharpe, Saint-Lambert, P.Q.).

150. BUILT-IN WALL CUPBOARD, WITH TWO DOORS. MID 18th C.
Built-in wall cupboard, with two doors, reminiscent of certain Breton armoires. The style of the console-shaped pediment is rarely found in France, but often in Italian churches. Made in 1755 when the *Hôtel-Dieu*, Quebec, was reconstructed after a fire.
w. 2' 3⅝''   H. 5' 6¼''
71 cm   168 cm
WOOD : pine   PROVENANCE : Quebec
(Coll. Hôtel-Dieu, Quebec).

151. ARMOIRE DOOR, IN THE LOUIS XV MANNER. LATE 18th C.
Armoire door, carved with a shell and a spiral derived from the Louis XV style.
w. 2'   H. 5' 3''
61 cm   160 cm

WOOD : pine
(Coll. Mr and Mrs Pierre Gouin, Saint-Sulpice, P.Q.).

152. BUILT-IN ARMOIRE, FROM A SACRISTY. LATE 18th C.
Built-in armoire, having two doors, from the private chapel of Monseigneur Jean Olivier Briand. Executed by the woodworker-carver Pierre Émond, about 1785.
w. 3' 7¾''   H. 7' 5¾''
111 cm   228 cm
WOOD : butternut   PROVENANCE : Quebec
(Coll. Seminary of Quebec, Quebec).

153. BUILT-IN CUPBOARD DOORS, IN THE HOPITAL-GÉNÉRAL, QUEBEC. LATE 18th C.
Doors of a built-in cupboard from the dispensary of the *Hôpital-Général*, Quebec, which were made by Pierre Émond about 1775. The shaping is in the Louis XV manner.
w. 3' 8¼''   H. 7' 1½''
112 cm   217 cm
WOOD : pine   PROVENANCE : Quebec
(Coll. Hôpital-Général, Quebec).

154. TWO DOORS, FROM AN ARMOIRE. LATE 18th C.
Two doors from an armoire, with the panels shaped in the Louis XV manner, but in a naive Canadian interpretation.

145

w. 1' 10''　　H. 5' 4¾''
　56 cm　　　165 cm

WOOD : pine

(Coll. Mr and Mrs J.W. McConnell, Saint-Sauveur des Monts, P.Q.).

155. TWO DOORS, FROM AN ARMOIRE. LATE 18th C.

Two doors from an armoire, with shaped panels and spirals ornamented with foliage, in the manner of the Liébert and Quevillon Schools.

w. 2' 6''　　H. 3' 5¾''
　76 cm　　　106 cm

WOOD : pine

(Coll. Mr and Mrs Cleveland Morgan, Senneville, P.Q.).

156. TWO DOORS, FROM AN ARMOIRE. LATE 18th C.

Two doors, from an armoire, with shaped panels carved with a shell. Colour : blue-green and white.

w. 1' 9''　　H. 4' 9''
　53 cm　　　145 cm

(Coll. Canada Steamship Lines, Tadoussac, P.Q.).

157. THREE ARMOIRE DOORS. EARLY 19th C.

Three doors from an armoire, with shaped panels. Floral motifs, spirals and *fleurs de lys.*

w. 1' 9''　　H. 5' 9¼''
　53 cm　　　176 cm

WOOD : pine

PROVENANCE : Sainte-Geneviève de Pierrefonds, P.Q.

(Coll. Mr and Mrs L.G. Johnson, Petit Fort, Sainte-Geneviève de Pierrefonds, P.Q.).

149. PORTES DE PLACARD, D'ESPRIT LOUIS XV. FIN
XVIIIe S.
DOORS OF BUILT-IN CUPBOARD, IN THE LOUIS XV
MANNER. LATE 18th C.

151. PORTE D'ARMOIRE, D'ESPRIT LOUIS XV. FIN XVIIIᵉ S.
ARMOIRE DOOR, IN THE LOUIS XV MANNER. LATE
18th c.

150. ARMOIRE-PLACARD A DEUX VANTAUX. MILIEU
XVIIIᵉ S.
BUILT-IN WALL CUPBOARD, WITH TWO DOORS. MID
18th c.

152. ARMOIRE-PLACARD DE SACRISTIE. FIN XVIIIe S.
BUILT-IN ARMOIRE, FROM A SACRISTY.   LATE 18th C.

153. PORTES DE PLACARD DE L'HOPITAL-GÉNÉRAL DE
QUÉBEC. FIN XVIIIe S.
BUILT-IN CUPBOARD DOORS, IN THE HOPITAL-GÉNÉRAL,
QUEBEC.   LATE 18th C.

154. DEUX PORTES D'ARMOIRE. FIN XVIIIe S.
TWO DOORS, FROM AN ARMOIRE. LATE 18th C.

155. DEUX PORTES D'ARMOIRE. FIN XVIIIe S.
TWO DOORS, FROM AN ARMOIRE. LATE 18th C

156. DEUX PORTES D'ARMOIRE. FIN XVIIIe S.
TWO DOORS, FROM AN ARMOIRE. LATE 18th C.

157. TROIS PORTES D'ARMOIRE. DÉBUT XIXe S
THREE ARMOIRE DOORS. EARLY 19th C.

DRESSERS AND BUCKET-BENCHES

The dresser or buffet-dresser *(vaisseliers* or *buffets-vaisseliers)* was very common in Canadian homes in the eighteenth century. It used to be called " a little buffet with upper shelves. "[1] It was also described as " a dresser with a food-locker in pine and having an iron lock and key. "[2]

In 1691, " the woodworker Parent undertook to do the woodwork at the house owned by the brothers Jean Baptiste and Pierre Charly on St. Paul Street in Montreal ... and to make a partition for a cupboard for dishes at the side of the lower room having a door and being tongued and grooved and whitened on the sides, on top of which he will make a dresser to keep dishes... "[3]

The dresser was divided into two parts, the lower being a low buffet (either without drawers or, more frequently, having drawers for cutlery), and was used for storing food and utensils, the top being used as a serving table. Above this were the shelves where the faience and pewter were displayed. The mistress of the household was proud to show her good faience pieces to visitors, it being particularly beautiful at this period, coming mainly from Rouen, La Rochelle, Marseilles, Strasbourg and Lunéville.

Another type of dresser had a low body fitted with drawers and a lower shelf for buckets and pots. It was very like the Norman *faux-palier* but its workmanship was more primitive.

Bucket-benches *(banc à seaux),* holding buckets and basins, were placed in the common room. There were not many references to them in the eighteenth century, but an inventory of 1760 does mention a " *Banc de Sciaux.* "[4] Those which have survived were made in the nineteenth century and were usually of primitive workmanship.

158. RUSTIC DRESSER. 18th C.
Rustic dresser, with a single central door set between two panels in the lower stage.

W. 4' 4"	H. 6' 4"	D. 9"
132 cm	193 cm	23 cm
		1' 8¾"
		53 cm

WOOD : pine

(Coll. Mr John H. Molson, Saint-Sauveur des Monts, P.Q.).

159. DRESSER, UNDER ENGLISH INFLUENCE. LATE 18th C.
Dresser, under English influence. The open upper stage is decorated with an arch and pilasters, the lower stage with two doors, and two drawers.

W. 4' 1½"	H. 6' 10½"	D. 10"
126 cm	210 cm	25 cm
		1' 7⅞"
		50 cm

WOOD : pine   PROVENANCE : Saint-Malachie, P.Q.

(Coll. Miss Barbara Richardson, Sainte-Agathe des Monts, P.Q.).

160. DRESSER. LATE 18th C.
Dresser, with two drawers, two doors and shaped panels in the lower stage.

W. 3' 11¾"	H. 6' 10"	D. 1' 4¾"
121 cm	208 cm	43 cm
4' 2"		10½"
127 cm		27 cm

WOOD : pine

(Coll. Mr and Mrs Victor M. Drury, Lake Anne, P.Q.).

161. DRESSER. 19th C.
Dresser, with two doors and two drawers. The cornice is festooned, and the uprights of the upper stage are shaped. The drawer handles and keyhole escutcheons have been replaced.

W. 4' 8½"	H. 6' 1½"	D. 10½"
144 cm	187 cm	27 cm
		1' 6¼"
		46 cm

WOOD : pine   PROVENANCE : Murray Bay, P.Q.

(Coll. Mrs Richard R. Costello, Sainte-Agathe des Monts, P.Q.).

(1) A J M, I O A. Inventaire de La Succession de deffun françois seguin du 19ᵉ juliet 1732. Greffe Coron.
(2) A J M, I O A. Inventaire des Biens de Deffunt Antoine Janote La Chapel, le 28 may 1746, Pointe aux Trembles. Greffe Comparet.
(3) A J M, I O A. Devis des ouvrages & marché fait Entre le Sr Charly & parent 13ᵉ May 1691, Montréal. Greffe Adhémar.
(4) A J M, I O A. Inventaire des biens de la Succession de feu François Leblanc et de deffunte Françoise Robert, le 9 octobre 1760 à Chambly. Greffe Grisé.

162. DRESSER, OF THE NORMAN "FAUX PALIER" TYPE. EARLY 19th C.

Dresser, with a structure very close to that of the Norman *faux-palier* type. The open shelf in the base, which has been replaced, served to hold buckets and cooking-pots. (Cf. p. 151.)

W. 4' 7" H. 6' ½" D.B. 1' 5¼" D.T. 8¾"
140 cm 184 cm 44 cm 22 cm

WOOD : pine PROVENANCE : Sorel, P.Q.

(Coll. Mr and Mrs Roland Leduc, Montreal).

163. RUSTIC BUCKET-BENCH. 19th C.

Rustic nineteenth-century bucket-bench. Note the grooves carved on the table top which served for drainage into a bucket.

W. 2' 5¾" H. 3' 3½" D. 13"
76 cm 100 cm 33 cm

WOOD : pine

(Coll. Mr and Mrs F.M. Hutchins, Pembroke, Ont.).

164. RUSTIC BUCKET-BENCH, FOLK ART. 19th C.

Rustic bucket-bench. The top shelf is shaped and decorated with openwork. Folk art.

W. 3' 6" H. 4' D. 1'
107 cm 122 cm 30 cm
6"
15 cm

WOOD : pine

PROVENANCE : Montée Saint-Charles, Pointe Claire, P.Q.

(Coll. Canada Steamship Lines, Tadoussac, P.Q.).

158. VAISSELIER RUSTIQUE. XVIIIe S.
RUSTIC DRESSER. 18th C.

159. VAISSELIER, D'ESPRIT ANGLAIS. FIN XVIIIᵉ S.
DRESSER, UNDER ENGLISH INFLUENCE. LATE 18th C.

160. VAISSELIER. FIN XVIIIᵉ
DRESSER. LATE 18th C.

161. VAISSELIER. XIXe S.
DRESSER. 19th C.

162. VAISSELIER DE TYPE
« FAUX-PALIER » NOR-
MAND. DÉBUT XIXᵉ S.
DRESSER, OF THE NORMAN
" FAUX-PALIER " TYPE.
EARLY 19th C.

163. BANC A SEAUX RUSTIQUE. XIXᵉ S.
RUSTIC BUCKET-BENCH. 19th C.

164. BANC A SEAUX RUSTIQUE, ART POPULAIRE. XIXᵉ S.
RUSTIC BUCKET-BENCH, FOLK ART. 19th C.

GLAZED BUFFETS, DOUGH-BOXES, FOOD-LOCKERS

GLAZED BUFFETS

The glazed buffet (*buffet vitré*, sometimes called *vitrau* in Canada) was constructed in either one or two tiers, the lower part being used for food and utensils, and the upper part for dishes. These pieces were found in large farmhouses and wealthy homes where they were used either as buffets or bookcases. They suggest a corner cabinet but were much wider and were intended to be placed against a wall. The majority of glazed buffets were influenced by English and American styles, although a few have shaped panels in the Louis XV style.

---

165. TWO-TIERED GLAZED BUFFET. 18th C.

Two-tiered glazed buffet, with four doors. The front and side panels are shaped in the Louis XV manner; the stiles and the centre-post have shaped panels. The glazed buffet is not found in French peasant homes but was used as a buffet-bookcase in bourgeois provincial houses. In Canada the glazed buffet is a transformation of the glazed corner cabinet. The fische hinges and keyhole escutcheons are original. An elegant and well-proportioned piece of furniture.

w. 4'	H. 7' 2''	D. 1' ⅝''
122 cm	218 cm	32 cm
4' 3½''		1' 8''
131 cm		51 cm

WOOD : pine   PROVENANCE : Isle of Orleans, P.Q.

(Coll. Mr and Mrs Jean-Paul Lemieux, Sillery, P.Q.).

166. RUSTIC GLAZED BUFFET. 18th C.

Rustic glazed buffet, with two shaped doors. The shaping of the upper cross-piece is a naive Canadian interpretation of Louis XV curves. Original rat-tail fische hinges. The cornice and the moulding at the base were added later.

| w. 3' 3¼'' | H. 7' 2¾'' | D. 1' 3¾'' |
| 100 cm | 220 cm | 40 cm |

WOOD : pine   PROVENANCE : Batiscan, P.Q.

(Coll. Mr Alexis Germain, farmer, Deschambault, P.Q.).

167. TWO-TIERED GLAZED BUFFET. LATE 18th C.

Two-tiered glazed buffet, with shaped panels. The bracket feet show English influence. The hinges are a later addition.

w. 3' 4''	H. 6' 5¾''	D. 1' 2''
102 cm	198 cm	36 cm
		1' 3¾''
		40 cm

WOOD : pine

(Coll. Senator and Mrs H. de M. Molson, Lac Violon, Sainte-Agathe des Monts, P.Q.).

168. SMALL GLAZED BUFFET, DECORATED WITH "GALETTES" IN THE BRETON MANNER. EARLY 19th C.

Small glazed buffet, decorated with discs or *galettes* in the Breton manner, ornaments which are found on armoires along the west coast of France, as far as the Pyrenees. Generally the discs are combined with lozenges or diamond points. This is a naive and rustic example, with its small *galettes* carved on the top rail.

| w. 2' 10½'' | H. 6' 10'' | D. 1' 4¾'' |
| 88 cm | 208 cm | 43 cm |

WOOD : pine

(Coll. National Museum of Canada, Ottawa, Ont.).

169. GLAZED BUFFET. LATE 18th C.

Glazed buffet, with four doors. The upper stage projects in the form of a prow. The lower panels of the doors are decorated with simplified linen folds, as are the eight lateral panels. The glazed doors are more rustic and of inferior workmanship than the rest, as if they had been replaced later. The cornice is carved with small lozenges. The moulding on the base is missing.

| w. 3' 9'' | H. 7' | D. 1' 4'' |
| 114 cm | 213 cm | 41 cm |

WOOD : pine   PROVENANCE : Saint-Hilarion, P.Q.

(Coll. of the author, Petite Rivière Saint-François, P.Q.).

157

170. GLAZED BUFFET, OF ENGLISH INSPIRATION. EARLY 19th C.

Glazed buffet, of English inspiration, decorated with many ornaments such as pastilles, fluting and cable moulding. The dentil cornice is a later addition. The bracket feet show the influence of Chippendale. The ornaments of the panels are in the Late Regency manner.

W. 4' ½''	H. 6' 7¾''	D. 1' 4''
123 cm	203 cm	41 cm
3' 10¼''		1' 1¼''
117 cm		34 cm

WOOD : pine

PROVENANCE : La Prairie de la Madeleine, P.Q.

(Coll. Mr and Mrs F.M. Hutchins, Pembroke, Ont.).

171. GLAZED BUFFET, WITH VARIEGATED DECORATION. EARLY 19th C.

Glazed buffet, with richly shaped lower doors. The decoration consists of cable mouldings, *entrelacs*, curves and countercurves with spirals, fluting, foliage and a carved ciborium on the central rail. The bevelled pilasters are fluted and reeded in a manner reminiscent of Adam and Regency styles. It has the structure of a corner cabinet. The shaped lower rail has been sawn. A piece of furniture derived from many styles with superabundant ornamentation.

W. 4' ¾''	H. 7' 5⅝''	D. 1' 3⅝''
124 cm	228 cm	40 cm
3' 3¾''		1' 1½''
101 cm		34 cm

WOOD : pine   PROVENANCE : Le Bic, P.Q.

(Coll. Mr and Mrs H.J. Godber, Sainte-Agathe des Monts, P.Q.).

172. TWO-TIERED GLAZED BUFFET, WITH TWO DRAWERS. 18th C.

Two-tiered glazed buffet, with two drawers and four doors. A rustic buffet with bracket feet of English derivation. The central knob on the lower rail of the upper stage is only an ornament. Rattail hinges.

W. 3' 11¼''	H. 6' 8½''	D. 1' 5¾''
120 cm	205 cm	46 cm
3' 9''		1' 1''
114 cm		33 cm

WOOD : pine   PROVENANCE : Saint-Gervais, P.Q.

(Coll. Canada Steamship Lines, Tadoussac, P.Q.).

173. GLAZED BUFFET-BUREAU. EARLY 19th C.

Glazed buffet-bureau in an English style. The upper stage was probably used as a bookcase. The lower portion served both as a commode and as an upright writing-desk for keeping papers. The stiles show English influence.

W. 3' 6''	H. 6' 4⅝''	D. 2'
107 cm	195 cm	61 cm
2' 11¼''		10''
90 cm		26 cm

WOOD : pine

(Coll. Provincial Museum, Quebec).

174. TWO-TIERED RUSTIC GLAZED BUFFET. 19th C.

Two-tiered rustic glazed buffet, with three doors and shaped top rails in the upper stage. The bottom doors are of primitive workmanship. Projecting cornices.

WOOD : pine

(Coll. Detroit Institute of Arts, Detroit, Mich., U.S.A.).

DOUGH-BOXES

The Canadian dough-box (*huche* or *pétrin*) was a chest on legs — a functional piece of furniture used to knead the dough and also to store bread or other food. It was to be found in every home from the beginning of the colony, " a pine dough-box with birch legs, valued at six livres. "[1] The shape varied little and was somewhat crude, as in Normandy. The beautifully carved types of the Pyrenees and Provence were not to be found in Canada, yet we know of the existence of a rather stylish one whose under-structure had been turned, the sides made of single planks dove-tailed together, and a shelf placed at the base (cf. no 177). Unfortunately the bun-feet are missing.

In order to make them watertight, their sides were made from whole, unjointed planks. Many trough-shaped dough-boxes were mentioned in inventories, and a few are still to be found

(1) A J M, I O A. Inventaire des Effets de Deffuns Silvestre proux et Thérèse ducharme sa femme, trouvez après le décès... 19ᵉ 8bre 1753, Montréal. Greffe Desmarest.

in attics. They were hollowed from a section of pine log with an adze, and have a very primitive appearance "... a part of a tree hollowed out to make a dough-box..." [1].

Since the development of village bakeries the dough-box has almost disappeared from Canadian homes except where home-made bread or bread baked in outdoor ovens is appreciated.

175. DOUGH-BOX. EARLY 19th C.

Rustic jointed dough-box, from the Montreal district. The lid is missing.

W. 3' 2⅝" H. 2' 5" D. 1' 7¾"
98 cm   74 cm   50 cm

WOOD : pine PROVENANCE : Sainte-Dorothée, P.Q.

(Coll. S. Breitman Antiques, Montreal).

176. DOUGH-BOX, WITH CURVED LEGS. 19th C.

A very common kind of dough-box, from the Montreal district, with an understructure reminiscent of Empire and American *Directoire* styles.

W. 2' 11⅝" H. 2' 6" D. 1' 7"
91 cm   76 cm   48 cm

WOOD : pine PROVENANCE : Saint-Hilaire, P.Q.

(Coll. Mr M.A. Dhavernas, Saint-Sauveur des Monts, P.Q.).

177. DOUGH-BOX, WITH TURNED LEGS. 18th C.

Dough-box, constructed with dove-tail joints, with turned legs of Louis XIII derivation and a shelf at the base. This is the most elegant Canadian dough-box, but unfortunately the bun-feet are missing.

W. 2' 11¾" H. 2' 4" D. 1' 9¼"
91 cm   71 cm   54 cm
                      1' 4⅝"
                      42 cm

WOOD : pine

PROVENANCE : Saint-André de Kamouraska, P.Q.

(Coll. Comte and Comtesse Bernard de Roussy de Sales, Montreal).

178. DOUGH-BOX. 19th C.

Dough-box, having a structure which was very common during the nineteenth century. Original black colouring.

W. 2' 7" H. 2' 4½" D. 1' 5¾"
79 cm   72 cm   44 cm

WOOD : pine

PROVENANCE : Saint-Denis-sur-Richelieu, P.Q.

(Coll. Mr and Mrs J.N. Cole, Montreal).

179. DOUGH-BOX, WITH PANELS AND FESTOONED APRON. MID 19th C.

Dough-box, with rectangular panels and a festooned apron. The feet are tapered in the English manner.

W. 4' H. 2' 8½" D. 1' 10"
122 cm 83 cm   51 cm

WOOD : pine

(Coll. Mr and Mrs J.N. Cole, Montreal).

FOOD-LOCKERS

Food-lockers *(garde-manger)* were mentioned in a number of eighteenth-century inventories, "a pine food-locker with hinges..." [2], but the few that have survived are very primitive. They usually had one or two doors, with vertical wooden bars or a grill inserted in the upper panel as ventilation to keep the food fresh.

There is still a food-locker built into the wall at the *Hôtel-Dieu*, Quebec. It was ventilated by a spindle grill (like the food-lockers found in French country houses), and was made in 1755 when the hospital was reconstructed after a fire. According to tradition, it was near the former refectory, and milk, butter and other fresh food would be placed there in the coolness of the stone wall, after each meal.

180. FOOD-LOCKER, WITH TWO DOORS. 18th C.
Food-locker, with two doors having a vertical grill

in the upper part. Generally this kind of furniture is of rustic manufacture.

(1) A J M, I O A. Inventaire des biens de feu Mr (pierre) Dupas, 10 au 15 octobre 1678 de Champlain. Greffe Adhémar.
(2) A J M, I O A. Inventaire d'André Demers le 19e fév. 1732, Montréal. Greffe Chaumont.

W. 5'   H. 5' 4''   D. 1' 8''
  152 cm   163 cm   51 cm
WOOD : pine   PROVENANCE : Neuville, P.Q.
(Coll. Dr and Mrs Claude Bertrand, Outremont, P.Q.).

181. FOOD-LOCKER, WITH ONE DOOR. 17th C.

Food-locker, with one door. It is the oldest known food-locker. The chamfered panel frames are identical with the chamfered side panels of a four-door armoire from Finistère, dated 1640, which figures as illustration no. 96 in Suzanne Tardieu's book, *Les Meubles régionaux datés.* This one was probably made by the resident woodworker of the *Hôtel-Dieu*, Quebec. Grey in colour.

W. 2' 9½''   H. 5' ½''   D. 1' 9''
  85 cm   154 cm   53 cm
WOOD : pine   PROVENANCE : Quebec.
(Coll. Musée de l'Hôtel-Dieu, Quebec).

182. BUILT-IN FOOD-LOCKER. 18th C.

Food-locker built into the interior partition-wall next to the old refectory of the Nuns of the *Hôtel-Dieu*, Quebec, in 1755. It has two doors and a central section of openwork with turned spindles. (Cf. p. 159.)

WOOD : pine   PROVENANCE : Quebec.

(Coll. Hôtel-Dieu, Quebec).

165. BUFFET VITRÉ A DEUX CORPS. XVIIIe S.
TWO-TIERED GLAZED BUFFET. 18th C.

166. BUFFET VITRÉ RUSTIQUE. XVIIIᵉ S.
RUSTIC GLAZED BUFFET. 18th c.

167. BUFFET VITRÉ A DEUX CORPS. FIN XVIIIᵉ S.
TWO-TIERED GLAZED BUFFET. LATE 18th c.

168. PETIT BUFFET VITRÉ, DÉCORÉ DE « GALETTES »
D'INFLUENCE BRETONNE. DÉBUT XIXᵉ S.
SMALL GLAZED BUFFET, DECORATED WITH "GALETTES"
IN THE BRETON MANNER.   EARLY 19th C.

169. BUFFET VITRÉ. FIN XVIIIᵉ S.
GLAZED BUFFET.   LATE 18th C.

170. BUFFET VITRÉ, D'INSPIRATION ANGLAISE. DÉBUT
XIXe S.
GLAZED BUFFET, OF ENGLISH INSPIRATION. EARLY
19th C.

171. BUFFET VITRÉ A DÉCORS MULTIFORMES. DÉBUT XIXᵉ S.
GLAZED BUFFET, WITH VARIEGATED DECORATION. EARLY 19th C.

172. BUFFET VITRÉ A DEUX CORPS, ORNÉ DE DEUX TIROIRS. XVIIIᵉ S.
TWO-TIERED GLAZED BUFFET, WITH TWO DRAWERS. 18th C.

173. BUFFET-BUREAU VITRÉ. DÉBUT XIXᵉ S
GLAZED BUFFET-BUREAU.   EARLY 19th C.

174. BUFFET VITRÉ RUSTIQUE A DEUX CORPS. XIXᵉ S.
TWO-TIERED RUSTIC GLAZED BUFFET.   19th C.

175. HUCHE A PAIN. DÉBUT XIXᵉ S.
DOUGH-BOX.   EARLY 19th C.

178. HUCHE A PAIN. XIXᵉ S.
DOUGH-BOX.   19th C.

176. HUCHE A PIEDS GALBÉS. XIXᵉ S.
DOUGH-BOX, WITH CURVED LEGS.   19th C.

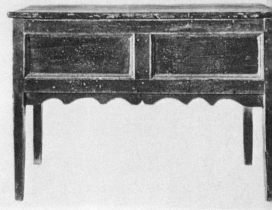

177. HUCHE A PIÈTEMENT TOURNÉ. XVIIIᵉ S.
DOUGH-BOX, WITH TURNED LEGS.   18th C.

179. HUCHE ORNÉE DE PANNEAUX ET D'UNE CEINTURE FESTONNÉE.
MILIEU XIXᵉ S.
DOUGH-BOX, WITH PANELS AND FESTOONED APRON.   MID 19th C.

180. GARDE-MANGER A DEUX VANTAUX. XVIIIᵉ S.
FOOD-LOCKER, WITH TWO DOORS. 18th C.

182. GARDE-MANGER-PLACARD. XVIIIᵉ S.
BUILT-IN FOOD-LOCKER. 18th C.

181. GARDE-MANGER A UN VANTAIL. XVIIᵉ S.
FOOD-LOCKER, WITH ONE DOOR. 17th C.

CORNER CABINETS

Corner cabinets or cupboards (*encoignures, buffets d'encoignure*, in Canada known as *armoires de coin, coinçons, écoinçons,* or simply *coins*) most often had a glazed upper section in which the best plates would be displayed as decoration. The lower section formed a buffet for storing food and utensils, and usually had one or two doors and sometimes one or two drawers.

Corner cabinets became popular in the rural districts of French Canada towards the end of the eighteenth century and continued to be made until the middle of the nineteenth century. The earliest ones were built at the same time as the house across one corner of the common room and consisted only of a front attached to the whitewashed wall of roughcast. Others dating from the end of the eighteenth century were finished with shaped panels in the Louis XV style. The most elegant corner cabinet I have seen has a bow front and dome top and was taken from the presbytery of *Notre-Dame de Québec* (dating from 1773-75) when the building was demolished in 1931. This very French-looking corner cabinet is a piece of skilled workmanship, and was probably made by one of the famous woodworker-carvers of the period.

Those of the early nineteenth century were influenced by many of the styles imported by the British cabinet-makers — Georgian, Adam, and Regency designs.

Corner cabinets were either two-tiered or built in one piece; some had a flat façade, some a bow front and others a serpentine front. In a few exceptional cases, the upper section had shelves or open steps which receded and became narrower towards the top. Some which had no lower section were little more than hanging shelves (with or without glass doors), and were attached to the wall.

The corner cabinet was given a place of honour in one corner of the common room, and later of the parlour. The housewife always took great pride in her corner cabinet in which she displayed her bibelots and prettiest dishes.

183. BOW-FRONT CORNER CABINET, IN THE " RÉGENCE " MANNER, WITH AN ARCHED CORNICE. 18th C.

Bow-front corner cabinet, in the *Régence* manner, with an arched cornice. The lower stage has two doors with shaped panels and a bottom rail carved with a shell. An enormous carved shell forms the interior vault underneath the arched top. A typically French model, made in Canada undoubtedly by a Master Woodworker and church carver. Formerly in the old Presbytery of Quebec Cathedral (built between 1773 and 1775, demolished in 1931).

w. 3' 7¾"   h. 8' 5"
111 cm   257 cm

WOOD : butternut

PROVENANCE : old Presbytery of the Cathedral, Quebec

(Coll. Mr and Mrs Antoine Dubuc, Chicoutimi, P.Q.).

184. DETAIL OF THE CARVED SHELL FORMING THE INTERIOR VAULT OF Nº 183.

185. DETAIL.

186. TWO-TIERED GLAZED CORNER CABINET, IN LOUIS XV MANNER. LATE 18th C.

Glazed corner cabinet with bevelled sides, in two tiers. The doors have shaped upper rails. Vertical and horizontal panels decorate the stiles and lower door. An eighteenth-century piece, of French derivation.

w. 3' 11½"   h. 7' 3½"
121 cm   222 cm
3' 9"
114 cm

WOOD : pine   PROVENANCE : Verchères, P.Q.

(Coll. Provincial Museum, Quebec).

187. CORNER CABINET, IN LOUIS XV MANNER. LATE 18th C.

Corner cabinet, in the Louis XV manner, having doors with prominent double mouldings and shaped upper rails. This corner cabinet was one of a pair which came from the old Presbytery of the place known today as *Vieille Église* in St Louis de Lotbinière.

w. 3' 1¾"   h. 7' 2⅜"
96 cm   219 cm

WOOD : pine

PROVENANCE : Saint-Louis de Lotbinière, P.Q.

(Coll. Miss Barbara Richardson, Sainte-Agathe des Monts, P.Q.).

188. TWO-TIERED CORNER CABINET, WITH BOW FRONT. LATE 18th C.

Two-tiered corner cabinet, with bow front, and four doors with shaped panels in the Louis XV manner. The small panels of the upper stage are squat, and upset the general balance of the piece. Nevertheless, it still has a very French provincial appeal. The cornice is missing.

W. 3' 9½"   H. 6' 11½"
116 cm   212 cm
3' 11½"
121 cm

WOOD : pine

PROVENANCE : Rivière Ouelle, P.Q.

(Coll. Mr and Mrs A.F. Culver, Pointe au Pic, P.Q.).

189. SMALL SERPENTINE-FRONTED CORNER CABINET, WITH OPEN SHELVES. LATE 18th C.

Small serpentine-fronted corner cabinet, with shelves in several tiers. It has two doors and a shaped and carved lower rail. The sides of the upper shelves are also shaped and carved with spirals, several of which are missing. The topmost part of the cabinet is also missing. The curved feet, terminating in *pieds de biche*, are surmounted with acanthus leaves. An agreeable small piece of furniture with a very French appeal, but interpreted in a Canadian manner.

W. 2' 10"   H. 7'
86 cm   213 cm

WOOD : pine   PROVENANCE : Lacolle, P.Q.

(Coll. Mrs Ross Sims, Saint-Sauveur des Monts, P.Q.).

190. DETAIL.

191. GLAZED CORNER CABINET, IN ONE PIECE. EARLY 19th C.

Glazed corner cabinet, in one piece with bevelled sides. The lower door has two shaped panels, and the glazed door has a festooned rail, reminiscent of Chinese Chippendale. Hinges in " H " form.

W. 2' 9½"   H. 6' 4"
85 cm   193 cm

WOOD : pine   PROVENANCE : Montreal district

(Coll. Mr and Mrs Pierre Gouin, St Sulpice, P.Q.).

192. BOW-FRONT TWO-TIERED CORNER CABINET, IN THE ADAM MANNER. LATE 18th C.

Bow-front corner cabinet, in two tiers, with panels in the Adam manner. Dentil cornice. The bracket

feet are a later addition. Fine example of the Adam brothers' influence.

W. 3' 5"   H. 7' 3½"
104 cm   222 cm

WOOD : pine

(Coll. Mr and Mrs Ross McMaster, Saint-Sauveur des Monts, P.Q.).

193. CORNER CABINET, WITH CARVED AND PAINTED DOOR. FOLK ART. EARLY 19th C.

Corner cabinet, with one door made from a single pine plank, painted and carved with a central motif of a plant in a vase. Folk art.

W. 2' 3½"   H. 7' 7"
70 cm   231 cm

WOOD : pine   PROVENANCE : Lacolle, P.Q.

(Coll. Mr and Mrs J.N. Cole, Montreal).

194. CORNER CABINET, WITH VARIEGATED DECORATION. LATE 18th C.

Corner cabinet, with variegated decoration. The dentils on the pediment are surmounted by Chinese Chippendale-style festoons. The fans recall Adam's " bat wings ". The *palmettes* suggest the wings of birds, and the two motifs on the upper rail are inspired by early door-knob plates. A fine corner cabinet with folk-art decoration.

W. 4' 5"   H. 7' 7¼"
135 cm   232 cm

WOOD : pine   PROVENANCE : Château-Richer, P.Q.

(Coll. Canada Steamship Lines, Tadoussac, P.Q.).

195. GLAZED TWO-TIERED CORNER CABINET, CARVED WITH GEOMETRIC REEDING. 19th C.

Glazed two-tiered corner cabinet. The door is framed with parallel reeding and fluting in the form of chevrons, a decoration peculiar to the Bresse region of Burgundy, although reeding in the form of chevrons could also give the impression of being inspired by Indian ceramics.

W. 3' 4½"   H. 7' 1¾"
103 cm   218 cm

WOOD : pine   PROVENANCE : Island of Montreal

(Coll. Mr and Mrs Louis G. Johnson, Petit Fort, Sainte-Geneviève de Pierrefonds, P.Q.).

196. GLAZED BOW-FRONT CORNER CABINET, IN TWO TIERS. 19th C.

Glazed bow-front cabinet, in two tiers, with four doors. The dentil cornice surmounts an upper rail with motifs reminiscent of Chinese Chippendale. The top rail of the lower stage, embellished with parallel and vertical fluting, shows a very marked English influence.

w. 3' 8''   H. 7' 2''
112 cm   219 cm

WOOD : pine

(Coll. Canadair Limited, Saint-Laurent, Montreal).

197. GLAZED CORNER CABINET, IN RUSTIC STYLE, WITH TWO DOORS. 19th C.

Glazed rustic corner cabinet, with two doors. Reeded dentils and carved rosettes are surmounted by a prominent pediment. The lower rail with its multiple mouldings is festooned, while the panels are ornamented with fans in the Adam manner. A naive and attractive piece.

w. 3' 1¾''   H. 6' 8''
96 cm   203 cm

WOOD : pine

PROVENANCE : St Paul de Joliette, P.Q.

(Coll. Mr and Mrs H.J. Godber, Sainte-Agathe des Monts, P.Q.).

198. SMALL GLAZED CORNER CABINET, IN RUSTIC STYLE, WITH BOW FRONT. 19th C.

Small bow-front glazed corner cabinet, with stiles and rails incised with waves and dots, of naive workmanship. The lower stage is missing. Hinges are in the " H " and " L " forms of the period.

w. 2' 6½''   H. 3' 4¾''
77 cm   104 cm

WOOD : pine

(Coll. Mr Paul Gouin, Montreal).

199. SMALL HANGING CORNER CABINET, WITH BOW-FRONT GLAZED DOORS. EARLY 19th C.

Small glazed bow-front corner cabinet, also known as " a hanging or suspended shelf " *(étagère),* because it is fixed to the wall and has no lower stage. The stiles and rails are festooned.

w. 2' 6¾''   H. 3' 6½''
77 cm   108 cm

WOOD : pine

PROVENANCE : Cap au Corbeau, Baie Saint-Paul, P.Q.

(Coll. Mr and Mrs Pierre Gouin, Saint-Sulpice, P.Q.).

200. RUSTIC GLAZED CORNER CABINET. EARLY 19th C.

Rustic glazed corner cabinet, with two doors. Very pronounced mouldings frame this piece of furniture. Carved inside the door of the lower stage is " 20 DC 1817 ". This does not necessarily mean that the cabinet was actually made then; the owner could have engraved these figures later. Original rat-tail fische hinges.

WOOD : pine

(Coll. Canada Steamship Lines, Tadoussac, P.Q.).

201. DETAIL OF ENGRAVED DATE INSIDE THE CORNER CABINET Nº 200.

202. GLAZED CORNER CABINET WITH BOW FRONT, SHOWING ENGLISH INFLUENCE. EARLY 19th C.

Glazed bow-front corner cabinet, with four doors. The top of the lower tier is surmounted by an arch in the form of a basket handle *(anse de panier)* and the base has bracket feet. It shows early nineteenth-century English influence.

w. 4'   H. 7' 8''
122 cm   234 cm

WOOD : pine

PROVENANCE : Sainte-Anne de la Pérade, P.Q.

(Coll. Mrs Richard R. Costello, Sainte-Agathe des Monts, P.Q.).

203. BOW-FRONT GLAZED CORNER CABINET IN TWO TIERS, IN THE REGENCY MANNER. EARLY 19th C.

Bow-front glazed corner cabinet. The shape of the appliqué moulding on the panels denotes the Regency style. Bracket feet. The lower rail is shaped in the characteristic manner of the period.

w. 4' 4''   - 3' 10½''   H. 7' 1''
132 cm - 118 cm   216 cm

WOOD : pine   PROVENANCE : Rivière Ouelle, P.Q.

(Coll. Mr and Mrs A.F. Culver, Pointe au Pic, P.Q.).

204. GLAZED CORNER CABINET, OF ENGLISH DERIVATION. EARLY 19th C.

Glazed corner cabinet, with bevelled sides. The rosettes and fans in the corner of the panels show Adam influence. The bracket feet have been restored. Original wrought-iron hinges.

w. 3' 5''   H. 7' 3''
104 cm   221 cm

WOOD : pine   PROVENANCE : Saint-Romuald, P.Q.

(Coll. Miss Barbara Richardson, Sainte-Agathe des Monts, P.Q.).

205. GLAZED CORNER CABINET, SHOWING ENGLISH INFLUENCE. EARLY 19th C.

Glazed corner cabinet, with four doors. The upper stage is framed with moulding and dentils. The bracket feet have been added. Rustic work showing English influence.

w. 3' 9½''   H. 7' 4½''
116 cm   225 cm

WOOD : pine   PROVENANCE : Isle of Orleans, P.Q.

(Coll. Canada Steamship Lines, Tadoussac, P.Q.).

206. OPEN CORNER CABINET WITH PILASTERS, IN THE ADAM MANNER. EARLY 19th C.

Open corner cabinet, with two doors. The upper

stage has fluted pilasters, with an *anse de panier* arch decorated with a small bracket called an *agrafe* and bat wings, in the Adam tradition.

w. 4' 9'' H. 7' 5½''
145 cm 227 cm

WOOD : pine

(Coll. Mr and Mrs F.M. Hutchins, Pembroke, Ont.).

207. LARGE CORNER CABINET, UNDER ENGLISH IN-FLUENCE. LATE 18th C.

Large corner cabinet, of English Chippendale derivation, having fluted and reeded pilasters, and a dentil cornice.

w. 5' 4½'' H. 7' 4½''
164 cm 225 cm

WOOD : pine

PROVENANCE : Saint Rémi de Napierville, P.Q.

(Coll. National Museum of Canada, Ottawa, Ont.).

208. OPEN CORNER CABINET, IN THE AMERICAN CHIP-PENDALE STYLE. LATE 18th C.

Open corner cabinet, with two doors, and an arch with two fluted pilasters. This piece, in the Chippendale manner, appeared in the United States about 1765. It is of rustic workmanship and must have been made in Canada towards the end of the eighteenth century.

w. 4' 1'' H. 7' 2''
124 cm 218 cm

WOOD : pine

PROVENANCE : Saint-Charles de Bellechasse, P.Q.

(Coll. National Museum of Canada, Ottawa, Ont.).

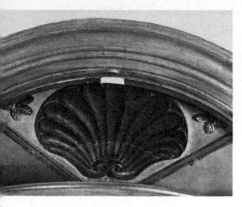

184. DÉTAIL DE LA COQUILLE SCULPTÉE FORMANT LA VOUTE
INTÉRIEURE DU Nº 183.
DETAIL OF THE CARVED SHELL FORMING THE INTERIOR VAULT
OF Nº 183.

183. ENCOIGNURE CINTRÉE A FRONTON CURVILIGNE, D'ESPRIT
RÉGENCE. XVIIIᵉ S.
LOW FRONT CORNER CABINET, IN THE " RÉGENCE " MANNER,
WITH AN ARCHED CORNICE. 18th C.

185. DÉTAIL.
DETAIL.

186. ENCOIGNURE A DEUX CORPS, D'ESPRIT LOUIS XV.
FIN XVIIIe S.
TWO-TIERED GLAZED CORNER CABINET, IN LOUIS XV
MANNER.   LATE 18th C.

187. ENCOIGNURE, D'ESPRIT LOUIS XV. FIN XVIIIe S.
CORNER CABINET, IN LOUIS XV MANNER.   LATE 18th C.

188. BUFFET D'ENCOIGNURE CINTRÉ, A DEUX CORPS.
FIN XVIIIᵉ S.
TWO-TIERED CORNER CABINET, WITH BOW FRONT.
LATE 18th C.

189. PETITE ENCOIGNURE GALBÉE A GRADINS. FIN XVIIIe S.
SMALL SERPENTINE-FRONTED CORNER CABINET, WITH OPEN SHELVES.
LATE 18th C.

190. DÉTAIL.
DETAIL.

192. ENCOIGNURE CINTRÉE A DEUX CORPS, DE STYLE
ADAM. FIN XVIIIe S.
BOW-FRONT TWO-TIERED CORNER CABINET, IN THE
ADAM MANNER. LATE 18th C.

193. ENCOIGNURE A PORTE PEINTE ET SCULPTÉE. ART
POPULAIRE. DÉBUT XIXe S.
CORNER CABINET, WITH CARVED AND PAINTED DOOR.
FOLK ART. EARLY 19th C.

194. BUFFET D'ENCOIGNURE A ORNEMENTS MULTIPLES.
FIN XVIIIe S.
CORNER CABINET, WITH VARIEGATED DECORATION.
LATE 18th C.

195. ENCOIGNURE VITRÉE A DEUX CORPS, ORNÉE DE
STRIES GÉOMÉTRIQUES. XIXᵉ S.
GLAZED TWO-TIERED CORNER CABINET, CARVED WITH
GEOMETRIC REEDING. 19th C.

196. BUFFET D'ENCOIGNURE VITRÉ ET CINTRÉ, A DEUX
CORPS. XIXᵉ S.
GLAZED BOW-FRONT CORNER CABINET, IN TWO TIERS.
19th C.

198. PETITE ENCOIGNURE RUSTIQUE, VITRÉE ET CIN
TRÉE. XIXᵉ S.
SMALL GLAZED CORNER CABINET, IN RUSTIC STYL
WITH BOW FRONT. 19th C.

197. ENCOIGNURE VITRÉE RUSTIQUE, A DEUX PORTES.
XIXᵉ S.
GLAZED CORNER CABINET, IN RUSTIC STYLE, WITH
TWO DOORS. 19th C.

199. PETITE ENCOIGNURE CINTRÉE. DÉBUT XIXᵉ S.
SMALL HANGING CORNER CABINET, WITH BOW-
FRONT GLAZED DOORS. EARLY 19th C.

202. ENCOIGNURE VITRÉE ET CINTRÉE, D'INFLUENCE
ANGLAISE. DÉBUT XIXᵉ S.
GLAZED CORNER CABINET WITH BOW FRONT, SHOWING
ENGLISH INFLUENCE. EARLY 19th C.

200. ENCOIGNURE VITRÉE RUSTIQUE. DÉBUT XIXᵉ S.
RUSTIC GLAZED CORNER CABINET. EARLY 19th C.

201. DÉTAIL DE LA DATE GRAVÉE A L'INTÉRIEUR DE
L'ENCOIGNURE Nº 200.
DETAIL OF ENGRAVED DATE INSIDE THE CORNER
CABINET Nₒ. 200.

203. ENCOIGNURE A DEUX CORPS, CINTRÉE ET VITRÉE,
D'ESPRIT REGENCY. DÉBUT XIXᵉ S.
BOW FRONT GLAZED CORNER CABINET IN TWO TIERS,
IN THE REGENCY MANNER. EARLY 19th C.

204. ENCOIGNURE VITRÉE, D'INFLUENCE ANGLAISE.
DÉBUT XIXᵉ S.
GLAZED CORNER CABINET, OF ENGLISH DERIVATION.
EARLY 19th C.

205. ENCOIGNURE VITRÉE, D'INFLUENCE ANGLAISE. DÉ-
BUT XIXᵉ S.
GLAZED CORNER CABINET, SHOWING ENGLISH INFLU-
ENCE. EARLY 19th C.

206. ENCOIGNURE OUVERTE A PILASTRES, D'ESPRIT ADAM.
DÉBUT XIXᵉ S.
OPEN CORNER CABINET WITH PILASTERS, IN THE ADAM
MANNER. EARLY 19th C.

207. GRANDE ENCOIGNURE, D'INSPIRATION ANGLAISE.
FIN XVIIIe S.
LARGE CORNER CABINET, UNDER ENGLISH INFLUENCE.
LATE 18th C.

208. ENCOIGNURE OUVERTE, D'ESPRIT CHIPPENDALE
AMÉRICAIN. FIN XVIIIe S.
OPEN CORNER CABINET, IN THE AMERICAN CHIPPEN-
DALE STYLE. LATE 18th C.

LATE EIGHTEENTH-CENTURY BEDROOM.

BEDS

Beds were given various names in Canada between 1650 and 1760 — *cabanes* (closed beds), *lits à quenouilles*, *lits à colonnes* (four posters), *châlits*, *bois de lit* (bedsteads), *couchettes* (cots), *roulettes* (truckle-beds).

The *cabane* was popular in the seventeenth and eighteenth centuries but disappeared when stoves, providing additional heat, were introduced. It was a type of enclosed bed, rougher than those of Brittany or Auvergne, and was built of spruce, balsam, or pine planks with one or two doors, " a *cabane* of balsam wood... " [1], " a *cabane* for sleeping in... " [2] Mother Marie de l'Incarnation recorded in 1644 that " ... our beds are made of wood, and close like armoires, and although they are lined with blankets or serge, it is difficult to keep warm. " [3]

In other words it was simply a large box or cabinet with one or two doors, made of planks and covered on top. The bed itself, with a plank bottom, was most often built all of a piece with the cabin; sometimes a four-poster bed or a cot was placed in the interior.

It was related in 1661 that Sister de Bresolles "... having gone to bed in one of the plank *cabanes* built in the Canadian fashion, the better to protect herself from the cold, heard three distinct knocks behind her head and some moaning... " [4] It was Sister Pilon, one of her companions who had died several days before and who had returned to give her a mysterious message.

These *cabanes* were designed in the early days of the colony as protection against the cold and the glacial draughts which blew in through every crack of the large common room, the only warmth being provided by one or two fires which however generally died down during the night. The *cabane* also provided more privacy for undressing and sleeping in early colonial common rooms where men and women, soldiers and clergy all lived side by side. The Abbé Charles Glandelet, in his Notes on Sister Marie Barbier of the Assumption, of the Congregation of Notre Dame, wrote that " a young man approached her with very wicked intentions while she was asleep, and tried to force open the doors of the *cabane* in which was her bed. He almost succeeded in doing so, being the stronger of the two, but she addressed herself to that Mother of Love and Purity, who instantly gave her such strength in holding the doors shut, that the other found himself obliged to withdraw." [5] Here is proof that *cabanes* had doors. They also served as wardrobes where clothing and personal belongings were kept.

M. de Maisonneuve, Governor of Montreal, must have felt nostalgia for Canada during a long sojourn in Paris as he had a *cabane* built in his Paris house. The blessed Marguerite Bourgeois, foundress of the Congregation of Notre Dame, wrote, " I went out to look for M. de Maisonneuve who was living on *Fossé St. Victor* near the Paris house of the Fathers of the Christian Doctrine, but I arrived rather late. Only a few days before he had equipped a little room with a *cabane* such as they have in Canada, to accommodate whatever guests may come from Montreal. " [6]

There may possibly have been partly enclosed beds but the only allusion I have found in an inventory reads, " Two tapestry curtains for use in front of a *cabane*. " [7]

Four-posters, bedsteads, and cots were to be found in nearly every house during and immediately after the colonial period. They had curtains which could be drawn for privacy and to keep out the cold. The high posts at each corner might be chamfered, tapering towards

---

(1) A J M, I O A. Inventaire de deffunt Pierre Gadoys, 3 novembre 1667. Greffe Basset.
(2) A J M, I O A. Inventaire par Lordre de Mrs Gausselin des meubles de la ferme. Greffe Coron.
(3) Letter from the Venerable Mother Marie de l'Incarnation to her son, 26 August 1644, letter XXXI.
(4) Morin, Sœur Marie, *Annales de l'Hôtel-Dieu de Montréal*. Montreal, 1921, p. 104.
(5) A S Q. Glandelet, Charles. *Notes sur Marie Barbier* (manuscript), p. 5.
(6) A A M. " *Mémoires de Marguerite Bourgeois* " (manuscript), p. 34.
(7) A J M, I O A. Procès Verbal de l'Estat des maisons et meubles de M. de Chambly à la reqte du Sr Gouyau 18 juillet 1678 (de l'Ile Saint-Louis). Greffe Adhémar.

the top (" pencil-point beds " in New England), or turned in spindles, or take the form of spiralled or twisted columns. On the upper frame was attached the linen canopy, called *ciel de lit*. Many had only two posts at the foot, and a large tapestry-covered panel at the head of the bed for extra warmth. Such a bed is still to be found at the *Hôpital-Général*, Quebec. While visiting this hospital in 1749, Peter Kalm, the Swedish botanist, noted that " the beds are surrounded by blue curtains. " [1]

Another type of bed, which may possibly have been the celebrated " *lit à la duchesse* ", was observed in 1776 in several country homes in the Batiscan region by a German officer in the Hessian troops during the American War of Independence. " There is at least one double bed in each bedroom and the bed-curtains usually hang from a square baldaquin which is attached to the ceiling. The beds are square and without posts. " [2]

Terminology led to some confusion in Canada in the seventeenth and eighteenth centuries. Four-poster beds *(lits à quenouilles)* were also termed *bois de lit*, " ... eight birch boards, three planks and two posts to make a bedstead *(bois de lit)*. All in birch, the ensemble is valued at 27 livres and six sols... " [3] *Châlit* was also confused with the four-poster, " ... a bedstead *(châlit)* with four posts in balsam wood, having enclosing curtains and a tapestry canopy... " [4] The *châlit* in France was a frame of wood on which a mattress was placed, and it had a wooden head-board.

In the records of receipts and expenses of the *Hôpital-Général*, Quebec, an entry for 1702 reads, " The sum of thirty-six livres for three bedsteads *(bois de lict)* at twelve livres apiece ", another for 1714, " a sum of 48 livres paid to Pierre Racine for four bedsteads *(châlits)* for the Sisters... the sum of 18 livres paid to the same person for three cots, one for Sister Colombe, Sister Gaucelin and the other for Sister de Saint Michel ", and for 1715, " The sum of 90 livres paid to Pierre Racine and his children for five bedsteads *(châlits)* for the Sisters, at 18 livres apiece... 90 livres. "

The four-posters of the Augustinian Sisters of the *Hôpital-Général*, Quebec, continued to be used until 1927, when they were replaced by iron cots. Birch cots with turned or plain legs are also mentioned, " A cot of birchwood, unturned... " [5] There is no mention of drapes or curtains in the description of these cots. They were low bedsteads with neither posts nor canopy — open beds in the style of nineteenth-century cots. No early specimens of these cots have been found.

There were also trestle-beds *(baudets)* and truckle-beds *(roulettes)*. The trestles were folding bed-frames covered with coarse linen, " ... a trestle bed of birch wood, with its linen cover, six livres. " [6] Truckle-beds were small, low children's cots, which probably had casters fitted to the feet to enable them to be pushed under larger beds during the day.

Sleigh beds or *carriole* beds (called *lits-bateaux* in Languedoc) were introduced in the nineteenth century. They took their design from the *Late Empire* period. Spindle beds were also to be found in many Canadian houses in the nineteenth-century and were still being made at Murray Bay about 1930 for the houses of summer visitors.

All these beds had bolsters, palliasses, and mattresses which were filled with straw, chicken or duck feathers, goose down, milkweed, or the feathers of carrier pigeons. The last seem to have been exceptional and only the more well-to-do bourgeois could afford them.

(1) Kalm, Peter. *Voyage en Amérique.* (Août 1749). Montréal, 1880, vol. 2, p. 114.
(2) Stone, W.L. *Letters of Brunswick and Hessian Officers during the American Revolution.* Albany, 1891, p. 13.
(3) A J M, I O A. Inventaire des meubles et esfectz de pierre busson subtil 25e avril 1689. Greffe Adhémar.
(4) A J M, I O A. Inventaire de Jacques Lemoine et agathe St Pere, 24 juillet 1685. Greffe Bourgine.
(5) A J M, I O A. Inuantaire de Jacques Cusson et Michelle Cholecq sa femme auparavant Veuve de feu françois Viger le 20 décembre 1729. Greffe Chaumont.
(6) A J M, I O A. Minutte de l'Inventaire et partage des biens meubles Et Succession de defunt Luc Dufresne. Du 27 Aoust 1760. Greffe Bouron.

In the nineteenth century when the bride brought a bed as part of her dowry, it could not be counted in the division of belongings, but had to remain in the house.

The bed has always played an important role in Canadian customs and continues to do so. It represents all stages of family life, being intimately linked with marriage and with the subsequent births (children of a first marriage are distinguished from those of a second by being called children from the first or second bed, *du premier lit, du deuxième lit, etc.*, as in France). The dying lie there for the last time, surrounded by the family, while the priest performs the last rites. It is there also that the body is laid out, according to custom.

209. BED, WITH SPIRALLY TURNED POSTS, IN LOUIS XIII MANNER. LATE 17th C.

Bed, having a large panel at the head and twisted or spirally turned posts of Renaissance derivation (much in favour under Louis XIII). This is the oldest bed known to me, and comes from the *Hôpital-Général*, Quebec, where it was probably a guest-bed. It may have been that of the Marquis de Frontenac, who often retired there. An attractive bed.

w. 6' 1"   H. 6' 1⅝"   D. 3' 5"
185 cm   187 cm   104 cm

WOOD : birch   PROVENANCE : Quebec

(Coll. Musée de l'Hôtel-Dieu, Quebec).

210. BED, WITH TURNED POSTS. LATE 18th OR EARLY 19th C.

Bed, having turned posts with small urns at their tips. This kind of bed was widespread. The headboard and the turning of the posts definitely show American influence.

w. 6' 11"   H. 7' 1¼"   D. 3' 7"
211 cm   217 cm   110 cm

WOOD : birch   PROVENANCE : Saint-Ours, P.Q.

(Coll. Mr Roch Rolland, Manoir de la Sapinière, Seigneurie de Saint-Ours, P.Q.).

211. BED, WITH TURNED POSTS. EARLY 19th C.

Bed with massive turned posts, typical of a great many Canadian poster beds. Note the canopy frame.

w. 6' 2"   H. 6' 8¼"   D. 4' 2"
188 cm   204 cm   127 cm

WOOD : birch   RAILS : ash

(Coll. Château de Ramezay, Montreal).

212. BEDSTEAD, WITH TURNED POSTS. EARLY 19th C.

Small bedstead, with turned half-posts, having a headboard surmounted by a roller and, at the foot, a chamfered and turned cross-piece. The heaviness of the uprights is inexplicable; perhaps it was intended to give greater solidity.

w. 6' 2¾"   H. 4' 8"   D. 2' 2½"
190 cm   142 cm   128 cm

WOOD : birch

PROVENANCE : L'Ange Gardien, P.Q.

(Coll. Mrs Colette P. Loranger, Montreal).

213. BEDSTEAD, WITH TURNED POSTS. EARLY 19th C.

Bedstead, with turned posts surmounted by urns. The head is topped by a turned rail and a chamfered roller and the front posts are joined by a turned rail. A scaled-down version of the poster bed.

w. 6' 1¾"   H. 3' 10¼"   D. 3' 7½"
187 cm   117 cm   110 cm

WOOD : birch

PROVENANCE : Sainte-Pétronille, Isle of Orleans, P.Q.

(Coll. Mrs Colette P. Loranger, Montreal).

214. BEDSTEAD WITH TURNED POSTS. EARLY 19th C.

Bedstead, with turned half-posts and having rollers at the head and foot. Note the pearls on the façade.

w. 6' 6"   H. 3' 8"   D. 4'
198 cm   112 cm   122 cm

WOOD : birch and ash   SIDES : pine

PROVENANCE : Sainte-Anne de la Pérade, P.Q.

(Coll. Mr and Mrs Georges-Étienne Gagné, Neuville, P.Q.).

215. " SLEIGH BED ", DERIVED FROM LATE EMPIRE STYLE. 19th C.

Sleigh bed (*carriole* as it is known in Canada). In France and particularly in Languedoc it bore the name of boat-bed *(lit bateau)*. This example is decorated with shaped frames and naive appliqué carvings. This kind of bed was widely found in all parts of Quebec during the first part of the nineteenth century, and dated from the reign of Napoleon, after the Italian campaigns. It was a return to ancient Roman forms.

w. 6' 5½"   H. 3' 6"   D. 3' 8"
197 cm   107 cm   112 cm

WOOD : pine and birch

PROVENANCE : Montreal district

(Coll. Mr and Mrs F.M. Hutchins, Pembroke, Ont.).

216. SPINDLE OR SPOOL BED. MID 19th C.

Bed, with turned spindles, decorated with acorns and turned rollers of an American type, and widely distributed during the nineteenth century.

W. 6' 3''   H. 3' 6¼''   D. 4' 4¼''
190 cm   108 cm   133 cm

WOOD : birch   PROVENANCE : Saint-Ours, P.Q.

(Coll. Mr and Mrs Armand Poupart, Seigneurie de Saint-Ours, P.Q.).

217. SPINDLE OR SPOOL BED, FROM CAP ROUGE. MID 19th C.

Bed, with vertical spindles at the head. Turned stiles and rails.

W. 6' 3''   H. 2' 8''   D. 4' 3''
190 cm   81 cm   130 cm

WOOD : maple and birch

PROVENANCE : Cap Rouge, P.Q.

(Coll. Mr and Mrs Georges-Étienne Gagné, Neuville, P.Q.).

218. BED FROM ST ANNE DE LA POCATIÈRE. LATE 19th C.

Bed, from St Anne de la Pocatière, with uprights and cross-pieces turned in spool form. The head is topped by a pediment, recalling that on seventeenth-century American bedsteads. It is the precursor of many beds made during the first part of the twentieth century.

W. 6' 8''   H. 3' 4¾''   D. 4' 7⅜''
203 cm   104 cm   141 cm

WOOD : UPRIGHTS : walnut

HEADBOARD AND FEET : BUTTERNUT

PROVENANCE : St Anne de la Pocatière, P.Q.

(Coll. Mr and Mrs Georges-Étienne Gagné, Neuville, P.Q.).

209. LIT A COLONNES TORSES, D'ESPRIT LOUIS XIII. FIN XVIIᵉ S.   BED WITH SPIRALLY TURNED POSTS, IN LOUIS XIII MANNER.   LATE 17th C.

210. LIT A COLONNES TOURNÉES.
FIN XVIIIᵉ-DÉBUT XIXᵉ S.
BED, WITH TURNED POSTS. LATE
18th OR EARLY 19th C.

211. LIT A COLONNES TOURNÉES.
DÉBUT XIXᵉ S.
BED, WITH TURNED POSTS. EARLY
19th C.

212. COUCHETTE A QUENOUILLES
TOURNÉES. DÉBUT XIXᵉ S.
BEDSTEAD, WITH TURNED POSTS.
EARLY 19th C.

213. COUCHETTE A QUENOUILLES
TOURNÉES. DÉBUT XIXᵉ S.
BEDSTEAD, WITH TURNED POSTS.
EARLY 19th C.

214. COUCHETTE A QUENOUILLES TOURNÉES. DÉBUT
XIXᵉ S.
BEDSTEAD WITH TURNED POSTS. EARLY 19th C.

215. LIT « CARRIOLE », D'INSPIRATION FIN EMPIRE.
XIXᵉ S.
" SLEIGH BED ", DERIVED FROM LATE EMPIRE STYLE.
19th C.

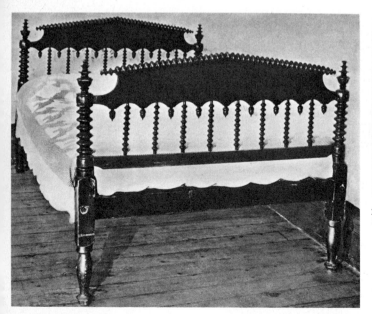

218. LIT DE SAINTE-ANNE DE LA POCATIÈRE. FIN XI
BED FROM ST ANNE DE LA POCATIÈRE.   LATE 19th

216. LIT A FUSEAUX. MILIEU XIXᵉ S.
SPINDLE OR SPOOL BED.   MID 19th C.

CRADLES

The cradle *(berceau* or *ber* in Canada) was found in all houses from the beginning of the colony, " a cradle of pine, with birch posts."[1] Most of them have four turned posts and heavy curved rockers, which were given regional names — *berces* or *chanteaux*. The latter term was used particularly in the lower St Lawrence region, the rockers resembling the halfmoon boards *(chanteaux)* used in making barrel tops.

The cradle was rocked by pushing one of the posts with the hand, or a rocker with the foot. Cradles with vertical spindles which form open-work sides are found in the Quebec region and in the western provinces of France. There were also a few cradles on legs, or suspended between two uprights at the same height as the early four-poster bed. The mother without leaving her bed could rock the cradle by means of an attached cord if the child cried during the night. The hooded cradle which had a curved shelter *(têtière)* above the headboard was probably influenced by those of the United States, as it so closely resembled the Mennonite cradles of Pennsylvania and New Jersey. Some cradles were ornamented with geometric designs or had panelling on the sides, and a few were decorated with paintings.

Canadian cradles were usually rather bulky but pleasant in their general appearance. Small holes were made in the sides through which a cord could be passed to secure the child. Cradles are now disappearing from use because pediatricians condemn them on the grounds that rocking a child encourages its whims, but they remain very popular with American collectors and are to be found all over the United States, sometimes being used as fireside woodboxes, magazine racks, or even turned upside-down and used as coffee tables.

---

219. DOLL'S CRADLE. 18th C.

Doll's cradle, with four turned posts on curved rockers, carved with geometric designs and incised with a flower basket.

w. 1' 6½"	H. 1' 3"	D. 9"
47 cm	38 cm	23 cm

WOOD : pine   PROVENANCE : Châteauguay, P.Q.

(Coll. Mrs Nettie Sharpe, Saint-Lambert, P.Q.).

220. HANGING OR SUSPENDED CRADLE. 18th C.

Cradle on feet or suspended between two uprights with two dowelled stretchers. This type is rare in Canada, but was found in France during the seventeenth and eighteenth centuries. Placed at the height of the poster bed, the mother could rock her child by means of a cord. Other cords were used to fasten the child firmly inside the cradle. A date : " 1820 ", is carved underneath this one.

w. 2' 1½"	H. 3' 11'	D. 1' 5½"
65 cm	119 cm	44 cm

WOOD : pine and birch

PROVENANCE : Saint-François, Isle of Orleans, P.Q.

(Coll. National Museum of Canada, Ottawa).

221. CRADLE, CARVED WITH LOZENGES. EARLY 19th C.

Cradle, carved with lozenges and sun rays. It has four posts turned in the Queen Anne manner.

w. 3' 6¼"	H. 2' 3"	D. 1' 7"
107 cm	69 cm	49 cm

WOOD : pine and birch PROVENANCE : L'Islet, P.Q.

(Coll. Mrs Richard R. Costello, Sainte-Agathe des Monts, P.Q.).

222. CRADLE FROM CAUGHNAWAGA. 18th C.

Cradle, with turned posts, on curved rockers and decorated with painted flowers in the Indian papooseboard manner. This kind of cradle is typical of the period. Very probably made by a French Canadian woodworker and then painted by an Indian.

w. 2' 10½"	H. 2' 2"	D. 1' 5"
88 cm	66 cm	43 cm

WOOD : pine and birch

PROVENANCE : Caughnawaga, P.Q.

(Coll. Château de Ramezay, Montreal).

---

(1) A J M, I O A. Inventaire Entre Marguerite Robidou veufve de feu Jean Baptiste Varin, le 2ᵉ may 1733. Montréal. Greffe Chaumont.

223. CRADLE, WITH SMALL POSTS. EARLY 19th C.

Cradle, with four small posts, six panels, a headboard and shaped rockers.

W. 3' 3"	H. 2' 4"	D. 1' 9"
99 cm	71 cm	53 cm

WOOD : pine and birch

PROVENANCE : Sault-à-la-Puce, P.Q.

(Coll. of the author, Petite Rivière Saint-François, P.Q.).

224. PANELLED CRADLE, WITH POSTS. 18th C.

Cradle with turned posts, on curved rockers and with six plain panels. A very common model in the Lower St Lawrence district.

W. 3' ½"	H. 2' 7½"	D. 1' 7¾"
93 cm	80 cm	50 cm

WOOD : birch and pine

PROVENANCE : Tour l'Oignon, Baie Saint-Paul, P.Q.

(Coll. of the author, Petite Rivière Saint-François, P.Q.).

225. HOODED CRADLE. EARLY 19th C.

Cradle, with arched and shaped hood of Mennonite derivation, having shaped rockers with spirals. The centre stretcher is turned. The two handles are made of wrought iron and the whole is painted white.

WOOD : pine

PROVENANCE : Saint-Barthélémy, P.Q.

(Coll. Museum of Fine Arts, Montreal).

226. CRADLE, WITH CORNER POSTS. LATE 18th C.

Cradle, with four corner posts, a shaped headboard and horizontal mouldings.

W. 3' 1"	H. 1' 6¾"	D. 1' 5"
94 cm	48 cm	43 cm

WOOD : pine and birch PROVENANCE : Belœil, P.Q.

(Coll. Canada Steamship Lines, Tadoussac, P.Q.).

227. HOODED CRADLE. LATE 18th C.

Hooded cradle on rockers, having a hood decorated with a shaped edge.

W. 3' 1½"	H. 2' 3"	D. 1' 4½"
95 cm	69 cm	42 cm

WOOD : pine PROVENANCE : Lacolle, P.Q.

(Coll. Canada Steamship Lines, Tadoussac, P.Q.).

228. HOODED CRADLE, WITH POSTS. EARLY 19th C.

Hooded cradle, with an arched hood and four small posts. The hood is derived from those of the Pennsylvanian Mennonites. A transitional piece with its small posts and hood.

W. 3' 1"	H. 2' 10¾"	D. 1' 7"
94 cm	88 cm	48 cm

WOOD : pine PROVENANCE : Longueuil, P.Q.

(Coll. Mr Jean Dubuc, Quebec).

229. HOODED CRADLE, IN THE INDIAN MANNER. EARLY 19th C.

Cradle, with two posts and arched hood, recalling the curves on Indian *cabanes*.

W. 2' 5"	H. 2' ⅜"	D. 1' 6"
74 cm	62 cm	46 cm

WOOD : pine, birch and ash

PROVENANCE : Sorel, P.Q.

(Coll. Mr and Mrs Georges-Étienne Gagné, Neuville, P.Q.).

230. CRADLE, WITH FOUR FLUTED POSTS. 19th C.

Cradle, with four turned and fluted posts, of Regency derivation. It also has panels and arms, but the latter seem to be a later addition.

W. 2' 10"	H. 2' 6½"	D. 1' 5¾"
86 cm	77 cm	45 cm

WOOD : butternut

PROVENANCE : Saint-Eustache, P.Q.

(Coll. Detroit Institute of Arts, Detroit, Mich. U.S.A.).

231. CRADLE, WITH CORNER POSTS. 18th C.

Cradle, with four posts and shaped headboard.

W. 3' 6"	H. 2' 8"	D. 1' 1"
107 cm	81 cm	33 cm

WOOD : pine and birch

PROVENANCE : Maskinongé, P.Q.

(Coll. Dr and Mrs Herbert Schwarz, Montreal).

232. CRADLE, WITH VERTICAL TURNED SPINDLES, SHOWING POITOU INFLUENCE. EARLY 19th C.

Cradle, with four turned posts and vertical spindles, on shaped curved rockers. The roller at the headboard, in the Late Empire manner, dates it as nineteenth century. This kind of cradle, but without the roller, was widely distributed in Poitou in the eighteenth century.

W. 3 4'½"	H. 2' 7"	D. 1' 8"
103 cm	79 cm	51 cm

WOOD : pine and birch

PROVENANCE : Baie Saint-Paul, P.Q.

(Coll. Mrs Colette P. Loranger, Montreal).

233. LATE EMPIRE-STYLE CRADLE. 19th C.

Late Empire-style cradle. The curves are evocative of the Canadian sleigh bed or *carriole* bed of the same period. The small hole, bored in the roller at the head, was used as a parasol-holder.

WOOD : butternut

(Coll. Mr and Mrs Pierre Gouin, Saint-Sulpice, P.Q.).

234. CRADLE, WITH SPINDLES. EARLY 19th C.

Cradle, with vertical spindles turned in spool form. There are four posts and turned rollers.

w. 2' 11⅜" H. 2' 5" D. 1' 8¼"
86 cm 74 cm 51 cm

WOOD : ash, birch and pine

PROVENANCE : Yamachiche, P.Q.

(Coll. S. Breitman Antiques, Montreal).

235. HANGING CRADLE. EARLY 19th C.

Hanging cradle, with four posts, two turned uprights and flat vertical bars pierced with circles.

w. 3' H. 2' 3⅜" D. 1' 4¾"
91 cm 69 cm 43 cm

WOOD : pine and birch

(Coll. Mr and Mrs Victor Drury, Lake Anne, P.Q.).

219. PETIT BERCEAU DE POUPÉE. XVIIIe S.
DOLL'S CRADLE. 18th C.

220. BERCEAU SUSPENDU. XVIIIe S.
HANGING OR SUSPENDED CRADLE. 18th C.

221. BERCEAU A LOSANGES. DÉ-
BUT XIXᵉ S.
CRADLE, CARVED WITH LOZENGES.
EARLY 19th C.

222. BERCEAU DE CAUGHNAWAGA.
XVIIIᵉ S.
CRADLE FROM CAUGHNAWAGA.
18th C.

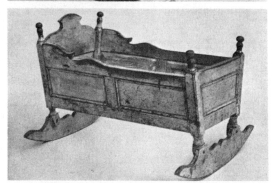

223. BERCEAU ORNÉ DE PETITES
QUENOUILLES. DÉBUT XIXᵉ S.
CRADLE, WITH SMALL POSTS.
EARLY 19th C.

224. BERCEAU A QUENOUILLES
ORNÉ DE PANNEAUX. XVIIIᵉ S.
PANELLED CRADLE, WITH POSTS.
18th C.

225. BERCEAU A TÊTIÈRE. DÉBUT XIXe S.
HOODED CRADLE. EARLY 19th C.

226. BERCEAU A QUENOUILLES. FIN XVIIIe S.
CRADLE, WITH CORNER POSTS. LATE 18th C.

227. BERCEAU A TÊTIÈRE. FIN XVIIIe S.
HOODED CRADLE. LATE 18th C.

228. BERCEAU A TÊTIÈRE ET A QUENOUILLES. DÉBUT
XIXe S.
HOODED CRADLE, WITH POSTS. EARLY 19th C.

229. BERCEAU A TÊTIÈRE, A L'INDIENNE. DÉBUT XIXe S.
HOODED CRADLE, IN THE INDIAN MANNER. EARLY 19th C.

230. BERCEAU A QUATRE QUENOUILLES CANNELÉES. XIXe S.
CRADLE, WITH FOUR FLUTED POSTS. 19th C.

231. BERCEAU A QUENOUILLES. XVIIIᵉ S.
CRADLE, WITH CORNER POSTS.   18th C.

232. BERCEAU A FUSEAUX VERTICAUX TOURNÉS, D'INFLUENCE POITEVINE. DÉBUT XIXᵉ S.
CRADLE, WITH VERTICAL TURNED SPINDLES, SHOWING POITOU INFLUENCE.   EARLY 19th C.

233. BERCEAU DE STYLE FIN EMPIRE XIXᵉ S.
LATE EMPIRE-STYLE CRADLE.   19th C.

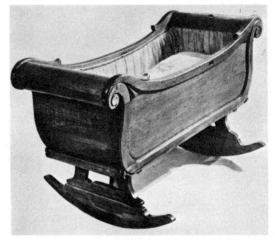

234. BERCEAU A FUSEAUX. DÉBUT XIXᵉ S.
CRADLE, WITH SPINDLES.   EARLY 19th C.

235. BERCEAU SUSPENDU. DÉBUT XIXᵉ S.
HANGING CRADLE.   EARLY 19th C.

SEATS

STOOLS, HIGH STOOLS, BENCHES, SETTLE-BEDS

Low and high stools and benches were in use in the colony from the beginning of the seventeenth century and were first mentioned in inventories of 1663. They were to be found in every household in French Canada, whether rich or poor. These simple seats had no backs and were easy to move about.

There were two types of stools *(tabourets)*. The smaller ones were used as footstools for resting and warming the feet near the fireplace. The others, somewhat higher, were used for sitting on. Most of them had turned legs in the Louis XIII manner or legs in the Louis XIV *os de mouton* style. The rest had plain legs.

The high stool *(escabeau)* was higher and often had a shaped hole in the top which was used as a hand-grip when moving it about. This stool served not only as a seat, but was also used by the housewife when reaching for articles on high shelves. Some were equipped with steps, but these were mostly used in churches.

Benches were placed on either side of the table in the common room, or against the walls for evening parties *(veillées)*.

Benches with backs made their appearance in country houses in the eighteenth century. The backs had a grill-work of shaped vertical splats or turned vertical spindles.

The coffer-bench *(banc-coffre)* (as in France, particularly Brittany), was placed beside the closed bed or the four-poster, and served both as a chest for storing linen and as a step for climbing into bed.

The bench-bed *(banc-lit)* was referred to by Havard in his dictionary [1] as having existed in the sixteenth century, but no specimen has been found in France. It appeared in Canada at the beginning of the nineteenth century, probably imported from Ireland where it was called a settle-bed. It was also known in Sweden and Finland and closely resembled the Bresse *arche-banc*, and the Breton coffer-bench from which it was derived. In Canada it was called a beggar's-bed.[2] It was used as both a seat and a storage chest during the day and as a bed at night.

These settle-beds were hinged to open into a bed-frame of about three feet in width and sometimes more than six feet in length. It was not unusual in the homes of large *habitant* families to put as many as four children in this bed and they would sleep " feet to feet " on a layer of straw or a palliasse. When not used for the children, it would be kept for wandering beggars (hence, its Canadian name : *banc du quêteux*) who would be offered hospitality for a night. It was quite popular in rural houses because it accommodated the large families of the time in the limited space available.

The settle-bed was unknown in France, and was very rare in the United States; however, there is a specimen in George Washington's home at Mount Vernon, Virginia, which is said to have served as a seat during the day, and as a soldier's cot at night. A few settle-beds were made in *Late Empire* style and others were influenced by English and American styles.

236. SMALL CHURCH STOOL. 18th C.

Small church stool, resembling the small stools found in Flemish paintings of the 17th and 18th centuries. There is a handhold pierced in the top, and the base has an openwork design. A stool in the old Flemish tradition, which was widely known in France and also in Canada. It was used equally as a seat and as a stepping-stool.

(1) Havard, Henry. *Dictionnaire de l'ameublement et de la décoration.* Paris, 1887.
(2) *Banc du quêteux.* It was also called *bède*, possibly from the English or perhaps from an old French word. Also *rabat* from the French verb *rabattre*, to fold.

201

w. 1' 2''   H. 1' 5¼''
   36 cm   44 cm

WOOD : pine

PROVENANCE : Church of l'Acadie, P.Q.

(Coll. Mrs Richard R. Costello, Sainte-Agathe des Monts, P.Q.).

237. HIGH STOOL, FROM THE OLD SEMINARY OF ST SULPICE, MONTREAL. 17th C.

High stool, having turned legs in the Louis XIII manner and stretchers with mouldings in quadrilateral form. This kind of seat was also used as a stepping-stool and was frequently found in churches, monasteries and homes in the seventeenth and eighteenth centuries.

w. 1' ⅝''   H. 1' 10⅝''
   32 cm   57 cm
   9¾''
   25 cm

WOOD : birch

PROVENANCE : old Seminary of St Sulpice, Notre-Dame, Montreal.

(Coll. Mr and Mrs J.N. Cole, Montreal).

238. CHURCH HIGH STOOL, IN THE LOUIS XIII MANNER. LATE 17th C.

High stool, with two steps, and a turned understructure in the Louis XIII manner. This is primarily a piece of church furniture, and was used as a portable step, either in the sacristy or the chancel. Only rarely found in private homes.

w. 1' 9¾''   H. 1' 9''   D. 1' 7½''
   55 cm   53 cm   50 cm

WOOD : birch   PROVENANCE : Quebec

(Coll. Hôtel-Dieu, Quebec).

239. STOOL, WITH CHAMFERED LEGS AND SHAPED SEAT RAIL. 18th C.

Stool, with chamfered legs, a shaped seat rail and four shaped stretchers in quadrilateral form. The top or upholstery is missing. A common eighteenth-century piece.

WOOD : pine

(Coll. Canada Steamship Lines, Tadoussac, P.Q.).

240. SMALL RUSTIC STOOL. 19th C.

Small rustic stool, with two turned stretchers. Original colouring of red ochre.

w. 1' 1''   H. 1' 2½''
   33 cm   37 cm

WOOD : pine

(Coll. Canada Steamship Lines, Tadoussac, P.Q.).

241. STOOL-BENCH, WITH CHAMFERED LEGS. 18th C.

Stool-bench, with chamfered legs, and stretchers and apron with mouldings. It was a toddler's walking aid, but is now used as a coffee table.

w. 2' 8''   H. 1' 3''   D. 1' 8'' - 1' 1½''
   81 cm   38 cm   51 cm - 34 cm

WOOD : pine

PROVENANCE : L'Abord à Plouffe, P.Q.

(Coll. Canada Steamship Lines, Tadoussac, P.Q.).

242. SMALL STOOL, WITH SEAT RAIL CARVED WITH SPIRALS. 18th C.

Small stool, with chamfered legs and seat rail carved with spirals on all four sides. The top is a later addition.

w. 1' 6''   H. 1' 9''   D. 1' 5''
   46 cm   53 cm   43 cm

WOOD : pine   PROVENANCE : Varennes, P.Q.

(Coll. Mr and Mrs A.M. Laurie, Longueuil, P.Q.).

243. SMALL STOOL, WITH '' PIEDS DE BICHE ''. EARLY 19th C.

Small stool, with *pieds de biche* and a serpentine-shaped seat rail. Prominently curved feet of English derivation. The upholstery is missing.

w. 1' 2''   H. 1' 7''
   35 cm   48 cm

WOOD : ash

PROVENANCE : Presbytery of St Augustin, Portneuf, P.Q.

(Coll. Miss Barbara Richardson, Sainte-Agathe des Monts, P.Q.).

244. STOOL OF WAVY MAPLE, WITH CURVED LEGS, IN THE LOUIS XV MANNER. 18th C.

Stool, with a shaped apron and curved legs terminating in double-scrolled *pieds de biche*. A small and charming classical piece.

w. 1' 10¼''   H. 1' 4''   D. 1' 6''
   56 cm   41 cm   46 cm

WOOD : tiger maple

(Coll. Mr and Mrs Maurice Corbeil, Boucherville, P.Q.).

245. STOOL-BENCH, WITH CURVED LEGS. 18th C.

Stool-bench, with curved legs and shaped apron. Transformed into a coffee table. This kind of stool is rare.

w. 3' 6''   H. 1' 2½''   D. 1' 4''
   107 cm   37 cm   41 cm

WOOD : birch

(Coll. Mrs Ross Sims, Saint-Sauveur des Monts, P.Q.).

246. WORK-BENCH, WITH DRAWER, FROM THE HOTEL-DIEU, QUEBEC. 18th C.

Small work-bench, with shaped feet in simplified lyre form. It has a drawer and a dowelled stretcher.

This little bench also served as a work-table, and was much in use in convents.

w. 2' 1½"   H. 1' 4⅝"   D. 1' 2¼"
65 cm   42 cm   36 cm

WOOD : pine   PROVENANCE : Quebec

(Coll. Musée de l'Hôtel-Dieu, Quebec).

247. SMALL CHEST-BENCH, RESTING ON A SHAPED BASE. 19th C.

Small chest-bench, *banc-coffre*, resting on a shaped base, and used both as a seat and as a box in which to keep shoe polish.

w. 1' 5"   H. 1' 2⅝"   D. 9"
43 cm   37 cm   23 cm

WOOD : pine   PROVENANCE : Quebec

(Coll. Musée de l' Hôpital-Général, Quebec).

248. BENCH, WITH RUSTIC LYRE-SHAPED FEET. 18th C.

Bench, with rustic lyre-shaped feet and a dowelled stretcher, reminiscent of Lorraine and Flemish benches.

w. 4' 3⅜"   H. 1' 7¾"   D. 10¼"
131 cm   50 cm   26 cm

WOOD : pine   PROVENANCE : Quebec

(Coll. Musée de l' Hôpital-Général, Quebec).

249. SHOEMAKER'S BENCH. 19th C.

Shoemaker's bench, made by an unskilled hand, but in a typical form.

w. 3' 9"   H. 1' 1¼"   D. 1' 8"
114 cm   34 cm   51 cm

WOOD : pine

(Coll. Canada Steamship Lines, Tadoussac, P.Q.).

250. SLANT-TOP PRAYER-STOOL (PRIE-DIEU). LATE 17th C.

Slant-top praying-stool, *prie-dieu*, with two doors and a drawer. This type of *prie-dieu* was placed in every cell of the Augustinian nuns of the *Hôpital-Général*, Quebec. Genuine ironwork.

w. 2' 3¾"   H. 2' 9¼"   D. 2' 3½"
70 cm   84 cm   70 cm

WOOD : butternut

PROVENANCE : Hôpital-Général, Quebec.

(Coll. Provincial Museum, Quebec).

251. CHURCH PEW, WITH BALUSTER BACK. LATE 18th C.

Church pew, having turned balusters in the back, shaped armrests and a chamfered understructure.

w. 6' 6"   H. 2' 9⅝"   D. 1' 1¾"
198 cm   85 cm   35 cm

WOOD : birch and pine

PROVENANCE : Church of Deschambault, P.Q.

(Coll. Miss Barbara Richardson, Sainte-Agathe des Monts, P.Q.).

252. CHURCH PEW, WITH OPENWORK LYRE-BACK. LATE 18th C.

Small church pew, with a shaped top rail in the back and three lyres in openwork. The posts and understructure are turned in the Louis XIII manner.

w. 3' 5"   H. 2' 10"   D. 1' 4"
104 cm   86 cm   41 cm

WOOD : birch and pine

PROVENANCE : Church of Sault-au-Récollet, P.Q.

(Coll. Provincial Museum, Quebec).

253. SMALL THREE-PANELLED RUSTIC BENCH. LATE 18th C.

Small rustic bench, with three panels in the back and chamfered feet.

w. 3' 10"   H. 1' 3¼"   D. 1' 2½"
117 cm   39 cm   37 cm

WOOD : pine

(Coll. Senator and Mrs H. de M. Molson, Lac Violon, Sainte-Agathe des Monts, P.Q.).

254. SMALL RUSTIC BENCH, WITH BALUSTER-SHAPED SPLATS. EARLY 19th C.

Rustic bench, with baluster-shaped splats in the back and a shaped seat rail. Armrests derived from Queen Anne and Windsor chairs. Although rustic this piece has fine proportions.

w. 5' 2½"   H. 2' 11¼"   D. 1' 3½"
159 cm   90 cm   39 cm

WOOD : pine

PROVENANCE : From a church of the Quebec district

(Coll. Miss Barbara Richardson, Sainte-Agathe des Monts, P.Q.).

255. RUSTIC BENCH, WITH CONSOLE FEET, IN THE LATE EMPIRE MANNER. MID 19th C.

Rustic bench, with console or bracket feet and armrests in the *Late Empire* manner, with flat and shaped balusters in the back. The stretchers are derived from the arrow-back designs of American chairs. The back posts are curved in the *Directoire* manner. Festooned seat rail.

WOOD : birch

(Coll. Detroit Institute of Arts, Detroit, Mich, U.S.A.).

256. CHURCH PEW, WITH PANELLED BACK. 19th C.

Church pew, having lateral uprights shaped in the *Late Empire* style, with *appliqué* mouldings on the four panels.

w. 6' 3½"   H. 3' 1"   D. 1' 2"
192 cm   94 cm   36 cm

WOOD : butternut

PROVENANCE : Protestant Church of St Canute, P.Q.

(Coll. Mr and Mrs Gerald Wilkinson, Sainte-Agathe des Monts, P.Q.).

257. SMALL RUSTIC PEW, FROM THE CHURCH OF CAUGHNAWAGA. 19th C.

Small rustic pew, from the Church of Caughnawaga, with a back of cut-out vertical bars.

W. 3' ⅝"	H. 2' 9¼"	D. 1' 2¼"
93 cm	84 cm	36 cm

WOOD : pine

PROVENANCE : Church of Caughnawaga, P.Q.

(Coll. Miss Barbara Richardson, Sainte-Agathe des Monts, P.Q.).

258. SETTLE-BED, IN THE LATE EMPIRE MANNER. 19th C.

Settle-bed, in the *Late Empire* manner, with wings and a shaped, openwork back. (Cf. p. 201.)

W. 6' 2⅝"	H. 3' 4"	D. 1' 8¼"
190 cm	102 cm	51 cm

WOOD : pine   PROVENANCE : Lanoraie, P.Q.

(Coll. Canada Steamship Lines, Tadoussac, P.Q.).

259. SETTLE-BED, WITH SHAPED OPENWORK BACK. 19th C.

Settle-bed, having a shaped, openwork baluster back and a festooned top rail pierced with a circle. The lateral uprights are of *Late Empire* derivation. The mouldings of the panels and the frame of the façade are all in *appliqué* work. A curious and picturesque piece.

W. 6' 1"	H. 3' 1¾"	D. 1' 9"
185 cm	96 cm	53 cm

WOOD : butternut

(Coll. Mr L.V. Randall, Montreal).

260. SETTLE-BED, WITH TURNED SPINDLES. 19th C.

Settle-bed, decorated with turned spindles in the back and a top rail carved with spirals. The *appliqué* columns on the façade are reminiscent of seventeenth-century Dutch furniture. The piece also shows American influence.

W. 5' 10"	H. 3' 2½"	D. 1' 7½"
178 cm	98 cm	50 cm

WOOD : pine   PROVENANCE : Montreal district

(Coll. Provincial Museum, Quebec).

261. COFFER-BENCH, WITH TURNED BALUSTERS. 19th C.

Coffer-bench, with turned balusters in the back and a top rail decorated with wave motifs or Grecian scrolls. There are three front panels with *appliqué* mouldings. The coffer-bench was found in all parts of France, being used to store clothes and also as a step for climbing into the high closed-bed or poster bed. This one recalls the Bresse *archebanc*.

W. 6' 2"	H. 3' 2"	D. 1' 8"
188 cm	97 cm	51 cm

WOOD : pine   PROVENANCE : Montreal district

(Coll. Mrs Richard R. Costello, Sainte-Agathe des Monts, P.Q.).

262. SETTLE-BED, DECORATED WITH AN APPLIQUÉ LOZENGE. 19th C.

Settle-bed, having an *appliqué* lozenge on the façade, and shaped and flat balusters in the back.

WOOD : pine   PROVENANCE : Montreal district

(Coll. Sir Robert and Lady Watson-Watt, Toronto, Ont).

263. RUSTIC SETTLE-BED, WITH INCISED GOUGE WORK. 19th C.

Rustic settle-bed, with a shaped splat carved with incisions by a burin. The shaped wings and the armrests are in *Late Empire* manner.

W. 5' 3⅝"	H. 2' 9¼"	D. 1' 4"
162 cm	84 cm	41 cm

WOOD : pine   PROVENANCE : Montreal district

(Coll. Mr and Mrs Fred Mulligan, Pleasant Valley, Henrysburg, P.Q.).

264. SETTLE-BED, IN THE LATE EMPIRE MANNER. 19th C.

Settle-bed, with multiple panels in the façade and back. The back is prolonged by curves and countercurves and recalls the shape of the Canadian *Late Empire* sleigh bed. This excrescence makes the piece too heavy.

W. 5' 11¼"	H. 3'	D. 1' 4"
181 cm	91 cm	41 cm

WOOD : pine   PROVENANCE : Quebec district

(Coll. Dr and Mrs Wilfrid Caron, Cap Rouge, P.Q.).

236. PETIT TABOURET D'ÉGLISE. XVIIIᵉ S.
SMALL CHURCH STOOL. 18th C.

237. ESCABEAU, DU VIEUX SÉMINAIRE DE SAINT-SULPICE
DE MONTRÉAL. XVIIᵉ S.
HIGH STOOL, FROM THE OLD SEMINARY OF ST SULPICE,
MONTREAL. 17th C.

238. ESCABEAU D'ÉGLISE, D'ESPRIT LOUIS XIII. FIN
XVIIᵉ S.
CHURCH HIGH STOOL, IN THE LOUIS XIII MANNER. LATE
17th C.

239. TABOURET A PIÈTEMENT CHANFREINÉ ET A CEINTURE CHAN-
TOURNÉE. XVIIIe S.
STOOL, WITH CHAMFERED LEGS AND SHAPED SEAT RAIL.   18th C.

240. PETIT TABOURET RUSTIQUE. XIXe S.
SMALL RUSTIC STOOL.   19th C.

241. TABOURET-BANC A' PIÈTEMENT CHANFREINÉ. XVIIIe S.
STOOL-BENCH, WITH CHAMFERED LEGS.   18th C.

242. PETIT TABOURET A CEINTURE ORNÉE DE SPIRALES
XVIIIe S.
SMALL STOOL, WITH SEAT RAIL CARVED WITH SPIRALS.
18th C.

243. PETIT TABOURET GALBÉ A PIEDS DE BICHE.
DÉBUT XIXᵉ S.
SMALL STOOL, WITH " PIEDS DE BICHE ".
EARLY 19th C.

244. TABOURET D'ÉRABLE ONDÉ A PIEDS GALBÉS,
D'ESPRIT LOUIS XV. XVIIIᵉ S.
STOOL OF WAVY MAPLE, WITH CURVED LEGS, IN THE
LOUIS XV MANNER. 18th C.

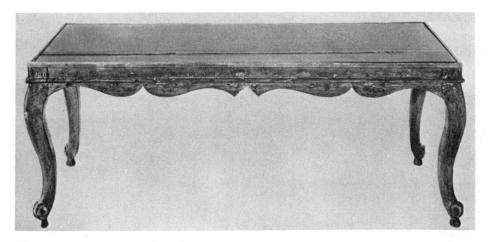

245. BANC-TABOURET A PIEDS GALBÉS. XVIIIᵉ S.
STOOL-BENCH, WITH CURVED LEGS. 18th C.

246. BANC-TRAVAILLEUSE ORNÉ D'UN TIROIR, DE L'HOTEL-DIEU DE QUÉBEC. XVIIIᵉ S.
WORK-BENCH, WITH DRAWER, FROM THE HOTEL-DIEU, QUEBEC. 18th C.

247. PETIT BANC-COFFRE REPOSANT SUR UNE BASE CHANTOURNÉE. XIXᵉ S.
SMALL CHEST-BENCH, RESTING ON A SHAPED BASE. 19th C.

248. BANC A PIEDS DE LYRE. XVIIIᵉ S.
BENCH, WITH RUSTIC LYRE-SHAPED FEET. 18th C.

249. BANC DE CORDONNIER. XIXᵉ S.
SHOEMAKER'S BENCH. 19th C.

250. PRIE-DIEU EN PENTE. FIN XVIIᵉ S.
SLANT-TOP PRAYER-STOOL (PRIE-DIEU). LATE 17th C.

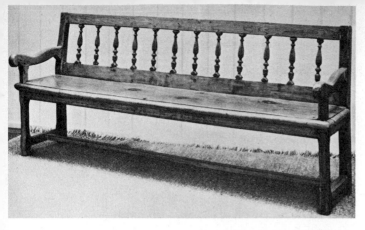

251. BANC D'ÉGLISE A DOSSIER A BALUS-
TRES. FIN XVIIIᵉ S.
CHURCH PEW, WITH BALUSTER BACK. LATE
18th C.

252. BANC D'ÉGLISE A DOSSIER ORNÉ DE
LYRES AJOURÉES. FIN XVIIIᵉ S.
CHURCH PEW, WITH OPENWORK LYRE-
BACK. LATE 18th C.

253. PETIT BANC RUSTIQUE ORNÉ DE TROIS
PANNEAUX. FIN XVIIIᵉ S.
SMALL THREE-PANELLED RUSTIC BENCH.
LATE 18th C.

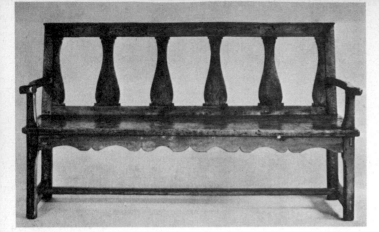

254. BANC RUSTIQUE ORNÉ D'UN DOSSIER
A BALUSTRES APLATIS. DÉBUT XIXᵉ S.
SMALL RUSTIC BENCH, WITH BALUSTER-
SHAPED SPLATS. EARLY 19th c.

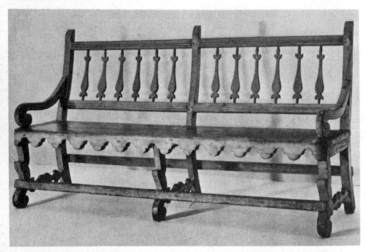

255. BANC RUSTIQUE A PIÈTEMENT EN
CONSOLE, D'INSPIRATION FIN EMPIRE. MI-
LIEU XIXᵉ S.
RUSTIC BENCH, WITH CONSOLE FEET, IN THE
LATE EMPIRE MANNER. MID 19th c.

256. BANC D'ÉGLISE A DOSSIER ORNÉ DE
PANNEAUX. XIXᵉ S.
CHURCH PEW, WITH PANELLED BACK.
19th c.

257. PETIT BANC RUSTIQUE, DE L'ÉGLISE DE
CAUGHNAWAGA. XIXᵉ S.
SMALL RUSTIC PEW, FROM THE CHURCH
OF CAUGHNAWAGA. 19th c.

258. BANC-LIT, D'INSPIRATION FIN EMPIRE.
XIXe S.
SETTLE-BED, IN LATE EMPIRE MANNER. 19th C.

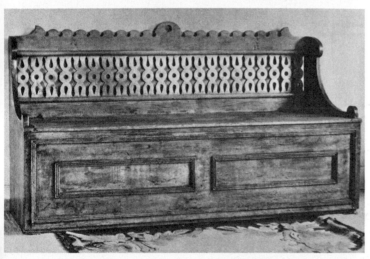

259. BANC-LIT AU DOSSIER CHANTOURNÉ
ET AJOURÉ. XIXe S.
SETTLE-BED, WITH SHAPED OPENWORK BACK.
19th C.

260. BANC-LIT ORNÉ DE FUSEAUX TOUR-
NÉS. XIXe S.
SETTLE-BED, WITH TURNED SPINDLES.
19th C.

261. BANC-COFFRE ORNÉ DE BALUSTRES
TOURNÉS. XIXe S.
COFFER-BENCH, WITH TURNED BALUSTERS.
19th C.

262. BANC-LIT ORNÉ D'UN LOSANGE APPLI-
QUÉ. XIXe S.
SETTLE-BED, DECORATED WITH AN APPLIQUÉ
LOZENGE. 19th C.

263. BANC-LIT RUSTIQUE DÉCORÉ A LA
GOUGE. XIXe S.
RUSTIC SETTLE-BED, WITH INCISED GOUGE
WORK. 19th C.

264. BANC-LIT, D'ESPRIT FIN EMPIRE. XIXe S.
SETTLE-BED, IN LATE EMPIRE MANNER. 19th C.

CHAIRS

Chairs were uncommon in peasant homes in seventeenth-century France, yet in Canada they were widely used to supplement benches and stools, " Six turned chairs with seats of straw ",[1] " two medium-sized chairs of jointed wood ".[2]

The types of chair most often mentioned in inventories are jointed chairs, straw or rush-bottomed chairs, and chairs with turned legs.

The jointed chairs were generally made of birch and had a pine-board seat. The back had the form of an open frame without spindles. They resembled the French *Lorraine* chairs which had chamfered or turned legs and " H " stretchers in the Louis XIII style. In Canada, they were called *Côte de Beaupré* or *Ile d'Orléans* chairs as they were found in every house in that region of the Lower St Lawrence.

Other jointed chairs had cross rails in the back frame joined by balusters or turned spindles, such as the chairs given to the *Hôtel-Dieu*, Quebec, by Madame d'Ailleboust, widow of the third Governor of New France, who retired there in 1672 to spend her last years, taking with her all her personal furniture. On her death in 1685 she left the nuns " ... several properties, a house in Quebec, another in Montreal, some funds in France and a considerable quantity of furniture. "[3]

The rush-seat chair (*chaise à la capucine*), with slightly inclined back-posts, straight legs and turned rungs, was to be found everywhere in Canada but was particularly common in the Montreal region. It was a light chair with cut-out or shaped slats in the back and could easily be moved about the room when chatting with friends. This chair was still made until recently and only a few years ago could be bought on a Friday in the Bonsecours Market, Montreal. Many varieties of these chairs, from all periods, and from all parts of French Canada, still exist today, as will be seen from the illustrations. These chairs, which are more than two hundred years old, are as solid as if they had been made yesterday. The early woodworkers used wood that was almost green for the back posts and legs, and well-dried wood for the rails, rungs, and stretchers. As the green wood dried, the grip on the rails and stretchers tightened like a vice, with the result that although glue was never used these chairs never wobbled nor came apart.

Specialist chair-makers such as Simon Audy dit Roy, " *faiseur de chaises* " in 1798, of Saint Augustin near Quebec[4] used to travel along all the country roads or " *rangs* " selling their chairs from door to door. They moved about in carts filled with chairs, thus spreading widely their own local styles. American and English designs were added at the end of the eighteenth and the beginning of the nineteenth centuries.

265. CHAIR, FORMERLY OWNED BY MGR DE ST VALLIER. LATE 17th C.

Chair, formerly owned by Monseigneur de St Vallier, which was given after his death to the Jesuit Fathers by the nuns of the *Hôpital-Général*, Quebec. The turning is completely in the Louis XIII manner. The back posts, heavily chamfered, are connected by three cross-rails shaped like bird wings.

w. 1' 6"   H. 3' 2½"   D. 1' 2½"
46 cm   98 cm   37 cm
WOOD : birch   PROVENANCE : Quebec
(*Coll. Art Institute, Detroit, Mich. U.S.A.*).

266. TURNED CHAIR, IN THE LOUIS XIII MANNER, FORMERLY OWNED BY MADAME D'AILLEBOUST. 17th C.

Turned chair, in the Louis XIII manner, with cross-rails in the back linked by turned balusters. This is one of ten chairs which were formerly owned by Madame d'Ailleboust, widow of the third Governor of New France, who spent her last years in retirement at the *Hôtel-Dieu*, Quebec, and who left all her furniture to the nuns. She entered the *Hôtel-Dieu* in 1672 and died there in 1685. A robust and well-made chair, reminiscent of Lorraine chairs. Note that the back feet are turned in column form.

(1) A J M, I O A. Inventaire des biens de Monsieur de Bel Estre, 12e Xbre 1684. Greffe Basset.
(2) A J M, I O A. Inventaire des biens meubles, titres et enseignements de deffunte Damoiselle Jeanne Mance vivant administratrice de l'hospital de Montréal, le 19 juin 1673. Greffe Basset.
(3) Juchereau de Saint-Ignace, Mère. *Les Annales de l'Hôtel-Dieu de Québec*, Québec, 1939, p. 26.
(4) Béchard, A. *Histoire de la Paroisse de Saint-Augustin* (Portneuf), p. 141.

Colour : dark brown.

w. 1' 5½"   H. 3' 2"   D. 1' ¾"
  44 cm   97 cm   32 cm

WOOD : birch   PROVENANCE : Quebec

(Coll. Musée de l'Hôtel-Dieu, Quebec).

267. " ILE D'ORLÉANS " TYPE OF CHAIR, WITH
TURNED FEET. LATE 17th C.

Jointed chair, of *Ile d'Orléans* type, but with turned understructure in the Louis XIII manner. These chairs were widely used in rural homesteads and in the towns of the Quebec region during the seventeenth and eighteenth centuries.

w. 1' 4⅝"   H. 2' 9⅜"   D. 1' 2⅜"
  42 cm   85 cm   37 cm

WOOD : birch

PROVENANCE : Saint-Pierre de Montmagny, P.Q.

(Coll. Provincial Museum, Quebec).

268. CHAIR, IN THE LOUIS XIII MANNER. LATE 17th C.

Chair, with an understructure in the Louis XIII manner, but with more simplified turning than that of Madame d'Ailleboust's chair. There are turned spindles in the back. A very sturdy chair.

w. 1' 2"   H. 3' 2"   D. 1' 1¾"
  36 cm   96 cm   35 cm

WOOD : maple

PROVENANCE : Hospice of the Grey Nuns, Quebec

(Coll. of the author, Montreal).

269. CHAIR, REPUTEDLY FROM THE OLD JESUIT HOUSE
AT SILLERY. 18th C.

Upholstered chair, with a turned understructure in the Louis XIII manner, which, according to oral tradition handed down by the Dobell family of Quebec, belonged to the Jesuits of Sillery. The upholstery is new.

w. 1' 8"   H. 3' 6"   D. 1' 5"
  51 cm   107 cm   43 cm

WOOD : maple   PROVENANCE : Sillery, P.Q.

(Coll. Mr Louis Mulligan, Montreal).

270. CHAIR, WITH TURNED SPINDLES AND FEET, IN
THE LOUIS XIII MANNER. 17th C.

Chair, with turned spindles and understructure, in the Louis XIII manner. The turning on the back posts is a deviation from the conventions of the period, and the balusters are simplified. Recently upholstered with an " Assomption sash " *(ceinture fléchée).*

w. 1' 4½"   H. 3' ½"   D. 1' 3"
  42 cm   93 cm   38 cm

WOOD : birch   PROVENANCE : Isle of Orleans, P.Q.

(Coll. Dr and Mrs Claude Bertrand, Outremont, P.Q.).

271. " ILE D'ORLÉANS " TYPE OF CHAIR, WITH A
BACK OF SHAPED RAILS. EARLY 18th C.

A jointed chair of the *Ile d'Orléans* or *Côte de Beaupré* type, with mouldings on the understructure, and shaped back rails. Strong and pretty period chair.

w. 1' 4"   H. 3'   D. 1' ¾"
  41 cm   91 cm   32 cm

WOOD : birch   SEAT : pine

PROVENANCE : Quebec district

(Coll. Mr and Mrs J.N. Cole, Montreal).

272. JOINTED CHAIR, OF " ILE D'ORLÉANS " TYPE.
EARLY 18th C.

A rustic jointed chair of *Ile d'Orléans* type. This is the most common chair of the Quebec district. The very robust ones are the earliest. Note the width of the chamfers, and the front cross-rail, which is not set square.

w. 1' 4"   H. 2' 7¼"   D. 1' ¼"
  41 cm   99 cm   31 cm

WOOD : birch   SEAT : pine

PROVENANCE : Isle of Orleans, P.Q.

(Coll. of the author, Montreal).

273. CHAIR, IN THE LOUIS XIII MANNER, WITH BA-
LUSTER BACK. 18th C.

Chair, in the Louis XIII manner, with turned legs and shaped rails linking balusters. The turning on the front rung, the stretchers and the balusters is slightly unconventional. Upholstered seat.

w. 1' 7½"   H. 3' 5½"   D. 1' 4½"
  49 cm   105 cm   42 cm

WOOD : birch   PROVENANCE : Quebec district

(Coll. Mrs Richard R. Costello, Sainte-Agathe des Monts, P.Q.).

274. JOINTED CHAIR, FROM THE HOTEL-DIEU, QUEBEC.
LATE 17th C.

Jointed chair, from the *Hôtel-Dieu*, Quebec, of the *Ile d'Orléans* type, with simplified turning and cross-rails and stretchers with mouldings. A robust chair.

w. 1' 6½"   H. 2' 6⅝"   D. 1' 1¾"
  47 cm   78 cm   35 cm

WOOD : maple   PROVENANCE : Quebec

(Coll. Musée de l'Hôtel-Dieu, Quebec).

275. CHAIR, IN THE LOUIS XV MANNER, FROM BOURG-
ROYAL. 18th C.

Jointed chair, with curved legs terminating in *pieds de biche.* The seat rail, the posts and the back rails are all shaped in the Louis XIV and Louis XV manners. According to oral tradition, this chair was taken from the *Ermitage* at the same time as armchair no. 304. They were carried off by the *habitants* of Bourg-Royal during the siege of Quebec in 1759. The *Ermitage* was the *Intendants'* country residence and was situated in the spot today known as *Château Bigot*. An elegant and original chair.

w. 1' 6"   H. 3' ½"   D. 1' 4½"
   46 cm   93 cm   42 cm

WOOD : birch SEAT : pine
PROVENANCE : Bourg-Royal, P.Q.
(Coll. Provincial Museum, Quebec).

276. " OS DE MOUTON " CHAIR. 18th C.
Upholstered chair, with an *Os de mouton* understructure, and shaped back rails linked by balusters. It is unusual to see back posts shaped in console or bracket form on this type of chair. A rare example.

w. 1' 7"   H. 3' 4½"   D. 1' 6"
   48 cm   103 cm   46 cm

WOOD : birch PROVENANCE : Quebec district
(Coll. Dr and Mrs Claude Bertrand, Outremont, P.Q.).

277. " OS DE MOUTON " CHAIR. 18th C.
Upholstered chair, of *Os de mouton* type.

w. 1' 8"   H. 3' 2"   D. 1' 8"
   51 cm   97 cm   51 cm

WOOD : birch
PROVENANCE : Ile aux Coudres, P.Q.
(Coll. Dr and Mrs Herbert T. Schwarz, Montreal).

278. TURNED CHAIR, SHOWING AMERICAN INFLUENCE. LATE 18th C.
Turned chair *à la capucine*, which shows American influence. The rungs as well as the back rails are turned and reveal American rather than Louis XIII influence, because the chamfered cubes are lacking. Rawhide seat.

w. 1' 5¾"   H. 2' 7"
   45 cm   79 cm

WOOD : birch PROVENANCE : Montreal
(Coll. Hôtel-Dieu, Montreal).

279. TURNED CHAIR, SHOWING VARIOUS INFLUENCES. LATE 18th C.
Turned chair, showing French and American influence. The turning on the feet is of American derivation, while that on the rungs is in the Louis XIII manner. The rungs enter the posts like dowels, in place of tenons which were more usual on Louis XIII chairs. The back also shows both French and American influence. The cord seat woven in diamond pattern is recent.

w. 1' 5½"   H. 2' 8¾"   D. 1' 3½"
   44 cm   83 cm   39 cm

WOOD : birch PROVENANCE : Quebec
(Coll. Musée des Ursulines, Quebec).

280. CHAIR " A LA CAPUCINE ". LATE 17th C.
Chair *à la capucine*, with two back rails, one of which is shaped. This is the oldest chair *à la capucine* known. New rush seat. One lateral rung has been replaced.

w. 1' 2"   H. 2' 11¼"   D. 1' 2"
   36 cm   90 cm   36 cm

WOOD : birch PROVENANCE : Quebec district
(Coll. Mr and Mrs Jean-Paul Lemieux, Sillery, P.Q.).

281. CHAIR " A LA CAPUCINE ". LATE 18th C.
Chair, *à la capucine*. The shaping of the back rails resembles that on chairs from Auvergne. Recent rawhide seat. A fine rustic chair.

w. 1' 5½"   H. 2' 8¾"   D. 1'
   44 cm   83 cm   31 cm

WOOD : oak, ash, birch and pine
PROVENANCE : Montreal district
(Coll. Canada Steamship Lines, Tadoussac, P.Q.).

282. TURNED CHAIR " A LA CAPUCINE ". 18th C.
Turned chair, with back rails having the same design as those of the armchairs *à la capucine*. Straw seat. Painted in black.

w. 1' 6¼"   H. 1' 1½"   D. 1' 2⅜"
   47 cm   34 cm   37 cm

WOOD : birch PROVENANCE : Quebec
(Coll. Musée de l'Hôpital-Général, Quebec).

283. SMALL CHAIR " A LA CAPUCINE ", WITH CHAMFERED FEET. EARLY 19th C.
Small chair, *à la capucine*, with shaped flat splats and a chamfered understructure. Seat of elm bark in basket-weave pattern.

w. 1' 5¾"   H. 2' 11¾"   D. 1' 2½"
   45 cm   91 cm   37 cm

WOOD : birch PROVENANCE : Quebec district
(Coll. of the author, Montreal).

284. CHILD'S CHAIR. LATE 18th C.
Child's high chair, with two shaped back rails. A model widely distributed in the eighteenth and nineteenth centuries. The rush-seat is missing.

w. 11 ¾"   H. 3' ¼"   D. 10 ¾"
   30 cm   92 cm   27 cm

WOOD : birch
(Coll. Château de Ramezay, Montreal).

285. CHAIR " A LA CAPUCINE ", IN THE CHIPPENDALE MANNER. EARLY 19th C.
Chair, *à la capucine*. The two back rails are shaped and are in openwork, in the manner of certain Chippendale chairs.

WOOD : birch

PROVENANCE : Caughnawaga, P.Q.

(Coll. Canada Steamship Lines, Tadoussac, P.Q.).

286. SMALL CHAIR, WITH AN OPENWORK BACK. EARLY 19th C.

Small chair, *à la capucine*. The upper back rail is pierced with two crosses. Recent seat, woven with cord.

w. 1' 5⅜"   H. 2' 10"   D. 1' 1⅝"
44 cm   86 cm   35 cm

WOOD : birch PROVENANCE : Montreal district

(Coll. Mr and Mrs J.N. Cole, Montreal).

287. CHAIR FROM CHAMBLY, OF NEW ENGLAND TYPE. EARLY 19th C.

Turned chair, with two back rails typical of New England, also found in St Jean d'Iberville, Chambly, St Hubert, and in the eastern townships. It was influenced by " Shaker " furniture. A very popular model during the nineteenth century. Rawhide seat.

WOOD : birch PROVENANCE : Chambly district

(Coll. Château de Ramezay, Montreal).

288. CHAIR, WITH HEAVILY CURVED BACK POSTS. 19th C.

Chair, with exaggeratedly curved back posts, a caricature of *Directoire* or " American Sabre-Leg " chairs. A curious and not at all comfortable chair. Many have been found in the Kamouraska, Cap St Ignace and Montmagny districts. Recent rawhide seat.

w. 1' 4½"   H. 2' 7½"   D. 1' 1¼"
42 cm   80 cm   34 cm

WOOD : birch

PROVENANCE : Ile aux Coudres, P.Q.

(Coll. Mr and Mrs J.N. Cole, Montreal).

289. RUSTIC CHAIR, WITH " CROISILLON " BACK RAILS. EARLY 19th C.

Rustic chair, with two back rails, one of which is decorated with *croisillons* or the St Andrew's cross, showing Sheraton influence. The rawhide seat is of recent date.

WOOD : birch PROVENANCE : Joliette, P.Q.

(Coll. Mr and Mrs J.N. Cole, Montreal).

290. CHAIR " A LA CAPUCINE ", WITH SHAPED BACK RAILS. 19th C.

Chair, *à la capucine*, with turned legs of American influence. The back has three shaped rails. Colour : deep red.

w. 1' 5½"   H. 2' 11⅝"   D. 1' 1½"
44 cm   90 cm   35 cm

WOOD : ash

(Coll. Provincial Museum, Quebec).

291. ORDINARY CONVENT CHAIR. EARLY 19th C.

Small chair, *à la capucine*, with original rush seat and splayed back posts. It was made in large quantities for convents.

w. 1' 4¾"   H. 2' 7"   D. 1' 1½"
43 cm   89 cm   35 cm

WOOD : birch and ash

PROVENANCE : Quebec

(Coll. Musée de l'Hôtel-Dieu, Quebec).

292. CHAIR, INSPIRED BY THE ENGLISH WINDSOR CHAIR. EARLY 19th C.

Chair, inspired by the English Windsor chair, with curved back posts, a wooden seat and splayed feet. The shaping on the upper back rail is in *Late Empire* manner.

w. 1' 2¼"   H. 2' 9¾"   D. 1' 3"
36 cm   86 cm   38 cm

WOOD : maple and beech

PROVENANCE : Montreal district

(Coll. Mr and Mrs P.T. Molson, Lac Violon, Sainte-Agathe des Monts, P.Q.).

293. ARROW-BACK CHAIR, INSPIRED BY AN AMERICAN MODEL. EARLY 19th C.

Chair, derived from the American Windsor chairs, but with vertical back slats like arrowheads (arrow back), a motif found in New England. The three horizontal back rails are reminiscent of those on Regency and Hitchcock chairs. These chairs were very popular in Canada and the United States at the beginning of the nineteenth century.

w. 1' 2"   H. 2' 8¼"   D. 1' 3¼"
35 cm   82 cm   39 cm

WOOD : birch PROVENANCE : Quebec district

(Coll. Mr and Mrs Jean-Paul Lemieux, Sillery, P.Q.).

294. RUSTIC CHAIR, FROM ST HILARION. 20th C.

Rustic chair, from St Hilarion, designed and executed by an old *habitant* woodworker who made traditional furniture. The birch seat is three and a half inches thick. A robust chair with sober lines. The artisan unknowingly anticipated the Swedish furniture designer Carl Mamstein, who created a practically identical chair a few years ago.

w. 11½"   H. 2' 9"   D. 1' 4¼"
29 cm   81 cm   41 cm

WOOD : birch PROVENANCE : Saint-Hilarion, P.Q.

(Coll. of the author, Petite Rivière Saint-François, P.Q.).

216

295. SMALL RUSTIC CHAIR, FROM THE BAIE ST PAUL AREA. 20th C.

Small rustic chair, from Charlevoix; particularly found in the Baie St Paul, St Urbain and St Hilarion areas. It is called the *violon* chair. The back recalls the small convent chairs of the period. The seat is of pine.

w. 1' 5"   H. 2' 9½"   D. 1' 2"
43 cm   83 cm   35 cm
WOOD : birch
PROVENANCE : Saint-Urbain, Charlevoix, P.Q.
(Coll. Mr and Mrs J.N. Cole, Murray Bay, P.Q.).

296. " COTE DE BEAUPRÉ " CHAIR, WITH SHAPED BALUSTERS. 19th C.

Côte de Beaupré type of chair, with an understructure of rungs. The back is assembled with mortise and tenon joints. Curious combination of two distinct techniques of construction. The two back splats are shaped, and vaguely reminiscent of English models. This kind of chair is quite widely distributed along the Côte de Beaupré.

w. 1' 7"   H. 2' 6¼"   D. 1' 1½"
48 cm   77 cm   34 cm
WOOD : maple
PROVENANCE : Côte de Beaupré, P.Q.
(Coll. Mr and Mrs J.N. Cole, Montreal).

297. " ILE D'ORLEANS " CHAIR, WITH BACK IN THE ENGLISH MANNER. 19th C.

Ile d'Orléans type of chair, with a splat which is a rustic borrowing from Queen Anne chairs. Canadian woodworkers were very strongly influenced by the furniture brought over by the English and Scots, above all in the Murray Bay district, where officers and soldiers who had served under General Wolfe settled. American families who spent their summers at the resort introduced other trends.

w. 1' 2¼"   H. 3'   D. 1' ½"
36 cm   91 cm   32 cm
WOOD : maple PROVENANCE : Murray Bay, P.Q.
(Coll. Mr and Mrs J.N. Cole, Montreal).

298. RUSTIC CHAIR, IN THE ENGLISH CHIPPENDALE MANNER. EARLY 19th C.

Chair, under English influence. The two splats in the back and the understructure show Chippendale influence.

w. 1' 6½"   H. 2' 8½"   D. 1' 2¾"
47 cm   83 cm   37 cm
WOOD : maple
PROVENANCE : The Manor, Nairne Seigniory, Murray Bay, P.Q.
(Coll. Mr and Mrs J.N. Cole, Montreal).

265. CHAISE DE MGR DE SAINT-
VALLIER. FIN XVIIᵉ S.
CHAIR, FORMERLY OWNED BY MGR
DE ST VALLIER.   LATE 17th C.

266. CHAISE TOURNÉE, D'ESPRIT LOUIS XIII, AYANT
APPARTENU A MADAME D'AILLEBOUST. XVIIᵉ S,
TURNED CHAIR, IN THE LOUIS XIII MANNER, FORMERLY
OWNED BY MADAME D'AILLEBOUST.   17th C.

269. CHAISE, DITE DES JÉSUITES DE
SILLERY. XVIIIᵉ S.
CHAIR, REPUTEDLY FROM THE
OLD JESUIT HOUSE AT SILLERY.
18th C.

270. CHAISE A PIÈTEMENT ET A
FUSEAUX TOURNÉS, D'ESPRIT
LOUIS XIII. XVIIᵉ S.
CHAIR, WITH TURNED SPINDLES
AND FEET, IN THE LOUIS XIII
MANNER. 17th C.

271. CHAISE DE TYPE « ILE D'ORLÉANS »,
A TRAVERSES DU DOSSIER CHANTOURNÉES.
DÉBUT XVIIIᵉ S.
" ILE D'ORLÉANS " TYPE OF CHAIR, WITH A
BACK OF SHAPED RAILS. EARLY 18th C.

272. CHAISE D'ASSEMBLAGE, DE
TYPE « ILE D'ORLÉANS ». DÉBUT
XVIIIᵉ S.
JOINTED CHAIR, OF " ILE D'OR-
LÉANS " TYPE. EARLY 18th C.

273. CHAISE D'ESPRIT LOUIS XIII,
A DOSSIER A BALUSTRES. XVIIIᵉ S.
CHAIR, IN THE LOUIS XIII MANNER,
WITH BALUSTER BACK. 18th C.

274. CHAISE DE MENUISERIE D'AS-
SEMBLAGE, DE L'HOTEL-DIEU DE
QUÉBEC. FIN XVIIᵉ S.
JOINTED CHAIR, FROM THE HOTEL-
DIEU, QUEBEC. LATE 17th C.

275. CHAISE GALBÉE, D'ESPRIT
LOUIS XV, PROVENANT DE BOURG-
ROYAL. XVIIIᵉ S.
CHAIR, IN THE LOUIS XV MANNER,
FROM BOURG-ROYAL. 18th C.

276. CHAISE A PIÈTEMENT « OS DE
MOUTON ». XVIIIᵉ S.
" OS DE MOUTON " CHAIR. 18th C

278. CHAISE TOURNÉE, D'IN-
FLUENCE AMÉRICAINE. FIN XVIIIᵉ S.
TURNED CHAIR, SHOWING AMERI-
CAN INFLUENCE. LATE 18th C.

279. CHAISE TOURNÉE, AUX DI-
VERSES INFLUENCES. FIN XVIIIᵉ S.
TURNED CHAIR, SHOWING VARIOUS
INFLUENCES. LATE 18th C.

280. CHAISE « A LA CAPUCINE ».
FIN XVIIᵉ S.
CHAIR " A LA CAPUCINE ". LATE
17th C.

281. CHAISE « A LA CAPUCINE ». FIN XVIIIᵉ S.
CHAIR " A LA CAPUCINE ". LATE 18th C.

282. CHAISE TOURNÉE « A LA CAPUCINE ».
XVIIIᵉ S.
TURNED CHAIR " A LA CAPUCINE ". 18th C.

283. PETITE CHAISE « A LA CAPUCINE »,
A PIÈTEMENT CHANFREINÉ. DÉBUT XIXe S.
SMALL CHAIR " A LA CAPUCINE ", WITH
CHAMFERED FEET.   EARLY 19th C.

284. CHAISE D'ENFANT. FIN XVIIIe S.
CHILD'S CHAIR.   LATE 18th C.

285. CHAISE « A LA CAPUCINE », D'INS-
PIRATION CHIPPENDALE. DÉBUT XIXe S.
CHAIR " A LA CAPUCINE ", IN THE
CHIPPENDALE MANNER.   EARLY 19th C.

286. PETITE CHAISE, A TRAVERSE
DU DOSSIER AJOURÉE. DÉBUT
XIXe S.
SMALL CHAIR, WITH AN OPENWORK
BACK.   EARLY 19th C.

287. CHAISE DE CHAMBLY, DE TYPE
NOUVELLE-ANGLETERRE. DÉBUT
XIXe S.
CHAIR FROM CHAMBLY, OF NEW
ENGLAND TYPE.   EARLY 19th C.

288. CHAISE A FORTES COURBES DU DOSSIER. XIXe S.
CHAIR, WITH HEAVILY CURVED BACK POSTS. 19th c.

289. CHAISE RUSTIQUE, A CROISILLONS. DÉBUT XIXe S.
RUSTIC CHAIR, WITH "CROISILLON" BACKRAILS. EARLY 19th c.

290. CHAISE « A LA CAPUCINE ». AVEC TRAVERSES DU DOSSIER CHANTOURNÉES. XIXe S.
CHAIR "A LA CAPUCINE ", WITH SHAPED BACKRAILS. 19th c.

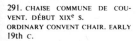

291. CHAISE COMMUNE DE COUVENT. DÉBUT XIXe S.
ORDINARY CONVENT CHAIR. EARLY 19th c.

292. CHAISE DE TYPE WINDSOR. DÉBUT XIXe S.
CHAIR, INSPIRED BY THE ENGLISH WINDSOR CHAIR. EARLY 19th c.

293. CHAISE DE TYPE « ARROWBACK », D'INFLUENCE AMÉRICAINE. DÉBUT XIXe S.
ARROW-BACK CHAIR, INSPIRED BY AN AMERICAN MODEL. EARLY 19th c.

294. CHAISE RUSTIQUE DE SAINT-HILARION. XXe S.
RUSTIC CHAIR, FROM ST HILARION. 20th C.

295. PETITE CHAISE RUSTIQUE, DE LA RÉGION DE BAIE-SAINT-PAUL.
XXe S.
SMALL RUSTIC CHAIR, FROM THE BAIE ST PAUL AREA. 20th C.

296. CHAISE DE TYPE « COTE DE BEAU-
PRÉ », A BALUSTRES DU DOSSIER CHAN-
TOURNÉS. XIXe S.
" COTE DE BEAUPRÉ " CHAIR, WITH
SHAPED BALUSTERS. 19th C.

297. CHAISE DU TYPE «ILE D'ORLÉANS»,
AVEC DOSSIER D'INFLUENCE ANGLAISE.
XIXe S.
" ILE D'ORLÉANS " CHAIR, WITH BACK IN
THE ENGLISH MANNER. 19th C.

298. CHAISE RUSTIQUE D'INSPIRATION
CHIPPENDALE. DÉBUT XIXe S.
RUSTIC CHAIR, IN THE ENGLISH CHIP-
PENDALE MANNER. EARLY XIXe C.

ARMCHAIRS

Chairs with arms *(chaises à bras)* are mentioned in several inventories from 1657, and armchairs *(fauteuils)* a little later. An entry in 1673 reads, "Two armchairs covered with cloth and a fringe."[1] In the years which followed, large numbers of armchairs of turned birch, or with turned legs, are listed in inventories, "the frame of an armchair of turned birch."[2] These are the classical turned armchairs in the Louis XIII style, with baluster understructure, chamfered cubes, and long, curved armrests designed to follow the line of the human arm. They had high backs, either a square or an arched top rail and nearly all were upholstered. It was the ideal fireside seat, the high back covered with tapestry or *gros point* offering good protection against any draughts in the room. It was the armchair of the master of the house.

Another chair which was quite popular in all parts of French Canada in the eighteenth century was the *os de mouton* armchair of which no dated specimens are to be found in the mother country before 1670.[3] This was a transitional piece leading from the Louis XIII to the Louis XIV style, in which scrolls replaced rectilinear forms. In Canada, the *os de mouton* was called the *fauteuil du seigneur*.

The *habitants*, having seen this type of chair in the Seigneur's manor, quickly imitated it for use in their own homes. A great variety of specimens exist, some roughly made and some the work of craftsmen. At first, they were made with bracket posts, the two front legs rising to a certain height then curving back in a continuous line to form the armrests of the chair. In the early eighteenth century, the armrests were supported by brackets *(supports d'accoudoir en console)* set back a little from the front of the chair, to allow the ladies, whose skirts had taken on more ample proportions, to seat themselves elegantly without feeling confined. This armchair was another stylish piece which found its way into the Canadian peasant's home but it does not seem to have been in use in the rural districts of France.

Another chair that was very popular in French Canada was the straw or rush-seat armchair *(fauteuil à la Capucine*, almost identical with the *Bonne femme* armchair of Orléanais, and the Loire Valley). This had elegantly shaped back rails as well as set-back arm-supports which went through the seat frame and were pegged into the first lateral rung.

The Canadian armchair *(à la capucine)* is distinguished, however, from the French armchair *(à la capucine* or *Bonne Femme)* of the period by its greater number of chamfered cubes on the front legs and back posts, and also by the very special turnings on the stretchers. I have seen no specimens of these chairs in France, either in museums or antique shops; however, I did come across an illustration in a French magazine[4] of an armchair with front legs and back posts suggesting the Canadian *capucine* armchair except that it had a wooden seat and the armrests were not set back but were in the Louis XIII style.

The *Capucine* chair could never have the solidity of the jointed chairs which were put together with mortise and tenon. It was made with dowelled rungs, like the little rush-seat chairs which were so common in all periods. However, it is one of the most beautiful Canadian pieces, and all the more charming for its rustic air.

In the United States it was believed for a long time that these armchairs came from New England, simply because many of them found their way into that region. Some American books on furniture even attribute this type of chair to certain craftsmen of New England. But the idea is difficult to accept as the lines of the chair are too clearly French. Many American

(1) A J M, I O A. Inv. des biens meubles, titres et Enseignemens de deffunte Damoiselle Jeanne Mance vivante administratrice de l'hospital de Montréal, le 19 juin 1673. Greffe Basset.
(2) A J M, I O A. Inv. des biens de la communauté qui a esté entre Denis Benard Sr la Terreur et Catherine Dene sa deffunte femme 5 may 1731. Greffe St-Romain.
(3) Feray, Jean. *Le dix-septième siècle français*, Paris, Hachette, 1958, p. 37.
(4) *Vie à la campagne, Meubles normands d'autrefois* (numéro extraordinaire). Paris, Hachette. Déc. 15, 1920, p. 40.

collectors admired and bought them in Canada, and it is more than possible that a certain number of them were manufactured in the United States not very long ago!

A whole range of Canadian armchairs have appeared since the eighteenth century and these now arouse the admiration of connoisseurs. All of them were in some way a modification of the *capucine* armchair, but were rougher and more naive in their workmanship. It is in these designs that we find proof of the originality and inventiveness of the Canadian chair-makers and woodworkers who excelled in the production of country-style chairs. At the time that the elaborate *Régence* and Louis XV armchairs were introduced in Paris, Canadian woodworkers were not familiar with such intricate techniques and fine workmanship. Very few specimens of these handsome chairs were made in Canada. I have included plates of the small number that I have found. All these chairs were probably made by church woodworker-carvers who must have had a carpenter's " green thumb ".

All armchairs of beech wood, upholstered or caned, in the Late Louis XIV, *Régence*, or Louis XV styles which have been found in Canada were imported from France. The official Customs regulations of 1748 show that Canadians had to pay duty for this type of imported chair... " Armchairs and chairs with cane-work, each to be paid six sols. "[1] Another armchair is sometimes mentioned in inventories, " a *bergère* with its backing and pillow, 12 livres. "[2] This chair, wide and deep, sometimes had wings, the seat was fitted with a cushion, and the space below the armrests was upholstered. However, I have not been able to find a single specimen which has survived the too numerous fires.

299. ARMCHAIR, IN THE LOUIS XIII MANNER. 18th C.

Armchair, having an understructure in the Louis XIII manner and flat, recessed armrests. Flat armrests are in the Louis XIII-Louis XIV traditions, but recessed armrests only appeared later in the eighteenth century.

| w. 2' 2" | H. 3' | D. 1' 7" |
| 66 cm | 91 cm | 48 cm |

WOOD : birch

PROVENANCE : Rivière Ouelle, P.Q.

(Coll. Mr and Mrs Ross McMaster, Saint-Sauveur des Monts, P.Q.).

300. ARMCHAIR, WITH SERPENTINE TOP RAIL, IN THE LOUIS XIII MANNER. 18th C.

Armchair, with feet and stretchers in the Louis XIII manner, almost identical with French armchairs of the same period, except for the elongated chamfered cubes on the front posts. There should be an open space in between the upholstered back and the seat. Note the back posts, which are nearly always chamfered.

| w. 1' 10½" | H. 3' 9" | D. 1' 7" |
| 57 cm | 114 cm | 48 cm |

WOOD : birch   PROVENANCE : Quebec district

(Coll. Royal Ontario Museum, Toronto, Ont.).

301. ARMCHAIR " A CRÉMAILLÈRE ", IN THE LOUIS XIII MANNER. 17th C.

Armchair, *à crémaillère*, derived from the adjustable toothed rack of a fireplace. It has a Louis XIII understructure and was formerly owned by Monseigneur de St Vallier, according to the oral tradition of the nuns of the *Hôpital-Général*, Quebec. This kind of armchair was widely distributed in seventeenth-century France. Molière's armchair, preserved at the Comédie-Française, is of a similar kind. The back can be adjusted to obtain a more comfortable position. It was also used as an invalid's chair. Although made of walnut, its unskilled workmanship confirms its Canadian origin. The bun feet were replaced.

| w. 2' 3¼" | H. 4' 3¾" | D. 1' 9" |
| 69 cm | 131 cm | 53 cm |

WOOD : walnut   PROVENANCE : Quebec

(Coll. Mr and Mrs Scott Symons, Toronto, Ont.).

302. ARMCHAIR, WITH DOUBLE-BALUSTER BACK, IN THE LOUIS XIII MANNER. LATE 17th C.

Armchair, in the Louis XIII manner, with double-baluster back, practically unknown in French Louis XIII armchairs which were panelled or upholstered. The bun feet have been worn away.

| w. 2' ½" | H. 3' 10" | D. 1' 9½" |
| 62 cm | 117 cm | 55 cm |

(1) *Edits et Ordonnances Royaux, Déclarations et Arrêts du Conseil d'Etat.* Québec, 1854, p. 598.
(2) A J M, I O A. Inventaire à la requeste de joseph letourneau du 24e de may 1757. Greffe Grisé.

LIVING-ROOM OF A MODERN HOUSE WITH TRADITIONAL FURNITURE.

WOOD : birch

PROVENANCE : Old Jesuit College, Quebec.

(Coll. Château de Ramezay, Montreal).

303. ARMCHAIR, WITH PANEL AND BALUSTER BACK, IN THE LOUIS XIII MANNER. 17th C.

Large and typically Canadian armchair, with a back of panels and balusters. It is truly the armchair of the master of the house. All these Louis XIII armchairs are of a superb solidity, since they were assembled with mortise and tenon joints.

w. 2' 1⅝"	H. 3' 10"	D. 1' 8½"
65 cm	117 cm	52 cm

WOOD : birch   PROVENANCE : Quebec district

(Coll. Mr Jean Dubuc, Quebec).

304. ARMCHAIR, WITH CHAMFERED FEET, IN THE LOUIS XIII MANNER. 17th C.

Large armchair, coming, according to oral tradition, from the *Ermitage*, the house built by Jean Talon in the forest of Bourg-Royal, the ruins of which are still visible at *Château Bigot*, near Charlesbourg. This house was for nearly a century the retreat of the *Intendants* of New France, and no doubt was designed to be well away from the town and safe from all gossip. At the Conquest the *habitants* of the hamlets of Bourg-Royal and Bourg-la-Reine carried off its furniture to their own homes, to prevent it falling into the hands of the English. (Cf. chair no. 275, which also came from the *Ermitage*). A rough armchair of peasant make, which has many associations attached to it.

w. 2' 1½"	H. 4' 1½"	D. 1' 9"
65 cm	126 cm	53 cm

WOOD : birch   PROVENANCE : Bourg-Royal, P.Q.

(Coll. Provincial Museum, Quebec).

305. ARMCHAIR, OF LOUIS XIII TYPE, FROM JEUNE-LORETTE. 18th C.

Armchair, of Louis XIII form, with openwork geometric designs of Indian inspiration. According to oral tradition, it was made by a Huron from Jeune-Lorette. Note the naive design of the double spirals, which recall the Algonquin double curve. This seat is the admiration of connoisseurs on account of its originality and fine proportions. Original colouring : dark brown.

w. 2' 4¾"	H. 3' 4½"	D. 1' 6¼"
73 cm	103 cm	46 cm

WOOD : birch

PROVENANCE : Huron Church of Jeune-Lorette, P.Q.

(Coll. Château de Ramezay, Montreal).

306. RUSTIC ARMCHAIR, IN THE LOUIS XIII MANNER. 18th C.

Rustic armchair, in the Louis XIII manner, with a jointed back much more elegant than the base, which consists of crude rungs. The seat should have had a turned understructure. However, the back rails with their motifs of bird wings in flight are reminiscent of some Lorraine armchairs. Its fine proportions redeem its faults and make one admire it.

w. 1' 8"	H. 3' 5½"	D. 1' 2¾"
51 cm	105 cm	37 cm

WOOD : birch

PROVENANCE : Côte de Liesse, Montreal

(Coll. Mr and Mrs J.N. Cole, Montreal).

307. " OS DE MOUTON " ARMCHAIR. 18th C.

These armchairs are called *Os de mouton* because the rails and stretchers of the understructure suggest the curves of sheep bones. It is a transitional piece, coming after the rectilinear forms of the Louis XIII style, and presaging, by its volutes, the curves and countercurves of the Louis XIV, Regency and Louis XV styles. The bracket or console-shaped feet on the front posts were to give birth to the whole gamut of *cabriole* and bracket feet of the Louis XIV style. The armrests were set back for more comfort. The upper back is in curvilinear form and the frame covering the seat rail was probably added much later to accommodate a larger cushion.

w. 1' 11"	H. 3' 3½"	D. 1' 9"
58 cm	100 cm	53 cm

WOOD : birch

(Coll. Museum of Fine Arts, Montreal).

308. " OS DE MOUTON " ARMCHAIR. 18th C.

Another interesting *Os de mouton* armchair, with squat padded armrests, a detail rarely found in France.

w. 2' 2½"	H. 3' 8¾"	H. 1' 10½"
67 cm	114 cm	57 cm

WOOD : birch   PROVENANCE : Quebec

(Coll. Miss Barbara Richardson, Sainte-Agathe des Monts, P.Q.).

309. " OS DE MOUTON " ARMCHAIR. 18th C.

Os de mouton armchair, with bracket or console-shaped front posts. The style is earlier than that of other *Os de mouton* armchairs with set-back armrests. Made by an unskilled hand.

w. 1' 1½"	H. 3' 3½"	D. 1' 9½"
34 cm	100 cm	55 cm

WOOD : birch   BACK POSTS : butternut

PROVENANCE : Bécancourt, P.Q.

(Coll. of the author, Montreal).

310. ARMCHAIR, WITH CONSOLE LEGS AND ARBALÈTE-FRONTED SEAT RAIL. 18th C.

Armchair, having bracket or console-shaped legs as in *Os de mouton* chairs, and an arbalète-fronted seat rail. A curious mixture of styles. The back is in Louis XIV curvilinear form, while the set-back armrests are in the Louis XV manner. The incurved front seat rail of arbalète form is very rare. The cross-stretcher is of the type known as a *double chapeau de gendarme*. This armchair was once owned by the family of Jacques Viger, the first Mayor of Montreal.

w. 2'   H. 3' 6½"   D. 2'
61 cm   108 cm   61 cm
WOOD : birch PROVENANCE : Montreal

(Coll. Dr and Mrs Herbert T. Schwarz, Montreal).

311. PEASANT ARMCHAIR. 18th C.

Peasant armchair, with chamfered front feet, and stretchers in quadrilateral form. The high-panelled back and the armrests relate it to the Louis XIII style. Note the curve of the armrest supports.

w. 1' 8"   H. 3' 5½"   D. 1' 5½"
51 cm   105 cm   44 cm
WOOD : birch SEAT : pine

PROVENANCE : Quebec district

(Coll. Canada Steamship Lines, Tadoussac, P.Q.).

312. RUSTIC CHAMFERED ARMCHAIR, WITH SPINDLE BACK. 18th C.

Rustic chamfered armchair, with spindle back. It is of the *Côte de Beaupré* or *Ile d'Orléans* type, and resembles Louis XIV seats in its square form and flat armrests. This armchair was used by the celebrant during High Mass. Colour : deep green.

w. 2' ¼"   H. 2' 10"   D. 1' 3¾"
61 cm   86 cm   40 cm
WOOD : birch SEAT : pine

PROVENANCE : Quebec district

(Coll. Canada Steamship Lines, Tadoussac, P.Q.).

313. LARGE ARMCHAIR FROM ILE D'ORLÉANS. 18th C.

Large rustic armchair, in the Louis XIII manner. The high back recalls the proportions of some upholstered Louis XIII armchairs. The chamfered understructure and the stretchers and rails are typical of the jointed chairs from the Côte de Beaupré and Ile d'Orléans. This armchair lacks elegance and shaped armrests would have been preferable.

w. 2'   H. 4'   D. 1' 6¼"
61 cm   122 cm   46 cm
WOOD : birch SEAT : pine

PROVENANCE : Isle of Orleans, P.Q.

(Coll. Canada Steamship Lines, Tadoussac, P.Q.).

314. RUSTIC ARMCHAIR, FROM PORTNEUF. LATE 18th C.

Rustic armchair, with shaped back rails and turned posts. Strong and elegant, it recalls some armchairs from the mountains of Savoie, although it shows a very Canadian character.

w. 1' 10"   H. 3' 9⅜"   D. 1' 5"
56 cm   115 cm   43 cm
WOOD : butternut

PROVENANCE : Portneuf, P.Q.

(Coll. Mr Louis Mulligan, Montreal).

315. RUSTIC ARMCHAIR, WITH TURNED LEGS. 18th C.

Country-type armchair, having a turned understructure, with shaped back rails and festooned front seat rail. The same type of back is to be found in some armchairs of Ile aux Coudres and Petite Rivière St François. The armrests are set at too great an angle.

w. 1' 11"   H. 3' 2"   D. 1' 7"
58 cm   97 cm   48 cm
WOOD : birch

PROVENANCE : Quebec district

(Coll. Dr and Mrs Herbert T. Schwarz, Montreal).

316. RUSTIC ARMCHAIR, WITH FESTOONED OPENWORK BACK RAILS. 18th C.

Jointed and chamfered rustic armchair, with back rails pierced with clover-leaves and circles. A charming example of a peasant armchair. It is very rare to find a chair made completely in pine.

w. 1' 8⅝"   H. 3' ¾"   D. 1' 5⅝"
52 cm   94 cm   44 cm
WOOD : pine

PROVENANCE : Les Éboulements, P.Q.

(Coll. Miss Barbara Richardson, Sainte-Agathe des Monts, P.Q.).

317. PRIEST'S CHAIR, FROM THE OLD CHURCH OF LOUISEVILLE, IN THE LOUIS XIII MANNER. 18th C.

Upholstered armchair, which was used by the celebrant during High Mass. The brackets or consoles of the armrest supports are *Os de mouton*, not in the same style as the chamfered understructure. The extremities of the feet have been sawn off.

w. 2' ¼"   H. 3' 1"   D. 2' 8"
61 cm   94 cm   81 cm
WOOD : birch

PROVENANCE : Old Church of Louiseville, P.Q.

(Coll. Miss Barbara Richardson, Sainte-Agathe des Monts, P.Q.).

318. RUSTIC ARMCHAIR, FROM ST SCHOLASTIQUE. 19th C.

Armchair, with shaped and openwork back. The upper back rail is of the Queen Anne and Windsor chair type, and seems to have been assembled with the wrong side up.

w. 1' 6¾" H. 3' 3" D. 1' 8¾"
48 cm   99 cm   53 cm

WOOD : birch

(Coll. Mrs Richard R. Costello, Sainte-Agathe des Monts, P.Q.).

319. RUSTIC ARMCHAIR, WITH OPENWORK ARMRESTS. EARLY 19th C.

Very original peasant armchair. The openwork armrest is undoubtedly a hand hold. The splayed back shows English influence.

w. 1' 7¾" H. 2' 10" D. 1' 4¾"
50 cm   86 cm   43 cm

WOOD : birch PROVENANCE : Montreal district

(Coll. Mr L.V. Randall, Montreal).

320. CURULE ARMCHAIR, IN THE ROMAN STYLE. 18th C.

Armchair, copied from a Roman curule chair. It has been said that it was a celebrant's armchair, but the narrowness and shallowness of the seat do not bear out this hypothesis. The upper back rail is of Windsor chair derivation.

w. 1' 10" H. 2' 9" D. 11"
56 cm   84 cm   28 cm

WOOD : birch PROVENANCE : Quebec district

(Coll. Royal Ontario Museum, Toronto, Ont.).

321. RUSTIC ARMCHAIR. 18th C.

Rustic armchair. The vertical slats in the back frame are cut out (a debased variation of the turned baluster back). The front seat rail is shaped. Painted in black. A primitive seat, but of agreeable proportions.

w. 1' 9" H. 3' 2" D. 1' 2¾"
53 cm   97 cm   38 cm

WOOD : birch PROVENANCE : Quebec district

(Coll. Canada Steamship Lines, Tadoussac, P.Q.).

322. CANADIAN ARMCHAIR " A LA CAPUCINE ". 18th C.

Canadian armchair *à la capucine*. It is the most elegant of our rush-seat chairs. Although it is related to the French provincial *Bonne Femme* armchair, it is distinguished from it by its profusion of chamfered cubes and its turned rungs. The armrest supports are fitted into the first lateral rung. The shaped back rails are conventional, being typical of the *Bonne Femme* armchairs from the Valley of the

Loire. A very popular chair in Canada especially in the Montreal district. (Cf. p. 227.)

w. 1' 6½" H. 3' 4" D. 1' 5"
47 cm   102 cm   43 cm

WOOD : birch PROVENANCE : New England

(Coll. Miss Barbara Richardson, Sainte-Agathe des Monts, P.Q.).

323. RUSTIC ARMCHAIR " A LA CAPUCINE ". 18th C.

This type of very simple and elegant armchair usually has four shaped back rails. Sometimes the armrests were set back as in no. 322. This one, although simple, is of pleasant proportions. The rush bottom has been replaced.

w. 1' 6½" H. 3' 4" D. 1' 5"
47 cm   102 cm   43 cm

WOOD : birch

PROVENANCE : Saint-Philippe de Laprairie, P.Q.

(Coll. Dr and Mrs Herbert T. Schwarz, Montreal).

324. RUSTIC ARMCHAIR, WITH WINGS. 18th C.

Fine Canadian rustic armchair, with armrests and wings, in the Louis XIII manner. Recent rawhide seat. The original green paint remains, but the feet have been worn away.

w. 2' 1" H. 3' 7½" D. 1' 5"
63 cm   110 cm   43 cm

WOOD : birch PROVENANCE : Montreal district

(Coll. Canada Steamship Lines, Tadoussac, P.Q.).

325. RUSTIC ARMCHAIR, WITH WINGS AND SHAPED RAILS. 18th C.

A very interesting peasant armchair which gives one the feel of the woodworker's craft. It brings to mind the robust peasant armchairs of the Savoie mountains. A very Canadian interpretation. The seat has been recovered in rawhide, and the feet have been worn away.

w. 1' 9½" H. 3' 4¼" D. 1' 9"
55 cm   102 cm   53 cm

WOOD : ash and birch

PROVENANCE : Quebec district

(Coll. Canada Steamship Lines, Tadoussac, P.Q.).

326. RUSTIC ARMCHAIR OF NAIVE WORKMANSHIP. EARLY 19th C.

Rustic armchair, with small wings and two shaped back splats of naive workmanship. The seat is of new rawhide.

w. 1' 8½" H. 3' 9¼" D. 1' 5"
52 cm   115 cm   43 cm

WOOD : birch PROVENANCE : Quebec district

(Coll. Canada Steamship Lines, Tadoussac, P.Q.).

327. RUSTIC ARMCHAIR, WITH WINGS AND SHAPED OPENWORK BACK. EARLY 19th C.

Rustic armchair, with wings. Two of the back rails are shaped, and one is in openwork. The beaded slats have arrowheads at their tips, derived from American arrow-back chairs. The seat is of elm bark, in basket-weave pattern. Original green colouring.

W. 1' 10" 56 cm | H. 3' 7¾" 111 cm | D. 1' 3¾" 40 cm

WOOD : birch PROVENANCE : Quebec district

(Coll. Canada Steamship Lines, Tadoussac, P.Q.).

328. RUSTIC ARMCHAIR, WITH ARMRESTS IN THE QUEEN ANNE MANNER. EARLY 19th C.

Country-type armchair. The upper back rail, with its spirals, recalls some Windsor chairs. The heavily inclined armrests, also spiralled, are derived from Queen Anne chairs. The seat has been recovered in rawhide. Original yellow colouring.

W. 1' 7⅜" 49 cm | H. 3' 3" 99 cm | D. 1' 2½" 37 cm

WOOD : birch PROVENANCE : Montreal district

(Coll. Canada Steamship Lines, Tadoussac, P.Q.).

329. RUSTIC ARMCHAIR, FROM ST FÉRÉOL. EARLY 19th C.

Typical armchair, from the St Joachim and St Féréol districts, with shaped flat slats in the back. The seat is woven with sea-grass from Cap Tourmente, and was recently restored by one of the last *habitant* rush-chair weavers in Canada.

W. 1' 10¾" 53 cm | H. 3' 6¾" 109 cm | D. 1' 7" 48 cm

WOOD : birch PROVENANCE : Saint-Féréol, P.Q.

(Coll. of the author, Petite Rivière Saint-François, P.Q.).

330. RUSTIC ARMCHAIR, WITH SHAPED AND PIERCED BACK RAILS. 19th C.

Rustic armchair, with three shaped and pierced back rails, reminiscent of the openwork in certain American Chippendale armchairs. The armrests are slightly curved. Original red colouring. Recent rawhide seat.

W. 1' 11⅝" 58 cm | H. 3' 2½" 98 cm | D. 1' 6" 46 cm

WOOD : birch

(Coll. Canada Steamship Lines, Tadoussac, P.Q.).

331. RUSTIC TURNED ARMCHAIR, OF AMERICAN DERIVATION. EARLY 19th C.

Rustic armchair, with turning in the American manner. The three back rails and the arched upper rail are typical of Pennsylvanian or "Shaker" armchairs. Seat of elm bark, in basket-weave pattern.

W. 1' 8⅝" 52 cm | H. 3' ¾" 94 cm | D. 1' 4" 41 cm

WOOD : birch and ash PROVENANCE : Montreal district

(Coll. Mr and Mrs Gordon Reed, Saint-Sauveur des Monts, P.Q.).

332. RUSTIC ARMCHAIR, WITH WINGS, AND SPINDLED ARMRESTS AND BACK. EARLY 19th C.

Rustic armchair, with wings, spindled armrests and a double row of spindles in the back, reminiscent of *Bergère* armchairs, but with turning of American derivation. Original rose colouring. Recent rawhide seat.

W. 2' 1½" 65 cm | H. 3' 2¾" 98 cm | D. 1' 6¾" 48 cm

WOOD : birch PROVENANCE : Isle of Orleans, P.Q.

(Coll. Canada Steamship Lines, Tadoussac, P.Q.).

333. RUSTIC ARMCHAIR, WITH WINGS AND BALUSTERS. LATE 18th C.

Rustic armchair, with wings and spindles in the back. The understructure recalls the turning of the first English jointed chairs, and American chairs of the "Brewster and Carver" type. It is a combination of two styles: the overall structure with its armrests and balusters is in the Louis XIII tradition but the turning is of American derivation. Recent cane seat.

W. 1' 11¾" 60 cm | H. 3' 7" 109 cm | D. 1' 5" 43 cm

WOOD : birch PROVENANCE : Grand'Mère, P.Q.

(Coll. Mr and Mrs Pierre Gouin, Saint-Sulpice, P.Q.).

334. RUSTIC ARMCHAIR, WITH OPENWORK BACK RAILS. EARLY 19th C.

Country-style armchair, with turned armrests and front posts. The back rails are pierced with upturned hearts, circles, houses, a *palmette*, a lozenge, and a spinning top. The turning and the armrests definitely show the influence of the first "Cromwell" period, and are widely distributed in New England. Recent rawhide seat.

W. 2' ½" 62 cm | H. 3' 4" 102 cm | D. 1' 6¼" 46 cm

WOOD : birch PROVENANCE : Berthier-en-Bas, P.Q.

(Coll. Canada Steamship Lines, Tadoussac, P.Q.).

335. RUSTIC ARMCHAIR, WITH TURNING OF NEW ENGLAND TYPE. LATE 18th C.

This armchair is visibly derived from the "Brewster and Carver" armchairs from New England. Note the sausages *(saucissons)* on the back rails. The general form, the armrests and the balusters are in the Louis XIII manner. Recent woven rush-seat.

| w. 2' 2" | H. 3' 4¾" | D. 1' 6⅜" |
| 66 cm | 104 cm | 47 cm |

WOOD : birch PROVENANCE : Montreal, P.Q.

(Coll. Miss Barbara Richardson, Sainte-Agathe des Monts, P.Q.).

336. RUSTIC ARMCHAIR, IN THE LOUIS XIV MANNER. 18th C.

Rustic armchair, with curved feet, in the Louis XIV manner. The seat rail, posts and back rails are shaped. The curved feet and armrests show English influence. According to oral tradition it came from the *Seigneurie de la Naudière*, in St Anne de la Pérade and would have been ceded by the *seigneur* to an ancestor of the present owner. See chair no. 275 which has the same type of back. A very fine regional armchair.

| w. 2' 1¼" | H. 3' 4¾" | D. 1' 6⅝" |
| 64 cm | 104 cm | 48 cm |

WOOD : birch PROVENANCE : Deschambault, P.Q.

(Coll. Mr Alexis Germain, farmer, Deschambault, P.Q.).

337. ARMCHAIR, IN THE LOUIS XIV MANNER, BUT WITH CABRIOLE ARM SUPPORTS IN THE CHIPPENDALE STYLE. 18th C.

Armchair, in the Late Louis XIV manner, with curved *pieds de biche*, and shaped seat rail and back. The accentuated curve of the cabriole arm supports shows Chippendale influence. Upholstered in horse-hair.

| w. 2' 2½" | H. 3' 5" | D. 1' 11½" |
| 67 cm | 104 cm | 60 cm |

WOOD : birch PROVENANCE : Quebec

(Coll. Mrs Paul Gouin, Montreal).

338. ARMCHAIR, IN THE RÉGENCE MANNER. LATE 18th C.

Canadian armchair, in the *Régence* manner, having curved feet, with seat rail and upper back rail carved with acanthus leaves and shells. One of the rare *Régence* armchairs made by a skilled hand, undoubtedly by a church woodworker and carver. Another one from the same woodworker is in the Church of the Hurons of Jeune-Lorette. Crosss-stretchers of the *double chapeau de gendarme* type.

| w. 2' 1" | H. 2' 4" | D. 1' 10" |
| 64 cm | 71 cm | 56 cm |

WOOD : birch

(Coll. David and Eleanor Morrice, Montreal).

339. ARMCHAIR, IN THE LOUIS XV MANNER, BUT IN CANADIAN ROCOCO STYLE. EARLY 19th C.

Armchair, in the Louis XV manner, having a serpentine-shaped seat rail carved with floral motifs and spirals. The back is also shaped and ornamented with spirals and a stylized shell. This seat has not the finesse of contemporary Louis XV furniture but suggests the work of the Quevillon School. The armrest supports are of Chippendale derivation.

| w. 2' 3" | H. 2' 2" | D. 1' 9" |
| 69 cm | 66 cm | 53 cm |

WOOD : birch PROVENANCE : Ile Bizard, P.Q.

(Coll. Detroit Institute of Arts, Detroit, Mich. U.S.A.).

340. ARMCHAIR, IN THE LOUIS XIV AND LOUIS XV MANNERS. LATE 18th C.

Armchair, in the Louis XV manner, with shaped seat rail. The serpentine-shaped back is of Louis XIV inspiration. The curves of the armrest supports do not harmonize with the shallow curve of the feet.

| w. 2' 2½" | H. 3' 7¼" | D. 1' 11" |
| 67 cm | 110 cm | 58 cm |

WOOD : birch PROVENANCE : Montreal district

(Coll. Mr Jean Dubuc, Quebec).

341. ARMCHAIR, IN THE RÉGENCE MANNER. LATE 18th C.

Armchair, in the *Régence* manner, with serpentine-shaped upper back rail in the Louis XIV manner. The bracket-type armrest supports belong to *Os de mouton* chairs. Curious combination of styles. A Canadian transitional piece. Very rare.

| w. 2' | H. 3' 9" | D. 1' 8¼" |
| 61 cm | 114 cm | 51 cm |

WOOD : birch PROVENANCE : Quebec district

(Coll. Mrs L.S. Bloom, Montreal).

342. ARMCHAIR, IN THE RÉGENCE MANNER. LATE 18th C.

Armchair, of *Régence* derivation, with cross-stretchers, and shaped seat rail and back. The shaped seat is typical of *Régence* caned chairs. The curve on the feet lacks finesse.

| w. 2' 1½" | H. 3' | D. 1' 8" |
| 65 cm | 91 cm | 51 cm |

WOOD : birch PROVENANCE : Montreal district

(Coll. Peter and William Dobell, Lac Memphremagog, P.Q.).

299. FAUTEUIL D'ESPRIT LOUIS XIII. XVIIIᵉ S.
ARMCHAIR, IN THE LOUIS XIII MANNER.
18th C.

300. FAUTEUIL, AU DOSSIER A DOUCINE,
D'ESPRIT LOUIS XIII. XVIIIᵉ S.
ARMCHAIR, WITH SERPENTINE TOP RAIL,
IN THE LOUIS XIII MANNER. 18th C.

302. FAUTEUIL AU DOSSIER A BALUSTRES,
D'ESPRIT LOUIS XIII. FIN XVIIᵉ S.
ARMCHAIR, WITH DOUBLE-BALUSTER BACK,
IN THE LOUIS XIII MANNER. LATE 17th C.

301. FAUTEUIL « A CRÉMAILLÈRE », D'ESPRIT
LOUIS XIII. XVIIᵉ S.
ARMCHAIR "A CRÉMAILLÈRE", IN THE
LOUIS XIII MANNER. 17th C.

303. FAUTEUIL AU DOSSIER A BALUSTRES ET A
PANNEAUX, D'ESPRIT LOUIS XIII. XVIIᵉ S.
ARMCHAIR, WITH PANEL AND BALUSTER BACK,
IN THE LOUIS XIII MANNER. 17th C.

304. FAUTEUIL AU PIÈTEMENT CHANFREINÉ,
D'ESPRIT LOUIS XIII. XVIIᵉ S.
ARMCHAIR, WITH CHAMFERED FEET, IN THE
LOUIS XIII MANNER. 17th C.

306. FAUTEUIL RUSTIQUE, D'ESPRIT LOUIS XIII.
XVIIIᵉ S.
RUSTIC ARMCHAIR, IN THE LOUIS XIII MANNER.
18th C.

305. FAUTEUIL DE FORME LOUIS XIII, DE JEUNE-
LORETTE. XVIIIᵉ S.
ARMCHAIR, OF LOUIS XIII TYPE, FROM JEUNE-
LORETTE. 18th C.

307. FAUTEUIL « OS DE MOUTON ». XVIIIe S.
" OS DE MOUTON " ARMCHAIR.   18th C.

308. FAUTEUIL « OS DE MOUTON ». XVIIIe S.
" OS DE MOUTON " ARMCHAIR.   18th C.

309. FAUTEUIL « OS DE MOUTON ». XVIIIe S.
" OS DE MOUTON " ARMCHAIR.   18th C.

310. FAUTEUIL A PIEDS EN CONSOLE ET A
CEINTURE ARBALÈTE. XVIIIe S.
ARMCHAIR, WITH CONSOLE LEGS AND
ARBALÈTE-FRONTED SEAT RAIL.   18th C.

FAUTEUIL PAYSAN. XVIIIᵉ S.
SANT ARMCHAIR. 18th C.

312. FAUTEUIL RUSTIQUE CHANFREINÉ AVEC
DOSSIER A FUSEAUX. XVIIIᵉ S.
RUSTIC CHAMFERED ARMCHAIR, WITH SPIN-
DLE BACK. 18th C.

313. GRAND FAUTEUIL, DE L'ILE D'ORLÉANS.
XVIIIᵉ S.
LARGE ARMCHAIR FROM ILE D'ORLÉANS.
18th C.

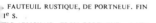

FAUTEUIL RUSTIQUE, DE PORTNEUF. FIN
Iᵉ S.
TIC ARMCHAIR, FROM PORTNEUF. LATE
C.

315. FAUTEUIL RUSTIQUE A PIÈTEMENT
TOURNÉ. XVIIIᵉ S.
RUSTIC ARMCHAIR, WITH TURNED LEGS.
18th C.

316. FAUTEUIL RUSTIQUE AUX TRAVERSES
DU DOSSIER FESTONNÉES ET AJOURÉES.
XVIIIᵉ S.
RUSTIC ARMCHAIR, WITH FESTOONED OPEN-
WORK BACKRAILS. 18th C.

317. FAUTEUIL DU PRÊTRE, DE L'ANCIENNE
ÉGLISE DE LOUISEVILLE, D'ESPRIT LOUIS XIII.
XVIIIe S.
PRIEST'S CHAIR, FROM THE OLD CHURCH
OF LOUISEVILLE, IN THE LOUIS XIII MAN-
NER. 18th C.

318. FAUTEUIL RUSTIQUE, DE SAINTE-SCHO-
LASTIQUE. XIXe S.
RUSTIC ARMCHAIR, FROM ST SCHOLASTIQUE.
19th C.

319. FAUTEUIL RUSTIQUE AVEC ACCOUD
AJOURÉS. DÉBUT XIXe S.
RUSTIC ARMCHAIR, WITH OPENWORK A
RESTS. EARLY 19th C.

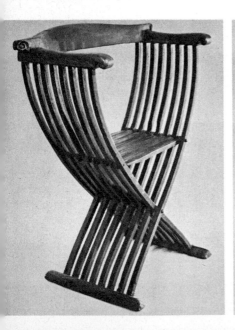

320. FAUTEUIL CURULE OU A TENAI
XVIIIe S.
CURULE ARMCHAIR, IN THE ROMAN ST
18th C.

321. FAUTEUIL RUSTIQUE. XVIIIe S.
RUSTIC ARMCHAIR. 18th C.

322. FAUTEUIL CANADIEN « A LA CAPUCINE ». XVIIIᵉ S.
CANADIAN ARMCHAIR " A LA CAPUCINE ". 18th C.

323. FAUTEUIL RUSTIQUE « A LA CAPUCINE ». XVIIIe S.
RUSTIC ARMCHAIR " A LA CAPUCINE ".   18th C.

324. FAUTEUIL RUSTIQUE A OREILLES. XVIIIe S.
RUSTIC ARMCHAIR, WITH WINGS.   18th C.

325. FAUTEUIL RUSTIQUE A OREILLES ET A TRAVERSES
CHANTOURNÉES. XVIIIe S.
RUSTIC ARMCHAIR, WITH WINGS AND SHAPED RAILS.
18th C.

326. FAUTEUIL RUSTIQUE, DE FACTURE NAIVE. DÉBUT XIXᵉ S.
RUSTIC ARMCHAIR OF NAIVE WORKMANSHIP. EARLY 19th C.

327. FAUTEUIL RUSTIQUE A OREILLES ET AU DOSSIER CHANTOURNÉ ET AJOURÉ. DÉBUT XIXᵉ S.
RUSTIC ARMCHAIR, WITH WINGS AND SHAPED OPENWORK BACK. EARLY 19th C.

328. FAUTEUIL RUSTIQUE AUX ACCOUDOIRS D'ESPRIT « QUEEN ANNE ». DÉBUT XIXᵉ S.
RUSTIC ARMCHAIR, WITH ARMRESTS IN THE QUEEN ANNE MANNER. EARLY 19th C.

329. FAUTEUIL RUSTIQUE, DE SAINT-FÉRÉOL. DÉBUT XIXᵉ S.
RUSTIC ARMCHAIR, FROM ST FÉRÉOL. EARLY 19th C.

330. FAUTEUIL RUSTIQUE AUX TRAVERSES DU DOSSIER CHANTOURNÉES ET AJOURÉES. XIXe S.
RUSTIC ARMCHAIR, WITH SHAPED AND PIERCED BACKRAILS. 19th C.

331. FAUTEUIL RUSTIQUE TOURNÉ, D'INSPIRATION AMÉRICAINE. DÉBUT XIXe S.
RUSTIC TURNED ARMCHAIR, OF AMERICAN DERIVATION. EARLY 19th C.

332. FAUTEUIL RUSTIQUE A OREILLES DOSSIER ET AUX ACCOUDOIRS ORNÉS FUSEAUX. DÉBUT XIXe S.
RUSTIC ARMCHAIR, WITH WINGS, SPINDLED ARMRESTS AND BACK. E. 19th C.

333. FAUTEUIL RUSTIQUE A OREILLES ET A BALUSTRES. FIN XVIIIe S.
RUSTIC ARMCHAIR, WITH WINGS AND BALUSTERS. LATE 18th C.

334. FAUTEUIL RUSTIQUE AUX TRAVERSES DU DOSSIER AJOURÉES. DÉBUT XIXe S.
RUSTIC ARMCHAIR, WITH OPENWORK BACKRAILS. EARLY 19th C.

335. FAUTEUIL RUSTIQUE, D'INFLUENC NOUVELLE-ANGLETERRE. FIN XVIIIe S.
RUSTIC ARMCHAIR, WITH TURNING NEW ENGLAND TYPE. LATE 18th C.

336. FAUTEUIL RUSTIQUE, D'ESPRIT LOUIS XIV.
XVIIIᵉ S.
RUSTIC ARMCHAIR, IN THE LOUIS XIV
MANNER. 18th C.

337. FAUTEUIL D'ESPRIT LOUIS XIV, AVEC SUPPORTS
D'ACCOUDOIRS D'INSPIRATION CHIPPENDALE. XVIIIᵉ S.
ARMCHAIR, IN THE LOUIS XIV MANNER, BUT WITH
CABRIOLE ARM SUPPORTS IN THE CHIPPENDALE STYLE.
18th C.

338. FAUTEUIL, D'ESPRIT RÉ-
GENCE. FIN XVIIIᵉ S.
ARMCHAIR, IN THE RÉGENCE
MANNER. LATE 18th C.

339. FAUTEUIL D'INSPIRATION LOUIS XV, MAIS DE STYLE
ROCOCO CANADIEN. DÉBUT XIXᵉ S.
ARMCHAIR, IN THE LOUIS XV MANNER, BUT IN CANA-
DIAN ROCOCO STYLE.   EARLY 19th C.

340. FAUTEUIL, D'INSPIRATION LOUIS XIV-
LOUIS XV. FIN XVIIIᵉ S.
ARMCHAIR, IN THE LOUIS XIV AND LOUIS XV
MANNERS.   LATE 18th C.

341. FAUTEUIL, D'ESPRIT RÉGENCE. FIN
XVIIIᵉ S.
ARMCHAIR, IN THE RÉGENCE MANNER.
LATE 18th C.

342. FAUTEUIL, D'INSPIRATION RÉGENCE. FIN
XVIIIᵉ S.
ARMCHAIR, IN THE RÉGENCE MANNER.
LATE 18th C.

ROCKING CHAIRS

According to two American authors [1] the rocking chair (called *chaise berceuse, chaise berçante* in French Canada) was invented by Benjamin Franklin who had one made as early as 1763. No mention is made of English rocking chairs in the important *Dictionary of English Furniture* by Macquoid and Edwards. William Savery, a woodworker in Philadelphia, added rockers to a straight chair in 1774,[2] and it soon became fashionable to convert existing Windsor chairs into rocking chairs.

The account books of the woodworkers Nathaniel Dominy IV and V of East Hampton, Long Island, show that they were adding rockers to chairs from 1801 [3] but it was not until after 1820 that the celebrated Boston rocker, the first rocking chair to be specifically designed as such, made its appearance [4]. It is clear that Canadian woodworkers imitated American designs by adding rockers to the straight country chairs and armchairs. In France it was unknown, except in the châteaux and in the homes of the upper bourgeoisie, where one would be kept for the wet-nurse while she rocked the infant, hence the name, *fauteuil de nourrice* (nurse's armchair). This chair was square, and had a high back of cross rails. No other model is known. I have seen only one of these French rocking chairs in a museum. It seems however that the rocking chair has quite recently won popularity in Paris, although of course it has long been used in Finland and Sweden.

In French Canada, rocking chairs eliminated the straight armchair and became the standard chair for all the family. There are curved rockers like cradles, some with arms, others without. Grandpa's chair *(chaise à pépère)* was placed beside the stove where grandfather smoked his pipe and poked the fire while rocking. Grandma's chair *(chaise à mémère)* was placed by the window in the summertime. It was narrower and the armrests were lower, making it easier for her to sew or to take the children in her arms and rock them. There is also a two-seated rocking chair, one for the suitor *(cavalier)* and the other for his girl *(blonde)*.

The armchair in olden times and the rocking chair today are symbols of good hospitality in Quebec country homes. If a complete stranger wishes to enter a house, he has only to knock and walk in. He will find the housewife alone in the kitchen, and she will usually leave her rocking chair and politely offer it to the visitor as the most comfortable seat in the house, without asking questions, and an atmosphere of confidence and cordiality is established by this simple gesture of welcome.

Even nowadays when you pass through a French Canadian village on a Sunday afternoon, the sight of ten to twenty people of all ages rocking together on the veranda, each in his own rhythm, has an almost hallucinatory character.

In the United States and Canada, people of all levels of society are united into a single class by this rocking movement, which resembles to soulless swinging of a pendulum, whose purely mechanical rhythm consumes time.

This does not alter the fact that this chair, whose original purpose was to enable the mother or nurse to rock an infant, gave free rein to the imagination of the country woodworker

---

(1) Esther Stevens and Walter A. Dyer.

(2) According to Charles F. Hummel, Associate Curator of the Henry Francis Du Pont Winterthur Museum, Winterthur, Delaware.

(3) Idem.

(4) Neither the invention of the rocking chair nor of the " Boston Rocker " can necessarily be attributed to the Americans. In Morazzoni's valuable book " Il Mobile Veneziano " (1958), a rocking chair of the type " Boston Rocker " is reproduced amongst examples of typically 18th c. Venetian furniture.

which he used with joy to produce the infinitely varied forms of this piece of furniture that became so closely integrated with daily life.

This chair is now produced on the assembly line in chrome tubing and loud-coloured plastic. The rocker has lost its charm.

343. RUSTIC ROCKING CHAIR, THE SPLATS PIERCED WITH HEARTS. 19th C.

Rustic rocking chair, with splats pierced with hearts. The majority of rocking chairs were assembled with rungs, which were inserted into the posts, in the same way as *à la capucine* chairs, and were in most cases made by *habitants*. The great naivety of this piece renders it odd and amusing.

W. 1' 4'' H. 3' 10½''
41 cm 118 cm

WOOD : birch and elm

PROVENANCE : Sainte-Geneviève de Batiscan, P.Q.

(Coll. National Museum of Canada, Ottawa).

344. RUSTIC ROCKING CHAIR, WITH SHAPED OPEN-WORK BACK RAILS. 19th C.

Rustic rocking chair, with shaped openwork back rails. Typical example of a chair made by a *habitant* woodworker who gave free rein to his imagination. Elm-bark seat in basket-weave pattern. A charmingly naive model.

W. 1' 8'' H. 3' 1¾'' D. 1' 1''
51 cm 96 cm 33 cm

WOOD : birch

(Coll. Mr and Mrs Victor M. Drury, Lake Anne, P.Q.).

345. RUSTIC ROCKING CHAIR, WITH FOUR BACK RAILS. 19th C.

Rustic rocking chair, with a high back and four shaped back rails. The seat has been renovated. A naive but elegant rocking chair.

W. 1' 7½'' H. 3' 8½'' D. 1' 2¼''
50 cm 113 cm 36 cm

WOOD : birch and oak

PROVENANCE : Saint-Denis-sur-Richelieu. P.Q.

(Coll. Mrs Nettie Sharpe, Saint-Lambert, P.Q.).

346. RUSTIC ROCKING CHAIR, WITH SIX BACK RAILS. 19th C.

Rustic rocking chair, with six shaped back rails. The splayed armrest supports allow for greater room. Rawhide seat. A fine example of a *habitant*-made rocking chair.

W. 1' 5½'' H. 3' 6'' D. 1' 5''
44 cm 107 cm 43 cm

WOOD : birch and ash

PROVENANCE : Lavaltrie, P.Q.

(Coll. Dr and Mrs Herbert T. Schwarz, Montreal).

347. RUSTIC ROCKING CHAIR, WITH SHAPED ROCKERS. 19th C.

Rustic rocking chair, with two back slats and shaped rockers. The armrest crosiers are carved with spirals on the outside, and geometric designs on the inside. The seat has been renovated.

W. 1' 7¾'' H. 3' 3½'' D. 1' 2''
50 cm 100 cm 36 cm

WOOD : birch and ash

PROVENANCE : Saint-Jean-Baptiste de Rouville, P.Q.

(Coll. Mrs Nettie Sharpe, Saint-Lambert, P.Q.).

348. RUSTIC ROCKING CHAIR, WITH OPENWORK BACK RAILS. 19th C.

Rustic rocking chair, with shaped openwork back rails and chamfered spindles. The front posts are splayed so as to allow for more room. The turned rungs recall those of more recent chairs. Wooden seat. A very original model.

W. 1' 8'' H. 4' 5½''
51 cm 136 cm

WOOD : birch

PROVENANCE : Saint-Jean Port Joli, P.Q.

(Coll. Mr Marius Barbeau, Ottawa).

349. RUSTIC ROCKING CHAIR, WITH OPENWORK BACK RAILS. 19th C.

Rustic rocking chair, having curved back posts with broad back rails shaped and in openwork. The openwork motif is reminiscent of sea-gulls in flight. Pinewood seat.

W. 1' 7'' H. 2' 6½'' D. 1' 2¼''
48 cm 77 cm 36 cm

WOOD : birch PROVENANCE : Beaumont, P.Q.

(Coll. Canada Steamship Lines, Tadoussac, P.Q.).

350. RUSTIC ROCKING CHAIR, WITH RAILS AND CROSS-STRETCHERS, IN THE SHERATON MANNER. 19th C.

Rustic rocking chair, with cross-rails and cross-stretchers of Sheraton derivation. The inclined armrests are similar to those on certain English armchairs. The finial in the Louis XIII manner clashes with the rest of the piece. Upholstered seat. A curious piece of furniture.

W. 1' 3½'' H. 1' 8''
39 cm 51 cm

WOOD : birch

(Coll. Mrs Richard R. Costello, Sainte-Agathe des Monts, P.Q.).

351. DETAIL.

Detail of the upper back rail of rocking chair no. 352. Stars, scrolls, curves, countercurves and flutings. Folk art.

352. RUSTIC ROCKING CHAIR, WITH WINGS DECORATED WITH SPIRALS. 19th C.

Rustic rocking chair, having wings decorated with spirals, and a shaped openwork back. The openwork designs of the upper rail are rather unusual. Rawhide seat. Black in colour.

w. 1' 10"	H. 3' 5½"	D. 1' 6"
56 cm	105 cm	46 cm

WOOD : birch and ash

(Coll. Canada Steamship Lines, Tadoussac, P.Q.).

353. RUSTIC ARROW-BACK ROCKING CHAIR. 19th C.

Rustic rocking chair, with vertical slats cut out in arrowhead form, an interpretation of the American arrow-back chair. Rawhide seat. Original colouring of red ochre.

w. 1' 8¼"	H. 3' 2¾"	D. 1' 2"
51 cm	98 cm	36 cm

WOOD : birch and pine

PROVENANCE : Baie Saint-Paul, P.Q.

(Coll. Canada Steamship Lines, Tadoussac, P.Q.).

354. RUSTIC ROCKING CHAIR, WITH SHAPED BACK. 19th C.

Rustic rocking chair, with four shaped vertical slats in the back frame, and a violin-shaped seat peculiar to Charlevoix county. Dark brown in colour.

WOOD : birch   PROVENANCE : Murray Bay, P.Q.

(Coll. Mr and Mrs J.N. Cole, Montreal).

355. HIGH-BACKED RUSTIC ROCKING CHAIR. 19th C.

Rustic rocking chair having a high back with three vertical slats. Chair of primitive character.

w. 1' 4¼"	H. 3' 5½"	D. 1' 4"
41 cm	105 cm	41 cm

WOOD : birch   PROVENANCE : Saint-Hilarion, P.Q.

(Coll. of the author, Petite Rivière Saint-François, P.Q.).

356. CHILD'S ROCKING HORSE. 19th C.

Child's rocking horse, with saddle-chair of American derivation. A toy of peasant workmanship.

w. 2' 6"	H. 1' 7"
76 cm	48 cm

WOOD : birch and pine

PROVENANCE : Saint-Vallier, P.Q.

(Coll. Mrs Nettie Sharpe, Saint-Lambert, P.Q.).

357. RUSTIC DOUBLE ROCKING CHAIR. 19th C.

Rustic rocking chair for two, with shaped back and pierced lozenges. This kind of seat is frequently found in the Quebec area, and was primarily used by courting couples, *le cavalier et sa blonde*, who rocked together on Sunday afternoons on the veranda. This seat is the precursor of the modern garden swing.

w. 3' 4"	H. 2' 3½"	D. 1' 4½"
102 cm	70 cm	42 cm

WOOD : birch and ash

PROVENANCE : Quebec district

(Coll. National Museum of Canada, Ottawa).

358. ROCKING-BENCH. 19th C.

Rocking-bench. A very unusual piece of furniture.

w. 6' 6⅜"	H. 2' 4"	D. 1' 5¼"
199 cm	71 cm	44 cm

WOOD : birch and pine

(Coll. Mr and Mrs Cleveland Morgan, Senneville, P.Q.).

359. ROCKING CHAIR, WITH SHAPED BACK IN MARQUETRY WORK.

Rocking chair, of a rather recent form, but with a seat in the form of unrolled parchment (phylactery) and inspired by the " Boston rocker ". The shaped back is decorated with hearts, clover-leaves and spades in inlaid work, made by the *habitant* woodworker Joseph Mailloux, of Baie St Paul, with oak staves taken from a barrel. Folk art.

w. 1' 5½"	H. 3' 6"	D. 1' 5"
44 cm	107 cm	43 cm

WOOD : oak and birch

PROVENANCE : Cap au Corbeau, Baie Saint-Paul, P.Q.

(Coll. Mr Marius Barbeau, Ottawa).

360. ROCKING CHAIR, OF THE " BOSTON ROCKER " TYPE. 19th C.

Rocking chair in the style known as the American " Boston rocker ". Note the curve of the unrolled scroll on the seat, and of the spirals on the armrests and upper back rail.

w. 1' 5¼"	H. 3' 6"	D. 1' 7½"
44 cm	107 cm	50 cm

WOOD : birch

(Coll. Provincial Museum, Quebec).

361. RUSTIC DOUBLE ROCKING CHAIR, WITH THREE ARMRESTS. 19th C.

Rustic rocking chair for two, having three armrests. Note that the front end posts are splayed to provide more room. The back posts show American influence.

w. 2' 8''   H. 3' 2''   D. 1' 5⅝''
   81 cm   97 cm   45 cm

WOOD : birch

PROVENANCE : Saint-Jean Port Joli, P.Q.

(Coll. Musée Provencher, Cap Rouge, P.Q.).

362. RUSTIC ROCKING CHAIR, WITH SHAPED SPINDLE BACK. 19th C.

Rustic rocking chair, with three shaped, openwork vertical slats surmounting four turned spindles. The general appearance of the chair suggests American influence, although the rails and spindles are turned in the Louis XIII style. The festoons recall Chinese Chippendale.

w. 1' 4¾''   H. 2' 10''   D. 1' ¾''
   43 cm   86 cm   32 cm

WOOD : birch   PROVENANCE : Murray Bay, P.Q.

(Coll. Miss Barbara Richardson, Sainte-Agathe des Monts, P.Q.).

363. RECENT RUSTIC ROCKING CHAIR.

Recent rustic rocking chair, having rails decorated with foliage and geometric designs and shaped back slats in openwork. Contemporary folk art.

w. 1' 6½''   H. 3' 4¼''   D. 1' 6''
   47 cm   102 cm   46 cm

WOOD : birch PROVENANCE : Lower St Lawrence

(Coll. Sir Wilfrid Laurier's house, Saint-Lin, P.Q.).

364. RUSTIC ROCKING CHAIR, OF AMERICAN DERIVATION, FROM ILE D'ORLÉANS. 19th C.

Rustic rocking chair, having characteristics of the jointed *Ile d'Orléans* chair in the understructure and features borrowed from the " Boston rocker " type in the back. Unbalanced in appearance.

w. 1' 4½''   H. 3'   D. 1' 7''
   42 cm   91 cm   48 cm

WOOD : birch SEAT : pine

PROVENANCE : Isle of Orleans, P.Q.

(Coll. Miss Emily Le Baron, North Hatley, P.Q.).

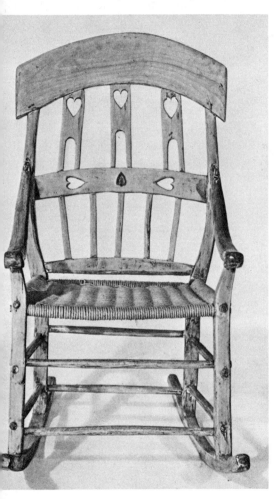

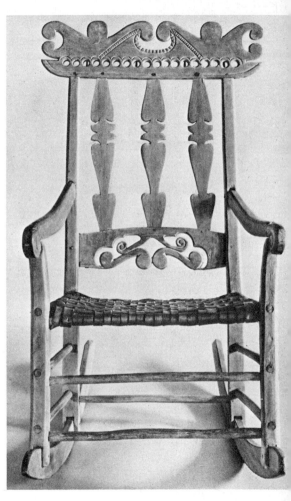

343. BERCEUSE RUSTIQUE, AVEC CŒURS
AJOURÉS. XIXᵉ S.
RUSTIC ROCKING CHAIR, THE SPLATS
PIERCED WITH HEARTS.   19th C.

344. BERCEUSE RUSTIQUE, A TRAVERSES DU
DOSSIER AJOURÉES ET CHANTOURNÉES.
XIXᵉ S.
RUSTIC ROCKING CHAIR, WITH SHAPED
OPENWORK BACKRAILS. 19th C.

346. BERCEUSE RUSTIQUE, A SIX TRAVERSES
DU DOSSIER. XIXᵉ S.
RUSTIC ROCKING CHAIR, WITH SIX BACK-
RAILS. 19th C.

345. BERCEUSE RUSTIQUE, A QUATRE TRAVERSES DU
DOSSIER. XIXᵉ S.
RUSTIC ROCKING CHAIR, WITH FOUR BACKRAILS.
19th C.

347. BERCEUSE RUSTIQUE, A PATINS CHAN-
TOURNÉS. XIXᵉ S.
RUSTIC ROCKING CHAIR, WITH SHAPED
ROCKERS. 19th C.

348. BERCEUSE RUSTIQUE, A TRAVERSES
DU DOSSIER AJOURÉES. XIXe S.
RUSTIC ROCKING CHAIR, WITH OPENWORK
BACKRAILS. 19th C.

350. BERCEUSE RUSTIQUE A TRAVERSES ET ENTRETOISES
D'ESPRIT SHERATON. XIXe S.
RUSTIC ROCKING CHAIR, WITH RAILS AND CROSS-
STRETCHERS, IN THE SHERATON MANNER. 19th C.

349. BERCEUSE RUSTIQUE, A DOSSIER AJOU-
RÉ. XIXe S.
RUSTIC ROCKING CHAIR, WITH OPENWORK
BACKRAILS. 19th C.

351. DÉTAIL. DETAIL.

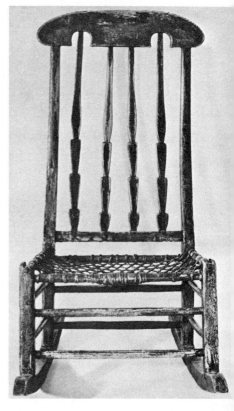

352. BERCEUSE RUSTIQUE A OREILLES ORNÉES DE SPIRALES. XIXᵉ S.
RUSTIC ROCKING CHAIR, WITH WINGS DECORATED WITH SPIRALS.   19th C.

353. BERCEUSE RUSTIQUE A « POINTES DE FLÈCHE ». XIXᵉ S.
RUSTIC ARROW-BACK ROCKING CHAIR. 19th C.

354. BERCEUSE RUSTIQUE A DOSSIER CHANTOURNÉ.
XIXe S.
RUSTIC ROCKING CHAIR, WITH SHAPED BACK.   19th C.

355. BERCEUSE RUSTIQUE A HAUT DOSSIER. XIXe S.
HIGH-BACKED RUSTIC ROCKING CHAIR.   19th C.

356. CHEVAL D'ENFANT, A BASCULE. XIXe S.
CHILD'S ROCKING HORSE.   19th C.

357. BERCEUSE RUSTIQUE A DEUX PLACES XIXᵉ S.
RUSTIC DOUBLE ROCKING CHAIR. 19th C.

358. BANC BERÇANT. XIXᵉ S.
ROCKING-BENCH. 19th C.

359. BERCEUSE A DOSSIER CHANTOURNÉ ET MARQUETÉ.
ROCKING CHAIR, WITH SHAPED BACK IN MARQUETRY
WORK.

360. BERCEUSE, DITE « BOSTON ROCKER ». XIXᵉ S.
ROCKING CHAIR, OF THE "BOSTON ROCKER" TYPE.
19th C.

361. BERCEUSE RUSTIQUE A DEUX SIÈGES ET TROIS
ACCOUDOIRS. XIXᵉ S.
RUSTIC DOUBLE ROCKING CHAIR, WITH THREE ARM-
RESTS. 19th C.

362. BERCEUSE RUSTIQUE A DOSSIER CHANTOURNÉ ET A FUSEAUX. XIXᵉ S
RUSTIC ROCKING CHAIR, WITH SHAPED SPINDLE BACK. 19th C.

363. BERCEUSE RUSTIQUE RÉCENTE
RECENT RUSTIC ROCKING CHAIR.

364. BERCEUSE RUSTIQUE DE L'ILE
D'ORLÉANS, D'INFLUENCE AMÉRI-
CAINE. XIXᵉ S.
RUSTIC ROCKING CHAIR, OF AMERI-
CAN DERIVATION, FROM ILE D'OR-
LÉANS. 19th C.

TABLES, WASH-STANDS, CONSOLE TABLES

TABLES

Square, round and oval tables were to be found in the homes of Canadian *habitants*, according to inventories of the period 1650-1760, but the long tables which were common in the homes of French peasants are rarely mentioned. " A square table of pine, without turnings, partly worn... "[1], " ... an old round table, with pine leaf... "[2], " ... an oval pine table, with flaps... a large oval table of pine with leaves. "[3]

Folding tables *(tables pliantes* or *tables ployantes)* were most popular because they occupied little space when folded between meals and placed against a wall in the common room, which naturally had been reduced in size by the erection of partitions to form bedrooms. The top of the table was usually made of three large pine boards, or narrow planks with tongue and groove joints, and had a moulding around the edge. Sometimes the top would be framed and also tongued and grooved to prevent the planks from warping. Wooden pegs were inserted into the legs and apron to strengthen the top. The apron, legs, and stretchers were of birch (although occasionally they were made of pine) and were held together with mortise and tenon joints.

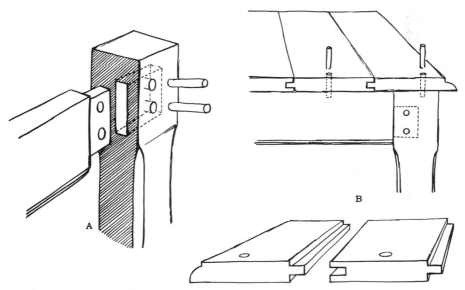

Fig. 6 - *Joints. A) Tenon and mortise joints, with pegs.*
B) Tongued and grooved joints.

(1) A J M, I O A. Invantaire de Jacques Cusson et Michelle Cholecq sa femme auparavant veuve de feu françois Viger le 20 décembre 1729, Montréal. Greffe Chaumont.

(2) A J M, I O A. Inventaire par Guillaume Tartre le 4 Xbre 1732, Montréal. Greffe Chaumont.

(3) A J M, I O A. Inventaire des biens de Pierre Buisson et de Françoise Levasseur sa femme, 30 septembre 1732, aubergiste à Montréal. Greffe Saint-Romain.

Folding tables had hinged leaves which were held in position by sliding supports, or by a pivoting leg or gate-leg on one or both sides of the table (*table à abattant*). A large number of these tables were fitted with one or two drawers: " Paid to Jean Gagnié for making four pine tables with two drawers... Six livres each at Quebec, the thirty-first of August 1740." [1] The legs of all these tables were plain, turned or chamfered. (A chamfer is a bevel cut made on the square edges or corners of a leg or rail to lighten its appearance.) An inventory of 1745 mentions the first table with *cabriole* legs (*pieds de biche*). There were also numerous trestle tables. The simplest tables were made by the peasants, the others by the village woodworkers.

It was around the common room table that the family assembled several times a day, as in our times. The father would sit at one end of the table, and cut the bread, passing it to each member of the family. With his left hand he would hold the large home-made loaf against his heart, cutting with his right hand and using his thumb to hold the slices, which he then distributed to the family with a broad symbolic gesture. It was not so long ago in Quebec that the mother was the servant and according to the custom of French peasants never sat at table with the family.

The three most common types of table-leg (all derived from Renaissance and Louis XIII styles) were turned legs, with matching stretchers (*à piètement tourné*) in Louis XIII style, found in most houses of the seventeenth and eighteenth centuries; single or double twisted spiral legs, with spiralled stretchers surmounted by a flame finial (*flambeau*) or by several finials on long tables, usually found in wealthier homes or in institutions; legs composed of a series of spheres (ball turning) in Renaissance style, but these were very rare.

There were several types of refectory table used in convents and monasteries. The legs were usually turned, or shaped in the form of lyres, pilasters or columns. Most of these tables had individual drawers. Peter Kalm noted during a visit to the Ursulines in Quebec in 1749, that in the refectory " ... the tables are fitted underneath with little drawers in which each nun keeps her napkin, knife and fork, and other small objects. " [2] These tables are also found in the *Hôtel-Dieu* and *Hôpital-Général*, Quebec.

There are also a number of little tables with a variety of curved legs in the *Régence* and Louis XV manners as well as demi-lune serving-tables, and little dressing-tables in the *Régence* manner, with cabriole legs. These were quite common in the home of the Canadian *habitant* after 1750, although they were rarely found in French peasant homes.

A table which was very popular in *habitant* homes in the nineteenth century was the table-chair (*table à bascule*). It had a round or square top which, when lifted, formed the back of a chair and was placed against the wall when not required as a table. The seat rail was often fitted with a drawer where food or cutlery could be kept. This table seems to have been unknown in France except for a few rare specimens of Norman origin, the tops of which however do not open. It would appear that the table-chair came from New England and Pennsylvania where it was called a hutch-table or monk's-chaise.

Another small table that was found in a few homes, and particularly in convents, was the sewing-table (*travailleuse*) with single or coupled legs. It sometimes had a lower shelf, and was often fitted with a drawer to hold needlework equipment.

Pedestal tables or candle tables (*guéridons*) were widespread in the seventeenth and eighteenth centuries but have almost completely disappeared today. They were round and had a single central leg that terminated in a tripod or turned disc. Candelabras, candlesticks or saucer-shaped candle holders (*martinets*) would be placed upon them, and as they were easy to carry, they would often be moved to the bedside for reading. There were also small country tables, perhaps the most interesting of all, to which peasant woodworkers added all sorts of naive touches, particularly in the shaping of the frieze.

(1) Quinsonas, Comte de. *Monseigneur de Laubérivière*. Paris, 1936, p. 175.
(2) Kalm, Peter. *Voyage en Amérique* (August 1749). Société Historique de Montréal, 1880, vol. 2, p. 114.

365. TABLE, IN THE HENRI IV AND LOUIS XIII MANNERS. 17th C.

Table, with legs turned in the form of superimposed spheres (also known as ball turning), held together by a double Y-shaped connecting stretcher. The frieze is in console form, with a prominent moulding at the base. This table was wholly inspired by the Henri IV and Louis XIII styles, and is the oldest table I know.

w. 3' 4''	H. 2' 3¾''	D. 2' 3¼''
102 cm	70 cm	69 cm

WOOD : pine   LEGS : birch

PROVENANCE : Quebec

(Coll. Musée de l'Hôpital-Général, Quebec).

366. TABLE, WITH SPIRALLY TURNED LEGS, IN THE LOUIS XIII MANNER. 17th C.

Table, with spirally turned legs, in the Louis XIII manner. The bun feet are in the shape of flat balusters *à la Bourguignonne*. The finial is missing. The drawer and pine-wood top are unfortunate later additions. A table typical of Burgundy and Lorraine.

w. 3' 3¼''	H. 2' 4''	D. 2' 2''
100 cm	71 cm	66 cm

WOOD : birch   PROVENANCE : Quebec

(Coll. Musée de l'Hôpital-Général, Quebec).

367. TABLE, WITH LEGS TURNED IN A DOUBLE SPIRAL, IN THE LOUIS XIII MANNER. 17th C.

Table, having legs turned in a double spiral and three finials; the centre one in openwork, a rare thing in France. Some of these tables were saved from the fire of the *Hôtel-Dieu*, Montreal, in 1695, and others were made after the same pattern by the woodworker Vincent Lenoir dit Le Tourangeau in 1697 to replace those which had been destroyed. Feet in flattened baluster form. The flame on one of the finials is missing; the top and the drawer are later additions.

w. 3' 4''	H. 2' 4¾''	D. 2' 2½''
102 cm	73 cm	67 cm

WOOD : birch

PROVENANCE : Hôtel-Dieu, Montreal

(Coll. Royal Ontario Museum, Toronto, Ont.).

368. TABLE, WITH FLAME FINIALS, IN THE LOUIS XIII STYLE. 17th C.

Table, with turned feet and three flame finials, in the Louis XIII style. The frieze has two drawers in the façade and lozenges on the back and sides. The drawers are a later addition; the original one would undoubtedly have been carved with lozenges as well. Another typical piece of Louis XIII derivation widely found in France and Canada. The

baroque element in the finials is a Canadian characteristic. A robust table.

w. 4' 3½''	H. 2' 4⅝''	D. 2' 7½''
131 cm	73 cm	85 cm

WOOD : birch and pine

PROVENANCE : Montreal

(Coll. Château de Ramezay, Montreal).

369. RUSTIC TABLE, IN THE LOUIS XIII MANNER. LATE 17th C.

Rustic table, with turned legs in the Louis XIII manner. The frieze decorated with lozenges has small finials. The feet are in bun or flattened baluster form. The colouring is original but the top is a later addition. A small and charming peasant table of the late seventeenth century.

w. 2' 7''	H. 2' 1½''	D. 1' 9½''
79 cm	65 cm	55 cm

WOOD : birch and pine

PROVENANCE : Gentilly, P.Q.

(Coll. Museum of Fine Arts, Montreal).

370. TABLE, WITH TURNED LEGS, IN THE LOUIS XIII MANNER. LATE 17th C.

Table, with turned legs and with two finials in the Louis XIII manner. The top and drawer were replaced a long time ago.

w. 2' 8¼''	H. 2' 4¼''	D. 1' 8½''
82 cm	72 cm	52 cm

WOOD : birch

PROVENANCE : Hôtel-Dieu, Montreal

(Coll. Dr and Mrs Claude Bertrand, Outremont, P.Q.).

371. TABLE, WITH TURNED LEGS, IN THE LOUIS XIII MANNER. 18th C.

Table, having turned legs in the Louis XIII manner, and horizontal mouldings along the drawer and frieze. The top is a later addition. A pretty little table, typical of seventeenth and eighteenth-century tables in the Louis XIII tradition.

w. 2' 6½''	H. 2' 3''	D. 1' 9¾''
77 cm	69 cm	55 cm

WOOD : birch.

PROVENANCE : Hôtel-Dieu, Montreal.

(Coll. Dr and Mrs Claude Bertrand, Outremont, P.Q.).

372. SMALL TABLE, WITH TURNED LEGS, IN THE LOUIS XIII MANNER. EARLY 18th C.

Small table, with turned legs in the Louis XIII manner, having drawers carved with lozenges and an upturned finial. Original hinged rings. Three finials are missing on the stretcher. Elegant turning. The pine-wood top is a later addition.

w. 3'	H. 2' 4''	D. 1' 11''
91 cm	71 cm	58 cm

WOOD : birch and wavy birch
PROVENANCE : Hôtel-Dieu, Montreal
(Coll. Dr and Mrs Claude Bertrand, Outremont, P.Q.).

373. TABLE, WITH TURNED LEGS AND ARBALÈTE-
FRONTED DRAWER. 18th C.
Table, with turned legs of Louis XIII derivation.
The extremities of the feet have bevelled edges.
The shaped frieze has two drawers in arbalète form.
One finial is missing and the top has been replaced.
Country-type turning.

| W. 3' 3¾" | H. 2' 2" | D. 1' 11¾" |
| 101 cm | 66 cm | 60 cm |

WOOD : elm core and hickory
PROVENANCE : Saint-Barnabé (near Saint-Hyacinthe)
(Coll. Mrs Nettie Sharpe, Saint-Lambert, P.Q.).

374. LARGE TABLE, IN THE LOUIS XIII MANNER, FOR-
MERLY OWNED BY THE CHARON BROTHERS. LATE
17th C.
Large table, with turned baluster legs and stretchers
with a finial in the centre. The frieze has two large
drawers. This table, according to an oral tradition of the Grey Nuns, came from the Charon
Brothers' Hospital *(Frères Hospitaliers de St Joseph
de la Croix),* which was founded in 1692, before
Madame d'Youville took it over in 1747. A massive table absolutely in the Louis XIII tradition.
Original hinged rings.

| W. 8' 7" | H. 2' 5" | D. 2' 8⅝" |
| 262 cm | 74 cm | 83 cm |

WOOD : birch PROVENANCE : Montreal
(Coll. Hôpital-Général of the Grey Nuns, Montreal).

375. LARGE TABLE, FROM THE DISPENSARY OF THE
HOTEL-DIEU, MONTREAL. EARLY 18th C.
Large dispensary table, having six drawers, turned
legs in the Louis XIII manner, and a profusion of
finials on the stretchers and frieze. It is believed
that this table at some time stood in a public ward
where it was used for the preparation of dressings, etc.
It came from a hospital and was called a *table
d'apothicairerie,* because it was used when preparing
medicaments. The top has been restored, but the
drawers and hinged rings are original. Another
such table, almost similar except that it has spirally
turned legs, is to be found in the Provincial Museum,
Quebec. It is contemporary to this one and to
other small tables of the same provenance. (Cf.
no. 370, 371, 372.) I have seen another fairly similar specimen of the same height and style at Nancy.

| W. 6' 6½" | H. 3' 1" | D. 2' 4¾" |
| 199 cm | 94 cm | 73 cm |

WOOD : birch PROVENANCE : Hôtel-Dieu, Montreal
(Coll. Detroit Institute of Arts, Detroit, Mich. U.S.A.).

376. REFECTORY TABLE, FROM THE URSULINE CON-
VENT, QUEBEC. 18th C.
Refectory table, with pilaster-shaped legs and five
drawers. This is the one described by Peter Kalm,
the Swedish botanist, on his visit to the Ursuline
Convent in Quebec in 1749. (Cf. p. 260.)

| W. 10' 1" | H. 2' 6½" | D. 2' ¾" |
| 307 cm | 77 cm | 62 cm |

WOOD : TOP, birch; BASE, pine
PROVENANCE : Ursuline Convent, Quebec
(Coll. Mr and Mrs L. Glen, Baie d'Urfé, P.Q.).

377. REFECTORY TABLE, FROM THE BROTHERS OF THE
CHRISTIAN SCHOOLS. 19th C.
Refectory table, with three pilaster-shaped legs,
bracket feet and fourteen drawers. This table
was widely used during the nineteenth century in
the Colleges run by the Brothers of Christian Schools
and was derived from the seventeenth-century Italian monastic tables. The brothers sat at both
sides and at both ends of the table. The drawer
handles are not the original ones; they are too heavy
and spoil the general appearance of the piece.
Wooden knobs or iron hinged rings would have
been more suitable.

| W. 12' 1" | H. 2' 6½" | D. 3' 6½" |
| 368 cm | 77 cm | 108 cm |

WOOD : pine
PROVENANCE : College of the Brothers of Christian
Schools, Laval des Rapides, P.Q.
*(Coll. Mr and Mrs Fred Mulligan, Pleasant Valley,
Henrysburg, P.Q.).*

378. KITCHEN TABLE, FROM THE HOTEL-DIEU, QUEBEC.
LATE 17th C.
Long kitchen table, having a turned understructure
and three drawers. It is a massive table with deep
drawers and heavy rails with mouldings. The very
thick maple top was probably used as a butcher's
table. Of Louis XIII derivation.

| W. 7' 11⅜" | H. 2' 5½" | D. 2' 5½" |
| 242 cm | 75 cm | 75 cm |

WOOD : maple PROVENANCE : Quebec
(Coll. Musée de l'Hôtel-Dieu, Quebec).

379. REFECTORY TABLE, FROM THE HOTEL-DIEU, QUE-
BEC. LATE 17th C.
Refectory table, having six drawers, three legs in
baluster form and a foot-rail. Each nun would
have her own drawer in which she would keep her
cutlery and pewter porringer. The Augustinian
Nuns of the *Hôtel-Dieu,* Quebec, have preserved
their old refectory tables. They are generally
placed along the refectory walls and the nuns sit
on benches with their backs to the wall. A typical
and very interesting piece of conventual furniture.

w. 8' 1¼''   H. 2' 5½''   D. 2'
    247 cm   75 cm   61 cm
WOOD : maple PROVENANCE : Quebec
(Coll. Hôtel-Dieu, Quebec).

380. REFECTORY TABLE, WITH TURNED LEGS AND DOUBLE STRETCHERS. LATE 18th C.
Refectory table, with turned legs and double stretchers. It is said to have come from the Trappist Monastery at Oka. New bun feet have been added to the original ones.
w. 6' 11½''   H. 2' 4''   D. 2' 8''
    212 cm   71 cm   81 cm
WOOD : pine and birch
PROVENANCE : Oka, P.Q.
(Coll. Mr and Mrs F.M. Hutchins, Pembroke, Ont.).

381. TABLE, WITH TURNED LEGS, IN THE LOUIS XIII MANNER. 18th C.
Table, with turned legs, stretchers and two drawers. It is typical of tables from the Bresse region of Burgundy. This one came from a convent. The top is a later addition.
w. 5' 2''   H. 2' 3½''   D. 3' 3''
    157 cm   70 cm   99 cm
WOOD : birch PROVENANCE : Sainte-Perpétue, P.Q.
(Coll. of the author, Montreal).

382. GATELEG TABLE, WITH LEGS IN THE LOUIS XIII MANNER. LATE 17th C.
Gateleg table, with turned legs in the Louis XIII manner. The top is supported by a pivoting leg called " gateleg ". This is the seventeenth and eighteenth-century common-room table mentioned in nearly all the inventories of the period. It did not take up much room when folded.
w. 3' 11½''   H. 2' 3½''   D. 3' 11½''
    121 cm   70 cm   121 cm
WOOD : pine
(Coll. Museum of Fine Arts, Montreal).

383. SMALL BEDSIDE TABLE, WITH TURNED LEGS. EARLY 18th C.
Small bedside table, with turned legs of Louis XIII derivation and stretchers in quadrilateral form. According to an oral tradition of the nuns of the *Hôtel-Dieu*, Quebec, these tables were used not long ago in the operating theatre to hold basins and instruments. I have seen some in the *Hospice de Beaune*, Burgundy, where they once served as bedside tables for the poster beds occupied by patients. The top is a later addition.
w. 1' 8''   H. 2' 2⅝''   D. 1' 9½''
    51 cm   68 cm   55 cm
WOOD : birch PROVENANCE : Quebec
(Coll. Musée de l'Hôtel-Dieu, Quebec).

384. RUSTIC FOLDING TABLE, WITH TURNED LEGS. LATE 18th C.
Rustic folding table, with turned legs of Louis XIII derivation, but in a peasant interpretation. It is a debased version of the conventional turnings of the Louis XIII style.
w. 3' 1''   H. 2' 3½''   D. 2'
    94 cm   70 cm   61 cm
WOOD : birch TOP : pine
PROVENANCE : Quebec district
(Coll. Provincial Museum, Quebec).

385. RUSTIC GATELEG TABLE, WITH TURNED LEGS. LATE 18th C.
Rustic gateleg table, with turned legs of Louis XIII derivation. Another very common eighteenth-century table found in *habitant* homes.
w. 4' ½''   H. 2' 4¼''   D. 3' 6''
    123 cm   72 cm   107 cm
WOOD : birch TOP : pine
PROVENANCE : Gentilly, P.Q.
(Coll. Mr and Mrs Scott Symons, Toronto, Ont.).

386. RUSTIC FOLDING OR GATELEG TABLE, WITH OVAL TOP. EARLY 19th C.
Rustic folding or gateleg table, with oval top, chamfered feet and stretchers in quadrilateral form. A type of table commonly found in rural homesteads from the seventeenth to the nineteenth centuries. The frieze has been raised two inches.
w. 5' 6¼''   H. 2' 2''   D. 3' 8⅝''
    168 cm   66 cm   113 cm
WOOD : pine
PROVENANCE : Saint-Jacques l'Achigan, P.Q.
(Coll. Mr and Mrs Roland Leduc, Montreal).

387. SMALL RUSTIC TABLE, WITH TURNED LEGS. LATE 18th C.
Small rustic table, with a single drawer. The turning on the feet is embellished with rings, and the stretcher has a finial in the centre. The turning is a debased variation of the Louis XIII style. The hinged ring on the drawer is original.
w. 3' 7''   H. 2' 2½''   D. 2' 3½''
    109 cm   67 cm   70 cm
WOOD : birch and pine
PROVENANCE : Saint-Henri de Lévis, P.Q.
(Coll. Mrs Nettie Sharpe, Saint-Lambert, P.Q.).

388. TABLE-CHAIR, WITH CUTLERY DRAWER, FROM RIVIÈRE OUELLE. EARLY 19th C.
Table-chair or hutch-table, with turned legs and double stretchers and a drawer for cutlery and dishes. (Cf. no. 389.)

w. 4'   H. 2' 1⅜''   D. 3' ¾''
122 cm   64 cm   101 cm

WOOD : birch and pine

PROVENANCE : Rivière Ouelle, P.Q.

(Coll. Canada Steamship Lines, Tadoussac, P.Q.).

389. TABLE-CHAIR, FROM LA MALBAIE. EARLY 19th C.

Table-chair (or hutch-table), with turned legs and stretchers in quadrilateral form. This type of table was very popular during the nineteenth century in the Lower St Lawrence Valley, especially along the Côte de Beaupré, and in Charlevoix county, where it was the only table in the common room. Nearly all the houses on Ile aux Coudres possessed one. The top can be lifted to form an armchair which could be set against the wall during *veillées* (Cf. p. 260). I have found this kind of table in Normandy, and in the Épernay district in Champagne, but there the top is more often elliptical and does not lift up. It is called a " food-locker table " in France, since it had a drawer in which food, cutlery and dishes could be kept. In New England and Pennsylvania where it was widely known, it is called " hutch-table " or " bench-table ". I believe that this table, in the form we know it, was borrowed from the United States, although the type existed in England. This particular one was found in the municipal rubbish dump of Murray Bay.

w. 4'   H. 2' 1½''   D. 3'
122 cm   65 cm   91 cm

WOOD : birch and pine

PROVENANCE : Murray Bay, P.Q.

(Coll. Mr and Mrs Patrick Morgan, Cap à l'Aigle, P.Q.).

390. SMALL TABLE, WITH CURVED LEGS, IN THE LOUIS XV MANNER. LATE 18th C.

Small table, having curved legs, one drawer and a shaped frieze in the Louis XV manner. This is a table which was not found in lower-class homes in France, and still less in the rural homes of the eighteenth century. It was, however, found among the provincial semi-bourgeoisie and the well-to-do farmers. In Canada it was frequent enough in rural surroundings. It is reminiscent of French dressing tables *(coiffeuses)*, and is an elegant piece of furniture with very French curves. The top is a later addition.

w. 2' 3½''   H. 2' 1¾''   D. 1' 8½''
70 cm   65 cm   42 cm

WOOD : birch and pine

PROVENANCE : Quebec district

(Coll. Dr and Mrs Claude Bertrand, Outremont, P.Q.).

391. SMALL RUSTIC TABLE, WITH CURVED LEGS. LATE 18th C.

Small rustic table, with curved legs and one drawer decorated with two rectangular panels. The frieze is carved with spirals and there are two lateral panels. The curve of the feet is more accentuated than on the two preceding tables. The extremities of the feet are missing.

w. 2' 5''   H. 2' 2''   D. 1' 7''
74 cm   66 cm   48 cm

WOOD : birch and pine

PROVENANCE : Three Rivers, P.Q.

(Coll. Dr and Mrs Herbert T. Schwarz, Montreal).

392. SMALL TABLE, WITH CURVED LEGS, IN LOUIS XV MANNER. LATE 18th C.

Small table, with a single drawer, curved legs and a shaped frieze carved with spirals and *palmettes.* The curved feet terminate in *pieds de biche* with double volutes. The drawer is a later addition. It is a piece with very graceful and very French lines.

w. 2' 7½''   H. 2' 3½''   D. 1' 9''
80 cm   70 cm   53 cm

WOOD : maple   PROVENANCE : Quebec

(Coll. Musée de l'Hôpital-Général, Quebec).

393. CANADIAN CHIPPENDALE TABLE. EARLY 19th C.

Small table, with curved Chippendale legs terminating in claw-and-ball feet, and carved with floral motifs on the knees. The colouring of the frieze and drawer imitates veneered wood.

w. 2' 6½''   H. 2' 5½''   D. 2' 5''
77 cm   75 cm   74 cm

WOOD : pine   PROVENANCE : Quebec

(Coll. Hôpital-Général, Quebec).

394. SMALL TABLE, WITH CURVED LEGS SHOWING ENGLISH INFLUENCE. LATE 18th C.

Small table, with curved legs showing English influence, and a festooned frieze with a drawer at one end. The countercurve of the lower part of the foot shows definite English influence. A marble or slate slab is missing from the top.

w. 2' 2¼''   H. 2' 4''   D. 1' 9¼''
67 cm   71 cm   54 cm

WOOD : butternut   PROVENANCE : Quebec

(Coll. Musée de l'Hôtel-Dieu, Quebec).

395. SMALL RUSTIC TABLE, WITH CURVED LEGS, IN THE RÉGENCE MANNER. LATE 18th C.

Small rustic table, having curved legs and shaped frieze carved with two spirals and a shell. A pleasant and naive piece.

w. 2' 9¾"   H. 2' 2"   D. 2' ½"
86 cm   67 cm   62 cm
WOOD : pine   LEGS : wavy maple
PROVENANCE : Saint-Jérome, P.Q.

(Coll. Miss Barbara Richardson, Sainte-Agathe des Monts, P.Q.).

396. SMALL TABLE, WITH CURVED LEGS, IN THE QUEEN ANNE MANNER. LATE 18th C.

Small table, with curved legs terminating in claw feet, of Queen Anne derivation. The festooned frieze is decorated with three small drawers and three small finials. The accentuated curve of the legs brings to mind English tables of the same period.

w. 2' 1"   H. 2' 1⅝"   D. 1' 8⅝"
63 cm   65 cm   52 cm
WOOD : birch   PROVENANCE : Quebec

(Coll. Musée de l'Hôpital-Général, Quebec).

397. TABLE, WITH ARBALÈTE-FRONTED FRIEZE. LATE 18th C.

Table, having two drawers and curved legs decorated with acanthus leaves at the knees and an arbalète-fronted frieze carved with a shell. Hardly noticeable *pieds de biche*. A small and narrow elongated table which stood by the wall in the entrance hall. The frieze is very close in style to a commode drawer, while the legs recall certain *Provençal* tables, particularly from the Grasse region.

w. 3'   H. 2' 4¼"   D. 1' 8"
91 cm   72 cm   51 cm
WOOD : pine   LEGS : ash

(Coll. Canadair Limited, Saint-Laurent, Montreal).

398. SMALL TABLE, WITH CURVED LEGS, IN THE QUEEN ANNE MANNER. EARLY 19th C.

Small table, having curved legs, a shaped frieze and one drawer, of Queen Anne derivation.

w. 2' 10"   H. 2' 4"   D. 1' 6"
86 cm   71 cm   46 cm
WOOD : oak   TOP : pine
PROVENANCE : L'Assomption P.Q.

(Coll. Dr and Mrs Herbert T. Schwarz, Montreal).

399. SMALL RUSTIC TABLE, WITH CURVED LEGS. LATE 18th C.

Small rustic table, having curved legs, a shaped frieze, one drawer and an overlapping top.

w. 2' 10¼"   H. 1' 11"   D. 2' 1¼"
87 cm   58 cm   64 cm
WOOD : pine   PROVENANCE : Montreal district

(Coll. Mr L.V. Randall, Montreal).

400. FOLDING TABLE, WITH CURVED LEGS. LATE 18th C.

Folding table, with curved legs terminating in *pieds de biche*, showing English Queen Anne influence. Elliptical top.

w. 4' 3"   H. 2' 2¾"   D. 2' 11½"
130 cm   68 cm   90 cm
WOOD : maple   PROVENANCE : Joliette, P.Q.

(Coll. Canada Steamship Lines, Tadoussac, P.Q.).

401. TABLE, WITH CURVED AND SHAPED FRIEZE IN LOUIS XV MANNER. 18th C.

Table, with curved legs and shaped frieze which is in console form. A very French and elegant table, in the Louis XV style. A rose is carved on the knee of each leg. Original handles and keyhole escutcheon. The colour is an imitation of marble.

w. 3' 6"   H. 2' 4½"   D. 1' 9¾"
107 cm   72 cm   55 cm
WOOD : pine   LEGS : birch
PROVENANCE : Quebec

(Coll. Musée de l'Hôpital-Général, Quebec).

402. TABLE, WITH CURVED LEGS, SHOWING ENGLISH INFLUENCE. MID 19th C.

Table, with curved legs flush with the shaped frieze. The accentuated curves of the legs recall some Regency furniture. The single drawer has two panels.

w. 3' 6"   H. 2' 2½"   D. 1' 10"
107 cm   67 cm   56 cm
WOOD : pine and birch
PROVENANCE : L'Assomption, P.Q.

(Coll. Canada Steamship Lines, Tadoussac, P.Q.).

403. LARGE RUSTIC TABLE, WITH CURVED LEGS. 19th C.

Large rustic table, with curved legs and a shaped frieze with openwork in its centre. Note the width of the border of the frieze and the naiveté of the central motif. It is a debased and very rustic interpretation of the Louis XV style. The heavily curved legs show English influence.

w. 5' 1¾"   H. 2' 4¼"   D. 2' 7½"
157 cm   72 cm   80 cm
WOOD : birch and pine
PROVENANCE : Carleton, P.Q.

(Coll. Canada Steamship Lines, P.Q.).

404. SMALL TABLE, WITH A DRAWER AND CHAMFERED LEGS. LATE 18th C.

Small table, with chamfered legs and one drawer. A very common type of table used from the seventeenth to the nineteenth centuries. The chamfer

265

is a bevel obtained by cutting the square edges or corners of a leg, an upright or a stretcher in order to lighten the general appearance.

w. 2' 3¾"	H. 2' 2¾"	D. 1' 4¾"
70 cm	68 cm	42 cm

WOOD : pine   PROVENANCE : Montreal district

(Coll. Canada Steamship Lines, Tadoussac, P.Q.).

405. SMALL RUSTIC TABLE, WITH FESTOONED FRIEZE. EARLY 19th C.

Small rustic table, with a festooned frieze. An agreeable peasant table.

w. 2' 5"	H. 2' ½"	D. 1' 8"
74 cm	62 cm	33 cm

WOOD : pine   PROVENANCE : Montreal district

(Coll. Mr and Mrs Antoine Dubuc, Chicoutimi, P.Q.).

406. SMALL RUSTIC TABLE, WITH NAIVE DECORATION. MID 19th C.

Small rustic table, having tapered legs and a shaped frieze naively carved with spirals, roundels and a shell. Charming example of country workmanship.

w. 2' 8¾"	H. 1' 11¾"	D. 2"
83 cm	60 cm	61 cm

WOOD : pine and birch

PROVENANCE : Carleton, P.Q.

(Coll. Canada Steamship Lines, Tadoussac, P.Q.).

407. RUSTIC TABLE, WITH CURVED LEGS. MID 19th C.

Rustic table, with curved legs and a shaped frieze. A piece of very simple form and made by an un-skilled hand. The feet on this table recall those of an ox.

w. 4' 6⅜"	H. 1' 1"	D. 2' 7⅜"
138 cm	33 cm	80 cm

WOOD : pine   PROVENANCE : Chambly, P.Q.

(Coll. Mr and Mrs M.M. Allan, Baie d'Urfé, P.Q.).

408. RUSTIC TABLE, WITH FESTOONED FRIEZE. MID 19th C.

Rustic table, with tapered legs and a shaped frieze having one drawer. It has an overlapping top. A naive piece of furniture.

w. 3'	H. 1' 11½"	D. 1' 10¼"
91 cm	60 cm	57 cm

WOOD : pine

(Coll. Canada Steamship Lines, Tadoussac, P.Q.).

409. SMALL RUSTIC TABLE, WITH FESTOONED FRIEZE. EARLY 19th C.

Rustic table, with chamfered legs and festooned frieze of unusual design.

w. 3' 2"	H. 2' 6"	D. 1' 10"
97 cm	76 cm	56 cm

WOOD : birch and pine

PROVENANCE : Sainte-Ursule, P.Q.

(Coll. Dr and Mrs Herbert T. Schwarz, Montreal).

410. RUSTIC TABLE, WITH THREE DRAWERS. EARLY 19th C.

Rustic table, with chamfered legs and three drawers. The central one is real, the two others are false, undoubtedly designed to create a balance in the piece. Note the wooden keys inserted under the top to prevent warping. A table of attractive proportions.

w. 3' 9⅜"	H. 2' 2¼"	D. 2' 7⅝"
115 cm	67 cm	80 cm

WOOD : pine   PROVENANCE : Quebec district

(Coll. Miss Barbara Richardson, Sainte-Agathe des Monts, P.Q.).

411. SMALL RUSTIC DEMI-LUNE TABLE, OR " TABLE-SOLEIL ". LATE 18th C.

Small demi-lune table, also called *table-soleil* or sun-table. It has tapered legs and one drawer. The top is assembled with tongued-and-grooved joints, and the design suggests sun rays. A pleasant table with a very rustic appearance. Original wrought-iron knob. The top has been restored.

w. 2' 6¾"	H. 2' 1¼"	D. 1' 1¼"
78 cm	64 cm	34 cm

WOOD : pine

PROVENANCE : La Rémi, Baie Saint-Paul, P.Q.

(Coll. Mr and Mrs Jean-Paul Lemieux, Sillery, P.Q.).

412. SMALL DEMI-LUNE TABLE. EARLY 19th C.

Small demi-lune table, with tapered legs, one drawer and a shaped frieze. The great majority of these tables were used as serving tables and placed against the wall. Often they were put at the ends of a large rectangular table so as to accommodate more guests.

w. 3' ¾"	H. 2'	D. 1' 7"
93 cm	63 cm	48 cm

WOOD : pine

(Coll. Mrs Ross Sims, Saint-Sauveur des Monts, P.Q.).

413. DEMI-LUNE TABLE, WITH BOWED AND FESTOONED FRIEZE. EARLY 19th C.

Demi-lune table, having a bowed and festooned frieze and tapered legs, of Sheraton derivation. A small elegant serving table.

w. 3'	H. 2' 3"	D. 1' 6"
91 cm	69 cm	46 cm

WOOD : pine

(Coll. Mrs Ross Sims, Saint-Sauveur des Monts, P.Q.).

414. DEMI-LUNE TABLE, WITH CROSS-STRETCHERS, IN THE REGENCY MANNER. MID 19th C.

Demi-lune table, having a bow-front frieze and tapered legs, in the Sheraton manner. The cross-stretcher is of Regency derivation.

W. 4' 1"   H. 2' 5"   D. 2' ½"
125 cm   74 cm   62 cm

WOOD : birch and butternut

(Coll. Mr and Mrs Ross McMaster, Saint-Sauveur des Monts, P.Q.).

415. SMALL RUSTIC DEMI-LUNE TABLE, WITH OPEN-WORK FRIEZE. MID 19th C.

Small rustic demi-lune table, having an openwork frieze decorated with pierced and flat spindles and a flower with incurved petals. The design is inspired by the Bresse *molette* or small muller with incurved rays, and is a rare motif in Canada. A small, naive yet charming serving table.

W. 3' 4¼"   H. 2' 2"   D. 1' 6"
102 cm   67 cm   46 cm

WOOD : pine   PROVENANCE : Isle of Orleans, P.Q.

(Coll. Miss Emily Le Baron, North Hatley, P.Q.).

416. RUSTIC TABLE, WITH CURVED LEGS. MID 19th C.

Rustic table, with curved legs and two leaves. The frieze has a moulding and a drawer at each end. The curved legs are of naturalistic inspiration and recall the legs of an ox. A curious piece of furniture.

W. 3' 4¾"   H. 2' 1¼"   D. 2' 11"
103 cm   64 cm   89 cm

WOOD : TOP : maple; FRIEZE : pine; LEGS : ash
PROVENANCE : Murray Bay, P.Q.

(Coll. Mrs Richard R. Costello, Sainte-Agathe des Monts, P.Q.).

417. RUSTIC CANDLE TABLE. LATE 18th C.

Rustic candle table *(guéridon)* with one central leg resting on a tripod. This rare piece was widely known in the seventeenth and eighteenth centuries, and was used for different purposes but especially for candlesticks. A small piece, easy to move. Unskilled workmanship. (Cf. p. 260.)

WOOD : pine

(Coll. Mr and Mrs Anthony Hays, London, England).

418. SMALL RUSTIC WORK-TABLE. EARLY 19th C.

Small work-table, having lyre-shaped legs and a drawer carved with geometric designs. (Cf. p. 260.)

W. 1' 6"   H. 1' 7"   D. 10"
46 cm   48 cm   25 cm

WOOD : birch and ash

PROVENANCE : Saint-Pierre les Becquets, P.Q.

(Coll. Dr and Mrs Herbert T. Schwarz, Montreal).

419. SMALL RUSTIC TABLE, NAIVELY DECORATED. MID 19th C.

Small rustic table, with one drawer and tapered feet which show Sheraton influence, and a frieze carved with naive designs. The work of an unskilled hand, but nevertheless an attractive piece.

W. 2' ¼"   H. 2' 3½"   D. 1' 4¾"
62 cm   70 cm   42 cm

WOOD : pine

(Coll. Mr and Mrs J.N. Cole, Montreal).

420. WORK-TABLE, WITH COUPLED LEGS. EARLY 19th C.

Work-table, with coupled legs in lyre form, having one drawer and shelf. The work-table with coupled legs is also found in France. Of *Late Empire* derivation. (Cf. p. 260.)

W. 1' 11"   H. 2' 2¼"   D. 1' 3"
59 cm   67 cm   38 cm

WOOD : pine

PROVENANCE : a convent, Quebec district

(Coll. Dr and Mrs Marcel Carbotte, Petite Rivière Saint-François, P.Q.).

WASH-STANDS

Wash-stands *(lave-mains* in French Canada) were very common in the nineteenth century. A few specimens which seem to have the most original shape have been chosen as illustrations for this book. They were small and light, and in many homes were placed near the bucket-bench. The men, coming in from the fields at noon, would wash their hands there in a basin near which there would be a soap dish containing home-made soap *(savon du pays)*. The small wash-stand however would usually be found in the parents' bedroom or in the guest room, with a faience basin and water jug placed upon it. It was usually made of pine, birch, or ash, and would have one or two drawers, and sometimes a lower shelf. Some had a hole in the top to hold the basin, and often there would be a shaped splash-board around three sides of the top, and towel-rails on the sides. A few were designed to fit into the corner of a room, their shape resembling certain French serving-tables and Burgundy bedside tables. Like the rocking chair, this small table gave free rein to the imagination of the French Canadian woodworker who produced a number of structural variants. Over the past years, wash-stands have been steadily replaced by wash-basins with running water in most rural houses of French Canada.

421. WASH-STAND, WITH ONE DRAWER. 19th C.
Wash-stand, with tapered legs showing Sheraton influence, having one drawer and two rows of festooned friezes. The top is serpentine-shaped, and is cut to hold a basin. A finely proportioned wash-stand.

w. 1' 1''   H. 2' 7''   D. 1' 4''
33 cm   79 cm   41 cm

WOOD : butternut and pine

(Coll. Mr and Mrs Ross McMaster, Saint-Sauveur des Monts, P.Q.).

422. SMALL WASH-STAND, WITH TURNED LEGS. 19th C.
Small wash-stand, with turned legs and two rows of festooned friezes. The splash-board on the top is shaped and in openwork.

w. 1' 4½''   H. 2' 8¾''   D. 1' 4½''
42 cm   83 cm   42 cm

WOOD : pine

PROVENANCE : Saint-Charles de Bellechasse, P.Q.

(Coll. Mrs Richard R. Costello, Sainte-Agathe des Monts, P.Q.).

423. SMALL CORNER WASH-STAND. 19th C.
Small corner wash-stand, with three-lobed rails and chamfered legs.

w. 2' 3½''   H. 2' 7''
70 cm   79 cm

WOOD : pine

(Coll. Miss Barbara Richardson, Sainte-Agathe des Monts, P.Q.).

424. NAIVE WASH-STAND, WITH THREE DRAWERS. 19th C.
Naive wash-stand, with three drawers, tapered legs and a shaped splash-board.

w. 2' 5¼''   H. 2' 4''   D. 1' 6''
74 cm   72 cm   46 cm

WOOD : pine

(Coll. Mr and Mrs J.W. McConnell, Saint-Sauveur des Monts, P.Q.).

425. WASH-STAND, WITH CHAMFERED LEGS. 19th C.
Wash-stand, with chamfered legs and a single drawer. The shaped splash-board is pierced and is carved with three hearts and the craftsman's signature : '' P.A.C. MAKER ''.

w. 2' 6½''   H. 2' 9''   D. 1' 7½''
78 cm   84 cm   50 cm

WOOD : pine   PROVENANCE : L'Assomption, P.Q.

(Coll. Mr and Mrs J.N. Cole, Montreal).

426. RUSTIC WASH-STAND. 19th C.
Rustic wash-stand, with curved legs, a single drawer, a shaped rail and a splash-board.

WOOD : pine   PROVENANCE : Montreal district

(Coll. Canada Steamship Lines, Tadoussac, P.Q.).

427. SMALL WASH-STAND-COMMODE, IN FOLK ART STYLE. 19th C.
Small wash-stand-commode, with four drawers, a shaped lower rail and a door pierced with upturned hearts, a crescent, etc. Very primitive.

w. 3'   H. 2'   D. 1' 4''
91 cm   61 cm   42 cm

WOOD : pine

(Coll. Mrs E. Thornley Hart, Sainte-Agathe des Monts, P.Q.).

428. '' CANADIAN ROCOCO '' WASH-STAND, OF LATE EMPIRE STYLE. 19th C.
Rococo wash-stand, having a drawer, with towel-rails and a roller of Late Empire style. Turned and tapered feet.

w. 2' 5¾''   H. 2' 11⅝''   D. 1' 8¼''
75 cm   90 cm   52 cm

WOOD : pine and birch

(Coll. Mr and Mrs Victor M. Drury, Lake Anne, P.Q.).

429. '' CANADIAN ROCOCO '' WASH-STAND. 19th C.
Rococo wash-stand, debased version of Late Empire and Restauration styles, having two convex-fronted drawers, turned feet, a shaped lower rail and splash-board. Folk art.

w. 3' ⅝''   H. 3' ¼''   D. 1' 9''
93 cm   92 cm   53 cm

WOOD : pine

(Coll. Musée Provencher, Cap Rouge, P.Q.).

EARLY NINETEENTH-CENTURY ARMOIRE, DECORATED WITH VARIEGATED GEOMETRIC DESIGNS.

365. TABLE, D'INSPIRATION HENRI IV ET LOUIS XIII. XVIIe S.
TABLE, IN THE HENRI IV AND LOUIS XIII MANNERS.
17th C.

366. TABLE A TORSADE, D'INSPIRATION LOUIS XIII.
XVIIe S.
TABLE, WITH SPIRALLY TURNED LEGS, IN THE LOUIS XIII
MANNER. 17th C.

367. TABLE A DOUBLE TORSADE, D'INSPI-
RATION LOUIS XIII. XVIIᵉ S.
TABLE, WITH LEGS TURNED IN A DOUBLE
SPIRAL, IN THE LOUIS XIII MANNER.
17th C.

368. TABLE, AVEC FLAMBEAUX, DE STYLE
LOUIS XIII. XVIIᵉ S.
TABLE, WITH FLAME FINIALS, IN THE
LOUIS XIII STYLE. 17th C.

369. TABLE RUSTIQUE, D'INSPIRATION
LOUIS XIII. FIN XVIIᵉ S.
RUSTIC TABLE, IN THE LOUIS XIII MANNER.
LATE 17th C.

370. TABLE A PIÈTEMENT TOURNÉ, D'ESPRIT
LOUIS XIII. FIN XVIIᵉ S.
TABLE, WITH TURNED LEGS, IN THE LOUIS XIII

371. TABLE A PIÈTEMENT TOURNÉ, D'ESPRIT
LOUIS XIII. XVIIIᵉ S.
TABLE, WITH TURNED LEGS, IN THE LOUIS XIII

372. PETITE TABLE A PIÈTEMENT TOURNÉ
DE STYLE LOUIS XIII. DÉBUT XVIIIᵉ S.
SMALL TABLE, WITH TURNED LEGS, IN THE
LOUIS XIII MANNER. EARLY 18th C.

373. TABLE A PIÈTEMENT TOURNÉ, ORNÉE
D'UN TIROIR DE FORME ARBALÈTE.
XVIIIᵉ S.
TABLE, WITH TURNED LEGS AND ARBA-
LÈTE-FRONTED DRAWER. 18th C.

374. GRANDE TABLE, D'ESPRIT
LOUIS XIII, DES FRÈRES CHARON.
FIN XVIIᵉ S.
LARGE TABLE, IN THE LOUIS XIII
MANNER, FORMERLY OWNED BY THE
CHARON BROTHERS. LATE 17th C.

375. GRANDE TABLE D'APOTHICAIRE-
RIE, DE L'HOTEL-DIEU DE MONTRÉAL.
DÉBUT XVIIIᵉ S.
LARGE TABLE, FROM THE DISPENSARY
OF THE HOTEL-DIEU, MONTRÉAL.
EARLY 18th C.

376. TABLE DE RÉFECTOIRE, DES URSULINES DE QUÉBEC.
XVIIIᵉ S.
REFECTORY TABLE, FROM THE URSULINE CONVENT,
QUEBEC. 18th C.

377. TABLE DE RÉFECTOIRE, DES FRÈRES DES ÉCOLES
CHRÉTIENNES. XIXᵉ S.
REFECTORY TABLE, FROM THE BROTHERS OF THE
CHRISTIAN SCHOOLS. 19th C.

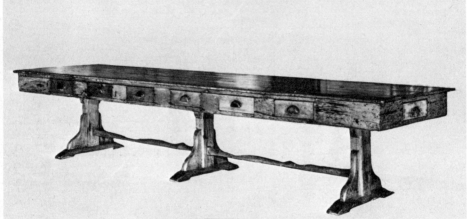

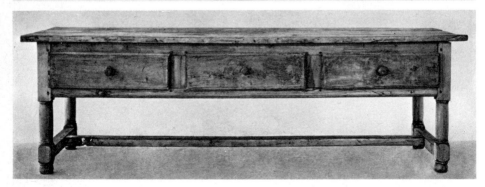

378. TABLE DE CUISINE, DE L'HOTEL-DIEU DE QUÉBEC.
FIN XVIIᵉ S.
KITCHEN TABLE, FROM THE HOTEL-DIEU, QUEBEC. LATE
17th C.

379. TABLE DE RÉFECTOIRE,
DE L'HOTEL-DIEU DE QUÉ-
BEC. FIN XVIIᵉ S.
REFECTORY TABLE, FROM THE
HOTEL-DIEU, QUEBEC. LATE
17th C.

380. TABLE DE RÉFECTOIRE,
A PIÈTEMENT TOURNÉ ET A
DOUBLES TRAVERSES. FIN
XVIIIᵉ S.
REFECTORY TABLE, WITH
TURNED LEGS AND DOUBLE
STRETCHERS. LATE 18th C.

381. TABLE A PIÈTEMENT
TOURNÉ, D'INSPIRATION
LOUIS XIII. XVIIIᵉ S.
TABLE, WITH TURNED LEGS,
IN THE LOUIS XIII MANNER.
18th C.

382. TABLE PLIANTE OU A ABATTANT,
A PIÈTEMENT D'INSPIRATION LOUIS XIII.
FIN XVIIᵉ S.
GATELEG TABLE, WITH LEGS IN THE LOUIS XIII
MANNER. LATE 17th C.

383. PETITE TABLE DE CHEVET, A PIEDS
TOURNÉS. DÉBUT XVIIIᵉ S.
SMALL BEDSIDE TABLE, WITH TURNED LEGS.
EARLY 18th C.

384. TABLE PLIANTE RUSTIQUE, A PIÈTE-
MENT TOURNÉ. FIN XVIIIᵉ S.
RUSTIC FOLDING TABLE, WITH TURNED LEGS.
LATE 18th C.

385. TABLE PLIANTE OU A ABATTANT, A
PIÈTEMENT TOURNÉ. FIN XVIIIᵉ S.
RUSTIC GATELEG TABLE, WITH TURNED
LEGS. LATE 18th C.

386. TABLE PLIANTE OU A ABATTANT RUS-
TIQUE, A PLATEAU ELLIPTIQUE. DÉBUT
XIXᵉ S.
RUSTIC FOLDING OR GATELEG TABLE, WITH
OVAL TOP. EARLY 19th C.

387. PETITE TABLE RUSTIQUE, A PIÈTEMENT
TOURNÉ. FIN XVIIIᵉ S.
SMALL RUSTIC TABLE, WITH TURNED LEGS.
LATE 18th C.

388. TABLE A PLATEAU BASCULANT, DE
RIVIÈRE OUELLE. DÉBUT XIXᵉ S.
TABLE-CHAIR, WITH CUTLERY DRAWER,
FROM RIVIÈRE OUELLE. EARLY 19th C.

389. TABLE A PLATEAU BASCULANT, DE LA
MALBAIE. DÉBUT XIXᵉ S.
TABLE-CHAIR, FROM LA MALBAIE. EARLY
19th C.

390. PETITE TABLE A PIEDS GALBÉS, D'ES-
PRIT LOUIS XV. FIN XVIIIᵉ S.
SMALL TABLE, WITH CURVED LEGS, IN
LOUIS XV MANNER. LATE 18th C.

391. PETITE TABLE RUSTIQUE, A PIEDS GAL-
BÉS. FIN XVIIIᵉ S.
SMALL RUSTIC TABLE, WITH CURVED LEGS.
LATE 18th C.

392. PETITE TABLE A PIEDS GALBÉS,
D'ESPRIT LOUIS XV. FIN XVIIIᵉ S.
SMALL TABLE, WITH CURVED LEGS,
IN LOUIS XV MANNER. LATE 18th C.

393. TABLE CHIPPENDALE CANADIENNE. DÉ-
BUT XIXᵉ S.
CANADIAN CHIPPENDALE TABLE. EARLY
19th C.

394. PETITE TABLE, AU GALBE D'INFLUENCE
ANGLAISE. FIN XVIIIᵉ S.
SMALL TABLE, WITH CURVED LEGS SHOWING
ENGLISH INFLUENCE. LATE 18th C.

395. PETITE TABLE RUSTIQUE A PIEDS CAM-
BRÉS, D'ESPRIT RÉGENCE. FIN XVIIIe S.
SMALL RUSTIC TABLE, WITH CURVED LEGS,
IN THE RÉGENCE MANNER. LATE 18th C.

396. PETITE TABLE A PIEDS GALBÉS, D'INSPIRATION QUEEN ANNE.
FIN XVIIIe S.
SMALL TABLE, WITH CURVED LEGS, IN THE QUEEN ANNE
MANNER. LATE 18th C.

397. TABLE, A CEINTURE ARBALÈTE. FIN
XVIIIe S.
TABLE, WITH ARBALÈTE-FRONTED FRIEZE.
LATE 18th C.

398. PETITE TABLE A PIEDS GALBÉS, D'ESPRIT
QUEEN ANNE. DÉBUT XIXe S.
SMALL TABLE, WITH CURVED LEGS, IN THE
QUEEN ANNE MANNER. EARLY 19th C.

399. PETITE TABLE RUSTIQUE, A PIEDS CAM-
BRÉS. FIN XVIIIe S.
SMALL RUSTIC TABLE, WITH CURVED LEGS.
LATE 18th C.

400. TABLE PLIANTE, A PIEDS GALBÉS.
FIN XVIIIe S.
FOLDING TABLE, WITH CURVED LEGS. LATE
18th c.

401. TABLE A PIEDS ET A CEINTURE GALBÉS, DE STYLE LOUIS XV. XVIIIe S.
TABLE, WITH CURVED AND SHAPED FRIEZE, IN THE LOUIS XV MANNER.
18th c.

402. TABLE A PIEDS GALBÉS, D'INFLUENCE ANGLAISE. MILIEU XIXe
TABLE, WITH CURVED LEGS, SHOWING ENGLISH INFLUENC
MID 19th c.

403. GRANDE T
RUSTIQUE, A P
GALBÉS. XIXe S.
LARGE RUSTIC TA
WITH CURVED L
19th c.

404. PETITE TABLE A PIEDS CHANFREINÉS ET UN
TIROIR. FIN XVIIIᵉ S.
SMALL TABLE, WITH A DRAWER AND CHAMFERED
LEGS. LATE 18th C.

405. PETITE TABLE RUSTIQUE, A CEINTURE
FESTONNÉE. DÉBUT XIXᵉ S.
SMALL RUSTIC TABLE, WITH FESTOONED
FRIEZE. EARLY 19th C.

406. PETITE TABLE RUSTIQUE. A DÉCORA-
TION NAÏVE. MILIEU XIXᵉ S.
SMALL RUSTIC TABLE, WITH NAIVE DECORA-
TION. MID 19th C.

407. TABLE RUSTIQUE A PIEDS CAMBRÉS. MILIEU XIXe S.
RUSTIC TABLE, WITH CURVED LEGS. MID 19th C.

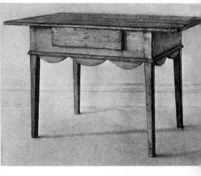

408. TABLE RUSTIQUE, A CEINTURE FESTON-NÉE. MILIEU XIXe S.
RUSTIC TABLE, WITH FESTOONED FRIEZE. MID 19th C.

409. TABLE RUSTIQUE, A CEINTURE FES-TONNÉE. DÉBUT XIXe S.
SMALL RUSTIC TABLE, WITH FESTOONED FRIEZE. EARLY 19th C.

410. TABLE RUSTIQUE, A TROIS TIROIRS. DÉBUT XIXe S.
RUSTIC TABLE, WITH THREE DRAWERS. EARLY 19th C.

411. PETITE TABLE RUSTIQUE DEMI-LUNE OU « TABLE-SOLEIL ». FIN XVIIIᵉ S.
SMALL RUSTIC DEMI-LUNE TABLE, OR " TABLE-SOLEIL ".
LATE 18th C.

412. PETITE TABLE DEMI-LUNE. DÉBUT XIXᵉ S.
SMALL DEMI-LUNE TABLE.   EARLY 19th C.

413. TABLE DEMI-LUNE, A CEINTURE CINTRÉE ET FESTONNÉE. DÉBUT XIXᵉ S.
DEMI-LUNE TABLE, WITH BOWED AND FESTOONED FRIEZE.
EARLY 19th C.

414. TABLE DEMI-LUNE, A ENTRETOISE D'ESPRIT REGENCY. MILIEU XIXᵉ S.
DEMI-LUNE TABLE, WITH CROSS-STRETCHERS, IN THE REGENCY MANNER.   MID 19th C.

415. PETITE TABLE DEMI-LUNE RUSTIQUE, A CEINTURE AJOURÉE. MILIEU XIXᵉ S.
SMALL RUSTIC DEMI-LUNE TABLE, WITH OPENWORK FRIEZE.   MID 19th C.

416. TABLE RUSTIQUE A PIEDS CAMBRÉS. MILIEU XIXᵉ S.
RUSTIC TABLE, WITH CURVED LEGS. MID 19th C.

418. PETITE TRAVAILLEUSE RUSTIQUE. DÉBUT XIXᵉ S.
SMALL RUSTIC WORK-TABLE. EARLY 19th C.

420. TRAVAILLEUSE A PIEDS
DOUBLES. DÉBUT XIXᵉ S.
WORK TABLE, WITH COUPLED
LEGS. EARLY 19th C.

417. GUÉRIDON RUSTIQUE. FIN XVIIIᵉ S
RUSTIC CANDLE TABLE. LATE 18th C.

419. PETITE TABLE RUSTIQUE A DÉCOR NAIF. MILIEU
XIXᵉ S.
SMALL RUSTIC TABLE, NAIVELY DECORATED. MID 19th C.

421. TABLE DE TOILETTE, A UN TIROIR. XIXe S.
WASH-STAND, WITH ONE DRAWER. 19th C.

422. PETITE TABLE DE TOILETTE, A PIEDS TOURNÉS.
XIXe S.
SMALL WASH-STAND, WITH TURNED LEGS. 19th C.

423. PETITE TABLE DE TOILETTE D'ENCOIGNURE. XIXe S.
SMALL CORNER WASH-STAND. 19th C.

424. TABLE DE TOILETTE NAÏVE A TROIS TIROIRS. XIXe S.
NAIVE WASH-STAND, WITH THREE DRAWERS. 19th C.

426. TABLE DE TOILETTE RUSTIQUE. XIXᵉ S.
RUSTIC WASH-STAND. 19th C.

427. PETITE TABLE-COMMODE DE TOILETTE.
ART POPULAIRE. XIXᵉ S.
SMALL WASH-STAND-COMMODE, IN FOLK
ART STYLE. 19th C.

425. TABLE DE TOILETTE, A PIÈTEMENT CHANFREINÉ. XIXᵉ S.
WASH-STAND, WITH CHAMFERED LEGS. 19th C.

428. TABLE DE TOILETTE « ROCOCO CANA-
DIEN ». FIN EMPIRE. XIXᵉ S.
"CANADIAN ROCOCO" WASH-STAND, OF LATE
EMPIRE STYLE. 19th C.

429. TABLE DE TOILETTE « ROCOCO CANA-
DIEN ». XIXᵉ S.
"CANADIAN ROCOCO" WASH-STAND. 19th C.

CONSOLE TABLES

Console tables (*consoles d'appui, tables consoles,* almost always called *crédences* in French Canada) were not common in the *habitant* home. Most of them had two console or bracket legs, and were placed against a wall. Others, somewhat longer and rather narrow, were also placed by the wall but rested on four curved legs. The first reference to a console table reads, " March 1736, paid to Jean François Godin for a credence, 6 livres for the church of Cap Santé. "[1] Console tables were usually to be found in churches, placed to the right of the altar. Sometimes there would be one on either side of the altar. They were used as serving-tables during the celebration of mass.

The design of these consoles was similar to the shape of the tomb altar *(tombeau)* dating from the end of the eighteenth and beginning of the nineteenth centuries, the corners of which were shaped in a receding curve.

In 1789, there was a console table in the church of St François de l'Ile d'Orléans made by Pierre Émond. And in the church of St Roch l'Achigan, before the fire of a few years ago, there was a lovely pair of console tables in *rococo* style derived from Louis XV, made by Joseph Pépin in 1819. There is still a console table in the chapel of the Mother House of the Grey Nuns of Montreal, which was the work of Philippe Liébert, the woodworker-carver. It is embellished at the two corners with cherubins' heads instead of the grotesque, half-human masks *(mascarons)* which were in vogue in the Louis XIV period.

In many cases these tables had an openwork frieze carved with shells and foliated motifs. At the beginning of the nineteenth century, Louis Quevillon, François Normand and other carvers created a number of console tables in *rococo* manner, but unfortunately they lacked some of the delicacy of the *rocaille* of the Louis XV style.

In Canada, console tables were not usually found in private houses, except occasionally in wealthy homes, and the Canadian console table is highly valued by collectors. A Canadian *seigneur* of 1786 had a console of gilded wood with a marble top[2] which was undoubtedly imported from France. But in Canada they were mainly regarded as church furniture, whereas in France console tables often surmounted by a mirror or a pier-glass were to be found in the living-room or entrance hall of the homes of the nobility and the upper middle-class.

The console tables illustrated in this book all date from the end of the eighteenth and the first half of the nineteenth centuries.

430. CONSOLE TABLE, IN THE LOUIS XV MANNER. LATE 18th C.

Console table, of serpentine shape, in the Louis XV manner, with an openwork frieze carved with classic motifs of acanthus leaves, *rocaille*, spirals, foliage and flowers. The *cartel* on the stretcher has been damaged. According to an oral tradition of the descendants of the Ranvoyzé family, this console table is said to have been made by François Ranvoyzé, the famous Quebec silversmith (1739-1819), and was given by him to his brother the Abbé Ranvoyzé, then *Curé* of St Anne de Beaupré. When the old church was demolished, the console is said to have been given to the third brother, the notary Louis Ranvoyzé. Does this indicate that François Ranvoyzé had a hobby?

WOOD : pine top; FRIEZE and LEGS : curly maple

PROVENANCE : Quebec
(Coll. Mr and Mrs Charles Couture, Quebec).

431. DETAIL.

432. CONSOLE TABLE, IN THE LOUIS XV MANNER. LATE 18th C.

Serpentine-fronted console table·in the Louis XV manner, having an openwork frieze carved with *rocaille* motifs and flowers (eglantines and oak leaves). This kind of furniture served to receive holy vessels during mass and was placed in the chancel, near the altar. Only a skilled hand, such as that of a church woodworker-carver, could make such tables. An elegant and finely proportioned console table.

W. 3' 2''; 3' 5''   H. 2' 8¼''   D' 1' 6¾''
97 cm; 104 cm   82 cm   47 cm

(1) I O A. Livre de Comptes de La Fabrique de Cap Santé. 1736.
(2) B R H. Massicotte, E.Z. Vol. XLVIII, Feb. 1942 (extract from an inventory) pp. 33-42.

WOOD : pine   PROVENANCE : Saint-Cuthbert, P.Q.
(Coll. Mrs Paul Gouin, Montreal).

433. DETAIL.

434. CONSOLE TABLE, IN THE LOUIS XV MANNER. LATE 18th C.

Console table, in the Louis XV manner, with an openwork frieze carved with foliage and an upturned shell. The legs are decorated with small *rocaille* motifs. The top is of *Brèche d'Alep* marble. The side friezes of these pieces are generally shaped in concave and convex profile. A curious combination of motifs.

w. 3' 1"   H. 2' 6"
94 cm   76 cm

WOOD : butternut   PROVENANCE : Saint-Vallier, P.Q.
(Coll. Mrs Howard W. Pillow, Montreal).

435. CONSOLE TABLE. 19th C.

Console table, having a shaped frieze carved with a shell, and curved legs carved with an acantlius leaf at the knee. The stretcher and balls have been restored, as have the side stretchers. Another example of *Canadian rococo.*

w. 1' 11"   H. 2' 3¾"   D. 1' 8"
58 cm   70 cm   51 cm

WOOD : pine   PROVENANCE : Montreal district
(Coll. Canadair Limited, Saint-Laurent, Montreal).

436. CONSOLE TABLE, IN " CANADIAN ROCOCO " STYLE. EARLY 19th C.

Serpentine-fronted console table, with claw-and-ball feet. It is carved with an openwork shell on the stretcher, acanthus leaves and a *cartel* on the frieze. These motifs are debased variations of Louis XV *rocaille* forms. The exaggerated curves of the bracket or console feet, the heaviness of the ornaments and of the claw-and-ball feet recall the work of the Quevillon workshops and apprentices. A typical example of *Canadian rococo.*

w. 3' 8½"   H. 2' 4"   D. 1' 7¾"
113 cm   71 cm   50 cm

WOOD : pine   PROVENANCE : Montreal district
(Coll. Mrs L.S. Bloom, Westmount, P.Q.).

437. CONSOLE TABLE, WITH CLAW-AND-BALL FEET. EARLY 19th C.

Serpentine-fronted console table, with claw-and-ball feet of Chippendale derivation. The frieze and stretcher are carved with foliage, acanthus leaves and a *cartel* in *rocaille* manner. A very Canadian interpretation.

w. 2' 10½"   H. 2' 5⅜"   D. 1' 7⅝"
88 cm   75 cm   50 cm

WOOD : pine

PROVENANCE : Sainte-Rose, Laval, P.Q.

(Coll. Mrs Richard R. Costello, Sainte-Agathe des Monts, P.Q.).

438. CONSOLE TABLE, MADE BY PHILIPPE LIÉBERT. LATE 18th C.

Console table, made by the woodworker-carver Philippe Liébert for the Grey Nuns' old Chapel at the *Hôpital-Général*, Place d'Youville, Montreal. It is a serpentine-fronted console table, in a debased variation of the Louis XIV and Louis XV styles. There are spirals, acanthus leaves, bunches of grapes, vine leaves and a *palmette* surmounted by a *cartel* in *rocaille* framed with acanthus leaves. Each corner of the console has a carved cherubin's head (in place of the grotesque semi-human masks, *mascarons*, found on Louis XIV console tables). The top has been replaced and the acanthus leaves mutilated. The dark brown colour and the bronze gilding disfigure a piece which was already heavily proportioned.

w. 2' 10½"   H. 2' 6"   D. 1' 6⅜"
88 cm   76 cm   47 cm

WOOD : pine   PROVENANCE : Montreal
(Coll. Chapel of the Grey Nuns' Hospital, Montreal).

439. CONSOLE TABLE, MADE BY FRANÇOIS NORMAND, OF THREE RIVERS. EARLY 19th C.

Serpentine-fronted console table, carved with acanthus leaves, flowers and *rocaille* motifs showing Louis XV influence. It also has claw-and-ball feet of English derivation. Heavy curves and countercurves. It was said to have been made by François Normand about 1807, according to the Ursuline Sisters of Three Rivers. It is reminiscent of the rococo designs of the English joiner and architect Henry Flitcroft (1697-1769).

w. 3' 8"   H. 2' 8"   D. 1' 9½"
95 cm   81 cm   55 cm
112 cm

WOOD : pine   PROVENANCE : Three Rivers, P.Q.
(Coll. Chapel of the Ursulines, Three Rivers, P.Q.).

440. CONSOLE TABLE, IN " CANADIAN ROCOCO " STYLE. 19th C.

Console table, in *Canadian rococo* style, which is a debased variation of Louis XV *rocaille*. It is a four-legged console table with claw-and-ball feet and a shaped frieze carved with floral motifs and spirals. Typical of the work of Quevillon's apprentices.

w. 3' 4⅝"   H. 2' 5⅜"   D. 2' 3¼"
103 cm   75 cm   69 cm

WOOD : butternut

PROVENANCE : Notre-Dame de Bonsecours Church, Montreal

(Coll. Peter and William Dobell, Lake Memphremagog, P.Q.).

431. DÉTAIL.
DETAIL.

430. CONSOLE D'APPUI, D'ESPRIT LOUIS XV. FIN XVIIIᵉ S.
CONSOLE TABLE, IN THE LOUIS XV MANNER. LATE 18th C.

432. CONSOLE D'APPUI, D'ESPRIT
LOUIS XV. FIN XVIIIᵉ S.
CONSOLE TABLE, IN THE LOUIS XV
MANNER. LATE 18th C.

433. DÉTAIL.
DETAIL.

434. CONSOLE D'APPUI, D'ESPRIT
LOUIS XV. FIN XVIIIᵉ S.
CONSOLE TABLE, IN THE LOUIS XV
MANNER. LATE 18th C.

435. CONSOLE D'APPUI. XIXᵉ S.
CONSOLE TABLE.   19th C.

436. CONSOLE D'APPUI « ROCOCO
CANADIEN ». DÉBUT XIXᵉ S.
CONSOLE TABLE, IN " CANADIAN
ROCOCO " STYLE.   EARLY 19th C.

437. CONSOLE D'APPUI ORNÉE DE
PIEDS A GRIFFES ET A BOULE.
DÉBUT XIXᵉ S.
CONSOLE TABLE, WITH CLAW-AND-
BALL FEET.   EARLY 19th C.

438. CONSOLE D'APPUI, DE
PHILIPPE LIÉBERT. FIN XVIIIᵉ S.
CONSOLE TABLE, MADE BY
PHILIPPE LIÉBERT. LATE 18th C.

439. CONSOLE D'APPUI, DE FRAN-
ÇOIS NORMAND, DE TROIS-RIVIÈRES.
DÉBUT XIXᵉ S.
CONSOLE TABLE, MADE BY FRAN-
ÇOIS NORMAND OF THREE RIVERS.
EARLY 19th C.

440. TABLE-CONSOLE « ROCOCO
CANADIEN ». XIXᵉ S.
CONSOLE TABLE, IN " CANADIAN
ROCOCO " STYLE. 19th C.

DESKS

Desks were not usually to be found in the rural districts of French Canada, while in France they were most common in middle-class homes. The first desks in Canada were owned by bishops, *seigneurs*, army officers, etc., for whom the secretary desk was the most practical. This piece was first mentioned in 1711: " a table or desk with eight drawers made of local maple wood, the drawers locking with a key, the base being of jointed wood in relief and the top being covered with green cloth, valued at 75 livres. "[1]

The earliest known specimen was a knee-hole desk (often called *bureau Mazarin*) in the Louis XIII style, which had eight tapered legs jointed by double Y-shaped stretchers. There was a chest of three bow-fronted drawers on each side, and a panel enclosing a small cabinet at the back of the knee-hole.

Other secretary desks have turned legs, as the wavy-grained birch desk made by Pierre Émond, master woodworker and carver, for Monseigneur Briand, Bishop of Quebec. The bishop gave this desk to the nuns of the *Hôpital-Général* of Quebec in 1770, " for the prescription of medicines ... Monseigneur settled the account which amounted to 60 livres. "[2]

A more common type of desk was the slant-top or slope-fronted secretary. The sloping lid rested on two sliding supports when opened. These desks were made like a commode with three or four drawers and a bracket base, under the English influence of the eighteenth century. The inside of the desk was fitted with small drawers and pigeon-holes *(le pigeonnier)* and sometimes with a secret compartment for hiding important or compromising papers.

Another desk consisted of a small cupboard, in which books and documents were kept. The door of the cupboard was hinged at the bottom and formed a writing table when opened.

The tall desk at which the writer would either stand or be seated on a high stool was found particularly in presbyteries for the collections of tithes, or in army offices for the distribution of pay.

---

441. KNEE-HOLE DESK, OF " MAZARIN " TYPE. LATE 17th C.

Knee-hole desk of the *Mazarin* type, having seven bow-front drawers and resting on eight tapered legs. It has a small cupboard at the back of the knee-hole recess. This type was inspired by the furniture made during the regency of Cardinal Mazarin (1639-1661). An Italian by birth, he greatly influenced the arts in France during the mid-seventeenth century, by surrounding himself with Italian artists and craftsmen. Stuck to the back of the desk, there is an ink inscription on a piece of fine linen, which reads : " I have given and give to Madame St Martin, Mother Superior of the Hôtel-Dieu, this bureau or commode as it is, such as it is and to this effect I sign. At Quebec this day 16th August 1768. Chavigny. " Made by a skilled hand, it is a unique Canadian piece.

w. 3' 10"   H. 2' 4½"   D. 1' 1¼"
117 cm   72 cm   34 cm

WOOD : birch   PROVENANCE : Quebec

(Coll. Musée de l'Hôtel-Dieu, Quebec).

442. KNEE-HOLE DESK, OF " MAZARIN " TYPE, WITH TURNED LEGS. LATE 17th C.

Desk, or bureau, of the *Mazarin* type, with seven bow-front drawers and turned legs in the Louis XIII manner. There is a small cupboard at the back of the knee-hole recess. According to oral tradition among the Augustinian Nuns of the *Hôpital-Général*, Quebec, this desk was formerly owned by Monseigneur de St Vallier, second bishop of Quebec, who lived in retirement at the Hospital from 1713 until his death in 1727.

w. 3' 1¾"   H. 2' 6"   D. 1' 10¼"
96 cm   77 cm   57 cm

WOOD : butternut   PROVENANCE : Quebec

(Coll. Musée de l'Hôpital-Général, Quebec).

443. KNEE-HOLE DESK, IN THE LOUIS XIII MANNER. LATE 18th C.

Desk or bureau, having five drawers, inspired by the *Mazarin* type, with turned legs in the Louis XIII manner, and a finial in the middle of the stretcher.

---

(1) A J M, I O A. Inventaire des biens de la succession de feu Mr Demuy 17 & 18 Juin 1711. Greffe Adhémar.
(2) Annales de l'Hôpital-Général de Québec.

It has a festooned frieze and Gothic four-leaf motifs (*quartefeuilles*) in the centre of the drawers (a motif often used by Pierre Émond). There are panels on the sides. The arch in the kneehole is of English influence. According to the Annals of the *Hôpital-Général*, Quebec, this desk was made by the woodworker Pierre Émond for Monseigneur Jean Olivier Briand who gave it to the Nuns " for the writing of prescriptions " (see p. 291). The brass hinged rings are original but the knobs are a later addition. This piece has never left the hospital dispensary.

w. 3'	H. 2' 5¾"	D. 1' 10½"
91 cm	75 cm	57 cm

WOOD : wavy maple   PROVENANCE : Quebec

(*Coll. Hôpital-Général, Quebec*).

444. KNEE-HOLE DESK, WITH DIAMOND-POINT CARVING ON THE DOORS. 18th C.

Knee-hole desk, having two drawers and two doors carved with diamond points.

w. 5' 4¾"	H. 2' 5¼"	D. 1' 9"
164 cm	74 cm	53 cm

WOOD : pine   PROVENANCE : Quebec district

(*Coll. Mr and Mrs Victor Drury, Montreal*).

445. SMALL SLANT-TOP DESK. LATE 18th C.

Small slant-top desk, with one drawer. It was used in a Presbytery for the collection of the tithe. The general structure and legs are of English derivation. Festooned framework around the top.

w. 2' 3"	H. 3' 4¾"	D. 1' 5¼"
69 cm	104 cm	44 cm

WOOD : pine

PROVENANCE : Saint-Marc-sur-Richelieu, P.Q.

(*Coll. Canada Steamship Lines, Tadoussac, P.Q.*).

446. SMALL SLANT-TOP DESK, CARVED WITH GEOMETRIC DESIGNS. 19th C.

Small slant-top desk, having curved legs. It is carved with foliated scrolls and geometric designs (roundels with petals inserted in a hexagon, stars and wheels or mullers with incurved rays). The front legs are derived from the *Late Empire* style. The side frieze is shaped.

w. 2' 7"	H. 3' 2½"	D. 1' 1"
79 cm	98 cm	33 cm

WOOD : pine and ash

PROVENANCE : Saint-Augustin, Two Mountains, P.Q.

(*Coll. Mrs Nettie Sharpe, Saint-Lambert, P.Q.*).

447. SLANT-TOP DESK, WITH CURVED LEGS, IN THE LOUIS XV MANNER. LATE 18th C.

Slant-top desk, with curved legs and stretchers derived from English and Louis XV styles. Original English brass fittings.

w. 3' 4"	H. 3' ¾"	D. 1' 10"
102 cm	43 cm	56 cm

WOOD : butternut   PROVENANCE : Quebec

(*Coll. Musée de l'Hôtel-Dieu, Quebec*).

448. SLANT-TOP DESK, WITH FOUR DRAWERS. MID 19th C.

Slant-top desk, with a structure of English derivation.

w. 3'	H. 3' 4¾"	D. 1' 5½"
91 cm	103 cm	44 cm

WOOD : pine   PROVENANCE : Montreal

(*Coll. Canada Steamship Lines, Tadoussac, P.Q.*).

449. SLANT-TOP DESK, WITH THREE DRAWERS. EARLY 19th C.

Slant-top desk, with three drawers. There are multiple panels on the side.

w. 3' 4"	H. 3' 10"	D. 1' 6"
102 cm	117 cm	46 cm

WOOD : pine

(*Coll. Mr and Mrs Paul Meredith, Toronto, Ont.*).

450. KNEE-HOLE DESK, INSPIRED BY ENGLISH MODELS. EARLY 19th C.

Knee-hole desk, of English derivation, with Chippendale legs and drawers flush with the stiles. The feet have been extended at a later date.

w. 4' 6"	H. 2' 3¼"	D. 2' 9"
137 cm	64 cm	84 cm

WOOD : pine

(*Coll. Musée Provencher, Cap Rouge, P.Q.*).

451. KNEE-HOLE DESK, WITH SIX DRAWERS. EARLY 19th C.

Knee-hole desk, with six drawers, of English derivation. It was probably used as a teacher's desk. There is a shelf in the kneehole.

w. 3' 7⅜"	H. 2' 4¼"	D. 1' 7"
110 cm	72 cm	48 cm

WOOD : pine

PROVENANCE : old school, Saint-Cuthbert, P.Q.

(*Coll. Provincial Museum, Quebec*).

452. WRITING DESK-COMMODE, INSPIRED BY " SHAKER " TYPE FURNITURE. 19th C.

Writing desk-commode, with two drawers and a drop leaf. The door in the upper stage drops down to form a writing table. This piece, except for the shaping of the lower rail, is highly reminiscent, in its simplicity, of " Shaker " furniture from New England.

w. 2' 10¾"   H. 4' 5¾"   D. 1' 7¼" - 9"
88 cm   136 cm   49 cm - 23 cm
WOOD : butternut and pine
(Coll. Mr L.V. Randall, Montreal).

453. UPRIGHT WRITING DESK, IN THE ADAM AND REGENCY MANNERS. EARLY 19th C.

Upright slant-top writing desk, with five drawers decorated with Adam and Regency motifs. The upper part served to hold papers, and one could sit in front of it on a high stool. The carved elliptical medallions are in *appliqué* work. Original knobs.

w. 3' 6¼"   H. 4' 6½"   D. 1' 7¾"
107 cm   138 cm   50 cm
WOOD : pine

PROVENANCE : Saint-Jean, Isle of Orleans, P.Q.

(Coll. Mrs J.C. Pouliot, Manoir Mauvide-Genest, Saint-Jean, Isle of Orleans, P.Q.).

454. TWO-TIERED SLANT-TOP DESK. EARLY 19th C.

Two-tiered slant-top desk. The upper part served to keep books or papers. The tapered feet are in the Sheraton manner.

w. 2' 8⅝"   H. 4' 10½"   D. 10½" - 1' 8¼"
83 cm   149 cm   27 cm - 51 cm
WOOD : pine

(Coll. Canada Steamship Lines, Tadoussac, P.Q.).

455. SLANT-TOP DESK, INSPIRED BY ENGLISH MODELS. LATE 18th C.

Slant-top desk, with a single drawer, of English derivation. The turned legs are inspired by early Queen Anne country style. A rustic piece.

w. 3' 4"   H. 3' 4½"   D. 1' 8"
102 cm   103 cm   51 cm
WOOD : pine

(Coll. Canada Steamship Lines, Tadoussac, P.Q.).

441. BUREAU, DIT « MAZARIN ». FIN XVIIe S.
KNEE-HOLE DESK, OF " MAZARIN " TYPE.
LATE 17th C.

442. BUREAU DU GENRE « MAZARIN », MAIS
A PIÈTEMENT TOURNÉ. FIN XVIIe S.
KNEE-HOLE DESK, OF " MAZARIN " TYPE,
WITH TURNED LEGS. LATE 17th C.

443. BUREAU, D'ESPRIT LOUIS XIII. FIN
XVIIIe S.
KNEE-HOLE DESK, IN THE LOUIS XIII MAN-
NER. LATE 18th C.

444. BUREAU A CAISSONS ORNÉS DE POINTES
DE DIAMANT. XVIIIe S.
KNEE-HOLE DESK, WITH DIAMOND-POINT
CARVING ON THE DOORS. 18th C.

445. PETIT BUREAU EN PENTE. FIN XVIIIe S.
SMALL SLANT-TOP DESK. LATE 18th C.

446. PETIT B
EN PENTE, O
DESSINS GÉO
QUES. XIXe S
SMALL SLA
DESK, CARV
WITH GEOM
DESIGNS. 1

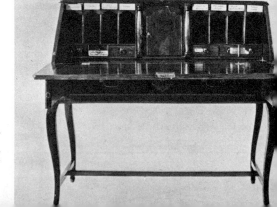

447. BUREAU EN PENTE, A PIEDS GALBÉS,
D'ESPRIT LOUIS XV. FIN XVIIIe S.
SLANT-TOP DESK, WITH CURVED LEGS,
IN THE LOUIS XV MANNER. LATE 18th C.

448. SECRÉTAIRE-BUREAU EN PENTE, A QUA-
TRE TIROIRS. MILIEU XIXᵉ S.
SLANT-TOP DESK, WITH FOUR DRAWERS.
MID 19th C.

449. SECRÉTAIRE-BUREAU EN PENTE, A TROIS
TIROIRS. DÉBUT XIXᵉ S.
SLANT-TOP DESK, WITH THREE DRAWERS.
EARLY 19th C.

450. BUREAU, D'INSPIRATION ANGLAISE. DÉ-
BUT XIXᵉ S.
KNEE-HOLE DESK, INSPIRED BY ENGLISH
MODELS. EARLY 19th C.

451. BUREAU A CAISSONS, A SIX TIROIRS.
DÉBUT XIXᵉ S.
KNEE-HOLE DESK, WITH SIX DRAWERS.
EARLY 19th C.

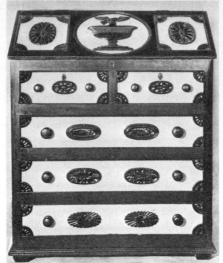

454. BUREAU EN PENTE, A DEUX CORPS. DÉBUT XIXᵉ S.
TWO-TIERED SLANT-TOP DESK. EARLY 19th C.

452. SECRÉTAIRE-COMMODE RUSTIQUE, A PLATEAU RABATTANT, D'INSPIRATION « SHAKERS ». XIXᵉ S.
WRITING DESK-COMMODE, INSPIRED BY " SHAKER " TYPE FURNITURE. 19th C.

453. SECRÉTAIRE A ÉCRIRE DEBOUT, D'INSPIRATION ADAM ET REGENCY. DÉBUT XIXᵉ S.
UPRIGHT WRITING DESK, IN THE ADAM AND REGENCY MANNERS. EARLY 19th C.

455. BUREAU EN PENTE, D'INSPIRATION ANGLAISE. FIN XVIIIᵉ S.
SLANT-TOP DESK, INSPIRED BY ENGLISH MODELS. LATE 18th C.

COMMODES

Havard asserts that the commode, like the armoire, was derived from the coffer, and was first introduced in Paris between 1700 and 1705.[1] The beginning of this evolution was the introduction of a drawer at the bottom of the coffer. Later, the interior of the coffer was entirely fitted with drawers. A typical specimen of this transitional commode is the small coffer with two drawers and turned legs and stretchers in the Louis XIII manner, which according to the nuns of the *Hôtel-Dieu*, Quebec, was left to them in 1685 by Madame d'Ailleboust. If this piece was actually made before 1685, it would be the first commode in existence, as the first French commode was attested to have appeared in 1695. If true, this is an important and very interesting discovery concerning the origins of the commode, which so far have been confused and disputed. But perhaps it should be noted that in the absence of undisputed documentary evidence, the turning of the legs and stretchers may well be of a later type dating from the eighteenth century. Nevertheless, this piece resembles a dower-chest on legs, with two drawers in place of the lid. This was the piece that anticipated the classical commode as we know it today and was the sole early transitional coffer to be found in Canada. Its wrought-iron handles suggest that it was used when travelling, in the same way as the dome-topped chest.

In France the commode was never very popular in peasant homes and only appeared in country districts after 1750.

M. de Salverte maintains on the other hand that the commode is derived from the " *Mazarin* " desk, whose drawers were extended, giving it the appearance of a commode but still serving as a place for keeping papers. Such pieces could not have been made before 1690 according to M. de Salverte, who quotes the deliveries made to Louis XIV, entered in the " *Journal du Garde-meuble* ", the first reference being dated 17th May 1692. Another, dated 1695, reads " ... a large writing-desk with three drawers. "[2]

M. Guillaume Janneau, former Director of the *Mobilier National*, Paris, holds that the first commodes were made by Charles-André Boulle, the master cabinet-maker, and only appeared about 1695.[3] At the time this was a great innovation.

The late Mr E.Z. Massicotte stated that the commode did not appear in Canada until after 1750, when " there were some of walnut with three drawers, three locks, and brass handles ... ", and later " of European woods, inlaid, with marble tops. "[4]

I have found in my own researches that some commodes existed in Canada as early as 1745, " ... in the room was found a commode of walnut with brass ornaments including six handles and fittings, appraised and valued at thirty-five livres. "[5]

In January 1749, Madame Élisabeth Bégon (née Rocbert de la Morandière), Canadian born, wished to sell some furniture to Monsieur Varin who was furnishing Monsieur de Senneville's house for the *Intendant* Bigot who was coming to live in Montreal " ... I could not persuade him to take dining tables or commodes. He preferred to have them made. "[6]

Madame Bégon was preparing to go to live in France at the time and was selling all her furniture before her departure.

A third reference to the existence of the commode in Canada is an extract from an inventory dated 1753 : " a commode of birch with four drawers, thirty livres ... "[7]

(1) Havard, Henry. *Dictionnaire de l'ameublement et de la décoration*. Paris, 1887.
(2) Salverte, le Comte de. *Le meuble français d'après les ornemanistes de 1660 à 1789*. Paris, 1930, p. 8.
(3) Janneau, Guillaume. *Les beaux meubles français anciens*. Ch. Moreau, ed. Paris, 1923, p. 5.
(4) B R H. Vol. XLVIII, February 1942, pp. 33-42.
(5) A J Q, I O A. Inventaire de Jean Boucher dit Belleville, entrepreneur en maçonnerie à Québec le 3 mai 1745. Greffe Barolet (1386).
(6) R A P Q. Correspondance of Madame Élisabeth Bégon (Letter of January 15, 1749). Québec, 1934-35, p. 198.
(7) A J M, I O A. Inventaire fait après le décès dud. Sr De Bouat. Des 12, 14 et 15 Xbre 1753. Greffe Bouron.

Commodes seem to have been rare, but they were mentioned more frequently in inventories· at the end of the eighteenth and the beginning of the nineteenth centuries. They were increasingly found in *habitant* homes during the period of prosperity which followed the Conquest and which lasted until 1830. Although they were a luxury item, this did not prevent the *habitant* from having them made for himself, just as he ordered spoons, forks and goblets of solid silver from native silversmiths.

This same sort of luxury was quite beyond the means of the French peasant of the period. Only the bourgeoisie and the nobility possessed such furniture and utensils.

Louis Franquet, the Royal Engineer, visited Canada on official business in 1753. Travelling by sleigh from Montreal to Quebec, he and his entourage stopped for the night at La Chesnaye where they " ... stayed at the inn of Madame Lamothe, store-keeper; best reception; ate well and slept even better; efficient service; passed a comfortable night in clean beds of the " *Duchesse* " type. Judging from the furnishings of this house, one must conclude that the country folk here are too well off ... "[1]

The way of life of the Canadian *habitant* was of great interest to Franquet, who continually made comparisons with the condition of the French peasant of the time. Although his stay in New France was brief, he noticed how slight the difference was between the standard of living of the *habitant* and that of the well-to-do. He also remarked on the fact that class distinctions were not nearly as sharp as in France.

Peter Kalm, the famous Swedish botanist who visited New France in 1748, was astonished by the affluence of the Canadian *habitant*, an affluence comparable only to that of the bourgeoisie in France. He noticed particularly the clothes of the Canadian country-wife, which were very much richer than those of her French cousins.

Louis Hémon expressed the same astonishment more than 160 years later when he described in *Maria Chapdelaine* the fur coats worn by Canadian country women as they left church in Péribonka after high mass.

However, according to my observations, commodes were not considered to be a luxury in Canada as they were in France. The earliest commodes had a flat front with three drawers of equal size, one above the other, or two large drawers surmounted by two small ones side by side. The latter design were sturdy pieces with strong stiles, and a slightly shaped bottom rail. The drawers had moulding all around them, and the feet were straight.

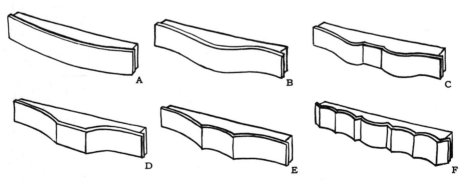

Fig. 7 — *DRAWER FRONTS* - A. *bow-front*; B. *serpentine-front*; C. *arbalète-front* (*cross-bow form*); D. *breakfront*; E. *break-front with concave centre*; F. *broken-front.*

(1) Franquet, Louis. *Voyages et Mémoires sur le Canada.* Québec, 1889, p. 157-158.

Next to appear were commodes with rounded corners, serpentine-fronted with plain sides, or with shaped panels on the side. A few took on sinuous lines, with a dip in the curve of the façade : the so-called " arbalète-fronted " or cross-bow commode. Others had bow fronts, or projecting fronts, the latter being derived from the Anglo-American break-front model. A few had a concave projection. Others, called *Régence* commodes, had the serpentine front and shaped sides and stiles with cabriole feet.

By examining the structure of these commodes, it can be seen that the stiles have been carved from a single thick piece of wood. Opening a drawer, it is evident that the front has been cut by a shaping-saw from a single thick plank. Canadian woodworkers did not take the trouble to shape the interior as was done in the drawers of French commodes. There was no reason to skimp on wood. On the other hand, Canadian commodes were rather small, or at most medium in size, unlike most French commodes of the same period which were large and sometimes bulky.

The sides of the drawers were generally dove-tailed, with one enormous dove-tail in the middle and two half dove-tails, one at the top and one at the bottom, the whole being consolidated with a big hand-forged nail. Nearly two centuries later, the joints are still sound and have not loosened.

The backs of Canadian commodes are generally made of wide planks, tongued and grooved, and assembled horizontally. Channels are cut in the back stiles of the commode, and the boards are slid into position from top to bottom. The ends of these boards are either thinned, to make a flat moulding like those around the edges of an armoire panel, or simply bevelled with a gouge or axe.

There were very few commodes of the " tombeau " type, the façade and sides of which swelled out considerably (called the " *bombée* " commode in Canada). The lower rails were extravagantly curved, with a central decoration of carved shells and flowers.

In another type of commode, the drawers were embellished with small rectangular panels, with a tiny panel in the centre for the keyhole. Although it had Canadian characteristics, it resembled the French commodes of the Dauphiné and Lyonnais districts.

Later, at the beginning of the nineteenth century, the commode with a pierced or open-work lower rail decorated with Louis XV *rocaille* appeared. This commode was made by church carvers who, after a considerable lapse of time, drew upon the *rocaille* designs but gave them a heavy rococo appearance. The *cartels*, whether openwork or not, were probably inspired

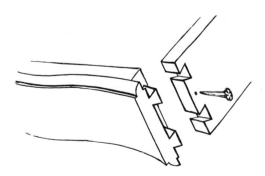

Fig. 8 — *Dove-tail joints of Canadian commode drawers.*

by the designs of Nicolas Pineau, architect and ornament designer.[1] The façade of these commodes was generally serpentine-fronted but projecting in the centre — Canadian in character, but inspired by the American break-front.

The cabriole feet were invariably in the Louis XV style — a long " S " with curve and countercurve, decorated with shaped floral motifs. On the stiles and lower rails of some of these commodes there were sometimes floral designs of the Louis XVI period, such as interlacing *(entrelacs)*, fluting, palmettes, etc. This type was too elaborate, and lacked the simplicity expected in regional furniture. Such commodes were typical of the work of Quevillon and his apprentices.

The type of Canadian commode which was very popular especially in the Montreal region, at the end of the eighteenth and the beginning of the nineteenth centuries, was the arbalète-fronted commode whose feet, instead of being straight or curved, were carved in claw-and-ball design — the claw of a lion or griffin, the talons of an eagle or some other bird, or even an old human hand with sinewy, knotted fingers gripping a ball.

For many years I was quite intrigued by this strange feature, not knowing from where Canadian woodworkers had got the idea. For a while I thought they might have been inspired by the large church candlesticks, or from tomb-shaped altars with bracket feet ending in a claw and ball. This might have made sense if I had not discovered that this type of altar did not make its appearance until the end of the eighteenth century, long after the Conquest, when the English and Scottish woodworkers and cabinet-makers had set up shop in Montreal and Quebec, bringing with them the templates of past and current English styles with which they were familiar. In the English styles of those days there was an enormous variety of spiral and claw-and-ball feet. They appear on the William and Mary, Queen Anne, and especially on Chippendale designs, which spread throughout England in the middle of the eighteenth century and reached the American colonies around 1760. This type is known as *Rococo Chippendale* and its influence can be traced as far as the Low Countries. The Dutch were themselves influenced by Chinese bronzes which they brought from the East. In turn, the English borrowed the motifs from their Dutch allies.[2]

This type of foot was almost unknown in France except in the Bordeaux region where, even today, a few serpentine-fronted commodes with claw-and-ball feet are found. The flourishing commerce between Bordeaux and England encouraged such exchanges, and many pieces of English furniture found a home in this region of France where French woodworkers were quick to imitate them.

Canadian woodworkers borrowed freely from English designs in making the feet of *tombeau* altars, and arbalète-fronted commodes.

Two strange commodes survive today, one in the Museum of Public Archives, Ottawa, which was said to have belonged to the Marquis de Montcalm, the other in the collection of Miss Barbara Richardson of Ste-Agathe des Monts. Both of them are arbalète-fronted but their feet are enormous carved spirals which project beyond the line of the commode. These feet resemble those of a rococo commode in the Philadelphia Museum of Arts which was made by Thomas Chippendale. There is also a likeness to a baroque piece from the middle of the eighteenth century, a *secrétaire* bearing the stamp of K.M. Mattern, the famous German cabinet-maker of Würzburg. The spiral feet are also related to the Queen Anne and William and Mary designs from England. These two commodes date from the same period as the other arbalète-fronted models, and I very much doubt that the Marquis de Montcalm owned the first one.

It is a pity that all these beautiful commodes were spoiled by adding such clumsy features to such typically French bodies. As my friends in France say, it shows a lack of taste. Nevertheless these pieces are interesting as examples of a combination of two styles.

(1) See plate XX of Salverte's book.
(2) The Venetians seem also to have been influenced by oriental motifs.

Generally speaking, there is an amazing variety of Canadian commodes, all of which are interesting, in spite of the frequent touches of naivety or heaviness. Canadian craftsmen differ from those of France in showing more fantasy in their work and much less respect for the traditional designs. This difference is particularly noticeable with the commode, which is one of the most curious pieces of all French Canadian traditional furniture.

456. SMALL COMMODE, FORMERLY OWNED BY MADAME D'AILLEBOUST. 17th c.

Small commode having two drawers resting on a Louis XIII base. The lower cross-rail has *fleur de lys* and volute carvings. This coffer-commode is the forerunner of the commode proper, said to have been formerly owned by Madame d'Ailleboust and left to the Nuns of *l'Hôtel-Dieu*, Quebec, in 1685 (see p. 299). This piece resembles the 17th c. coffer mounted on feet. The coffer lid was replaced by a top, and two drawers were added. (Later more drawers were added, and the cross-stretchers were replaced by short feet.) Original hinged rings with petal-shaped plates and wrought-iron handles on the sides. The keyhole escutcheons were added later and the finial of the cross-stretcher is missing.

w. 2' 2¾"	H. 2' 5½"	D. 1' 5"
68 cm	75 cm	43 cm

WOOD : butternut; FEET : birch

PROVENANCE : Quebec

(Coll. Musée de l'Hôtel-Dieu, Quebec).

457. SERPENTINE-FRONTED COMMODE, WITH FOUR DRAWERS. 18th c.

Serpentine-fronted commode, with four drawers. The two lower drawers are made in one piece, but the moulding and the recess of the central section give the impression of double drawers. The upper keyhole escutcheon is only decorative. This is one of the oldest forms of the commode, and was widely distributed during the eighteenth century. The sides are generally flat and only rarely panelled. Original drop handles, rosettes and keyhole escutcheons. Two of the drawers have been restored.

w. 3' 9"	H. 2' 9½"	D. 1' 11½"
114 cm	85 cm	60 cm

WOOD : butternut

(Coll. Museum of Fine Arts, Montreal).

458. RUSTIC SERPENTINE-FRONTED COMMODE, OF WAVY BIRCH, IN THE LATE LOUIS XIV MANNER. LATE 18th c.

Serpentine-fronted commode in wavy birch, having three drawers. The central motif on the lower rail is a *campane* (upturned bell or upturned gendarme's hat), peculiar to the veneered commodes of the later Louis XIV style.

w. 3' 6½"	H. 2' 10¼"	D. 1' 10"
108 cm	87 cm	56 cm

WOOD : birch   PROVENANCE : Quebec district

(Coll. Mrs Richard R. Costello, Sainte-Agathe des Monts, P.Q.).

459. COMMODE, WITH PALMETTES, IN THE LOUIS XVI MANNER. LATE 18th c.

Commode, with a flat three-drawer façade ornamented with small moulded and shaped panels derived from Dauphiné or Lyonnais. The central panel has a relief-carved *palmette* in the Louis XVI manner. There is a suggestion of a curve on the feet.

w. 3' 5¾"	H. 2' 11¼"	D. 2' ½"
106 cm	90 cm	62 cm

WOOD : pine   PROVENANCE : Neuville, P.Q.

(Coll. Mr and Mrs F.M. Hutchins, Montreal).

460. RUSTIC COMMODE, WITH THREE DRAWERS. EARLY 19th c.

Rustic commode, with flat façade and three drawers decorated with gouge-work and naive rosettes, in the Adam manner. The feet are straight, but curved on the inside. The lower rail is rather heavy and is ornamented with spirals and a naively carved shell. Original wooden knobs. Made by an unskilled hand, but still a pleasing piece.

w. 3' 4¼"	H. 2' 11"	D. 2' ½"
103 cm	89 cm	62 cm

WOOD : pine

(Coll. Mr and Mrs Pierre Gouin, Saint-Sulpice, P.Q.).

461. SERPENTINE-FRONTED COMMODE, WITH FOUR DRAWERS, IN THE LOUIS XV MANNER. LATE 18th c.

Commode with serpentine façade and sides. It has four drawers and a shaped bottom rail decorated with a *palmette*. The diminutive and squat curved feet upset the balance of the piece.

w. 3' 9⅝"	H. 4' 7⅜"	D. 1' 5½"
116 cm	141 cm	44 cm

WOOD : birch   PROVENANCE : Saint-Vallier, P.Q.

(Coll. Miss Barbara Richardson, Sainte-Agathe des Monts, P.Q.).

462. SMALL RUSTIC COMMODE, WITH THREE DRAWERS. LATE 18th c.

Rustic commode, having three drawers and shaped side panels and lower rail. The feet are in lion-claw form. The front rails are heavy, in Canadian fashion. This type of commode was used on journeys, as the original wrought-iron handles on the sides indicate. The shaped apron is a later addition. Attractive but with a naive structure and decoration.

w. 1' 10½"   H. 2' 4½"   D. 1' 9½"
57 cm   72 cm   55 cm

WOOD : butternut

(Coll. Mr and Mrs A.F. Culver, Pointe-au-Pic, P.Q.).

463. SERPENTINE-FRONTED COMMODE, WITH UNUSUAL BOTTOM RAIL. LATE 18th C.

Commode with serpentine front, having three drawers. The unexpected form of the lower rail, which is a peasant creation, has a folk art appeal. The rounded stiles show Louis XV influence.

w. 3' 6¼"   H. 2' 5½"   D. 2' 4½"
108 cm   75 cm   72 cm

WOOD : birch; TOP : pine

PROVENANCE : Saint-Denis-sur-Richelieu, P.Q.

(Coll. Mr and Mrs F.M. Hutchins, Pembroke, Ont.).

464. FOUR-DRAWER COMMODE, FROM ST GERVAIS. LATE 18th C.

Commode, with small elliptical panels with mouldings on the flat façade, a shaped lower rail and the suggestion of a curve on the legs. A simple commode.

w. 4'   H. 2' 10¾"   D. 2' 1⅝"
122 cm   88 cm   65 cm

WOOD : pine   PROVENANCE : Saint-Gervais, P.Q.

(Coll. Canada Steamship Lines, Tadoussac, P.Q.).

465. SERPENTINE ARBALÈTE-FRONTED COMMODE, WITH THREE DRAWERS, IN THE LOUIS XV MANNER. LATE 18th C.

Commode, with massive stiles and curved feet. A very French commode, despite the typically Canadian sturdiness of the stiles and feet. The drawers have been restored.

w. 3' 10"   H. 2' 9¼"   D. 1' 10¾"
117 cm   85 cm   57 cm

WOOD : pine   PROVENANCE : Saint-Eustache, P.Q.

(Coll. Mr W.I. Hart, Sainte-Thérèse de Blainville, P.Q.).

466. SERPENTINE-FRONTED COMMODE, WITH THREE DRAWERS. LATE 18th C.

Serpentine-fronted commode, having small shaped panels and four-leaved *(quartefeuilles)* Gothic motifs. The stiles are decorated with rosettes and the lower rail with a shell. The straight feet with their double scrolls suggest a curve. Shaped side panels. It is in the Louis XV manner, but is very Canadian with its massive stiles and rails. Original iron handles

and wrought-iron petal-shaped rosettes. A robust and charming little piece.

w. 3' 2½"   H. 2' 5½"   D. 2' 1¼"
98 cm   75 cm   64 cm

WOOD : butternut

(Coll. Museum of Fine Arts, Montreal).

467. RUSTIC COMMODE, DECORATED WITH LOZENGES. LATE 18th C.

Rustic commode, having a flat façade and four drawers. The stiles are decorated with lozenges and discs and terminate in claw feet. Heavy rails in the façade. At the top of the rear left stile are carved the letters " P.P. ". The Louis XV brass handles are a later addition. It is a charming piece by an untrained hand.

w. 1' 3⅜"   H. 2' 8"   D. 1' 11⅝"
39 cm   81 cm   60 cm

WOOD : butternut

PROVENANCE : Montreal district

(Coll. Miss Barbara Richardson, Sainte-Agathe des Monts, P.Q.).

468. SERPENTINE-FRONTED COMMODE, IN THE LOUIS XV MANNER. LATE 18th C.

Serpentine-fronted commode, having curved feet terminating in *sabots*, with five drawers, three of them at the top, with a very small one in between. Slight curve on the sides. A very French commode. Original brass fittings and keyhole escutcheons. The top has been replaced. The moulding around the edges is missing.

w. 4' 1¼"   H. 2' 9¾"   D. 2' 1"
125 cm   86 cm   63 cm

WOOD : maple   PROVENANCE : Saint-Ours, P.Q.

(Coll. Mr and Mrs Armand Poupart, Seigneurie de Saint-Ours, P.Q.).

469. SERPENTINE-FRONTED COMMODE, WITH THREE DRAWERS, IN THE LOUIS XV MANNER. LATE 18th C.

Serpentine-fronted commode, with a lower rail and side panels shaped in the Louis XV manner. The curved feet with double volutes terminate in small *sabots*. Interesting shaping on the lower rail. The drawers have been restored.

w. 3' 6¼"   H. 2' 10½"   D. 2' ¼"
108 cm   88 cm   62 cm

WOOD : maple

(Coll. Mrs E. Thornley Hart, Sainte-Agathe des Monts, P.Q.).

470. SERPENTINE-FRONTED COMMODE, IN THE LOUIS XV MANNER, SHOWING DAUPHINÉ INFLUENCE. LATE 18th C.

Serpentine-fronted commode, with drawer façades having shaped panels and mouldings recalling certain commodes of Dauphiné and Lyonnais (see page 301).

w. 3' 8" H. 2' 9½" D. 1' 10½"
97 cm   85 cm   57 cm
WOOD : butternut

(Coll. Mrs L.S. Bloom, Westmount, P.Q.).

471. COMMODE, WITH THREE DRAWERS, OF ARBALÈTE TYPE. LATE 18th C.

Three-drawer commode, having a shaped lower rail decorated with *palmettes*, spirals, a flower and a shell.

w. 3' 9"   H. 3' 3"   D. 1' 10"
114 cm   99 cm   56 cm
WOOD : butternut

PROVENANCE : Ile Perrôt, P.Q.

(Coll. Mrs Nettie Sharpe, Saint-Lambert, P.Q.).

472. " RÉGENCE " SERPENTINE-FRONTED COMMODE, IN TIGER MAPLE. LATE 18th C.

Régence commode, having serpentine-shaped stiles and a shaped lower rail decorated with a shell. The realistic hoof *(sabot)* on the foot is very rare in France and is of Louis XIV derivation. I have seen a Louis XIV chair in the Museum of Decorative Arts in Paris, which has an identical hoof on the foot, this being a precursor of the delicate curved feet with curves and countercurves of the *Régence* and Louis XV styles. A highly successful use of tiger or wavy maple. One of the spirals on the bottom rail is missing.

w. 3' 9½"   H. 2' 11"   D. 1' 10"
116 cm   89 cm   56 cm
WOOD : tiger maple

PROVENANCE : Montreal district

(Coll. Museum of Fine Arts, Montreal, P.Q.).

473. BROKEN-FRONTED COMMODE, WITH THREE DRAWERS, IN THE LOUIS XV MANNER. LATE 18th C.

Serpentine-fronted commode, with three drawers of sinuous form, called " broken-fronted " and having heavy curved double-volute feet. The shaped bottom rails are decorated with shells. Shaped side panels. A robust piece of furniture of Louis XV derivation.

w. 3' 7"   H. 3'   D. 1' 1⅝"
110 cm   91 cm   35 cm
WOOD : pine; STILES : birch

(Coll. Mrs Richard R. Costello, Sainte-Agathe des Monts, P.Q.).

474. " TOMBEAU " COMMODE, WITH BOTTOM RAIL OF AMERICAN DERIVATION. LATE 18th C.

Tombeau commode, with three drawers, the stiles terminating in lions' claws. The bottom rail, of American derivation, is carved with three shells, copied from the Dunlaps, of New Hampshire. The general structure of the commode is in the Louis XV style. The drawer rails are fluted and the side panels are in relief.

w. 4' 2¾"   H. 1' 11¼"   D. 2' ½"
129 cm   59 cm   62 cm
WOOD : butternut   PROVENANCE : Quebec

(Coll. Miss Barbara Richardson, Sainte-Agathe des Monts, P.Q.).

475. DETAIL.

476. " TOMBEAU " COMMODE, WITH THREE DRAWERS. LATE 18th C.

Tombeau commode, with three drawers, each having three panels with prominent mouldings. The lower rail of the façade is incomplete. A commode reminiscent of Dutch Baroque. Photo C.S.L.

WOOD : birch

PROVENANCE : Sainte-Geneviève de Pierrefonds, P.Q.

(Formerly in the collection of Canada Steamship Lines, Tadoussac, P.Q.).

477. NARROW SERPENTINE-FRONTED COMMODE, IN LOUIS XV MANNER. LATE 18th C.

Narrow serpentine-fronted commode, with three drawers in break-front form. The shaped bottom rail is carved with *rocaille* motifs. The curved feet with double scrolls are surmounted by acanthus leaves. The projection of the drawers is inspired by American break-front. The narrow form of this commode is not French, and could well have been a little wider. An agreeable small piece.

w. 2' 7"   H. 2' 10"   D. 1' 7"
79 cm   86 cm   48 cm
WOOD : butternut

PROVENANCE : Baie d'Urfé, P.Q.

(Coll. Dr and Mrs Herbert T. Schwarz, Montreal).

478. SERPENTINE-FRONTED COMMODE, IN THE LOUIS XV MANNER, WITH PROJECTIONS SHOWING AMERICAN BREAK-FRONT INFLUENCE. LATE 18th C.

Serpentine-fronted commode, having three drawers with a central projection, derived from American break-front. The shaped side panels, curved feet and shaped lower rail carved with spirals and a *fleur de lys*, are very French. The height of the lower rail is definitely Canadian. The drawers and feet have been restored. A fine commode from the Montreal district.

w. 3' 3"   H. 2' 9"   D. 1' 11¾"
99 cm   84 cm   60 cm
WOOD : pine   PROVENANCE : Ile Perrôt, P.Q.

(Coll. of the author, Montreal).

479. COMMODE, WITH THREE DRAWERS OF ARBALÈTE TYPE. LATE 18th C.

Three-drawer commode, of arbalète form, in the Louis XV manner but having claw-and-ball feet in the Chippendale tradition and Canadian ornamentation on the lower rail. Shaped side panels. The central decoration of the lower rail is a mixture of *palmettes* and foliage twisted around spirals. (Cf. detail.) Once again the drawer rails are too heavy. A piece which is an interesting combination of styles. The extremities of the drawers have been restored.

w. 3' 1''	H. 2' 8⅜''	D. 1' 9⅜''
94 cm	82 cm	54 cm

WOOD : pine   PROVENANCE : Montreal district

(Coll. Mr and Mrs Thomas Caverhill, Montreal).

480. DETAIL.

481. DETAIL.

482. DETAIL.

483. COMMODE, WITH SERPENTINE FRONT AND FEET OF CHIPPENDALE DERIVATION. LATE 18th C.

Serpentine-fronted commode, having three drawers and feet showing Chippendale influence. There are unusual curves on the side panels and the shaped lower rail is carved with a shell, spirals and parallel gouge incisions (which recall Indian ceramics). The drawer rails are too heavy. Chippendale handles and period Hepplewhite keyhole escutcheons. Rods on the corners and multiple mouldings on the stiles. The feet are rather odd, and the shell has been mutilated. Original deep colouring. A bizarre and amusing commode.

w. 3'	H. 2' 8''	D. 1' 11⅜''
91 cm	81 cm	59 cm

WOOD : pine   PROVENANCE : Montreal

(Coll. Mr and Mrs H.W. Hingston, Montreal).

484. '' TOMBEAU '' OR '' BOMBÉE '' COMMODE, IN THE RÉGENCE MANNER. LATE 18th C.

Commode (called *bombée* in Canada), in the *Régence* style. The façade and the sides are in serpentine form. The bottom rail is shaped and decorated with a central shell. The general form of this piece is very French and recalls commodes of Dauphiné and Lyonnais. The singular curve of the stiles and feet make it very Canadian. A rare and curious piece of furniture.

w. 3' 2¾''	H. 2' 9½''	D. 1' 11¼''
98 cm	85 cm	59 cm

WOOD : birch

(Coll. Mr and Mrs J.W. McConnell, Dorval, P.Q.).

485. DETAIL.

486. COMMODE WITH FOUR DRAWERS, FROM VERCHÈRES. EARLY 19th C.

Commode, having four drawers, with gouge decoration. The shaped lower rail is carved with a shell and two enormous spirals as those on commode no. 474 (revealing Dunlap influence). The shaping of the side panels is very overladen. The drawers are flush with the stiles, a technique used in veneered cabinet-made commode drawers of the eighteenth century. Chippendale style handles.

w. 3' 3''	H. 3'	D. 1' 9¼''
99 cm	91 cm	54 cm

WOOD : pine   PROVENANCE : Verchères, P.Q.

(Coll. Mrs F. Curzon Dobell, Montreal).

487. COMMODE, WITH FOUR DRAWERS, SHOWING VARIOUS INFLUENCES. LATE 18th C.

Four-drawer commode, decorated with small shaped panels. The centre has a concave projection, while the side panels are shaped. The bottom rail and the claw feet are derived from Chinese Chippendale models. The drawers would gain from being decorated with Louis XV fixed brass foliage handles rather than English Sheraton handles. Curious combination of four styles : small drawer panels suggestive of Dauphiné or Lyonnais; very French side panels; a projection of American break-front derivation and a bottom rail and feet borrowed from the Chinese Chippendale rococo. A most interesting piece.

w. 3' 2''	H. 2' 8¾''	D. 1' 9''
96 cm	83 cm	53 cm

WOOD : birch; STILES : maple; TOP : pine

(Coll. Mr and Mrs A.R. Gillespie, Montreal).

488. DETAIL.

489. COMMODE, WITH ARBALÈTE FRONT AND FOUR DRAWERS, IN THE LOUIS XV MANNER. LATE 18th C.

Arbalète-fronted commode, with four drawers, two of which are in the upper portion. The arbalète drawers are decorated with small shaped panels, each ornamented with tiny stylized flowers. Shaped side panels. The lower rail is shaped and carved with acanthus leaves, bluebells, spirals and a *palmette*. Of Dauphiné derivation, but with a profusion of ornaments in the Canadian fashion. A small attractive commode.

w. 3' 1¼''	H. 2' 8''	D. 1' 9''
95 cm	81 cm	53 cm

WOOD : butternut   PROVENANCE : Quebec

(Coll. Dr and Mrs Herbert T. Schwarz, Montreal).

490. ARBALÈTE-FRONTED COMMODE, WITH FEET DERIVED FROM THE CHIPPENDALE STYLE. LATE 18th C.

Three-drawer arbalète commode, with claw-and-ball feet of Chippendale derivation. The lower rail is decorated with a shell. Original handles and keyhole escutcheons. Three badly cast rosettes were recently added. This model was widely distributed throughout French Canada at the end of the eighteenth century and the beginning of the nineteenth. A curious combination of Louis XV and Chippendale rococo styles.

w. 3' 10''　　　H. 2' 11''　　　D. 1' 11''
117 cm　　　　89 cm　　　　58 cm
WOOD : tiger maple

(Coll. Museum of Fine Arts, Montreal).

---

491. ARBALÈTE-FRONTED COMMODE, WITH BOOT-SHAPED FEET. LATE 18th C.

Three-drawer arbalète-fronted commode. The stiles terminate in carvings of boots, as worn by soldiers of the period. A naive and amusing interpretation. An ornament, most likely a *campane* (upturned bell or upturned gendarme's hat), is missing in the centre of the lower rail. A robust and naive piece.

w. 4' 3''　　　H. 2' 10''　　　D. 2' 3¾''
130 cm　　　　86 cm　　　　70 cm
WOOD : butternut
PROVENANCE : Saint-Basile, near Montreal

(Coll. Museum of Fine Arts, Montreal).

---

492. CANADIAN ARBALÈTE-FRONTED COMMODE. LATE 18th C.

Commode, having three arbalète-fronted drawers and feet shaped like realistic hooves, terminating in claws gripping a ball. The lower rail has a pierced rosette carving. The heaviness of the cross-rails, lower rail and the curve of the feet cause a certain lack of balance. A typically Canadian interpretation of Louis XV and Chippendale.

w. 3' 3⅜''　　　H. 2' 9¾''　　　D. 2'
100 cm　　　　86 cm　　　　61 cm
WOOD : pine　PROVENANCE : Montreal district

(Coll. Mr Gilles Corbeil, Saint-Hilaire, P.Q.).

---

493. COMMODE, WITH SHALLOW BOW FRONT, IN TIGER MAPLE. LATE 18th C.

Commode, with three doors flush with the stiles as in veneered cabinet-made commodes. The feet terminate in gnarled hands gripping a ball. The shaped lower rail has in the centre an upturned heart carved with a small flower next to enormous spirals recalling those of the Dunlaps of New Hampshire. The feet are inspired by Chippendale claw-and-ball style. Original Louis XV handles.

w. 3' 10¼''　　　H. 2' 9½''　　　D. 2'
118 cm　　　　85 cm　　　　61 cm
WOOD : tiger maple　PROVENANCE : Montreal

(Coll. Old Seminary of St Sulpice, Notre-Dame, Montreal).

---

494. " TOMBEAU " SERPENTINE-FRONTED COMMODE, IN TIGER MAPLE. LATE 18th C.

Tombeau commode, having three drawers and a shaped lower rail, carved with a shell and enormous spirals. A piece derived from traditional Dauphiné furniture. The spirals and the curve of the stiles are typically Canadian. The drawers have been restored.

w. 3' 4½''　　　H. 2' 11''　　　D. 1' 10¼''
103 cm　　　　89 cm　　　　57 cm
WOOD : maple　PROVENANCE : Three Rivers, P.Q.

(Coll. Mr and Mrs Harvey Rivard, Three Rivers, P.Q.).

---

495. COMMODE OF ARBALÈTE TYPE, WITH ELABORATE BRACKET AND CLAW-AND-BALL FEET, IN THE CHIPPENDALE STYLE. LATE 18th C.

Commode, having an arbalète façade and three drawers. The stiles have *appliqué* brackets or consoles in the Chippendale manner. The feet, in the form of a hand gripping a ball, are also of Chippendale derivation. The sides have prominently incurved doors, enclosing shelves. According to tradition, this commode came from the Old Presbytery of *Notre-Dame*, Montreal, and passed to the Langlois *seigneurie* in Portneuf. A bizarre and rococo commode. The English period handles do not suit this kind of drawer.

w. 3' ¾''　　　H. 2' 7''　　　D. 2'
93 cm　　　　79 cm　　　　61 cm
3' 11¼''
120 cm
WOOD : butternut　PROVENANCE : Montreal

(Coll. Mr and Mrs John Breakey, Breakeyville, P.Q.).

---

496. ARBALÈTE-FRONTED COMMODE, WITH SPIRALLED FEET. LATE 18th C.

Commode, with three drawers, in arbalète form, having stiles terminating in enormous spirals. This is the commode wrongly known as that of the " Marquis de Montcalm ", owned by the Public Archives of Canada. The commode itself is definitely French and is in the Louis XV manner, but with feet derived from the William and Mary and Chippendale styles. (Cf. p. 302.) Original brass handles and keyhole escutcheons (called *bronzes au page* or *bronzes au valet*). Original deep brown colour.

w. 3' 10''　　　H. 2' 9''　　　D. 2'
117 cm　　　　84 cm　　　　61 cm
WOOD : walnut

(Coll. Public Archives of Canada, Ottawa).

---

497. ARBALÈTE-FRONTED COMMODE, WITH SPIRALLED FEET. LATE 18th C.

Three-drawer arbalète-fronted commode, with spiralled feet and shaped lower rail derived from

William and Mary and Chippendale styles. The spiralled feet, surmounted by a *fleur de lys*, have been jointed to the stiles of the commode. Original drop handles, rosettes, and keyhole escutcheons. A curious and rare piece. (Cf. p. 302.)

w. 4' 4¼"	H. 2' 9"	D. 2' 3¼"
133 cm	84 cm	70 cm

WOOD : butternut   PROVENANCE : Iberville, P.Q.

(Coll. Miss Barbara Richardson, Sainte-Agathe des Monts, P.Q.).

498. NARROW COMMODE, WITH DRAWERS SHOWING AMERICAN " BREAK-FRONT " INFLUENCE. LATE 18th C.

Narrow commode, with three drawers and a projection of American break-front derivation. The shaped lower rail is carved with spirals and a central *rocaille* motif and the feet with acanthus leaves. The scrolls on the feet are missing. The drawers have been restored. A narrow commode, not really French in form, although the piece is of Louis XV derivation.

w. 2' 4"	H. 2' 9"	D. 1' 9"
71 cm	84 cm	53 cm

WOOD : butternut

PROVENANCE : Island of Montreal

(Coll. Mrs L.S. Bloom, Westmount, P.Q.).

499. RUSTIC COMMODE, IN THE LOUIS XV MANNER. LATE 18th C.

Commode, in the Louis XV manner, with three drawers, side panels, a shaped lower rail and curved feet. Heavy façade rails.

w. 2' 8⅝"	H. 3' ⅝"	D. 2'
83 cm	93 cm	61 cm

WOOD : pine

(Coll. Mr and Mrs Ross McMaster, Saint-Sauveur des Monts, P.Q.).

500. COMMODE, WITH ARBALÈTE FRONT, FROM DETROIT. LATE 18th C.

Commode, in arbalète form, from Detroit, with three drawers and showing multiple influences. The small panels are derived from Dauphiné commodes, while the *rocaille* motif on the feet and the shaped lateral panels show Louis XV influence. The *palmette* on the lower rail is in the Louis XVI manner. The feet have very French lines, but the general decoration is overladen and gives the piece a baroque look. It was the only piece saved from destruction by the Moran family in the Detroit fire, circa 1820. It is not known where it was made, perhaps in Quebec or in Detroit by a Canadian woodworker. (Cf. commode no. 489, apparently made by the same craftsman, the moulding of the small panels and the ornamentation of the lower rail being very similar.) The top has been replaced, and the moulding on its edge is inappropriate.

w. 2' 10¾"	H. 2' 8"	D. 1' 8¼"
88 cm	81 cm	52 cm

WOOD : butternut

PROVENANCE : Detroit, Mich., U.S.A.

(Coll. Detroit Historical Museum, Detroit, Mich., U.S.A.).

501. COMMODE, WITH FLORAL MOTIF FRIEZES. LATE 18th C.

Three-drawer commode, with carved friezes of flowers and foliage, in the Louis XV manner. Shaped side panels. Acanthus leaves are carved on the feet, but the volutes are missing. The shaped lower rail could well have been decorated. The top opens as the lid of a chest, and the upper drawer is false. The cheap handles have been happily replaced since the photograph was taken. Painted in white.

w. 3' 3¼"	H. 2' 10"	D. 2' ½"
100 cm	86 cm	62 cm

WOOD : pine   PROVENANCE : Pierreville, P.Q.

(Coll. Mr and Mrs W.G. McConnell, Montreal).

502. RUSTIC BROKEN-FRONTED COMMODE. 19th C.

Rustic commode, with six sinuous-fronted drawers and a central flat stile. The space wasted by the heavy rails is a very Canadian characteristic. There is a disparity between the flat uprights and the refined curves on the drawers. This commode, for all its faults, has a most pleasant country tang. Original wooden knobs.

w. 2' 10⅝"	H. 1' 11¾"	D. 1' 1¾"
88 cm	60 cm	35 cm

WOOD : butternut   PROVENANCE : Saint-Vallier, P.Q.

(Coll. Canada Steamship Lines, Tadoussac, P.Q.).

503. ECCLESIASTICAL ROBE CHEST, WITH SERPENTINE FRONT, IN THE MANNER OF THE QUEVILLON SCHOOL. LATE 18th C. OR EARLY 19th C.

Serpentine-fronted vestry commode, with two doors having false drawer fronts. The side panels and bottom rails are shaped with *rocaille* motifs in the Louis XV style, but interpreted in the *Canadian rococo* manner of the Quevillon School. (Cf. p. 302.) The feet, surmounted by acanthus leaves, have been badly worn. There is a false centre post on one of the doors. Inside are several shelves on which chasubles and other church vestments were placed. The surface of the wood has been ruined by the excessive use of strong paint remover. The handles of the false drawers are missing. The wooden knobs and latch are later additions.

w. 4' 5¼"	H. 2' 11⅝"	D. 2' 9½"
136 cm	90 cm	85 cm

WOOD : butternut

PROVENANCE : Sacristy of Notre-Dame de Lourdes Chapel, Montreal
(Coll. Provincial Museum, Quebec).

504. SERPENTINE-FRONTED COMMODE, WITH OPENWORK ROCAILLE BASE, IN THE LOUIS XV MANNER. LATE 18th C.

Serpentine-fronted commode, with three projecting drawers in break-front form. The side panels are shaped and in serpentine form and the rail is in openwork *rocaille*, carved with acanthus leaves, spirals and stylized flowers. Commodes having the base in openwork *rocaille* are found in Languedoc and Provence. This piece was found on the Island of Montreal, and inspired by the Quevillon School. The curved feet, topped by an acanthus leaf and a flower, have been worn away. Several of these commodes have come from St Geneviève de Pierrefonds. It is an example of the *Canadian rococo*-Louis XV style of the late eighteenth and early nineteenth centuries.

w. 2' 10"	H. 2' 9¼"	D. 1' 8¾"
86 cm	85 cm	52 cm
3' 6"		
107 cm		

WOOD : butternut
PROVENANCE : Montreal district, but found in New Hampshire
(Coll. Royal Ontario Museum, Toronto, Ont.).

505. SERPENTINE-FRONTED COMMODE, WITH OPENWORK ROCAILLE BASE. LATE 18th C. OR EARLY 19th C.

Commode, with serpentine front and base in openwork *rocaille*. The three drawers form a projection inspired by American break-front. The stiles are decorated with *entrelacs* in the Louis XVI manner. The openwork *rocaille* lower rail is ornamented with spirals, acanthus leaves and a tiny *palmette*. The curved feet, surmounted by floral motifs, are carved at the extremities in the shape of acanthus leaves. Another commode of Canadian interpretation, derived from the carvings of the Quevillon workshop. The top is made from a single plank of butternut. The drawers have been restored. The dovetails are missing. A small and agreeable baroque piece of furniture.

w. 3' 2¾"	H. 2' 9½"	D. 2' 1¼"
97 cm	85 cm	64 cm

WOOD : butternut   PROVENANCE : Ile Bizard, P.Q.
(Coll. Mr and Mrs Eliot S. Frosst, Westmount, P.Q.).

506. COMMODE, WITH THREE DRAWERS, OF AMERICAN INSPIRATION. LATE 18th C.

Small commode, with a flat façade, three drawers and curved feet in the Queen Anne manner. The shaped lower rail is carved with shells, derived from the patterns of the Dunlap family, woodworkers who flourished in Bedford, New Hampshire between 1750 and 1790. This type of lower rail is often found in French Canada at the end of the eighteenth century. The top has a serpentine front and sides. Original keyhole escutcheons.

w. 3' 4½"	H. 2' 3½"	D. 2' ½"
103 cm	70 cm	62 cm

WOOD : birch
(Coll. Mr and Mrs Peter Laing, Dorval, P.Q.).

507. SERPENTINE-FRONTED COMMODE, WITH TWO DRAWERS, IN THE LOUIS XV MANNER. LATE 18th C.

Commode, with a shaped rail carved with a shell. The curved feet terminate in *sabots*, a typical detail of some Louis XV style armchairs. The top moulding on the first drawer is missing. A small elegant piece of furniture.

w. 2' 11"	H. 1' 8"	D. 1' 11"
89 cm	51 cm	58 cm

WOOD : pine   PROVENANCE : Baie Saint-Paul, P.Q.
(Coll. Mr and Mrs F.M. Hutchins, Pembroke, Ont.).

508. SMALL COMPOSITE COMMODE. EARLY 19th C.

Small two-drawer commode, decorated with *guilloché* work and rosettes. The appliqué lower rail, shaped and having *guilloché* work, recalls Chinese Chippendale. Diamond-point side panels, in the Louis XIII manner. Rustic Louis XV curved feet, carved in four clawed scrolls. The brackets on the stiles are decorated with swans' heads, in the Regency manner. An interesting combination.

w. 3' 1"	H. 2' 8½"	D. 1' 10½"
94 cm	82 cm	57 cm

WOOD : butternut
PROVENANCE : Saint-Benoît-du-Lac, P.Q.
(Coll. Mrs L.S. Bloom, Westmount, P.Q.).

456. PETITE COMMODE, DE MME D'AIL-
LEBOUST. XVIIe S.
SMALL COMMODE, FORMERLY OWNED
BY MME D'AILLEBOUST. 17th C.

457. COMMODE GALBÉE, A QUATRE TIROIRS. XVIIIᵉ S.
SERPENTINE-FRONTED COMMODE, WITH FOUR DRAW-
ERS. 18th C.

458. COMMODE GALBÉE RUSTIQUE EN MERISIER ONDÉ,
D'ESPRIT FIN LOUIS XIV. FIN XVIIIᵉ S.
RUSTIC SERPENTINE-FRONTED COMMODE, OF WAVY
BIRCH, IN LATE LOUIS XIV MANNER. LATE 18th C.

459. COMMODE ORNÉE DE PALMETTES, D'INSPIRATION
LOUIS XVI. FIN XVIIIᵉ S.
COMMODE, WITH PALMETTES, IN THE LOUIS XVI
MANNER. LATE 18th C.

460. COMMODE RUSTIQUE, A TROIS TIROIRS.
DÉBUT XIXe S.
RUSTIC COMMODE, WITH THREE DRAWERS.
EARLY 19th C.

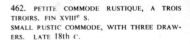

462. PETITE COMMODE RUSTIQUE, A TROIS
TIROIRS. FIN XVIIIe S.
SMALL RUSTIC COMMODE, WITH THREE DRAW-
ERS. LATE 18th C.

461. COMMODE GALBÉE, A QUATRE TIROIRS, D'ES-
PRIT LOUIS XV. FIN XVIIIe S.
SERPENTINE-FRONTED COMMODE, WITH FOUR
DRAWERS, IN THE LOUIS XV MANNER. LATE 18th C.

463. COMMODE GALBÉE, A CURIEUSE CEIN-
TURE. FIN XVIIIᵉ S.
SERPENTINE - FRONTED COMMODE, WITH
UNUSUAL BOTTOM RAIL. LATE 18th C.

464. COMMODE A QUATRE TIROIRS, DE SAINT-
GERVAIS. FIN XVIIIᵉ S.
FOUR-DRAWER COMMODE, FROM ST
GERVAIS. LATE 18th C.

465. COMMODE ARBALÈTE, A TROIS TIROIRS,
D'ESPRIT LOUIS XV. FIN XVIIIᵉ S.
ARBALÈTE-FRONTED COMMODE, WITH THREE
DRAWERS, IN THE LOUIS XV MANNER. LATE
18th C.

466. COMMODE GALBÉE, A TROIS TI-
ROIRS. FIN XVIIIᵉ S.
SERPENTINE-FRONTED COMMODE, WITH
THREE DRAWERS.   LATE 18th C.

467. COMMODE RUSTIQUE, ORNÉE DE
LOSANGES. FIN XVIIIᵉ S.
RUSTIC COMMODE, DECORATED WITH
LOZENGES.   LATE 18th C.

468. COMMODE GALBÉE, D'ESPRIT LOUIS XV. FIN XVIIIᵉ S.
SERPENTINE-FRONTED COMMODE, IN THE LOUIS XV MANNER. LATE 18th C.

469. COMMODE GALBÉE, A TROIS TIROIRS, D'ESPRIT LOUIS XV. FIN XVIIIᵉ S.
SERPENTINE-FRONTED COMMODE, WITH THREE DRAWERS, IN THE LOUIS XV MANNER. LATE 18th C.

470. COMMODE GALBÉE, D'ESPRIT LOUIS XV, D'INSPIRATION DAUPHINOISE. FIN XVIIIᵉ S.
SERPENTINE-FRONTED COMMODE, IN THE LOUIS XV MANNER, SHOWING DAUPHINÉ INFLUENCE. LATE 18th C.

471. COMMODE A TROIS TIROIRS DE
TYPE ARBALÈTE. FIN XVIIIᵉ S.
COMMODE, WITH THREE DRAWERS, OF
ARBALÈTE TYPE. LATE 18th C.

472. COMMODE GALBÉE, DITE « RÉGENCE »,
EN ÉRABLE ONDÉ. FIN XVIIIᵉ S.
"RÉGENCE" SERPENTINE-FRONTED COM-
MODE, IN TIGER MAPLE. LATE 18th C.

473. COMMODE SINUEUSE, A TROIS TIROIRS,
D'ESPRIT LOUIS XV. FIN XVIIIᵉ S.
BROKEN-FRONTED COMMODE, WITH THREE
DRAWERS, IN THE LOUIS XV MANNER.
LATE 18th C.

474. COMMODE « TOMBEAU », A
CEINTURE D'INFLUENCE AMÉRICAINE.
FIN XVIIIᵉ S.
" TOMBEAU " COMMODE, WITH BOT-
TOM RAIL OF AMERICAN DERIVATION.
LATE 18th C.

475. DÉTAIL.
DETAIL.

476. COMMODE « TOMBEAU », A TROIS
TIROIRS. FIN XVIIIᵉ S.
" TOMBEAU " COMMODE, WITH THREE
DRAWERS.   LATE 18th C.

477. COMMODE ÉTROITE ET GALBÉE, D'INSPIRATION LOUIS XV.
FIN XVIIIᵉ S.
NARROW SERPENTINE-FRONTED COMMODE, IN LOUIS XV
MANNER. LATE 18th C.

478. COMMODE GALBÉE, D'ESPRIT LOUIS XV, MAIS A
RESSAUT D'INFLUENCE AMÉRICAINE. FIN XVIIIᵉ S.
SERPENTINE-FRONTED COMMODE, IN THE LOUIS XV
MANNER, WITH PROJECTIONS SHOWING AMERICAN
" BREAK-FRONT " INFLUENCE. LATE 18th C.

479. COMMODE ARBALÈTE, A TROIS TIROIRS
FIN XVIIIᵉ S.
COMMODE, WITH THREE DRAWERS, OF
ARBALÈTE TYPE. LATE 18th C.

480. DÉTAIL.
DETAIL.

481. DÉTAIL.
DETAIL.

483. COMMODE GALBÉE, A PIÈTEMENT D'IN-
FLUENCE CHIPPENDALE. FIN XVIIIᵉ S.
COMMODE, WITH SERPENTINE FRONT AND
FEET OF CHIPPENDALE DERIVATION. LATE
18th C.

482. DÉTAIL.
DETAIL.

484. COMMODE DITE « TOMBEAU » OU « BOM-
BÉE » D'ESPRIT RÉGENCE. FIN XVIIIᵉ S.
"TOMBEAU" OR "BOMBÉE" COMMODE, IN
THE "RÉGENCE" MANNER.   LATE 18th C.

485. DÉTAIL.
DETAIL.

486. COMMODE A QUATRE TIROIRS, DE VER-
CHÈRES. DÉBUT XIXᵉ S.
COMMODE, WITH FOUR DRAWERS, FROM
VERCHÈRES. EARLY 19th C.

487. COMMODE A QUATRE TIROIRS, MARQUÉE DE MULTIPLES INFLUENCES. FIN XVIIIe S. COMMODE, WITH FOUR DRAWERS, SHOWING VARIOUS INFLUENCES. LATE 18th C.

488. DÉTAIL.
DETAIL.

489. COMMODE ARBALÈTE, A QUATRE TIROIRS, D'ESPRIT LOUIS XV. FIN XVIIIe S. COMMODE, WITH ARBALÈTE FRONT AND FOUR DRAWERS, IN THE LOUIS XV MANNER. LATE 18th C.

490. COMMODE ARBA-
LÈTE, A PIÈTEMENT D'ES-
PRIT CHIPPENDALE. FIN
XVIIIe S.
ARBALÈTE-FRONTED COM-
MODE, WITH FEET DE-
RIVED FROM THE CHIP-
PENDALE STYLE. LATE
18th C.

COMMODE ARBALÈTE, A PIÈTE-
T EN BOTTES. FIN XVIIIe S.
ALÈTE-FRONTED COMMODE, WITH
T-SHAPED FEET. LATE 18th C.

492. COMMODE ARBALÈTE CANADIENNE. FIN
XVIIIe S.
CANADIAN ARBALÈTE-FRONTED COMMODE
LATE 18th C.

493. COMMODE LÉGÈREMENT GALBÉE,
ÉRABLE ONDÉ. FIN XVIIIe S.
COMMODE, WITH SHALLOW BOW FRONT,
TIGER MAPLE. LATE 18th C.

494. COMMODE GALBÉE DE TYPE « TOM-
BEAU », EN ÉRABLE ONDÉ. FIN XVIIIᵉ S.
"TOMBEAU" SERPENTINE-FRONTED COM-
MODE, IN TIGER MAPLE. LATE 18th C.

495. COMMODE ARBALÈTE, ORNÉE DE CONSOLES
ET DE PIEDS ROCOCO CHIPPENDALE. FIN XVIIIᵉ S.
COMMODE, OF ARBALÈTE TYPE, WITH ELABORATE
BRACKET CORNERS AND CLAW-AND-BALL FEET,
IN THE CHIPPENDALE STYLE. LATE 18th C.

496. COMMODE ARBALÈTE, A PIÈTEMENT EN SPIRALES.
FIN XVIIIᵉ S.
ARBALÈTE-FRONTED COMMODE, WITH SPIRALLED FEET.
LATE 18th C.

497. COMMODE ARBALÈTE, A PIÈTEMENT EN SPIRALES.
FIN XVIIIᵉ S.
ARBALÈTE-FRONTED COMMODE, WITH SPIRALLED FEET.
LATE 18th C.

499. COMMODE RUSTIQUE, D'ESPRIT
LOUIS XV. FIN XVIIIᵉ S.
RUSTIC COMMODE, IN THE LOUIS XV MAN-
NER. LATE 18th C.

498. COMMODE ÉTROITE, A TROIS TIROIRS A
RESSAUT, D'INSPIRATION « BREAK-FRONT »
AMÉRICAIN. FIN XVIIIᵉ S.
NARROW COMMODE, WITH DRAWERS SHOW-
ING AMERICAN "BREAK-FRONT" INFLUEN-
CE. LATE 18th C.

500. COMMODE ARBALÈTE, DE DÉTROIT.
FIN XVIIIᵉ S.
COMMODE, WITH ARBALÈTE FRONT, FROM
DETROIT. LATE 18th C.

501. COMMODE ORNÉE DE FRISES A MOTIFS FLO-
RAUX. FIN XVIIIe S.
COMMODE, WITH FLORAL MOTIF FRIEZES. LATE
18th C.

502. COMMODE RUSTIQUE SINUEUSE.
XIXe S.
RUSTIC BROKEN-FRONTED COMMODE.
19th C.

503. COMMODE-CHASUBLIER GALBÉE,
DE L'ÉCOLE DE QUEVILLON. FIN
XVIIIe S. OU DÉBUT XIXe S.
ECCLESIASTICAL ROBE CHEST, WITH
SERPENTINE FRONT, IN THE MANNER
OF THE QUEVILLON SCHOOL. LATE
18th C. OR EARLY 19th C.

504. COMMODE GALBÉE, A BASE AJOURÉE EN ROCAILLE, D'ESPRIT LOUIS XV. FIN XVIIIᵉ S.
SERPENTINE-FRONTED COMMODE, WITH OPENWORK ROCAILLE BASE, IN THE LOUIS XV MANNER. LATE 18th C.

505. COMMODE GALBÉE, A BASE AJOURÉE EN ROCAILLE. FIN XVIIIᵉ S. OU DÉBUT XIXᵉ S.
SERPENTINE-FRONTED COMMODE, WITH OPENWORK ROCAILLE BASE. LATE 18th C. OR EARLY 19th C.

506. COMMODE A TROIS TIROIRS, D'INSPIRATION AMÉ-
RICAINE. FIN XVIIIᵉ S.
COMMODE, WITH THREE DRAWERS, OF AMERICAN
INSPIRATION. LATE 18th C.

507. COMMODE GALBÉE A DEUX TIROIRS, D'ESPRIT
LOUIS XV. FIN XVIIIᵉ S.
SERPENTINE-FRONTED COMMODE, WITH TWO DRAW-
ERS, IN THE LOUIS XV MANNER. LATE 18th C.

508. PETITE COMMODE COMPOSITE. DÉBUT XIXᵉ S.
SMALL COMPOSITE COMMODE. EARLY 19th C.

DOORS FROM A LATE EIGHTEENTH-CENTURY ARMOIRE,
IN THE LOUIS XV MANNER. ORIGINAL COLOURS.

DOORS

Early interior and exterior doors are to be found in old stone houses along the St Lawrence Valley, from Montreal to Cap Tourmente on the north shore, and to Rivière-du-Loup on the south shore. There are also more elaborate ones to be found in convents and churches, either in solid wood or partly glazed with two or more panels, " The sum of 80 livres paid to Messrs Reiche and Du bois for making two glazed doors for the Community. "[1] Most of them date from the end of the eighteenth or the beginning of the nineteenth centuries and are in the Louis XIII style, with lozenge or diamond-point motifs, or in the Louis XV style, with shaped panels decorated with spirals and rosettes.

Bedroom doors were glazed to allow light from the common room to enter the small bedrooms which were often poorly lit. The flickering rays of the dying fire, or the soft glow of a night-light in the common room perhaps comforted those who could not immediately fall asleep in the long winter nights.

Decorated and shaped doors were almost unknown in rural homes in France in the eighteenth and early nineteenth centuries, but the panelling and interior doors of churches were so highly regarded in French Canada at this time that the *habitants* wished their homes to have the same elaborate elegance. They wanted to beautify their houses like the people of the upper classes. The workmanship of these doors was often very simple and even primitive, and unfortunately most of them have been spoiled, having suffered many mutilations and transformations for almost two centuries.

509. DOORS, OF THE URSULINE CONVENT, QUEBEC. 18th C.

Two finely proportioned doors, with large projecting mouldings and deep panels. These doors are in the Community Hall of the Ursuline Nuns, Quebec. Original wrought-iron handles and keyhole escutcheons.

w. 5' 8¼"   h. 6' 7"
174 cm   201 cm

WOOD : pine   PROVENANCE : Quebec

(Coll. Monastère des Ursulines, Quebec).

510. BEDROOM DOOR, IN THE LOUIS XV MANNER. LATE 18th C.

Bedroom door, in the Louis XV manner, having four upper panels and a shaped lower panel with a top rail carved with a foliated scroll between two spirals. The double spirals on the lower rail are very French. Original forged-iron handle and latch. The door was made in 1775, at the same time as the building of the *Maison Marcile* which was then in the parish of Longueuil.

w. 2' 7"   h. 6' 1"
80 cm   185 cm

WOOD : pine   PROVENANCE : Saint-Lambert, P.Q.

(Coll. Mrs Nettie Sharpe, Saint-Lambert, P.Q.).

511. TWO SHAPED DOORS, IN THE LOUIS XV MANNER. 18th C.

Two doors, with shaped panels, in the Louis XV manner, having rails carved with flowers and incised spirals. It is of naive workmanship.

w. 2' ⅝"   h. 6' 1½"
63 cm   187 cm

WOOD : pine

(Coll. Mr and Mrs A.F. Culver, Pointe-au-Pic, P.Q.).

512. GLAZED AND DECORATED DOOR, FROM ST GENEVIÈVE DE PIERREFONDS. EARLY 19th C.

Glazed door, having shaped panels, with a middle rail carved with rosettes, *palmettes*, shells and the monogram " A M ", which stood for " Ave Maria " and was found in the houses of both the Congregation of *Notre-Dame* and the Sulpician Fathers. The doors probably came from a house belonging to one of these orders, in the St Geneviève district. The *palmettes* resemble those on no. 513. Original wrought-iron door handle.

w. 2' 4"   h. 5' 10¼"
71 cm   179 cm

WOOD : pine

PROVENANCE : Sainte-Geneviève de Pierrefonds, P.Q.

(Coll. Mr and Mrs David Yuile, Sainte-Geneviève de Pierrefonds, P.Q.).

(1) Livre des Recettes et dépenses de l'Hôpital-Général de Québec pour les années 1715-16.

513. TWO ARCHED DOORS, WITH VARIEGATED DECORATION. EARLY 19th C.

Two arched doors, with shaped panels in the Louis XV manner, carved with shells, *palmettes*, rosettes, raspberries, foliage and bluebells. The decoration is overladen and rather rococo. A very Canadian interpretation. These communicating *salon* doors come from an old stone house in St Théodosie, P.Q. They were made by a woodworker of St Jean Baptiste de Rouville about 1815 or 1816, when the house itself was built. This woodworker went from village to village making furniture and doors for 25 *sous* per day plus his keep. Sometimes he would stay in the same house for months. Much of his work is found in this district.

w. 3' 6¾''   H. 6' 7''
109 cm   201 cm

WOOD : pine   PROVENANCE : Sainte-Théodosie, P.Q.

(Coll. Mr and Mrs Larry Hart, Senneville, P.Q.).

514. BEDROOM DOOR. LATE 18th C.

Bedroom door, having five panels with arched relief motifs derived from simplified linen folds. Original wrought-iron handle.

w. 2' 7⅜''   H. 6' 1½''
80 cm   187 cm

WOOD : pine

(Coll. Miss Barbara Richardson, Sainte-Agathe des Monts, P.Q.).

515. BEDROOM DOOR, DECORATED WITH MULTIPLE SPIRALS. LATE 18th C.

Bedroom door, with shaped panels and rails carved with multiple spirals. The interpretation and the profusion of spirals give it a real Canadian regional appearance.

w. 2' 8¾''   H. 6' 2''
83 cm   189 cm

WOOD : pine

(Coll. Mr and Mrs Leslie E. Haslett, Sainte-Marguerite, P.Q.).

516. GLAZED BEDROOM DOOR, FROM ST ANNE DE LA PÉRADE. LATE 18th C.

Glazed bedroom door, with very gracious and elegant shaping in the Louis XV manner. It has been widened on all sides. A beautiful Canadian door.

w. 2' 7½''   H. 6' 6''
80 cm   198 cm

WOOD : pine

PROVENANCE : Sainte-Anne de la Pérade, P.Q.

(Coll. Mr and Mrs J.W. McConnell, Saint-Sauveur des Monts, P.Q.).

517. DOOR, FROM THE OLD CHAPEL OF NOTRE-DAME DE LA VICTOIRE, MONTREAL. LATE 18th C.

Door in Louis XV derivation, from the old chapel of *Notre-Dame de la Victoire*, Montreal, built in 1713 and demolished in 1900. The upper panel is decorated with foliated scrollwork. Elegant shaping. Unfortunately the bottom panel has been cut off.

w. 2' 10¼''   H. 6' 2''
87 cm   188 cm

WOOD : pine   PROVENANCE : Montreal

(Coll. Château de Ramezay, Montreal).

518. GLAZED DOOR, WITH THREE PANELS. LATE 18th C.

Glazed door, with a shaped top rail. Two of the three panels are carved with the cross of St Andrew. A combination of Louis XIII and Louis XV motifs.

w. 2' 4''   H. 6' ¾''
71 cm   185 cm

WOOD : pine

PROVENANCE : Sainte-Anne de la Pérade, P.Q.

(Coll. Mr and Mrs Gordon Reed, Saint-Sauveur des Monts, P.Q.).

519. DOOR, FROM ST GENEVIÈVE DE PIERREFONDS. LATE 18th C.

Door, from St Geneviève de Pierrefonds, with two shaped panels in the Louis XV tradition. This style of door is often seen in the old stone houses which line the St Lawrence between Montreal and St Anne de la Pocatière. The period iron knob is peculiar to these doors.

w. 2' 10''   H. 6' 2½''
86 cm   189 cm

WOOD : pine

PROVENANCE : Sainte-Geneviève de Pierrefonds, P.Q.

(Coll. Miss Barbara Richardson, Sainte-Agathe des Monts, P.Q.).

520. GLAZED DOOR, ORNAMENTED WITH A SHELL. LATE 18th C.

Glazed door, with a shaped top rail carved with a shell. There are also two shaped vertical panels. A classical door, except for the shell, which spoils the curve of the shaping and is clumsily placed.

w. 2' 8¼''   H. 5' 8¼''
82 cm   174 cm

WOOD : pine

PROVENANCE : Laprairie de la Madeleine, P.Q.

(Coll. Mr and Mrs Fred Mulligan, Pleasant Valley, Henrysburg, P.Q.).

521. DOOR, CARVED WITH DIAMOND POINTS AND SIMPLIFIED LINEN FOLDS. 18th C.

Door, having four vertical panels carved with diamond points and simplified linen folds. There are horizontal *caissons* or rectangular panels on the centre rail and vertical ones between the panels. An interesting combination of diamond points inspired by the medieval linen fold and the Louis XIII style.

w. 2' 6¾'' H. 5' 9⅝''
  78 cm   177 cm

WOOD : pine

PROVENANCE : Saint-Barthélémy, P.Q.

(Coll. Mr and Mrs Wilson Mellen, Sainte-Agathe des Monts, P.Q.).

522. GLAZED DOOR, ORNAMENTED WITH TWO ROSETTES. LATE 18th C.

Glazed door, having a shaped top rail carved with a rosette, and two shaped vertical panels. The central rail is carved with a larger rosette. As in door no. 520, the upper rosette breaks the flow of the line. The red and white colouring is recent.

w. 2' 5⅝'' H. 5' 6⅝''
  75 cm   169 cm

WOOD : pine

(Coll. Mr and Mrs Pierre Gouin, Saint-Sulpice, P.Q.).

523. GLAZED BEDROOM DOOR. LATE 18th C.

Glazed door, with shaped arches and panels. The panels are pleasantly decorated with spirals and stylized flowers. Attractive proportions. The base has been restored.

w. 2' 7¼'' H. 5' 7¼''
  80 cm   171 cm

WOOD : pine

(Coll. Senator and Mrs H. de M. Molson, Lac Violon, Sainte-Agathe des Monts, P.Q.).

524. GLAZED BEDROOM DOOR. LATE 18th C.

Glazed bedroom door, with shaped upper rails and panels, in the Louis XV manner. A common type of glazed door peculiar to the old houses of the St Lawrence Valley. Pretty pane mouldings. Typical iron knob of the period.

w. 2' 6'' H. 5' 10½''
  76 cm   179 cm

WOOD : pine

(Coll. Miss Barbara Richardson, Sainte-Agathe des Monts, P.Q.).

525. DOOR, WITH DECORATION REMINISCENT OF GOTHIC MOTIFS. 18th C.

Two-panelled bedroom door, with a motif of double spirals reminiscent of traditional French Gothic designs. Original wrought-iron handle.

w. 2' 5'' H. 5' 9''
  74 cm   175 cm

WOOD : pine

(Coll. Miss Barbara Richardson, Sainte-Agathe des Monts, P.Q.).

526. BEDROOM DOOR, CARVED WITH LOZENGES, IN THE LOUIS XIII MANNER. 18th C.

Bedroom door, with four rectangular panels decorated with lozenges, and a horizontal panel bearing the cross of St Andrew. A fine door in the Louis XIII tradition.

w. 2' 9¾'' H. 5' 7½''
  86 cm   171 cm

WOOD : pine

(Coll. Mr and Mrs J.W. McConnell, Saint-Sauveur des Monts, P.Q.).

527. GLAZED BEDROOM DOOR. LATE 18th C.

Glazed bedroom door, with a shaped panel of Louis XV derivation. The larger of the two spirals, with its carved foliage, recalls those on certain late eighteenth and early nineteenth century church doors and panels, made in the Quevillon or Liébert workshops. The uprights have been restored.

w. 2' 8'' H. 6' 11¾''
  81 cm   212 cm

WOOD : pine

(Coll. Mr and Mrs J.W. McConnell, Saint-Sauveur des Monts, P.Q.).

528. EXTERIOR DOOR, IN THE REGENCY MANNER. EARLY 19th C.

Exterior door, with six panels and a central pilaster ornamented with foliated scrollwork of Louis XV derivation. Both upper and lower panels are definitely Regency. The *appliqué* panels in the centre are shaped in the Louis XV manner and are decorated with a small foliated scroll bearing a *fleur de lys* resembling those on the small panels of the two-tiered buffet no. 126. Note the border of small lozenges. The rails are unbalanced.

w. 2' 11½'' H. 5' 8½''
  90 cm   174 cm

WOOD : pine PROVENANCE : Verchères, P.Q.

(Coll. Mr Russell J. Barrett, Baie d'Urfé, P.Q.).

529. DOOR PANEL, WITH ROCAILLE MOTIFS (DETAIL). EARLY 19th C.

Panel from a door, decorated with spirals, *rocaille* motifs and floral designs with foliated crosiers. This is the best example known of the work of the Quevillon or Liébert Schools. The spirals terminate in foliated crosiers, a characteristic of these workshops. This door comes from the old Church of St Laurent, Montreal.

w. 2' 8'' H. 3' 11''
  81 cm   119 cm

WOOD : butternut

PROVENANCE : Saint-Laurent, Montreal
(Coll. Mrs R.S. Bloom, Westmount, P.Q.).

530. EXTERIOR DOOR, IN ADAM STYLE. EARLY 18th C.
Exterior door, with six panels carved with rosettes and elliptical medallions derived from the Adam style, but of rustic workmanship.

w. 2' 9¾''   H. 6' 6''
  86 cm   198 cm

WOOD : pine
(Coll. Mrs Richard R. Costello, Sainte-Agathe des Monts, P.Q.).

531. EXTERIOR DOOR, IN FOLK ART STYLE. LATE 19th C.
Exterior door, with seven panels ornamented with folk-art motifs : suns, urns on tables decorated with linen folds, branches, and sun-rays surmounted by small birds, etc. Of naive workmanship.

w. 2' 8⅝''   H. 5' 10¾''
  83 cm   180 cm

WOOD : pine
PROVENANCE : Sainte-Hénédine, Dorchester, P.Q.
(Coll. Mr Russell J. Barrett, Baie d'Urfé, P.Q.).

532. CHURCH DOOR, IN THE LOUIS XIV MANNER. LATE 18th C.
Door, with four panels decorated with Louis XIV motifs. The top panel has a garland embellished with a ribbon. The *rosace* of the central panel is also decorated with ribbons and flowers. The motifs on the frames are pearls and *rais de cœur*. The two *rosaces* on the lower panels enclose vine leaves and bunches of grapes and are decorated with roses. This door was found in the Church of St Marie de Beauce and originally came from a church in Quebec City. It has been thought that it dates from the late seventeenth century and that it came from the old Jesuit Church in Quebec, which was partly destroyed by the bombardment of the town in 1759. This particular door must not be confused with the arched doors found in Short's engraving of the interior of the Jesuit Church after the siege of Quebec.

w. 2' 10''   H. 6' 11½''
  86 cm   212 cm

WOOD : butternut; UPRIGHTS : walnut
PROVENANCE : Quebec

(Coll. Provincial Museum, Quebec).

509. PORTES, DES URSULINES DE QUÉBEC. XVIIIᵉ S.
DOORS, OF THE URSULINE CONVENT, QUEBEC.   18th C.

510. PORTE DE CHAMBRE, D'ESPRIT LOUIS XV.
FIN XVIIIe S.
BEDROOM DOOR, IN THE LOUIS XV MANNER.
LATE 18th C.

511. DEUX PORTES CHANTOURNÉES, D'ESPRIT
LOUIS XV. XVIIIe S.
TWO SHAPED DOORS, IN THE LOUIS XV
MANNER. 18th C.

512. PORTE VITRÉE ET DÉCORÉE, DE SAINTE-
GENEVIÈVE DE PIERREFONDS. DÉBUT XIXᵉ S.
GLAZED AND DECORATED DOOR, FROM ST
GENEVIÈVE DE PIERREFONDS.   EARLY 19th C.

513. DEUX PORTES CINTRÉES A DÉCORS
MULTIPLES. DÉBUT XIXᵉ S.
TWO ARCHED DOORS, WITH VARIEGATED
DECORATION. EARLY 19th C.

514. PORTE DE CHAMBRE. FIN
XVIIIᵉ S.
BEDROOM DOOR. LATE 18th C.

515. PORTE DE CHAMBRE DÉCO-
RÉE DE MULTIPLES SPIRALES. FIN
XVIIIᵉ S.
BEDROOM DOOR, DECORATED WITH
MULTIPLE SPIRALS. LATE 18th C.

516. PORTE DE CHAMBRE VITRÉE, DE SAINTE-
ANNE DE LA PÉRADE. FIN XVIIIᵉ S.
GLAZED BEDROOM DOOR, FROM ST ANNE
DE LA PÉRADE. LATE 18th C.

517. PORTE DE L'ANCIENNE CHAPELLE DE
NOTRE-DAME DE LA VICTOIRE, MONTRÉAL.
FIN XVIIIᵉ S.
DOOR, FROM THE OLD CHAPEL OF NOTRE-DAME
DE LA VICTOIRE, MONTREAL. LATE 18th C.

518. PORTE VITRÉE, A TROIS PAN-
NEAUX. FIN XVIIIᵉ S.
GLAZED DOOR, WITH THREE
PANELS. LATE 18th C.

519. PORTE, DE SAINTE-GENEVIÈVE
DE PIERREFONDS. FIN XVIIIᵉ S.
DOOR, FROM ST GENEVIÈVE DE
PIERREFONDS. LATE 18th C.

20. PORTE VITRÉE, ORNÉE D'UNE COQUILLE.
N XVIIIᵉ S.
LAZED DOOR, ORNAMENTED WITH A SHELL.
ATE 18th C.

521. PORTE ORNÉE DE POINTES DE DIAMANT
ET DE PLIS DE SERVIETTE SIMPLIFIÉS. XVIIIᵉ S.
DOOR, CARVED WITH DIAMOND POINTS AND
SIMPLIFIED LINEN FOLDS. 18th C.

522. PORTE VITRÉE, DÉCORÉE DE DEUX RO-
SETTES. FIN XVIIIᵉ S.
GLAZED DOOR, ORNAMENTED WITH TWO
ROSETTES. LATE 18th C.

523. PORTE DE CHAMBRE VITRÉE.
FIN XVIIIᵉ S.
GLAZED BEDROOM DOOR. LATE
18th C.

524. PORTE DE CHAMBRE VITRÉE.
FIN XVIIIᵉ S.
GLAZED BEDROOM DOOR. LATE
18th C.

525. PORTE A MOTIF D'ESPRIT GOTHIQUE.
XVIIIᵉ S.
DOOR, WITH DECORATIONS REMINISCENT OF
GOTHIC MOTIFS.   18th C.

526. PORTE DE CHAMBRE DÉCORÉE DE LO-
SANGES, D'ESPRIT LOUIS XIII. XVIIIᵉ S.
BEDROOM DOOR, CARVED WITH LOZENGES,
IN THE LOUIS XIII MANNER.   18th C.

527. PORTE DE CHAMBRE VITRÉE. FIN XVIII
GLAZED BEDROOM DOOR.   LATE 18th C

528. PORTE D'EXTÉRIEUR, D'ESPRIT RE-
GENCY. DÉBUT XIXᵉ S.
EXTERIOR DOOR, IN THE REGENCY MANNER.
EARLY 19th C.

529. PANNEAU DE PORTE, A MOTIFS RO-
CAILLE (DÉTAIL). DÉBUT XIXᵉ S.
DOOR PANEL, WITH ROCAILLE MOTIFS (DE-
TAIL). EARLY 19th C.

530. PORTE D'EXTÉRIEUR, DE STYLE ADAM.
DÉBUT XIXᵉ S.
EXTERIOR DOOR, IN ADAM STYLE. EARLY
19th C.

531. PORTE D'EXTÉRIEUR. ART POPULAIRE.
FIN XIXᵉ S.
EXTERIOR DOOR, IN FOLK ART STYLE. LATE
19th C.

532. PORTE D'ÉGLISE, DE STYLE LOUIS XI
FIN XVIIIᵉ S.
CHURCH DOOR, IN THE LOUIS XIV MANNE
LATE 18th C.

CLOCKS, SPINNING-WHEELS, CHANDELIERS

CLOCKS

Long case clocks, or grandfather clocks, were usually found in the common room with the case screwed to the wall in order to balance the pendulum as the floors were not always level.

The first clocks appeared in Canada in the seventeenth century. The movement and face were made in France, but sometimes the pine case would be Canadian, as happened with the clock of Madame de la Peltrie.

Henry Solo, the first known clock-maker, established a business in Quebec in 1730, followed by Jean Ferment in 1734, and N. Gosselin in 1758. An inventory of 1738 mentions, " a clock with cords and weights, which does not chime, made by Dubois, the clockmaker in this town, valued with its pinewood case ... "[1]. None of these early clocks has been found. The oldest Canadian clocks that I have been able to discover are two clocks with steel mechanisms made by François Valin, master-locksmith and armourer of Quebec, around 1750. There used to be a mantel clock signed *Valin à Québec* in the presbytery at Baie St-Paul and there is another Valin clock at Boston. The violin-shaped case,[2] which was so popular in France at the end of the eighteenth century, was not known in Canada. It was only after Canada had been ceded to the English that clocks became more common in middle class and well-to-do *habitant* homes.

English clock-makers established themselves in Quebec, and introduced the popular designs which were current in England. James Godfrey Hanna and James Orkney began making clocks in Quebec city immediately after the conquest.

Other well-known clockmakers included C.S.H. Bellerose, the French Canadian, who made clocks at Three Rivers from the end of the eighteenth century until 1843; the five Twiss brothers of Connecticut, a family of American clock-makers, who moved to Montreal in 1821, and whose clocks were generally signed J.B. and R. Twiss. They were manufactured by a factory technique and the movements were made of cherry wood. A large number of these clocks found their way across the country. Joseph Balleray of Longueuil and C.J. Ardouin of Quebec manufactured clocks in the same style. Ardouin also imported clocks from France, and one of these can be seen in the visiting-room of the *Hôpital-Général*, Quebec. The *habitants* used a translation of the English term " grandfather clock " for these clocks (which are still called *horloge grand-père* in French Canada). They were considered a luxury and the most valuable piece of furniture in *habitant* homes. The clock-faces were usually decorated with floral designs, although a few with Canadian landscapes by the painter Cornelius Krieghoff have been found. Mantel clocks in veneered wood cases did not appear in Canada until the nineteenth century. Most of them were made in New England.

533. FRENCH CLOCK, WITH CANADIAN CASE. 17th C.
Clock, with a French steel and brass movement and a Canadian case. It is known as the *Horloge de Madame de la Peltrie*. (For more details cf. p. 28.)

w. 9¾"	H. 6' 8¾"	D. 8½"
25 cm	205 cm	22 cm

WOOD : pine   PROVENANCE : Cap-Rouge, P.Q.

(Coll. Mr and Mrs Gordon Reed, Saint-Sauveur des Monts, P.Q.).

534. GRANDFATHER CLOCK, IN THE ENGLISH MANNER. EARLY 19th C.
Grandfather clock case, in the English manner, made about 1820 and signed " James Godfrey Hanna ". The door is of Chippendale derivation.

w. 1' 5½"	H. 7' 1¾"	D. 8¼"
44 cm	218 cm	21 cm

WOOD : mahogany   PROVENANCE : Quebec

(Coll. Provincial Museum, Quebec).

(1) A J M. Inventaire fait à la Reqte du Sr Mocquin du 31e mars 1738, Montréal. Greffe Chêvremont.
(2) Cf. p. 9, preface of G.H. Rivière.

535. CLOCK, BY THE TWISS BROTHERS. EARLY 19th C.
Long case clock, with a movement of cherrywood and a case of pine. In the English tradition.

w. 1' 4¾" H. 7' 1" D. 9½"
42 cm 216 cm 24 cm
1' ¼"
31 cm

WOOD : pine PROVENANCE : Montreal

(Coll. Mr and Mrs Georges-Étienne Gagné, Neuville, P.Q.).

536. CLOCK, BY BELLEROSE. 19th C.
Long case clock made by Bellerose from Three Rivers, having a case reminiscent of certain French clocks, with a dome-top cut-away pediment. One rail is decorated with an inlaid shell. The movement is in brass.

w. 1' 6¼" H. 7' 5" D. 8"
47 cm 226 cm 20 cm
1' 4¼"
42 cm

WOOD : butternut PROVENANCE : Three Rivers, P.Q.
(Coll. Mr and Mrs Robertson Fleet, Montreal).

537. CLOCK, BY SAVAGE & SONS. 19th C.
Clock, signed " Savage & Sons ", Montreal. The movement is in metal and the case of mahogany. Made about 1830.

w. 1' 9" H. 6' 11½" D. 10"
53 cm 212 cm 25 cm

WOOD : mahogany PROVENANCE : Quebec
(Coll. Provincial Museum, Quebec).

SPINNING-WHEELS

The spinning-wheel is more properly classified as a handicraft instrument than as furniture, but it was to be found in many homes in the eighteenth and particularly the nineteenth centuries, and, being so much a part of daily life at that time, came to be regarded as furniture. When household duties allowed a moment of respite, the women would spin their wool and flax.

There were two principal types of spinning-wheels in the eighteenth century: one had a large hand-driven wheel which was operated while standing; the other had a small wheel, also hand-driven, but at which the woman would be seated. The spinning-wheel with a pedal, the most familiar today, did not appear until the end of the eighteenth and the beginning of the nineteenth centuries.

The spinning-wheel is a picturesque but obsolete piece, home-spinning having all but disappeared in Quebec in the last few years. American dealers have recently started to come to Canada with enormous trucks to buy all the spinning-wheels (as well as skein-winders and cradles) they can find in the province. They are then stripped and waxed and find a ready place in the homes of well-to-do Americans of the second or third generation who are beginning to feel the sentimental need of creating ancestors for themselves. I have often been shown a spinning-wheel near the fireplace in the living-room of American families, which was proudly claimed as an heirloom from great-grandmother. These ancestral relics were all too obviously spinning-wheels which had been found in the attics of French Canada.

538. PEDAL-OPERATED SPINNING-WHEEL. EARLY 19th C.
Pedal-operated spinning-wheel.

WOOD : birch PROVENANCE : Quebec
(Coll. Musée des Ursulines, Quebec).

539. SMALL PEDAL-OPERATED SPINNING-WHEEL, WITH DISTAFF. 18th C.
Small pedal-operated spinning-wheel, with distaff. It is practically identical with small Norman and Breton spinning-wheels.

WOOD : birch

PROVENANCE : Isle of Orleans, P.Q.
(Coll. Mrs J.C. Pouliot, Manoir Mauvide, Saint-Jean, Isle of Orleans, P.Q.).

540. PEDAL-OPERATED SPINNING-WHEEL. 19th C.
Pedal-operated spinning-wheel, the most common type of Quebec spinning-wheel. They were still being made in the same manner a few years ago.

w. 3' H. 3' 6¼"
91 cm 108 cm

WOOD : birch PROVENANCE : Quebec
(Coll. Musée de l'Hôtel-Dieu, Quebec).

541. SMALL PEDAL-OPERATED SPINNING-WHEEL. LATE 18th C.
Small pedal-operated spinning-wheel, with turned uprights.

w. 2' ½" H. 2' 8¾"
62 cm 83 cm

WOOD : birch   PROVENANCE : Quebec district

(Coll. Mrs Louis Vachon, Sainte-Marie, Beauce, P.Q.).

542. PEDAL-OPERATED SPINNING-WHEEL.   LATE 18th C.

Pedal-operated spinning-wheel; this particular type is as rare in Canada as in France.

W. 1' 6''   H. 5'
46 cm   152 cm

WOOD : birch

PROVENANCE : Les Éboulements, P.Q.

(Coll. Canada Steamship Lines, Tadoussac, P.Q.).

543. SMALL PEDAL-OPERATED SPINNING-WHEEL.   LATE 18th C.

Small pedal-operated spinning-wheel.

W. 2' 2''   H. 1' 11⅜''
66 cm   60 cm

WOOD : birch

PROVENANCE : Three Rivers district

(Coll. Musée du Séminaire, Three Rivers, P.Q.).

CHANDELIERS

Chandeliers do not, strictly speaking, belong in the category of furniture, but I wish to include them as they offer evidence of the strong aesthetic sense of church woodworker-carvers of French Canada.

Chandeliers are mentioned in the account books of the new church of St Augustin near Quebec, in 1731 : " ...Three wooden chandeliers for midnight mass, of which two are turned, and the other plain wood; one has only six branches, one has eight, and one has thirty-six, ''[1] and again in 1734, " paid to Jean Valin the sum of 100 l. for a chandelier of thirty branches of spiralled wood. ''[2]

Chandeliers were carved for the church of Saint-Pierre, Isle of Orleans, in 1734; for the church of Cap-Santé, by Jean-François Godin, in 1739; for Lachenaie, in 1741; for Charlesbourg, in 1749; and for a large number of churches up to 1833.   The purchase of chandeliers is shown in the account books of the different parishes, together with the names of the woodworker-carvers — François Baillairgé, François Lepage, George and Daniel Finsterer, André Achim, François-Xavier Berlinguet, André Paquet, Séraphin Bertrand and Honoré Lorrin.

The Canadian chandelier is related to the Dutch chandelier and the French brass chandelier of the Louis XIV style which had its origin in Holland and resembles those seen in Vermeer paintings of Dutch interiors.   No brass work was being made in Canada at the time, so the Canadian chandelier was carved in native woods in conventional designs and embellished with pine cones and acanthus leaves.   The curved iron rods terminating in candle sockets were decorated with balls in the middle.   The chandeliers had one, two or three tiers, one above the other, and could hold from eight to thirty-six candles.

They were all covered with gold leaf, and certain parts were painted a very deep green. Some churches had between ten and twenty such chandeliers which produced a very special light in which the candle flames seemed to dance in the soft play of shadows.   No lighting system of today can compare with it.

A large number of chandeliers were made of tin by blacksmiths and tinsmiths, but the design was somewhat different.   The branches were decorated with leaves having a pattern of veins in *repoussé* work.

Chandeliers were to be found only in the larger houses and in churches with particularly high ceilings.   In addition there were also candlesticks, including the saucer-shaped *martinets* made of silver or brass, and brass chandeliers, like the one shown in the picture " Canadian

---

(1) Livre de Comptes de la Fabrique de Saint-Augustin. Second Mémoire des ameublements qui sont venus à l'église de Saint-Augustin depuis la fin de l'année 1713 jusqu'à la Saint-Michel 1731.
(2) Livre de Comptes de la Fabrique de Saint-Augustin pour l'année 1734.

Minuet ", in the book *Travels through the Canadas* by George Heriot. Canadian and foreign connoisseurs consider the carved chandelier to be one of the most beautiful Canadian creations.

The iron lamp was the commonest form of lighting in the *habitant* home. This lamp was called a hearth lamp with a harpoon *(lampe d'âtre à harpon)* in France, Betty lamp in the United States, and crow's beak lamp *(bec de corbeau)* in Canada. It burnt white porpoise *(beluga)* or whale oil soaked in a wick and had a pointed hook which was driven into the beams of the room.

In every home, there would be a large number and variety of candlesticks, flat candlesticks *(bougeoirs, martinets)*, pewter *flambeaux*, wooden candelabras with iron wire branches, and tin lanterns. A *fanal* lantern was mentioned in an inventory of 1759. Lamps and storm lanterns would be used when going outside the house or when visiting the stable. These lanterns were turret-shaped and the light shone through small holes pierced in a geometric pattern, which also protected the flame from the wind.

544. THREE-TIERED CHANDELIER. EARLY 19th C.
Chandelier, in turned wood, having thirty branches and a shaft carved with acanthus leaves, gadroons, rings and pine cones. It is one of the rare chandeliers with three tiers of branches. Painted a deep green and gilded. The candle sockets have been replaced.
WOOD : pine
(Coll. of the author, Montreal).

545. THREE-TIERED TURNED CHANDELIER. EARLY 19th C.
Three-tiered gilded chandelier, with a turned shaft carved in gadroons and pearls. Sockets replaced.
WOOD : pine
(Coll. Dr and Mrs Herbert T. Schwarz, Montreal).

546. CARVED WOODEN CHANDELIER, WITH SIX BRANCHES. EARLY 19th C.
Chandelier, in carved wood, having a shaft carved with acanthus leaves, pine cones and an acorn. Painted in deep green and gilded. This type of chandelier was widely used in churches in the eighteenth and nineteenth centuries. Two branches are missing.
WOOD : pine
(Coll. Mr and Mrs Victor Drury, Lake Anne, P.Q.).

547. TURNED CHANDELIER, WITH MULTIPLE ORNAMENTS. EARLY 19th C.
Turned chandelier, with a shaft decorated with *appliqué* acanthus leaves, pearls, acorns and bluebells. The branches are ornamented with balls, acorns and sockets carved with cables. Probably made in the Quevillon workshop or by one of his apprentices. An almost identical chandelier is to be found in the McCord Museum, Montreal.
WOOD : pine

PROVENANCE : Old Church of Sainte-Thérèse de Blainville, P.Q.
(Coll. Dr and Mrs Herbert T. Schwarz, Montreal).

548. WOODEN CHANDELIER, FROM THE OLD CHURCH OF LONGUEUIL. EARLY 19th C.
Twenty-branched chandelier, made in 1826 by the carver-woodworker André Achim for the Church of Longueuil. Achim's entry in the parish account books reads : " Wooden chandelier, with iron wires. The shaft is in carved and gilded wood. The branches are decorated with little wooden balls. " It is the classic type of chandelier of the late eighteenth and early nineteenth centuries, decorated with acanthus leaves, grapes or pine cones, with numerous branches and balls, all either painted a deep green or gilded. A Canadian creation derived from the Louis XIV or Dutch chandeliers.
WOOD : pine
(Coll. Château de Ramezay, Montreal).

549. EIGHT-BRANCHED CHANDELIER, DERIVED FROM LOUIS XIV MODELS. 18th C.
Eight-branched chandelier, in carved and turned wood. The shaft is embellished with an urn and pine cone and the branches are carved with acanthus leaves and spirals, the candle sockets, with incurved foliage and pearls. According to oral tradition among the Ursuline Nuns, this chandelier was hung in front of the altar of the Sacred Heart in 1739. It is the only known example of an early eighteenth-century chandelier.
WOOD : pine
(Coll. Musée des Ursulines, Quebec).

550. RUSTIC CANDELABRA, WITH TWELVE BRANCHES, IN TURNED WOOD. LATE 18th C.
Candelabra, in turned wood with twelve iron branches and candle sockets in tin. A very pleasant piece.
(Coll. Mr and Mrs F.M. Hutchins, Pembroke, Ont.).

533. HORLOGE FRAN-
ÇAISE, A GAINE CA-
NADIENNE. XVIIᵉ S.
FRENCH CLOCK, WITH
CANADIAN CASE.
17th C.

535. HORLOGE
« TWISS ». DÉBUT
XIXᵉ S.
CLOCK, BY THE TWISS
BROTHERS. EARLY
19th C.

537. HORLOGE
« SAVAGE & SONS ».
XIXᵉ S.
CLOCK, BY SAVAGE
& SONS. 19th C.

534. HORLOGE A GAI-
NE, OU « GRAND-PÈ-
RE », D'ESPRIT AN-
GLAIS. DÉBUT XIXᵉ S.
GRANDFATHER
CLOCK, IN THE
ENGLISH MANNER.
EARLY 19th C.

536. HORLOGE
« BELLEROSE ». XIXᵉ S.
CLOCK, BY BELLE-
ROSE. 19th C.

538. ROUET A PÉDALE. DÉBUT XIXᵉ S.
PEDAL-OPERATED SPINNING-WHEEL.
EARLY 19th C.

539. PETIT ROUET A PÉDALE, AVEC
QUENOUILLE. XVIIIᵉ S.
SMALL PEDAL-OPERATED SPINNING-
WHEEL, WITH DISTAFF. 18th C.

540. ROUET A PÉDALE. XIXᵉ S.
PEDAL-OPERATED SPINNING-WHEEL.
19th C.

541. PETIT ROUET A PÉDALE. FIN
XVIIIᵉ S.
SMALL PEDAL-OPERATED SPINNING-
WHEEL. LATE 18th C.

542. ROUET A PÉDALE. FIN XVIIIᵉ S.
PEDAL-OPERATED SPINNING-WHEEL.
LATE 18th C.

543. PETIT ROULT A PÉDALE. FIN
XVIIIᵉ S.
SMALL PEDAL-OPERATED SPINNING-
WHEEL. LATE 18th C.

544. LUSTRE A TROIS RANGÉES DE BRANCHES.
DÉBUT XIXᵉ S.
THREE-TIERED CHANDELIER.   EARLY 19th C.

545. LUSTRE TOURNÉ, A TROIS RANGÉES DE
BRANCHES. DÉBUT XIXᵉ S.
THREE-TIERED TURNED CHANDELIER.   EARLY
19th C.

546. LUSTRE EN BOIS SCULPTÉ, A SIX BRAN-
CHES. DÉBUT XIXᵉ S.
CARVED WOODEN CHANDELIER, WITH SIX
BRANCHES.   EARLY 19th C.

547. LUSTRE TOURNÉ, AUX MULTIPLES ORNE-
MENTS. DÉBUT XIXᵉ S.
TURNED CHANDELIER, WITH MULTIPLE
ORNAMENTS. EARLY 19th C.

549. LUSTRE A HUIT BRANCHES, D'INSPIRA-
TION LOUIS XIV. XVIIIᵉ S.
EIGHT-BRANCHED CHANDELIER, DERIVED
FROM LOUIS XIV MODELS. 18th C.

548. LUSTRE EN BOIS, DE L'ANCIENNE ÉGLISE
DE LONGUEUIL. DÉBUT XIXᵉ S.
WOODEN CHANDELIER, FROM THE OLD
CHURCH OF LONGUEUIL. EARLY 19th C.

550. CHANDELIER RUSTIQUE EN BOIS TOURNÉ,
A DOUZE BRANCHES. FIN XVIIIᵉ S.
RUSTIC CANDELABRA, WITH TWELVE BRAN-
CHES, IN TURNED WOOD. LATE 18th C.

FUNCTIONAL AND DECORATIVE HOUSEHOLD OBJECTS AND MANTELPIECES

FUNCTIONAL AND DECORATIVE HOUSEHOLD OBJECTS

Many useful objects embellished the French Canadian home, and while these were primarily functional, the *habitant* took pleasure in making them attractive and decorative. Mirror frames, caskets, tiny chests, salt-boxes, knife-boxes, comb or pipe racks, dust-pans, shelves, etc., were made by the *habitants* in a naive and simple manner during the long winter evenings.

However, professional carvers also made some of these things, but their work is immediately recognizable by the decoration. A number of square, round, and oval boxes are also to be found which were made by Indians or in the Indian manner. These were decorated with geometric designs derived from Indian folk tradition, or, in some cases, with designs borrowed from the European settlers.

All the decorative and functional objects made by the *habitants* reflect the character of French Canada, and although these things were made in an unsophisticated manner, yet they reveal that the *habitants* possessed an instinctive aesthetic sense.

551. CASKET, CARVED WITH GEOMETRIC DESIGNS. 18th C.

Casket, carved with geometric designs, motifs found all over Europe. Note the mullers or small roundels carved with incurved rays. The majority of these designs were originated by the artisans when experimenting with a pair of compasses. The casket has a sliding lid. It was sometimes used as a candle box. Folk art which has its roots in the Middle Ages.

WOOD : pine   PROVENANCE : Saint-Joachim, P.Q.

(Coll. Miss Barbara Richardson, Sainte-Agathe des Monts, P.Q.).

552. SMALL CASKET, CARVED WITH GEOMETRIC DESIGNS. 19th C.

Small casket, carved with geometric designs, of a folk type, which include several popular motifs, such as sun roundels, stars, saw-teeth, *dents de loup*, simplified linen folds, and lozenges.

WOOD : pine

(Coll. Mrs L.S. Bloom, Westmount, P.Q.).

553. SMALL CASKET, WITH APPLIQUÉ CARVINGS. 18th C.

Small casket, with *appliqué* carvings of stars, swans, buckles, flowers and *cabochons*. Folk art.

w. 1'   H. 6''   D. 8''
  31 cm   15 cm   21 cm

WOOD : butternut

PROVENANCE : Three Rivers, P.Q.

(Coll. Musée du Séminaire des Trois-Rivières, P.Q.).

554. BOX, CARVED WITH DIAGONAL REEDING. 18th C.

Box, carved with checkered squares incised with diagonal grooves arranged in opposite directions, producing a special light effect. It recalls parallel or diagonal reeding found in some furniture from the Bresse region of Burgundy. Edges in *dents de loup*.

w. 5¼''   H. 2⅜''   D. 3⅜''
  13 cm   6 cm   8 cm

WOOD : pine

(Coll. Mr and Mrs Georges-Étienne Gagné, Neuville, P.Q.).

555. MINIATURE TRUNK. 18th C.

Miniature trunk, ornamented with balsam needles, *dents de loup*, *guilloché* work and lozenges. A pretty little dome-top casket.

WOOD : pine   PROVENANCE : Quebec

(Coll. Musée de l'Hôtel-Dieu, Quebec).

556. SMALL CARVED CASKET, FROM LES ÉBOULEMENTS. 19th C.

Small casket, having panels carved with swans, ducks, birds, branches and leaves.

w. 1' ¼''   H. 6½''   D. 8½''
  31 cm   16 cm   22 cm

WOOD : pine

PROVENANCE : Les Éboulements. P.Q.

(Coll. of the author, Montreal).

557. OVAL BOX, IN THE INDIAN MANNER. 18th C.

Oval box, made from thin, curved wood. The lid is carved with geometric designs and incised leaves in the Indian manner. Probably made by a Huron from Jeune Lorette.

w. 1' 1''   H. 8''   D. 7⅜''
33 cm   20 cm   19 cm

WOOD : LID, maple

PROVENANCE : Quebec

(Coll. Musée de l'Hôtel-Dieu, Quebec).

558. SMALL MIRROR FRAME, IN THE LOUIS XV AND LOUIS XVI MANNER. LATE 18th C.

Mirror frame, carved with a Louis XVI *palmette* and foliated scrolls in crosier form, in the Louis XV manner.

w. 1' 5''   H. 2' 3''
43 cm   69 cm

WOOD : butternut

(Coll. Miss Barbara Richardson, Sainte-Agathe des Monts, P.Q.).

559. CANADIAN RELIQUARY HOLDER. LATE 18th C.

Canadian reliquary holder, from a church. The oval medallion contained the relic and the lower frame held the parchment which certified its authenticity. A Canadian rococo frame carved with shells, stars, scrolls, foliage and a cherubin's head. There are other almost identical models in the churches of St Jean-Port-Joli and Notre-Dame, Montreal.

w. 1' 6½''   H. 2' 6½''
47 cm   77 cm

WOOD : pine

PROVENANCE : Saint-Roch l'Achigan, P.Q.

(Coll. Mr L.V. Randall, Montreal).

560. NAIVE FOLK-ART MIRROR FRAME. 19th C.

Naive folk-art mirror frame, with human and animal carvings.

w. 1' 8''   H. 2' 4''
51 cm   71 cm

WOOD : pine

(Coll. Mrs Richard R. Costello, Sainte-Agathe des Monts, P.Q.).

561. RUSTIC MIRROR FRAME. 19th C.

Rustic mirror frame, pierced with variegated circles and incised with wavy grooves.

w. 1' 4⅝''   H. 2' ⅝''
42 cm   62 cm

WOOD : pine

(Coll. Mr and Mrs J.N. Cole, Murray Bay, P.Q.).

562. SMALL SHELF FROM VERCHÈRES. LATE 18th C.

Small shelf, from Verchères, carved with rosettes and grooves.

w. 1' 10¼''   H. 8''   D. 4½''
57 cm   20 cm   11 cm

WOOD : pine

PROVENANCE : Petit Côteau, Verchères, P.Q.

(Coll. Mrs Nettie Sharpe, Saint-Lambert, P.Q.).

563. SHELF, FROM CHATEAUGUAY. LATE 18th C.

Shelf, from Châteauguay, with fine carvings of acanthus leaves, pearls, parallel reeding, foliated scrolls, vine leaves, rosettes and roses. It comes from the hand of a highly skilled carver and woodworker.

w. 4' 2''   H. 1' 1''   D. 7''
127 cm   33 cm   18 cm

WOOD : pine and birch

PROVENANCE : Châteauguay, P.Q.

(Coll. Mrs Nettie Sharpe, Saint-Lambert, P.Q.).

564. SHELF, WITH CARVED AND APPLIQUÉ MOTIFS. 19th C.

Shelf, carved with daisies, fern leaves, dentils and cabling.

w. 2' 8¼''   H. 1' 3''   D. 5¼''
82 cm   38 cm   13 cm

WOOD : pine   PROVENANCE : Caughnawaga, P.Q.

(Coll. Canada Steamship Lines, Tadoussac, P.Q.).

565. RUSTIC SHELF, IN FOLK ART STYLE. 19th C.

Rustic shelf in folk art, from the same hand as the previous one, but with an angel's head, apparently of Indian type and probably carved by an Iroquois from Caughnawaga.

w. 2' 3''   H. 1' 2½''   D. 5''
69 cm   37 cm   13 cm

WOOD : pine   PROVENANCE : Caughnawaga. P.Q.

(Coll. Mr and Mrs P.T. Molson, Lac Violon, Sainte-Agathe des Monts, P.Q.).

566. SMALL RUSTIC SHELF. 19th C.

Small rustic shelf, with festooned rails, and incised with a double sun roundel, the initials " A b ", garlands of foliage, and lozenges on the lower shelf.

WOOD : pine

(Coll. Mr and Mrs Bronson Culver, Montreal).

567. SHELF, FROM QUEBEC. 18th C.

Shelf from Quebec, carved with dentils, ovolos and festoons.

w. 2' 4¾''   H. 6⅝''   D. 4⅝''
73 cm   17 cm   12 cm

WOOD : pine   PROVENANCE : Quebec

(Coll. Miss Barbara Richardson, Sainte-Agathe des Monts, P.Q.).

568. SHELF, ORNAMENTED WITH VERTICAL REEDING. 18th C.
Shelf, carved with vertical and parallel reeding.

| w. 4' | H. 6¾'' | D. 4¾'' |
| 122 cm | 17 cm | 12 cm |

WOOD : pine
(Coll. Canada Steamship Lines, Tadoussac, P.Q.).

569. RUSTIC SHELF. 19th C.
Rustic shelf, carved with *guilloché* lozenges, dentils and gadroons. A very naive piece.

| w. 2' ¼'' | H. 5⅝'' | D. 4¾'' |
| 62 cm | 14 cm | 12 cm |

WOOD : pine
(Coll. Mr and Mrs J.N. Cole, Montreal).

570. SMALL RUSTIC SHELF. 18th C.
Small rustic shelf, carved with *rais de cœur* and ovolos.

| w. 1' 5⅜'' | H. 7'' |
| 44 cm | 18 cm |

WOOD : pine
(Coll. Mr and Mrs J.N. Cole, Montreal).

571. RUSTIC SALT-BOX. 19th C.
Rustic salt-box.
WOOD : pine
(Coll. Mrs L.S. Bloom, Westmount, P.Q.).

572. SALT-BOX, FROM ST DENIS-SUR-RICHELIEU. 19th C.
Salt-box, from St Denis-sur-Richelieu, with one drawer and surmounted by two geese.

| w. 10½'' | H. 1' 7'' | D. 7'' |
| 27 cm | 48 cm | 18 cm |

WOOD : pine
(Coll. Mrs Nettie Sharpe, Saint-Lambert, P.Q.).

573. RUSTIC SALT-BOX. 19th C.
Rustic salt-box, with shaped sides.
WOOD : pine   PROVENANCE : Quebec district
(Coll. Dr and Mrs Claude Bertrand, Outremont, P.Q.).

574. RUSTIC SALT-BOX, IN FOLK ART STYLE. 19th C.
Rustic salt-box, carved with three cocks and clover leaves. On the hinged lid are found the initials " LL ".
WOOD : pine   PROVENANCE : Quebec district
(Coll. Dr and Mrs Claude Bertrand, Outremont, P.Q.).

575. RUSTIC SALT-BOX. 18th C.
Rustic salt-box, with a hinged lid.
WOOD : pine   PROVENANCE : Quebec district
(Coll. Mrs L.S. Bloom, Westmount, P.Q.).

576. DUSTPAN. 18th C.
Dustpan.
WOOD : pine   PROVENANCE : Quebec
(Coll. Musée de l'Hôtel-Dieu, Quebec).

577. SMALL RUSTIC URN, WITH FLAT BACK. 18th C.
Small rustic urn or salt-box, carved with a shell and having a flat back and a shaped rim.
(Coll. Mr and Mrs P.T. Molson, Lac Violon, Sainte-Agathe des Monts, P.Q.).

578. RUSTIC KNIFE-BOX. 19th C.
Rustic knife-box, decorated with painted geometric designs. The upper part is shaped and pierced with circles.
WOOD : pine
(Coll. Canada Steamship Lines, Tadoussac, P.Q.).

579. RUSTIC SALT-BOX, WITH LONG BACK-BOARD. 19th C.
Rustic salt-box, with a long back-board used for grinding rock salt.
WOOD : pine
(Coll. Mr and Mrs H.J. Godber, Sainte-Agathe des Monts, P.Q.).

MANTELPIECES

Fireplaces were very simple in Canada, usually being made of stone and nearly always covered with white-washed rough-cast. Mantelpieces came into fashion at the end of the eighteenth century in the wealthier homes of Quebec and Montreal, in convents and to some extent in *habitant* houses.

The mantelpiece was made of wood as an embellishment for the fireplace, and while serving a utilitarian purpose, it became quite a decorative feature of the room. The opening of the fireplace would be covered during the warm weather with panels or summer doors *(portes d'été)*.

These summer doors kept out the cold, prevented the wind from blowing soot into the house, and acted as a screen against any birds which might find their way down the flue.

About the end of the eighteenth century, a few stone houses on Montreal Island had fireplaces fitted with lintels which were decorated with narrow horizontal panels. There were also vertical panels on the chimney, some of them shaped and forming a frame for a large central panel. A few mantelpieces, such as those found in an old house at Bout de l'Ile, Montreal, or the one by Pierre Émond in the dispensary of the *Hôpital-Général* of Quebec, or the one in the former presbytery of the basilica of Quebec, were finished with shaped lintels under the mantel shelf. These were derived from the marble chimneys in the Louis XV style which were then in vogue in France.

The supporting pilasters of some Canadian mantelpieces were often influenced by the English Adam style with its sun-bursts, shell-work and flutings, and subsequently by the Regency style. Almost all the houses of the bourgeois in Quebec and Montreal adopted these designs at the beginning of the nineteenth century.

580. MANTELPIECE, OF LOUIS XV DERIVATION. LATE 18th C.

Mantelpiece, in the Louis XV manner, built by Pierre Émond, woodworker-carver, for the Nuns of the *Hôpital-Général*, Quebec (c. 1770-80). Émond was undoubtedly inspired by the marble lintels of Louis XV mantelpieces. This piece can still be seen in the dispensary of the hospital. The handles of the " summer doors " are later additions.

w. 5' 1"   H. 4'
   155 cm   122 cm
WOOD : pine   PROVENANCE : Quebec
(*Coll. Hôpital-Général, Quebec*).

581. MANTELPIECE, FROM A HOUSE IN BOUT-DE-L'ILE, MONTREAL. LATE 18th C.

Mantelpiece, with shaped lintel in the Louis XV manner. The pilasters of the jambs are in the Louis XVI or Adam manner, with flutings and rosettes. The panels in the chimney-piece are decorated with paintings of flowers and birds. The large panels on the chimney-piece and hearth are ornamented with suns and rays. This mantelpiece comes from an old stone house in Bout-de-l'Ile, Montreal.

w. 5'   H. 8' 5"
   152 cm   257 cm
WOOD : pine
PROVENANCE : Bout-de-l'Ile, Montreal
(*Coll. Mr and Mrs Jean Raymond, Westmount, P.Q.*).

582. MANTELPIECE, IN ADAM MANNER. LATE 18th C.

Mantelpiece, with several panels decorated with *appliqué* mouldings, cornices and pilasters in the Adam manner. The pilasters on the chimney-piece are carved with lozenges, giving it a rustic appearance. This mantelpiece was installed in the Community Hall of the Ursulines Convent, Quebec.

w. 7'   H. 9' 6¾"
   213 cm   291 cm

WOOD : birch PROVENANCE : Quebec
(*Coll. Convent of the Ursulines, Quebec*).

583. MANTELPIECE, FROM ILE D'ORLÉANS. LATE 18th C.

Mantelpiece, with pilasters carved with grooved chevrons, reminiscent of arrowheads. . The carving on the cornice includes cabling, dentils and gouge work. The two panels are decorated with *fleurs de lys* and rosettes, but the pearls consist curiously enough of real dried peas embedded in the wood. The Adam influence predominates.

w. 4' 6"   H. 5' 5½"
   137 cm   166 cm
WOOD : pine   PROVENANCE : Isle of Orleans, P.Q.
(*Coll. Mr Russell J. Barrett, Baie d'Urfé, P.Q.*).

584. MANTELPIECE, IN THE ADAM AND REGENCY MANNERS. EARLY 19th C.

Mantelpiece, with panels and " summer doors " in the Adam manner. The fluted colonnades are carved with gadroons and simplified acanthus leaves in the Late Regency tradition. Foliated scrolls, flowers and water leaves are in *appliqué* work on the lintel.

w. 4' ½"   H. 4' 8⅝"
   123 cm   144 cm
WOOD : pine
(*Coll. Mr and Mrs Eliot S. Frosst, Westmount, P.Q.*).

585. MANTELPIECE, IN THE ADAM MANNER. EARLY 19th C.

Mantelpiece, with fluted and reeded pilasters. The lintel has *appliqué* foliated scrolls enclosing flowers and water leaves (as no. 584). The mantel and cornice are decorated with cabling of Adam derivation.

w. 4' 6½"   H. 4' 3¼"
   138 cm   131 cm
WOOD : pine
(*Coll. Mrs Richard R. Costello, Sainte-Agathe des Monts, P.Q.*).

551. COFFRET ORNÉ DE DESSINS GÉOMÉTRIQUES. XVIIIᵉ S. CASKET, CARVED WITH GEOMETRIC DESIGNS. 18th C.

552. COFFRET ORNÉ DE DESSINS GÉOMÉTRIQUES. XIXᵉ S. SMALL CASKET, CARVED WITH GEOMETRIC DESIGNS. 19th C.

553. PETIT COFFRET, AUX APPLIQUES SCULPTÉES. XVIIIᵉ S. SMALL CASKET, WITH APPLIQUÉ CARVINGS. 18th C.

554. BOITE ORNÉE DE STRIES DIAGONALES. XVIIIᵉ S. BOX, CARVED WITH DIAGONAL REEDING. 18th C.

555. PETIT COFFRET-BAHUT. XVIIIᵉ S. MINIATURE TRUNK. 18th C.

556. PETIT COFFRET SCULPTÉ, DES ÉBOULEMENTS. XIXᵉ S. SMALL CARVED CASKET, FROM LES ÉBOULEMENTS. 19th C.

557. BOITE OVALE, D'INSPIRATION INDIENNE. XVIIIᵉ S. OVAL BOX, IN THE INDIAN MANNER. 18th C.

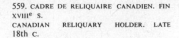

558. PETIT CADRE DE MIROIR, D'ESPRIT
LOUIS XV ET LOUIS XVI. FIN XVIIIe S.
SMALL MIRROR FRAME, IN THE LOUIS XV
AND LOUIS XVI MANNERS. LATE 18th C.

559. CADRE DE RELIQUAIRE CANADIEN. FIN
XVIIIe S.
CANADIAN RELIQUARY HOLDER. LATE
18th C.

560. CADRE DE MIROIR NAÏF. ART POPU-
LAIRE. XIXe S.
NAIVE FOLK ART MIRROR FRAME. 19th C.

561. CADRE DE MIROIR RUSTIQUE. XIXe S.
RUSTIC MIRROR FRAME. 19th C.

. PETITE CORNICHE, DE VERCHÈRES. FIN

ᵉ S.

LL SHELF, FROM VERCHÈRES. LATE

 C.

CORNICHE, DE CHATEAUGUAY. FIN

ᵉ S.

F. FROM CHATEAUGUAY. LATE 18th C.

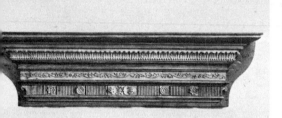

564. TABLETTE, A MOTIFS SCULPTÉS ET
APPLIQUÉS. XIXᵉ S.

SHELF, WITH CARVED AND APPLIQUÉ MOTIFS.
19th C.

565. TABLETTE RUSTIQUE. ART POPULAIRE.
XIXᵉ S.

RUSTIC SHELF, IN FOLK ART STYLE. 19th C.

566. PETITE TABLETTE RUSTIQUE. XIXᵉ S.
SMALL RUSTIC SHELF. 19th C.

567. CORNICHE, DE QUÉBEC. XVIIIᵉ S.
SHELF, FROM QUEBEC. 18th C.

568. CORNICHE A STRIES VERTICALES. XVIIIᵉ S.
SHELF, ORNAMENTED WITH VERTICAL REEDING. 18th C.

569. CORNICHE RUSTIQUE. XIXᵉ S.
RUSTIC SHELF. 19th C.

570. PETITE CORNICHE RUSTIQUE. XVIIIᵉ S.
SMALL RUSTIC SHELF. 18th C.

571. BOITE A SEL RUSTIQUE.
XIXᵉ S.
RUSTIC SALT BOX. 19th c.

572. BOITE A SEL, DE SAINT-DENIS-SUR-
RICHELIEU. XIXᵉ S.
SALT BOX, FROM ST DENIS-SUR-RICHE-
LIEU. 19th c.

573. BOITE A SEL RUSTIQUE. XIXᵉ S.
RUSTIC SALT BOX. 19th c.

574. BOITE A SEL RUSTIQUE, ART POPU-
LAIRE. XIXᵉ S.
RUSTIC SALT BOX, IN FOLK-ART STYLE.
19th c.

575. BOITE A SEL RUSTIQUE. XVIIIᵉ S.
RUSTIC SALT BOX. 18th c.

576. PELLE A POUSSIÈRE. XVIIIe S.
DUSTPAN. 18th C.

577. PETITE URNE RUSTIQUE, A DOS PLAT.
XVIIIe S.
SMALL RUSTIC URN, WITH FLAT BACK.
18th C.

578. BOITE A COUTEAUX RUSTIQUE. XIXe S.
RUSTIC KNIFE-BOX. 19th C.

579. BOITE A SEL RUSTIQUE, A LONGUE PLAN-
CHETTE. XIXe S.
RUSTIC SALT BOX, WITH LONG BACK-BOARD.
19th C.

581. MANTEAU DE CHEMINÉE, D'UNE MAISON
DU BOUT DE L'ILE, MONTRÉAL. FIN XVIIIᵉ S.
MANTELPIECE, FROM A HOUSE IN BOUT-DE-
L'ILE, MONTREAL. LATE 18th C.

582. MANTEAU DE CHEMINÉE, DE STYLE
ADAM. FIN XVIIIᵉ S.
MANTELPIECE, IN ADAM MANNER. LATE
18th C.

583. MANTEAU DE CHEMINÉE, DE L'ILE D'OR-
LÉANS. FIN XVIIIᵉ S.
MANTELPIECE, FROM ILE D'ORLÉANS.   LATE
18th C.

584. MANTEAU DE CHEMINÉE, D'ESPRIT ADAM
ET REGENCY. DÉBUT XIXᵉ S.
MANTELPIECE, IN THE ADAM AND REGENCY
MANNERS.   EARLY 19th C.

585. MANTEAU DE CHEMINÉE, D'ESPRIT
ADAM. DÉBUT XIXᵉ S.
MANTELPIECE, IN THE ADAM MANNER.
EARLY 19th C.

COMMON ROOM.

TECHNICAL
AND HISTORICAL ASPECTS

FURNITURE FABRICS

In order to complete the description of French Canadian traditional furniture in its original setting, it is essential to deal with the materials used to cover and enrich the chairs, armchairs, and beds of New France in the seventeenth and eighteenth centuries.

For many years materials were imported from France as the colony produced no wool, linen or cotton in the early period, and few people knew how to weave.

Consequently such materials were a luxury, and as such, were a sign of the prosperity of the French Canadian *habitant*. Looms and spinning-wheels were extremely rare in the early days, and home-weaving developed very slowly, only becoming general around 1700. Talon insisted that the habitants should learn to supply their own needs in this field as in all others.

Upholstery was consequently a most expensive item at the beginning of the colony, and naturally the quality of the cloth used depended on what the *habitant* could afford. The authorities in France continued to oppose the making of textiles in Canada in favour of the manufacturers and merchants of Paris, Rouen, Dieppe and La Rochelle. At the beginning of the seventeenth century, the Company of One Hundred Associates pledged themselves to encourage a Canadian textile industry and the establishment and support of weaving schools in Canada, but nothing came of it. They preferred to continue selling imported materials in their stores at exorbitant prices. Later, the Intendant Jean Talon and his successors made appeals to Louis XIV to endorse the manufacture of cloth in Canada, arguing that it would in no way compete with the textile industry in France. But it was only in 1704 that royal assent was given for linen and other fabrics to be made as a temporary measure, " It ought not to be encouraged if it is going to be to the detriment of French manufacturers. "[1]

Weavers were brought from France to instruct the young people of the villages in the craft, and looms had also to be imported from France as no one made them in Canada.

Madame Pierre Le Gardeur de Repentigny, a persevering widow, succeeded after many years of trial in establishing a little weaving business in Montreal around 1705. She made " coarse blankets, linen, twill serge, serge made with a warp of buffalo wool, and drugget of different colours ".[2] She made her dyes from wood bark and the roots of various plants, using recipes she had learned from the Indians. These crude materials could not replace the fine stuffs imported from France which however were becoming more and more expensive.

The *habitants* found they could buy materials much more cheaply in the English American colonies. English materials were smuggled across the border in such quantities in the eighteenth century that Louis XV ordered a search of all the houses in Montreal in 1731 and imposed a fine on any contraband goods which were found. Only fifty-three families escaped payment of a fine.

Furniture was upholstered in serge, tapestry, needle-point and painted linen *(toile de Jouy)* in lively colours, for the more prosperous colonists.

There are detailed descriptions of upholstery in inventories of the period, including armchairs trimmed " with *Crespine* (a woven fringe with a figured band at the top) of blue serge with a fringe of various colours ", an armchair with a " pillow covered with *Serge de Caen* " (this came in yellow, blue, green or red, and was also used for clothes), " four folding chairs covered

(1) A P C. Rapp. 1899, p. 194.
(2) A P C. Série F., vol. 22, p. 348.

363

with grey *drap de Sceaux* with a coloured fringe ", " six turned chairs covered with the same material as the bed, in green and white *moquette* " (a woollen material on a linen base, looped or cut — a type of cut velvet), and " four armchairs covered in *point de Hongrie* ".

The widespread use of cushions on chairs shows that comfort was demanded even in the early days. They were usually attached to *Capucine* chairs by strings. The seats were made of twisted straw or marsh-grass, woven in a diamond-point pattern, or of elm bark plaited in basket-weave pattern, or of rawhide (especially in the Montreal region).

Many forms of bed covers are mentioned in inventories, " a bed-covering of yellow *Aumale* serge ", " bed valances of *Bergamo* tapestry " (coloured wool on a woof of unbleached yarn), " *point de Paris* ", " *drap de Sceaux* ", " bed curtains of *point de Hongrie* " (a material using several colour combinations always in a dart pattern), and possibly the French Canadian *ceintures fléchées* were derived from this. Bed curtains of " blue-checked linen ", sheets, bedspreads, blankets and quilts of the period were also described in inventories, " a white bedspread of *Rouen* cloth ", " three bedspreads of *Montpellier* cloth ", " two *de Villé* blankets ", " three *Normandie* bed covers, one green, one yellow and one white " (made like *catalogne*), " a Bordeaux blanket ", " a painted linen quilt " (much of the linen was painted or printed like *toile de Jouy*), " a small English quilt ", " a pair of *Beaufort* linen sheets ", " a paillasse of *Meslye* linen " (a very strong linen made from the core of hemp, the thread being well washed in lye, in the Olonne region), " a wool mattress covered with checkered linen ", " a table with a green or blue cover ".

When Canadian materials began to appear, they were generally found in poorer homes. " A feather mattress covered with native linen ", " a beaded bed-valance ", " a mattress covered with ticking and a *catalogne* bedspread ". *Catalogne* (called *lirette* in Poitou) is often mentioned in inventories as a covering, not as a carpet as it later became. " Three sheets of homespun linen ", " a quilt of homespun drugget ", " a feather mattress covered with deer-skin ", " a steer-skin with a woollen blanket ", " a buffalo robe " *(robe de bœuf Illinois)*, " two old blankets made of dog's hair and a four poster bed ", " two cured moose skins with a rickety bedstead ", " a mattress stuffed with moose hair ".

Joseph Edmond Roy, a well-known former archivist of the Province of Quebec, after analysing the inventory of the estate of the *seigneur* Étienne Charest, who died in 1734 at Point Levy, was able to reconstruct a picture of the great hall of the manor, the furnishings and the surroundings in which the Canadian *seigneur* lived in the eighteenth century : " The house, which was built some time before by Bissot, near the bank of the river at Point Levy, in the shade of high luxuriant elms, had become the seigneurial manor. It was a large stone building, sixty feet long, with thick white-washed walls. A few hundred yards to the east stood a tannery, forty feet long, a water-mill, a bakehouse, an ice-house, a dove-cote, barns, and stables.

" On the walls of the great hall are hung tapestries of *point de Hongrie*. In the centre of the room stands a birch table with spiralled twisted legs, and an armchair of the same wood, covered with green baize. Around the room are six chairs covered with moquette, four stools upholstered with the same material, a fine clock in a tall walnut case, a large mirror in a gold frame, the glass alone measuring twenty-two inches by sixteen. The light from the windows is muted by green serge curtains held back by small iron rings.

" At the end of the room stands the *seigneur's* great bed made of birch, partly concealed by the green serge curtains which hang from the canopy. The mattresses are filled with the best down, and the covers are cariboo skins.

" The immense fire-place, in which maple logs are burnt is flanked on either side by built-in cupboards. In one is stored the table linen — table-cloths and napkins of linen from Rouen, Beaufort, or Herbé. The other cupboard holds a blue and white porcelain service and a great tray from the East on which stand eight cups... "[1]

(1) Roy, Joseph-Edmond. *Histoire de la Seigneurie de Lauzon.* Lévis, 1897-1904, 5 vol., pp. 132-133.

IRON AND BRASS WORK

All chests, dome-topped chests, and buffets were fitted with locks, in accordance with an ancient practice, still to be found in France, of keeping everything under lock and key.

Much of the early furniture had wooden locks. A long wooden key was inserted in a square hole cut through the door-frame of the furniture. Most of the locks, however, were made of iron, of the " ordinary " type. Many coffers or chests were fitted with locks of the snap-over fastener type *(à battant)* which were handmade by locksmiths. Unfortunately, these locks were bound to break sooner or later, and today if a key is missing, few collectors will take the trouble to have a new one made, nor are they likely to have the lock repaired, for it is easier to replace it with a shoddy wooden latch.

Keyhole escutcheons were generally made in a stylized dragon or sea-horse design, or a flame motif cut out of iron, often pierced. The lock was always on the right door of a buffet or an armoire. A false escutcheon was often placed on the left door as well, either to maintain balance and harmony of the design, or else as decoration. The right door opened first, and all that had to be done to open the left door was to release the retaining hook on one of the shelves.

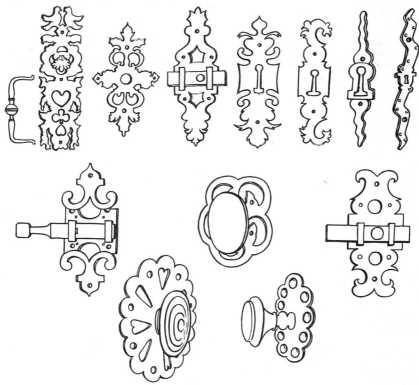

Fig. 9 - *Slide bolts or* targettes, *keyhole escutcheons, handles and knobs for doors and drawers.*

The same type of escutcheon was placed horizontally in the centre of the drawers of two-tiered buffets. Sometimes an iron knob would be forged to the escutcheon.

The over-lapping doors of early buffets and armoires required a special type of hinge called a fische hinge *(fiche)*. The pivot or pins of these hinges were made of cast iron and had wrought-iron tenons wrapped around them while red hot. The tenon of the upper part was fitted into a mortise on the side of the door while the tenon of the lower part was mortised into the side-posts of the furniture. The tips of the pins were shaped like balusters, or urns. It is obvious from a careful study of numerous inventories of the eighteenth century that these fische hinges were made in Canada as is found in the inventory of François Letourneau, master-locksmith in Quebec. " The said *Sieur* Letourneau, *père*, will have for his moiety the following objects ... forty pairs of *fische* hinges for casement windows, sixteen pairs of *fische* hinges for both doors and armoires. "[1] All the ironwork seems to have been conceived for this type of traditional furniture.

Another type of *fische* hinge that would frequently be found on armoires and buffets at the end of the eighteenth and beginning of the nineteenth centuries was called *queue de rat* by French Canadians, possibly after the English rat-tail. These hinges were also common in New England. French Canada may have adopted the rat-tail from New England or from Savoie and Lorraine, the only regions in France where I have found them on furniture of the eighteenth century.

Handles give the finishing touch to commodes just as hinges and escutcheons embellish armoires. A commode without handles is half-naked. The drop-handles for table and commode drawers were made of either iron or brass, the end pieces being usually decorated with rosettes. Almost all drop-handles, whether imported from France or cast in Canada, were taken from popular French designs, such as those with the end plates shaped like valets or pages

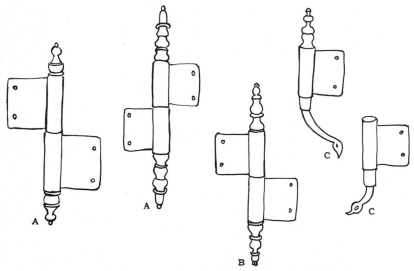

Fig. 10 - *Armoire fische hinges* — A. *Vase with pearls.* B. *Baluster.* C. *Rat-tail.*

(1) A J Q, I O A. Partage entre Jean Letourneau et les héritiers de Dame Marie Gaultier sa femme, 1er août 1783. Greffe J.A. Panet.

known as " *bronzes au page, bronzes au valet* " or the fixed handles with floral designs in the Louis XV style.

Locksmiths, silversmiths, and some blacksmiths were occasionally metal founders, being equipped to cast delicate objects in iron or brass. Silversmiths also cast the cherubins for sanctuary lamps and the Christ figures for processional crosses either in silver or brass. Although I have found no documentary evidence, I have reason to believe that brass and iron drawer handles were also cast by Canadian locksmiths and silversmiths. Today such delicate objects are still made by silversmiths as well as in foundries.

There was a great variety of slide bolts, latches, door-handles, door-knobs and door-escutcheons. Canadian craftsmen have left charming examples, mostly the work of blacksmiths. They are not always as interesting as those found in France, but most of them were copied from French models, and without doubt they add to the charm of French Canadian furniture and give it an unmistakable *province française* look.

FIREPLACE ACCESSORIES AND STOVES

Some fireplace accessories which were used by early French Canadians can be seen in the coloured illustration of an early kitchen. These articles were mentioned in nearly all inventories, " a fire shovel... a pair of fire-dogs... a pair of bellows... fire-tongs... tripods... an iron grill... round iron pans... kettles... roasting spits... a chimney-hook with a large iron grill placed against the back-plate of the fire, with four bars and two cross-pieces... three little copper pots... a copper cauldron taking two bucketfuls of water... two copper bed-warmers... a roasting fork... a revolving spit in iron, with all its fittings... "

In a country of severe cold, chimneys were not enough to heat the houses, and so stoves were brought into use in Canada in the seventeenth century. Mother Marie de l'Incarnation, writing to her son in 1644, gives us an excellent picture of what heating was like before the arrival of the stove, " Our fireplace is at the end of the dormitory to heat the cells which have pine partitions, otherwise we would not be warm; but don't think that it's possible to stay away from the fire for very long in winter; to be away from it for an hour would be too long, and besides you would need to be warmly-clothed with your hands protected. Besides the religious observances, the usual place for reading, writing, or studying is, by necessity, near the fire, which is a most inconvenient subjection, particularly for me, as I never used to warm myself in France... We burn 175 cords of fire-wood a year in the four fireplaces which we have : and even though it might be so severely cold, we go to chapel throughout the winter, but we do suffer a little. " [1]

The first stove was installed in the Ursuline Convent, Quebec in 1668 "... then a stove was placed in the large dormitory of the nuns by orders of the superiors... " [2]

These were the stoves made of very thick cast-iron plates which have continued to be popular in Canada up to the present day. The thick plates produced a great deal of heat, and the fire-boxes could hold a large number of maple or birch logs and drew very well. But such stoves were a luxury in the seventeenth century and always came from France. According to M. E.Z. Massicotte, only a few of the colonists owned them, and " they placed them inside the fireplaces because they were so afraid of them "

From the beginning of the eighteenth century stoves were listed in inventories, " an iron stove with palms and three lions. " [3] This *Palmier* stove is mentioned very often, and probably got its name from a design of palm leaves in relief on the plates. Another quite common stove

(1) *Lettres de la Vénérable Mère Marie de l'Incarnation*, Paris, 1681, p. 384-385.
(2) *Les Ursulines de Québec depuis leur établissement jusqu'à nos jours*. Québec, 1878, vol. I, p. 86.
(3) A J M, I O A. Inventaire des Biens de defunt Sieur Pierre Forestier, 26e aoust 1732. Greffe Chaumont.

was " an iron stove representing the Samaritan woman on the side plates, and three lions on the front and back plates. "[1]

There was also a stove of an altogether different type, " ... a brick stove with a hot plate, having a pipe in four sections (including the elbow), a stove door and a supporting-frame. "[2]

This model seems to have been used for cooking rather than heating. The first two stoves bore a strong resemblance to Canadian rectangular box stoves or double-decker stoves bearing relief designs and perhaps the French made them specially for Canada.

I have seen several of these stoves and stove-plates made of cast iron in the museums of Colmar and Nancy. Most of them were made at Zinsweiler, near Strasbourg, in the eighteenth century. The one in Colmar Museum had side plates decorated with bas-reliefs representing the biblical scene of the Marriage at Cana, and may possibly be the same model as the one described in an inventory of 1753, " an iron stove depicting the Marriage at Cana... "[3]

No stoves seem to have been made in Canada before 1744. A continuous search was made for iron ore for many years under the *Intendants* Talon, De Meules, Raudot, Dupuy, and Hocquart. Iron ore was eventually found at Baie-St-Paul and Three Rivers, but it took several years before foundries could be put into operation. The first trial castings of Canadian ore were made at Three Rivers about 1733. In 1744, 59 heating stoves were cast, " which were fairly successful for a first attempt. The habitants preferred them to the Dutch (enamelled stoves)

Fig. 11 - *CANADIAN IRON STOVES. - Three-decker stove, 19th c. (for heating and cooking). - Stove from the St Maurice Forge. Early 19th c. (for heating).*

(1) A J M, I O A. Inventaire des Biens de feu Sieur Jullien Trottier DesRivières faite a la Reqte et Dlle Marie Catherine Raimbault Sa veuve, le 30 avril 1738. Greffe Chevremont.

(2) A J M, I O A. Invantaire des Biens de La Communeauté dentre feu Michel Dufraine et Geneviève Caty. Le 22ᵉ Xbre 1751. Greffe Comparet.

(3) A J M, I O A. Invantaire des Biens de la Communauté qui a Esté Entre Sr pierre brien Et deffunte Elisabethe des Roche. Le Neuf 8bre 1753. Greffe Comparet.

because they were less breakable... "[1] In 1747 there were made " ... more than two hundred stoves for the habitants, which were bought even before they were cast, so great was the demand. "[2]

Sometimes they were called " single-decker stoves " or " double-decker stoves "; others, " à la balance, au balancier ".[3] I have seen only two examples of eighteenth-century work from the St Maurice Forge of Three Rivers and these were recently discovered in the town. One was an iron panel from a small stove belonging to the Ursuline Sisters of Three Rivers, and had a bas-relief that apparently represented the baptism of an Indian by a Jesuit missionary. However it was very worn and the figures were barely discernible as if the panel had been rescued from the ruins of a fire. The other, a chimney back-plate, with a curvilinear top, bore a medallion with crown, fleur de lys and laurel leaves, the emblem of the French monarchy.

I have seen several double-decker stoves bearing the stamp of the St Maurice Forge, but they all date from the first half or the middle of the nineteenth century. Since that time, foundries all over the country have turned out double-deckers and triple-deckers (poêles à deux ponts, poêles à trois ponts) always decorated with floral or geometric designs in bas-relief. The second and third decks formed ovens for roasting meat or baking bread and pastries. This type of stove has almost completely disappeared, having been replaced by the enamel and chrome models which the housewives found more practical. However, it is generally agreed that the early type of iron stoves were better for heating.

The stove was usually placed near a partition in the large common room of the *habitant* house. There would often be an opening in this partition to allow heat from the stove to warm the adjoining room. The stove-pipe usually entered the breast of the chimney near the ceiling.

THE WOODS USED

In the description of furniture found in inventories in the period 1650-1750, the woods most commonly used were pine, yellow birch and butternut. There were enormous quantities of these trees which grew very tall and very thick around the houses of the early settlers.

These were trees preferred in furniture making as they were high-branched and could be made into long, knot-free planks, from 16 to 25 inches in width, and up to 20 feet in length.

Yellow birch was an ideal wood, being hard, and yet workable because so supple. Pierre Boucher, a Canadian gentleman, gave this description of the wood in 1664, " the tree called *Merisier* (yellow birch) grows large, high, and very straight. Its wood is used to make furniture and gun stocks. It is red inside, and is most attractive for the sort of work done in this country. It bears no fruit. It is called *Merisier* because its bark resembles that of the *merisier* (wild cherry) of France. "[4]

The friezes and legs of tables were usually of yellow birch, while the top was often of pine or butternut.

Solid wood or rush-seat chairs were usually made of yellow birch; sugar maple or red maple were also used but the seats were generally made of pine. Armoires and low buffets were made of pine or butternut, with the exception of a few two-tiered buffets which date from the end of the seventeenth century and according to inventories were made of solid yellow birch. A few of these are still to be seen today.

There are exceptions, of course. Red oak was used in Montreal at the beginning of the colony. At the time this type of tree probably produced wider planks. Pierre Boucher describes

(1) Quoted by Mgr Albert Tessier : *Les Forges Saint-Maurice* 1729-1883, Trois-Rivières, 1952, page 89.
(2) A P C. Corr. Générale C11A, vol. 88, pp. 93-94.
(3) BRH. E.Z. Massicotte.
(4) Boucher, Pierre. *Histoire Véritable et Naturelle des Mœurs et Productions du Pays de la Nouvelle France.* Paris, 1664, p. 45.

it : " There are two types of oak, one more porous than the other.   The porous type is suitable for furniture, woodworking and rough carpentry; the other is suitable for vessels to travel on the water; these trees grow high, wide and straight, particularly near Mount Royal. "[1]

Oak was not used for very long, judging from references in inventories.   A very few early chairs were made of oak but no furniture of any importance has survived in this wood.

Nowadays, the oak of Quebec is small and produces only narrow planks.   It is difficult to dry, and it has a tendency to warp and split.   Modern Canadian furniture makers have for a long time imported oak from the United States.

A few small pieces of furniture made of elm are mentioned in inventories, but it seems that the wood was not popular.   This may explain the description which Pierre Boucher left, " There are elms which grow very large and high.   The wood is excellent, and the cartwrights of this country use it a great deal. "[2]

It is used nowadays only in building work where it can be firmly held in position, for example for skirting boards or frames, and is never used for furniture as it tends to warp and twist with each change of season according to the humidity.

At the beginning of the eighteenth century, furniture was also made from red or soft maple, which was called *plaine*.   Pierre Boucher wrote, " Another type of tree which is called *Plaine* is very like the maple; but it is softer and is used for fire-wood... "[3]   The wood of this tree is softer than the sugar maple and is more easily worked, and mostly those which produced a wavy, curly, or bird's eye grain were used.

It is only later that white maple (the alternative name for sugar maple) is mentioned in the inventories.   Pierre Boucher described it in 1664, this way : " There is another type of tree which they call maple, which grows large and high : the wood is most beautiful, although it is used only for fire-wood or tool-handles, for which it is most suitable as it is very smooth and strong. "[4]   White maple did not come into general use for furniture until the end of the eighteenth or the beginning of the nineteenth century.   It is as highly regarded for its appearance as red maple *(plaine)* with a curled or undulating grain or with a bird's eye pattern of tiny curled knots.   Its popularity is limited because it is difficult to work as it splits so easily.   Furniture makers are today faced with exactly the same problem and often find themselves obliged to scrap their work half way through.   In spite of these obstacles, a new piece of finely finished furniture in white maple has a character which no other Canadian wood possesses.   These trees are typical of eastern Canada and the United States, and were used for solid wood furniture. In France, they were used only as veneers.

Ash was rarely mentioned in the records and its wood was just as rarely used; however it became very popular in the middle of the nineteenth century as a material for tables, washstands, and other small pieces.

Furniture made of cedar, balsam, or bass-wood is mentioned only infrequently in inventories.   It seems that these woods were not regarded as practical, although bass-wood achieved wide popularity in the middle of the nineteenth century when the first factories began to turn out mass-produced furniture.

Black cherry wood (called *cerisier d'automne* by the French Canadians) was another material rarely used, for it was difficult to obtain wide planks and was as scarce as it is today, except in western Canada and in the United States.   The wood was used for a few small pieces of nineteenth-century furniture; it has a beautiful tone and grain, and greatly resembles French birch.

(1) Boucher, Pierre. *Histoire Véritable et Naturelle des Mœurs et Productions du Pays de la Nouvelle France.* Paris, 1664, p. 45-46.
(2) idem, p. 47.
(3) idem, p. 47.
(4) idem, p. 44.

The beech tree is very common in the Montreal region. It bears a strong resemblance to the French beech, but is much harder. Pierre Boucher wrote, " There is also beech wood of great beauty and fine quality, and the trees bear beechnuts as do those of France; but it is used here only as a fuel. " [1] Furniture makers and wood carvers maintain that it is too hard to work. The Canadian beech tree does not yield very large planks, and when sawed and planed, warps with every climatic variation, making it unsuitable for furniture-wood. It is used here only when it is backed by something more solid; for flooring and also for handles of tools, hammers, axes, etc., and occasionally for wheel-spokes and carriage shafts.

Canadian beech is a particularly difficult wood to dry, and I have not seen beech furniture mentioned in any inventory. It is safe to assume that all the Louis XIV and Louis XV beech wood chairs and armchairs found in Canada were made in France.

IDENTIFICATION OF WOODS

It is important for collectors to be able to distinguish traditional furniture made in Canada from European importations. Much of our furniture resembled that of France, although it was rarely an exact copy. It is often through the materials used that we are able to distinguish one from the other. Obviously, it is easier to identify a piece of furniture once the paint or the stain has been removed. If the piece is painted, a test-scraping must be made in some unexposed spot to identify the wood.

WHITE PINE

Canadian white pine has a texture which cannot be found in any of the resinous woods of France. It is less grained than resinous French woods and its surface is more regular. Woodworkers in the past had pine logs sawed in such a way, that the surface of the planks was neither grained nor veined. They called it yellow pine. The French coniferous wood which most closely resembles Canadian pine is a type of balsam (sapin) which was used in Normandy, particularly in the region of Caux, to make some beautiful furniture in traditional designs. The surface of this wood is richly veined and almost identical with Canadian hemlock (tsuga canadensis). A few pieces of Canadian hemlock furniture have been mistakenly identified as French. The veins of French balsam are darker, and the wood between is much lighter. French balsam cannot be confused with Canadian white pine as the difference is too obvious.

BUTTERNUT

The Canadian butternut wood (noyer tendre) can easily be mistaken for French or American walnut. The only way in which it can be distinguished from the others is by digging a finger-nail into the wood. If the finger-nail sinks into the wood and leaves a mark, it is Canadian butternut. If it slides across the surface without penetrating it, it is French or American walnut.

It will be noted in this experiment that the sap-wood of butternut is firmer than the core of the tree and is sometimes mistaken for walnut. The core of butternut has an undulating grain and is easier to dent with the finger-nail, while sap-wood has a straight grain and is much more difficult to mark. When paint or stain has been removed from a piece of butternut furniture, it has a beautiful tone and somewhat resembles the colour of straw. The butternut tree is not found in Europe.

Pierre Boucher wrote in the seventeenth century "... there are two types of walnut trees,

(1) Boucher, Pierre. *Histoire Véritable et Naturelle des Mœurs et Productions du Pays de la Nouvelle France*. Paris, 1664, p. 45.

both of which bear nuts. In one case the nuts are large and hard but the wood of the tree is very soft and is only used to make clogs, for which it is most suitable. There are quantities of this type of tree around Quebec and Three Rivers, but further up the river they are scarcer. The other type of walnut tree bears small round nuts which have a soft husk like those of France, but the wood is very hard and red inside. These trees are to be found on Mount Royal, and also exist in large numbers in the Iroquois country. '' [1] New York State was the centre of the Iroquois country, which may explain why walnut is now imported from the United States.

YELLOW BIRCH

Yellow birch (*bouleau jaune*, falsely called *merisier* in French Canada) should not be confused with the *merisier* (wild cherry) of France. It is lighter in colour than the cherry wood which has a reddish brown tinge. When it is finished with a stain, French wild cherry has a golden tone which resembles many other fruit-woods. A number of tiny deep-red knots are sometimes to be seen on the surface of a piece of furniture made of French wild cherry which are never found in Canadian birch.

Another characteristic of Canadian birch is the faint wavy grain in certain sections of the wood when examined closely under a strong light. Some Canadian furniture was made of birch wood chosen specially for this undulating grain and called " wavy " or " curly " birch.

PARASITES

A large number of early chairs, armchairs and tables imported from France have tiny, perfectly round worm-holes which can be seen on the surface of the wood. These were made by wood-worms (anobium tesselatum, of the coleopterous species) which feed on the wood and which can cause a piece of furniture to disintegrate completely. It is a scourge in France, but Canada is protected to a certain extent by the cold winters. These wood-worms are not found in walnut or butternut farther north than the lower part of Vermont.

Rare worm-holes are sometimes found in butternut wood imported from the United States, but never in the butternut of the Montreal or Three Rivers districts. These little holes in American butternut are identical to the ones found in French furniture, but once the wood has been made into a piece of furniture, the worms become inactive. Larger worms of another species are to be found just under the bark of resinous trees such as white pine, where they make long and sinuous channels in the sapwood. Apparently they do not survive once the wood has been dressed. Inferior-quality wood showing channel marks was often used for the backs of early Canadian commodes or armoires.

In many years of observation and research, I have come across only two pieces of Canadian furniture with worm-holes like those found in French furniture : a butternut console table of the eighteenth century, and a *habitant* armchair made of birch in the nineteenth century. According to experts whom I consulted, they could have been contaminated by contact with European furniture, particularly if they were kept in a damp place.

For these reasons it is possible to say that if a piece of furniture has worm-holes, it is almost certainly of European or possibly of American origin.

WORKMANSHIP

Let us imagine a *habitant* of Beauport, called Augustin Parent, on a stroll through his property one Sunday afternoon in the Fall of 1726, his fowling-piece under his arm and his dog at his heels. He is in a reflective mood. He has several daughters to marry off, which means

---

(1) Boucher, Pierre. *Histoire Véritable et Naturelle des Mœurs et Productions du Pays de la Nouvelle-France, Paris,* 1664, p. 47.

a good deal of wood to cut, since, according to the custom, his daughters will be expected to bring marriage chests and armoires as part of their dowry. The dog flushes a partridge, but Parent is too late with his gun and he watches the bird disappear through the branches of an enormous pine tree. That pine! He is struck with admiration for the tree. Perhaps it is the very one that can supply the wood he might soon need for the dower pieces.

This pine is a true masterpiece of nature. Its huge trunk rises skywards, straight and strong. Its boards will be wide, and free of knots.

The next day, Parent fells the tree, and cuts it into logs. A few months later, these are sledded over the fresh snow to the nearby river where they are soaked from spring to the following autumn to remove the sap. Next they are taken to the pit-sawyers, where they are cut into wide boards. Then the wood is stacked near the Parent stable where it is allowed to dry for a full year.

A few years later, one of Augustin Parent's daughters becomes engaged, and will now need the traditional dower armoire. The cured pine boards have already been given to Claude Filliau, one of his wife's cousins and a Master Woodworker, who has a workshop, Côte de la Canoterie, Quebec, and whose craftsmanship Parent has always admired. Filliau has already trimmed the boards and stacked them in his shed for further drying.

The father and daughter now pay the woodworker a visit to discuss the dowry armoire. Entering the workshop of Master Filliau, they are impressed by the orderliness and cleanliness all around them. A journeyman and two apprentices are busy putting together a four-poster bed. A great number of tools are arranged on the wall and on the side of the work-bench. On another wall, templets are to be seen hanging from nails. These are the patterns cut out of thin wood, for table legs, buffet stiles, chair backs, the arms of armchairs, etc. At the back of the shop the visitors can see the lathe with its big wheel and leather belt.

Leaning against the wall there are boards of a variety of woods, and still more are stored overhead, across poles which run between the beams. There are a number of trestles of different sizes, but the most imposing article in the workshop is the great work-bench, a massive table made of thick yellow birch, and supported by six sturdy legs. It is equipped with a bench-dog, vice, and hook, and in one corner is the grinding stone for sharpening the blades of cutting tools.

Claude Filliau, dressed in his apron of coarse homespun linen, greets his cousins. The exchange of family news over, the two men lean on a corner of the work-bench while the girl explains the sort of armoire she would like : one with two doors and panels carved with diamond points. The woodworker makes a rough sketch for her, at the same time suggesting two drawers at the base of the armoire, and three panels in each of the doors, with diamond points placed horizontally on the middle panel.

Next, the price is discussed, and they reach an agreement. The armoire is promised for the week before her marriage which is to take place in five months' time.

Claude Filliau sets to work on the armoire soon after their visit. First of all, he pencils the different parts of the armoire directly onto the wood with the aid of his templets and pouncing patterns. Next he saws the thicker wood for the stiles, then the planks for the upper, lower, and lateral rails. The wood for the doors and door-frames comes next, and the drawer fronts, cornices, and panels follow. Finally, he cuts from a lower-grade wood the backing of the armoire, the bottom and the top of the interior, and in most cases he does not plane the parts which do not show.

Claude Filliau is a serious and methodical craftsman. He cuts the wood along the grain with a rip-saw, and the boards are measured off at the desired length with the cross-cut saw. He then levels them with a scuffing-plane, removing the rough saw-marks, and finally planes them to a smooth surface.

Now that the parts are ready, Claude Filliau begins to assemble them with great care. This delicate operation consists of making the mortise and tenon joints and the dowelling for the doors, stiles and rails.   He taps the pieces together with his mallet for a trial assembly, checking all the while with his set-square and clamping them into position.   Once satisfied, he draws the outline of his mouldings, the cornice, the bottom rail, the two front feet, as well as the frame mouldings and the panels.

Claude Filliau then takes the armoire apart again.   The next stage is the carving of the diamond points on the doors and the side panels, each type of moulding requiring a special tool. Once this is finished, the final assembly takes place.   All the parts are fitted together again, with the back and bottom firmly set in the grooves of the rails and the stiles.   The pieces are then pegged in place, and the shelves are installed.   Finally, the doors and door-frames, which have been joined separately, are placed in position, with their hinges, keyholes, and escutcheons. The skilled woodworker then smooths the surfaces of the armoire carefully with pumice, and applies the final stain with a cork and woollen pads.   The stain most commonly used at the time was a deep brown.

Claude Filliau lavished both time and care on this armoire.   Besides making his living, he had earned the satisfaction of making a piece of furniture which was not only useful, but durable.   It is extraordinary to realize the great pride and affection the men of this period expressed in their workmanship.   In spite of the many uncertainties of the epoch — wars, plagues and famines, and the difficulties of living in a new and undeveloped continent — these people were concerned to create objects which would serve for generations.

Filliau has built a piece of furniture which will defy time; the father had the foresight to cut, years in advance, the tree from which the dower armoire was to be made and now the bride-to-be is planning her future.   Such people had profound faith in Providence.

Here are the tools which were listed in Claude Filliau's workshop :

" One pair of planes for tonguing and grooving planks; a moulding plane with its assorted shaped blades; a trying plane for mitre joints; a pair of small brass drawing compasses; a small iron square; flat-nosed pliers with a claw hook to match; a rabbet-plane with a tenon saw.   Two square rabbet-planes; a moulding-plane for rounding the moulding on window-frames; a plough-plane; a plough-plane for tongue and groove work; a curved moulding-plane; another moulding-plane; a pair of grooving planes; a dowel-saw; a pair of large iron compasses and a scraper.

Two square rabbet-planes; a rabbet-plane for bevelling panels; an ogee-plane; a small moulding-plane for window-frames.   Two moulding-planes; three rat-tail files; an ordinary rip-saw; a scroll-saw; and a coarse rip-saw; two small tenon saws; one large clamp; one medium clamp; one small clamp.

An iron brace and bit, and a wooden one fitted with an iron auger; a small iron vice; two mitre-triangles; two bevel triangles and a dove-tail triangle.

Two small hand-axes; seven marking and mortise gauges; two chisels; two mortise chisels; two gouges; two small augers; four rasps; two files; two bench-clamps; one adze; a copper pan for glue; a carpenter's bench; three grind-stones and two honing stones; sixteen pieces of three-inch wood roughed out for chairs; a new bedstead in pine. "[1]

THE WOODWORKERS

A considerable number of craftsmen came to Canada soon after the arrival of the first peasant settlers, and they brought with them a variety of skills.   Certain *seigneurs*, who had

(1) A J Q, I O A. Inventaire des biens feu Claude Filliau, 18 décembre 1730. Greffe Pinguet : « Suit ce qui s'est trouvé dans la susditte chambre et les outils cy après nommés et de par et par Lots assortis afin d'en procurer une hérite plus avantageuse par les Srs Cliche et gagnié menuisiers appellés a cet effet. »

been granted fiefs, brought their feudal tenants and some craftsmen with them.[1] They were masons, smiths, carpenters, woodworkers, etc., and they came from many different regions of France, including Paris. The first woodworker to come to New France and who is mentioned in a labour contract was called " Jehan Hanin, journeyman woodworker from Paris. " He joined the expedition of 1606 to Acadia, which was led by Monsieur de Monts. The prospect of adventure attracted craftsmen; perhaps they hoped for an easier life in a country with a future rich in possibilities.

Some of them signed up for a minimum of three years, bringing their families with them. Others came alone to establish themselves before their wives and children joined them, as still happens today.

In the earliest days, the colonist was obliged to be a jack-of-all-trades. He developed certain rudimentary skills, and made the most necessary utensils and furniture with his own hands. He had neither the training nor the tools to make complicated or important furniture.

Thus, in the first years of the colony, there were two types of furniture : the furniture of the skilled craftsman, *main de métier*, and the simple but sturdy furniture of the *habitant*, *main fruste et robuste*.

The professional woodworkers were experts thoroughly versed in their craft, who had served their apprenticeship and practised their profession in France. Those who wished to come to Canada were carefully selected before being given their contract.

In those days, woodworking and carpentry were much less specialized professions than they are now. For example, a number of carpenters and masons were also called architects, and they were qualified to draw up plans for a building. The same was true of the woodworker whose job it was to finish the interiors of the houses : joinery, wainscoting, ceilings, floors, frames, panels, cupboards, armoires and furniture of every description. A woodworker *(menuisier)* of that time was not someone who just knocked boards together. He had a thorough knowledge of all the joiner's techniques for locking and mitre joints, mortise and tenon, etc., " ... the sum of 300 Livres paid to the Sieurs Reiche for making five armoires, two large and three medium size, and six casement windows finished with panelled interior shutters for the convent and for the pantry. "[2]

We should also remember that in Canada most of the church carvers were also woodworkers who knew how to make chairs, furniture, and panel-work as well as statues and retables. In a country where the needs were so urgent and varied, the craftsmen could not afford to be specialists. We know that such woodworkers as Le Vasseur, Baillairgé, Émond and Quevillon excelled in every related field of work, and that François and Thomas Baillairgé and Louis Quevillon were even architects.

In some cases, the woodworker did not make the entire piece of furniture because he did not have a lathe to make the turnings, or because he preferred to assign the turning to a colleague with a flair for that type of work. In other cases, if carving were not one of his strong points, he might take this part of the work to a well-known wood-carver " ... December 17, 1793. Delivered to Mr McCutcheon a carved chair-back worth three shillings. "[3] Mr McCutcheon was an English cabinet-maker, recently arrived in Quebec, and the carver was François Baillairgé.

These skilled woodworkers had a permanent shop in a city or a town, although they sometimes set up a work-bench in the house of the person who had engaged them.

The travelling woodworker was another type, but much rarer; a sort of " *coureur de bois* " who moved about the country roads, unable or unwilling to stay put in one community.

(1) For example, Jean-Baptiste François des Champs, Sieur de la Bouteillerie, who established himself at Rivière Ouelle in 1671. — Saint-Pierre, Marquis de Grosourdy de. *Un cousin canadien en Normandie au XVIIIᵉ siècle. Nova Francia*, vol. II, nᵒ 1, Paris, 1926, p. 26.
(2) Compte de la Recette et Dépence des biens de l'Hôpital-Général, Québec, 1ᵉʳ janvier 1715.
(3) I O A. Journal de François Baillairgé, 1784-1800.

Today we sometimes find several pieces of furniture in houses along the same *rang* which were obviously made by one craftsman who in spite of his restlessness sometimes stayed several months in a *habitant* home where he was given board and lodgings, and paid either wages or an agreed sum for the individual piece of work. A considerable amount of traditional furniture was made in this way. I have often been told, when visiting *habitant* homes, about itinerant craftsmen. On one occasion when I admired an old armoire in a farmhouse, the owner related a story which had been passed down in his family about an itinerant woodworker who had stayed in the house for six months while making the armoire.

On another occasion, I was told about an itinerant woodworker from Saint Jean-Baptiste de Rouville who used to travel about with his tools around the beginning of the last century. He would stop off at farmhouses where he would make furniture at the rate of twenty-five sous a day, room and board included. Sometimes he would stay for several months in the same house.

This is the sort of information passed on orally, which makes it possible for us to compare the early Canadian woodworkers with the journeymen craftsmen in France, where the same practice flourished in the eighteenth century. In the mother country, these woodworkers were banded together in an association known as the *Compagnons du Tour de France*, and they used to travel from village to village, city to city, as they did here, learning the different techniques of the provinces in the workshops of Master Woodworkers.

These itinerant woodworkers have left us tangible proof that they used to make armoires in the house itself. The *habitant* generally knew in advance where he wanted to place the armoire, either in the large common room, or in a bedroom. When one of the sides of the armoire was to be placed next to a partition or against a wall, the woodworker would not take the trouble to make panels for the unexposed side, but used simple tongued-and-grooved boards, and left out the side of the cornice. This would be done only with the agreement of the *habitant*, of course, and the purpose was to save both time and material.

SCHOOLS OF ARTS AND CRAFTS

In the seventeenth century, Bishop Laval required a large number of woodworkers and carvers to work on several churches at the same time, but there was a shortage of such craftsmen, and the demands on their time were increasing as the population of the colony grew at a rapid rate. Because of this, Laval decided to found a school of Arts and Crafts, and in 1675 he sent to France for a staff of carpenters, woodworkers, wood-carvers, masons and stone-cutters. The list included the following :

" Guillaume Jourdain, called Labrosse, woodworker
Michel Fauchois, apprentice wood-carver, engaged for four years at 100 francs a year
Samuel Genner, wood-carver, engaged for three years, he earns 300 livres for each year
Dusmaret, rough carpenter
Léonard Lureken, woodworker
Pierre Rivière, woodworker, engaged for three years
Michel Leblond, called Le Picard, woodworker, engaged for three years. " [1]

These people all arrived on the same boat on September 21, 1675, to teach at two schools, one at Cap Tourmente, St-Joachim, and the other at the Seminary of Quebec.

It is almost certain that the school at the seminary had existed before this time since the *Intendant*, Jean Talon, wrote to Louis XIV on November 2nd, 1671, " the young men devote themselves, and attack their studies in the classes for science, the arts, crafts, and particularly

(1) A S Q. Livre de Raison, 1675-1676.

seamanship, with such enthusiasm that if their interest continues to grow there is reason to hope that this country will become a training ground for navigators, fishermen, sailors and craftsmen, all with a natural disposition for these professions. "[1]

Father de Charlevoix, after coming to Canada and observing the system of training for young Canadians, remarked that : " No one can deny that they have an unusual gift for mechanics; they hardly have need of instruction to excel in the field and every day one finds young men who are successful in their craft without having gone through an apprenticeship. "[2] Again, the Abbé Bertrand de la Tour wrote of the talent of the young Canadians, stating in particular, " they succeed much better in working with their hands; these arts are carried to a great perfection, and very good workers of all sorts are to be found; the least child shows skill... "[3]

These were the first schools of Arts and Crafts in either French Canada or the British colonies in North America. The teachers at the School of Arts and Crafts of Quebec Seminary and at the Cap Tourmente school were Guillaume Jourdain " called Labrosse ", who arrived in 1675, Jacques Le Blond de Latour, from Bordeaux, and Denis Mallet, who taught woodwork and carving. It was their students who did the carving and panelling of the seminary chapel as it was described by Bacqueville de la Potherie : " The carving, which is valued at ten thousand crowns, is very beautiful; it was done by the seminarists who spared nothing to make it a work of perfection. The High Altar is an architectural piece in the Corinthian style; the walls are covered with panelling and sculpture, and include several large paintings, and the ornamentation rises to the cornice of the many-sided vault which in turn is decorated with the lozenge pattern and with painted and gilded carving. "[4]

The *Intendant* de Meulles wrote in 1685, " We also plan to set up looms to provide instruction for the children of the country, and they are already being taught woodworking, carving, painting, gilding for the decoration of churches, masonry, and carpentry. "[5] Mgr de Saint-Vallier, during a pastoral visit to the Côte de Beaupré around 1685, wrote in his diary : " My principal concern in Cap Tourmente was to examine, one by one, the thirty-nine children whom two priests from the Quebec Seminary are training; nineteen are scholars, the others are being taught trades... " and later he says, " if we had the funds to support this little school, we would in time produce a good number of saintly priests and skilled craftsmen. "[6]

These arts and crafts schools unfortunately did not survive for very long. The Training School of Bishop Laval exercised its greatest influence between 1692 and 1701, according to Marius Barbeau.[7] The students passed on a tradition which affected not only the ornamentation of churches, but all aspects of the making of furniture. It is astonishing that in such a short time so many artisans could be trained and that they should have established a tradition in New France which lasted for several generations.

There were many famous family dynasties of woodworkers in French Canada during the eighteenth century. The family of Guillaume Jourdain, called Labrosse, is an example. His son Denis and his descendants, Paul-Raymond, Basile and Antoine, continued in the trade both at Quebec and Montreal. Eventually they dropped the name Jourdain, and were known only as Labrosse. The Labrosse family not only belonged to an important line of woodworkers and carvers, but their excellence in their crafts was widely recognized. In 1750, Madame Bégon, writing from Rochefort, France, to her son-in-law in Louisiana claimed " There is not one worker in this town worth Labrosse... "[8] Canadian by birth, and a resident of Montreal nearly all her life, Mme Bégon had had furniture made for her by Paul Labrosse who was the

(1) A P Q, A N C. "A3 Mémoire de Talon au Roi sur le Canada (2 novembre 1671).
(2) Charlevoix, François-Xavier de, S.J. *Histoire et Description Générale de la Nouvelle-France*. Paris 1744, p. 174.
(3) *Mémoires sur la Vie de M. de Laval*, Cologne 1761, p. 99.
(4) La Potherie, Bacqueville de. *Histoire de l'Amérique Septentrionale*. Paris, 1753, vol. 1, p. 235.
(5) Quoted by Abbé Amédée Gosselin in : *L'Instruction au Canada sous le régime français*. Quebec, 1911.
(6) M. l'Évêque de Québec. *Estat présent de l'Eglise et de la colonie françoise dans la Nouvelle-France*, pp. 53-54.
(7) Barbeau, Marius. *Québec où survit l'ancienne France*, p. 28.
(8) R A P Q. *Correspondance de Madame Élisabeth Bégon*. (*Letter of October* 29, 1750). Quebec, 1934-35, p. 247.

celebrated woodworker and carver of the time. The large wooden crucifix in Montreal's Notre-Dame Church was carved by him.

There were many other dynasties of Master Woodworkers and Master Carvers who plied their trade for several generations, and trained a large number of apprentices and masters. The most famous was the Le Vasseur family, of which the first was Jean Le Vasseur, Master Woodworker of Paris, who came to New France before 1660 and was the ancestor of a long line of woodworkers and sculptors. The best known of his descendants were Noël, François-Noël, Pierre-Noël and Jean-Baptiste-Antoine.

Another distinguished line of craftsmen was the Baillairgé family. The Master Woodworker Jean Baillairgé settled in Quebec in 1741 and his descendants, François, Pierre-Florent and Thomas, were among the most gifted of Canadian artisans. There was also the Berlinguet family, Louis-Thomas, Flavien and François-Xavier, who carried on the tradition of the Baillairgés well into the nineteenth century.

In France as in Canada, these skills were often passed on from father to son and it is tragic that this custom has all but disappeared in our times. Today it is rare to find the son of a craftsman following in his father's trade. The ties between father and son are no longer the same .

On April 14, 1694, Louis XIV gave his approval to François Charon de la Barre for the establishment of a charitable institution in Montreal " ...where they will provide a refuge for poor children and orphans... instruct the said children in the crafts, and give them the best possible education, all for the greater glory of God and the well-being of the colony. "[1]

Five years later, the Charon Brothers *(Frères Hospitaliers de Saint-Joseph de la Croix)* obtained letters patent from Louis XIV giving them " permission to establish Manufactories of Arts and Crafts in their building and grounds. "[2]

In 1701, the Master Woodworker Martin Noblesse, the painter Pierre Leber and the Master Woodworker and Carver Charles Chaboillez were the teachers in this school. Maître Chaboillez committed himself to the order of the Charon Brothers " to serve God and the poor in every way possible with his skill as a carver as well as directing the necessary woodwork in the community. "[3] The school of the Charon Brothers was short-lived, unfortunately. Charles Chaboillez, a bachelor, did not remain with the Charon Brothers' institution for long, possibly because the restrictions of conventual life did not appeal to such an artist. When he left the order he was over sixty, but he married a very young girl and fathered two sons whose descendants were to become famous. Chaboillez Square in Montreal was named after his grandson, a celebrated fur-trader.

Another churchman who showed an interest in the arts and crafts was Monseigneur Pierre Dosquet who was named Coadjutor to the Bishop of Quebec in 1729, and Bishop in 1734. Shortly after his arrival in Canada, he sent for several artisans from Flanders and the northeast of France.

It is obvious that there was really a great need to train craftsmen from among the Canadian population since it would reduce these constant appeals for skilled workers from the mother country.

APPRENTICESHIP

Apart from the schools that I have already mentioned, there were woodworkers and carvers with workshops in Montreal, Quebec, and Three Rivers who trained young men in their various

(1) *Édits, Ordonnances Royaux, Déclarations et Arrêts du Conseil d'État.* Québec, 1854, pp. 277-278.
(2) A S Q. Viger, Jacques. Saberdache E., p. 193.
(3) *Inventaire des greffes de notaire.* Frères Hospitaliers de Montréal. Conventions entre Charles Charon (le 6 mai 1701). Greffe Adhémar.

crafts. A quantity of apprenticeship articles, registered by the notaries, and preserved in the records of the Judicial Archives, support this evidence.

In seventeenth-century France, the acquisition of Master's papers was not simply a matter of talent but also of privilege. Even a good apprentice who graduated to the rank of Journeyman could not expect to become a Master automatically. In Canada, however, there was no question of privilege in the early days, talent being the only requirement. In fact, any young man who wished to practise the profession of woodworker, carver, etc., was welcomed in a Master's workshop, and could himself become a Master if he possessed sufficient skill. The needs of the country were too pressing to permit the exclusion of any gifted craftsman.

The period of apprenticeship in Canada generally lasted from three to seven years, and a youngster with natural ability would join the workshop of a Master between the ages of twelve and fourteen. Once the Master had accepted him, the articles of apprenticeship were registered with a notary. As an example of such a certificate, we have the articles of young Pierre Marin, who was engaged in Quebec in 1752 " by the Messrs Armand Joseph Chaussat and Jean Baillairgé, Master Woodworkers by profession, living in the Faubourg St-Jean of this town, partners in the same workshop... who promise severally and jointly to teach their said craft and profession of woodworker, and everything related and inter-related to the said profession, without concealing anything from him, and the said apprentice, for his part, promises to study as best he can, and to serve and obey faithfully anything which both of the said Masters, or either one of them, might command that is honest and lawful as both a student and a servant; to feed and lodge the said employee according to his state and condition, to wash and mend his clothing, and to treat him humanely. And to give him the necessary time on feast days and Sundays for religious observances and Christian instruction, and, besides, to consign and pay him as a wage during the said three years, namely, the sum of thirty Livres the first year, fifty Livres the second year, and seventy Livres the third and final year, all in coin of the realm... "[1]

Craftsmen's associations in Canada enjoyed much more freedom than they did in France where they were subjected to the many restrictions dictated by the " Jurande ", the body charged with the protection of the rights of the guild. Everyone was allowed to exercise his craft as he pleased in Canada, as long as he had the talent, and as long as he agreed to respect the rules required by good craftsmanship : " la belle ouvrage ". In doing this, Canadian craftsmen respected the statutes of Paris of 1581 and 1743 : " All writing-tables, commodes with cabriole legs, in the tomb shape or whatever shape or style may be, armoires, secretaries, desks of all kinds, clock cases, corner cabinets, toilet chairs, pedestal tables and all other woodwork made of wild cherry, walnut, oak, silver fir, beech, peartree, olive-wood, cedar... and any others which are not veneered must be well and truly made with respect to joinery, contours, shaping, profile, turnings, carving or ornamentation of whatever form, material or shape may be, respecting the tenons, mortises, tails, shouldering, slit-and-tongue and the other jointing which the art requires for good solidity and finish of the said works; and the drawers, for the above mentioned articles and for all others shall be well assembled with dove-tail joints; the bottoms of the said drawers as well as the tops of desks, tables, commodes, panels and other articles requiring several widths of boards together, shall be well and duly joined by tongue and groove, with the same care. " It is remarkable that the Canadian woodworkers always respected these statutes, although they were under no formal obligation to do so. The " belle ouvrage " was in some measure a question of honour for them. It is not by chance that the verb " chef-d'œuvrer " is still used in French Canada. I have often heard the praises sung of woodworkers, who had a reputation for making furniture with care and artistry : one says that they " chef-d'œuvrent " or that they are " chef-d'œuvreux". In other words, they are creators of perfection.

(1) A J Q, I O A. *Minutier de Mtre C. Barolet*, n° 2692, 22 octobre 1752. Engagement Pierre Marin.

THE CONFRÉRIE DE SAINTE ANNE

Each association of workers in France had its patron saint : St-Joseph was the patron of carpenters, and St-Anne the patroness of woodworkers. Marius Barbeau in his " *Mémoire sur la Confrérie de Sainte-Anne au Canada* " writes : " Some Master Woodworkers of Quebec, having belonged to the famous *Confrérie de Sainte-Anne* of Paris, soon decided to start a branch of the *Confrérie* in Canada.... "[1]

Like all other confraternities which commended themselves to the good graces of a patron saint, the members of the *Confrérie de Sainte-Anne* had to practise their religion, aid their fellow-members in need, and maintain the high standard of their craft.

In Quebec, in the early days of the colony, as was the custom in France, there was an annual procession of the Blessed Sacrament and each group of craftsmen would be preceded by a banner. The first procession in which the woodworkers are reported to have taken part was in 1648. " On the eleventh the feast of the Blessed Sacrament, the procession took place at the time and in the manner of the previous years... Our Brother Nicolas carried the cross, and Joliet and Costé, two little boys in surplices, walked on either side of the cross which bore a crown of flowers. Next came the Indians led by Father Le Jeune who was dressed in surplice and stole; there followed twelve torches carried by twelve craftsmen of different trades : turner, woodworker, cobbler, cooper, locksmith, armorer, carpenter, mason, toolmaker, baker, cartwright, and nailer... "[2]

The *Confrérie de Sainte-Anne* was formed in New France on the first of May, 1658, according to the evidence of this document : " ...In this land let us found and establish and declare founded and established the *Confrérie des Menuisiers de Madame Ste-Anne* their patroness, in our parochial church and in the chapel of Ste-Anne, also called Of the Rosary. "[3]

In 1660, the first members of this brotherhood at Quebec were the following Master Woodworkers : " Jean Le Vasseur, Master Woodworker of Paris, Dean of the *Confrérie de Sainte-Anne*, established in the parochial church of Our Lady of Quebec and Pierre Biron, Pierre Le Vasseur, at present my Confreres of the said *Confrérie*, Raymont Pagets called Carcy, Pierre Minville, Guillaume Loyer, former Masters... and Jean Le Messlin... "[4]

From the very beginning of the colony, woodworkers, like other craftsmen, took an active part in the life of New France. Through both their religious faith and their *esprit de corps* they perpetuated French traditions in America.

PRESERVATION AND RESTORATION

We have seen that from 1650 to 1750, the furniture of French Canada was inspired largely by the Louis XIII style. According to records, most furniture of this period was stained rather than painted. As soon as the woodworker had finished a piece he applied a colour, using transparent or opaque stains which imitated French walnut, or old oak, as was the custom in the French provinces. Since the native woods were very light in tone, they could not be left unstained as they would soon have become dirty and greasy. In rare cases, a piece of furniture would be finished in its natural colour, but it would be protected from finger marks or other contact with a thin coat of clear varnish. I have seen very few examples of this type of finish

(1) Barbeau, Marius. *La Confrérie des menuisiers de Madame Sainte-Anne.* (Les Archives de Folklore, vol. I). Montréal, 1946, pp. 72-96.
(2) *Journal des Jésuites.* Québec, June 1648, pp. 109-110.
(3) A S Q. Collection Faribault, quoted by Marius Barbeau.
(4) Barbeau, Marius. *Les Le Vasseur: maîtres-menuisiers, sculpteurs, statuaires.* (Les Archives de Folklore, vol. III). Montréal, 1948, pp. 35-52.

EIGHTEENTH-CENTURY KITCHEN.

but one of the exceptions is worth commenting upon. In the crypt of the chapel of the Grey Nuns of Montreal, the diamond-point armoire of Mother d'Youville has been preserved with its natural wood finish. Protected from the beginning by clear varnish, it has acquired a very beautiful golden tone. It is interesting to note that these sisters brought with them the complete room of the foundress of their order when they left their original building, the *Hôpital-Général*, on Youville Square. In their desire to be faithful to the original, they installed the same doors, floors, and beams, as well as the furniture of Mother d'Youville. It was recreated as they found it, in the crypt of their new building on Dorchester Street.

STAINED AND PAINTED FURNITURE

From 1745 we find painted furniture mentioned in inventories, and many of the pieces were painted red. Later, almost all furniture must have been painted. Some of the conventional colours used were the same as those found on pier-glass frames, chandeliers and armchairs of the eighteenth century in France : a very dark blue-green; a subtle blue-green suggesting a robin's-egg blue; a white, tinted with yellow ochre; a red ochre colour, or iron oxide (this last colour was very popular at the end of the eighteenth century, and the beginning of the nineteenth) " ... a little square wooden table painted red. "[1]

In certain parts of Quebec, especially in the region of Three Rivers, the *habitants* used to pulverize red earth from their fields and mix it with linseed oil or skimmed milk. Another type of painting widely used on furniture and woodwork during the last century and even today, particularly in churches and convents, is the kind which attempts to imitate wood grain. It is difficult to account for this ridiculous practice when the true grain of the wood is already there, except that the nineteenth century was inordinately fond of imitations. Perhaps the appalling efforts of today are simply a continuation of this pernicious practice.

LOCATION AND CONDITION OF OLD FURNITURE

Early Canadian furniture is usually found in the country homes but rarely in use in rooms. It might be stowed away in the attic or cellar, or in a shed or barn, or even in the henhouse !

Needless to say it is generally found in a pitiful state, covered with dirt, and encrusted with several layers of paint : house-paint, or enamel ranging from the gloomiest shades to screaming colours, and most of the furniture found in these places has been dreadfully mutilated. The pieces have lost either tops, cornices, and moulding, or feet, and if the fische hinges have been torn off they have been replaced by ugly strap-hinges or pieces of leather, screwed or nailed haphazardly on to the panels and stiles. Sometimes they may have been gnawed by rats, leaving enormous holes in the corners of drawers or doors. In almost every case you will find nail-holes, ink-stains, dye-stains, burns, deep hammer marks, and, for some mysterious reason, deep saw cuts. Bottom rails, when free from saw-marks, seem to have been kicked deliberately to remove the shaping. I once discovered, in the Côte de Beaupré, an armoire whose entire surface had been ornamented with incised geometrical designs. It was an armoire without equal in my experience, but it had been completely sawn through the doors and was irreparably damaged. Too often have I seen such examples of wanton mutilations !

ORIGINAL COLOURS

If you are lucky enough to find a piece of furniture with its original coat of paint intact, it is best not to strip it, but simply to clean or wash the surface, removing the superficial dirt without damaging the colour. In this way you will have a piece of furniture exactly as it was conceived and appreciated in its own period. An armoire that has had the paint stripped, revealing

(1) A J Q, I O A. Partage entre Jean Letourneau et les héritiers de Dame Marie Gauthier sa femme : 1er août 1783. Greffe J.A. Panet.

a slight orange tone caused when linseed oil originally penetrated the wood, can be very attractive and most effective when contrasted with a white or tinted wall. But the effect is just the opposite if the armoire is placed against wood panelling of the same tone.

Every effort should be made to keep the furniture as nearly as possible in its original state, as they do in some museums and homes of genuine collectors who respect the woodworkers' creation. The Museum of Detroit has even taken the bold step of restoring the paint of several pieces whose finish was in a sad state. If the original colour is attractive, it is best to try to preserve it. To expose the original coating is very delicate work, demanding extraordinary patience and a technique comparable to that of the oil-painting restorer. Every single square inch of the surface must be concentrated upon and cleaned with a pad and special solvents. I have seen statuettes cleaned in this way with great success. If you wish to recreate the original colour, you must not expect to find it ready mixed in a store; you must make the mixture yourself, and here again great patience and skill are required. Some of these ancient colours were also powder paints mixed with skimmed milk which produced a type of casein paint and a particularly hard, almost vitrified, surface difficult to remove without a scraper.

STRIPPING

Where all the paint has to be removed, there is a correct way of doing it. Avoid using a scraper, knife, or any sharp-edged object. Wash the furniture with solvents such as alcohol, a solution of caustic soda, or any good commercial solvent. But patience is a primary requirement, and a miracle must not be expected : not all the coats of paint will come off at the same time. Continue to brush the paint-remover over the surface to be cleaned until each coat comes off with the brush itself. A brush with synthetic bristles is recommended. Make sure that the surface that you are working on is flat so that the remover does not run off and is given time to penetrate the paint. Sometimes, with a particularly stubborn coat, the surface must be literally soaked with the remover, and it can take as much as two days to disintegrate paint which is almost vitrified. A scraper can be used on thicker coats, but it should be discarded before reaching the actual surface of the wood.

I realize that, with small country chairs, it is sometimes almost impossible to obtain the desired result with these methods as the remover cannot adhere to the rungs. In such cases a scraper must be used, but always with caution.

If the basic colour is not too dark, some pieces can be washed with lye or caustic soda. This method is not to be recommended unless great care is taken when preparing the solution. The lye and water are mixed in a bucket. I know some serious collectors who before using lye on an important piece of furniture, will first test their mixture on a piece of painted wood of no value because they are so afraid of lifting the grain of the wood or burning the surface.

When you are sure that the mixture is safe to use, it is best to work outside, as when washing the car, wearing rubber boots, goggles and rubber gloves. Coat the piece with the lye solution repeatedly, using a synthetic fibre broom, until all the paint has been removed. Remove the stubborn paint with a smaller brush and wash the piece down with a hose between different applications. It is important to keep working until all the paint is removed, because the lye may run down the wood and leave indelible stains if the operation is interrupted.

Once the piece of furniture is dry, a fine sand-paper and fine steel-wool can be used.

It must be emphasized, however, that this method of removing paint is a very dangerous one, and every precaution must be taken if it is used.

A blow-torch must never be used to remove paint from furniture, because it often scorches the wood so deeply that the damage is irreparable. There is a striking example in a Canadian museum of a beautiful French commode of the *tombeau* type which is streaked with blow-torch burns as a result of this foolish method. The sad part is that there was no apparent reason for removing the magnificent original stain and varnish.

A piece of furniture which has had its paint removed should be waxed frequently, not only to preserve the wood from dust and marking, but also to give the surface a fine tone. The connoisseurs favour a beeswax, which they prepare themselves.

RESTORATION

There are two schools of thought in Canada today on the problems of restoring traditional French Canadian furniture. One of them believes in retaining the signs of wear and age (marks left by hot plates, ink stains, scratches left by a pair of compasses or a marking-gauge, a design cut with a pen-knife by some child, flaking of the wood caused by humidity, and other such signs of long life and daily use). The other school prefers an immaculate piece of furniture, which is almost an impossibility if the piece was made two centuries ago. To obtain this effect, they are ready to sacrifice the ridges and cavities of the moulding and carved ornaments as well as the original tone of the wood which must then be simulated with a stain. In this case it would be far better to have the piece reproduced rather than to destroy the craftsman's touch and the patina of age which are the living witnesses of our ancestors.

When it is a question of restoring a piece of furniture, it is of the utmost importance that the work be placed in the hands of a craftsman who has experience in such matters. Above all, he should have a feeling for the character and style of the piece.

I have seen furniture irreparably spoiled by workers who were incapable of understanding its essential beauty. These are people who consider the creations of woodworkers of the past to be of little importance because they fail to grasp the aesthetic qualities and the love and care of many generations which these pieces silently reflect. They show no hesitation in removing the delicate relief of a piece of moulding with a scraper or in driving nails into some exposed surface. Where a piece of wood is missing it is often replaced with different type of wood.

If part of a piece of furniture is missing (a cornice, leg, or shaped bottom-rail) it is better to ask the woodworker to make a trial model with the aid of a pouncing pattern or templets if there is any doubt about the character of the missing part. In this way it can be ascertained whether the addition will harmonize with the rest of the piece. Only when an agreement has been reached on the desired solution should the actual restoration begin.

Decisions must never be made in haste. A large number of commode drawer-fronts are found in a mutilated condition — an overlapping end-moulding is missing, or a large sliver has broken off. If the wood is strongly veined, it is a particularly delicate job to make an insert or a joint with new wood, and sometimes a long and painstaking search must be made to find material which matches the original grain.

I recently saw a drawer-front which had had its ends replaced, and the veining of the new wood was so perfectly matched with the rest that it was almost impossible to distinguish the joint. The craftsman who had done the work was very proud of it, and with good reason.

Almost all the good pieces of early traditional furniture have already been tracked down, sold, or destroyed, but there are still a few fine examples of traditional furniture in the homes of Quebec farmers who remain attached to the heritage of their ancestors. They deserve our admiration because they are among the very few who genuinely appreciate their patrimony. But the bell has tolled! There are no more fine pieces on the market except for cradles, dough-boxes, spinning-wheels, little wash-stands, or armoires having square panels with applied moulding, dating from the middle of the nineteenth century. We could consider ourselves lucky if more than half a dozen pieces of importance were brought to light in a year in the entire province. Nevertheless, a collector can still add a fresh charm to his house with many of the humbler articles listed above, and at reasonable cost.

The care and restoration of early furniture can be summed up in the words of Pierre Verlet, Chief Curator of the Department of Objets d'Art of the Louvre : " Total conservation is impossible. The past cannot be arrested or recaptured but it is possible, with care, respect, and taste, to get close to the original state of the piece, and to maintain in good condition the pleasing appearance that has been acquired over the years. All this requires infinite care, attention, and understanding of the way in which old things have evolved, and a scrupulous conservation of the past which may seem practically impossible and paradoxical in this century. But this is the stern lesson of love which early furniture teaches to those who would live with it. ''[1]

IDENTIFICATION

No one can expect to learn in one lesson how to tell the true from the false in early French Canadian furniture. Years of experience and study are required in order to become an authority. But the conscientious person, with a love for these things, can develop an eye for the good pieces, sometimes picking them out at first sight and without examining them at close range.

There are cases, however, where the piece must be gone over practically with a microscope, or at least a magnifying glass, so cleverly has it been faked. I have met a number of collectors who own furniture which they believed to be authentic early Canadian, when in actual fact it was so restored or transformed that the traces of the original work had all but disappeared.

Panels of armoires or buffets are replaced, new rails are shaped, ornaments are added, etc. Sometimes armoires are cut in half and transformed into sideboards or low buffets. In the same way, long tables are cut through the middle in order to make two, but in such cases, new legs must be added at one end in imitation of the original ones.

Alterations are sometimes justified, of course. If an armoire or a table is too massive, or a corner cabinet or low buffet is ill-proportioned or too high, it may be rightly changed. When a piece of furniture is badly mutilated, there is nothing wrong in replacing part of it. However, the conscientious antique dealer who has the interest of his client at heart will indicate all the transformations that have been made, and will say when a piece is not authentic.

The following is a list of simple rules for identification of authentic French Canadian furniture.

1. PLANKS (THICK AND THIN)

The boards that were used in making traditional furniture in the seventeenth and eighteenth centuries were generally much thicker than those of today because they were pit-sawed. In those days, wood 1 ¼ to 1 ½ inches in thickness was used for tops, rails and doors. Sometimes it was even thicker as we find in the drawer-fronts of serpentine-shaped commodes, some measuring up to five inches in thickness, or the bottom rails of armoires which are often more than two inches in thickness.

Today, this same type of board may be less than an inch thick, say, $^7/_8$'', or perhaps less : $^{25}/_{32}$ of an inch, or even less. The standards changed with the introduction of the circular saw around 1840. Before that time, the *habitant* or woodworker had his planks sawed as he wanted them, which accounts for the variety of measurements in early furniture. This is the reason for the appreciable difference in thickness of planks used in each category of furniture.

If deception is the object, however, it is still possible to cut pine, yellow birch, or butternut from thick lumber in imitation of the early dimensions. But if there is any doubt about the age of the wood, the deception can be detected by scratching a small area with a penknife. If the wood under the surface is white, it is new. Old wood acquires a slightly warm orange tinge.

(1) Verlet, Pierre. *Les meubles français du XVIIIe siècle. II Ébénisterie.* Paris, Presses Universitaires de France, 1956 (Coll. L'Œil du Connaisseur), p. 96.

2. OLD WOOD

Some imitators can make fake pieces out of wood reclaimed from old uninteresting furniture, or from lumber obtained from demolition companies. The first thing to look for in a case like this is a trace of the circular or band-saw under the rails, on the reverse side of the rails, on the inside of drawer-fronts, or at the rail-joints and the dove-tails of drawers. Where the wood has been freshly cross-cut, no matter how old it is, it will look almost like new. And if any glue can be seen at the joints there is added reason for suspicion since the early woodworkers hardly ever used it.

In the façades of drawers made from thick boards of reclaimed pine, there are nearly always traces of nail holes which leave black or rusty spots. I once saw a fake commode made in this way and sold to a collector as an authentic piece at an astronomical price. One look at the drawers was all that was needed to detect the forgery.

3. SURFACE OF OLD WOODS

The wood in early traditional furniture has a surface quite different from that made after the introduction of the machine plane and the sanding machine around the middle of the nineteenth century. If the wood is examined in a cross light, traces of the hand-operated smoothing-plane will be seen. If the furrows or concavities caused by the smoothing-plane have disappeared with time from the worn areas, the reverse side of the board should be examined. Furrows will be seen on panels of armoires, as well as on side panels of commodes of the eighteenth century.

4. TOP SURFACES

For the tops of low buffets, tables, and the leaves of folding tables, etc., woodworkers of the past preferred to use boards measuring up to twenty-six inches or more in width, and over an inch thick, and they were generally selected from knot-free lumber. If a table-top required two or three boards, they were invariably tongued and grooved. This is one of the rare instances where a little glue would be used in the joints to prevent the planks from working loose or warping, but in most cases all superficial traces of glue have long since disappeared as the conscientious housewife often scrubbed the top with a solution of lye.

5. DOVE-TAILS

The early dove-tail joints were never symmetrical because they were hand cut with a chisel and saw. The sides of drawers of Canadian commodes were joined with an enormous central dove-tail, braced by a hand-forged nail, and two half dove-tails, one at the top, the other at the bottom. In some cases the drawer joint is made of four medium-sized dove-tails, but they are never identical. At the corners of eighteenth-century coffers or blanket chests, dove-tails of various sizes are also to be seen.

For some time now, special machinery for making dove-tails has been used in factories and in woodworking shops. When these joints are examined at close range, all the dove-tails are seen to be equally spaced and exactly the same. It should be remembered that early woodworkers were not concerned with symmetry. This can be seen in the joints and mouldings that vary from one armoire door to another, and even in the ornamentation where the absence of symmetry is a delight.

Of course it is still possible to make the early type of dove-tail by hand, and old wood can be used to imitate the antique. But it is always the fresh end-grain of the wood and the absence of the furrows caused by the smoothing-plane which betrays the fact that the work is recent.

6. LATHE-WORK

Irregular and asymmetrical turning is also characteristic of traditional furniture. If the legs of a table or of a Louis XIII armchair are examined closely, all the irregularities of the lathe can be seen. The reason they are never perfectly round is that the lathes at that time were operated by a treadle, or by an enormous wheel turned with a crank by an apprentice. The balusters, bevelled cubes, and bun feet of the furniture are never identical. Here and there you will find a flattened surface because the original wood was cut too thinly by mistake.

Finally, it is interesting to note that a set of chairs made at the same time are never exactly alike. Each one of the set will have its peculiarities.

7. BACKINGS AND BOTTOMS

The unexposed backs, tops, and bottoms of armoires, buffets and commodes are usually made of large boards, bevelled at the ends, or hewn with an axe and then slid horizontally into the grooves of the posterior stiles, from top to bottom. In most cases the wood was left rough in these unexposed places, and all the marks of the pit-saw or axe are still to be seen.

In some cases, where a more sophisticated kind of workmanship is found, the woodworker embellished the backing planks with flat mouldings like those found on simpler armoire panels. The backing planks would be slid into position in the grooves of the stiles in the usual way, although sometimes the back would be pegged to the sides with large tenon-and-mortise joints, and braced at intervals with sturdy rails.

The bottoms of drawers were always made of a wide board, or two boards tongued and grooved, bevelled around the four sides, and fitted into the grooves of the drawer-frame. Here again, the furrows of the smoothing-plane can be felt on the bottom.

The bottoms of armoires, buffets, and commodes are assembled in the same way as the drawer bottoms, fitted into the grooves of the rails and stiles.

8. DOORS

The doors of armoires and buffets of the seventeenth and eighteenth centuries were invariably made to overlap the rails, stiles, and centre-post, unlike later nineteenth-century doors which were flush with the frame. The French term for the earlier type is *porte à battement*.

The form of these earlier doors demanded fische hinges whereas later doors were flush with the frame and equipped with butt hinges screwed to the inside edges of the stiles and doors.

When doors are taken from another armoire and shortened to fit a low buffet, it is necessary to bore new hinge-mortises as the old ones will rarely fit. When a door has been substituted, traces of the old as well as the new mortises are apparent. Furthermore, the tenons of fische hinges were always held together by hand-forged nails which would have to be replaced, and new ones are easy to identify.

9. PEGS OR DOWELS

In the seventeenth and eighteenth centuries, all traditional furniture of jointed woodwork was assembled by means of tenons and mortises held by pegs. The pegs were driven into holes which had been drilled first through the stiles, then through the tenons, thus securing the joint. Early woodworkers cut their own faceted or even squarish pegs with a chisel or hatchet. Modern lumber suppliers now produce turned, perfectly round wooden dowels in long strips which woodworkers cut into the desired lengths for peg work.

10. MOULDINGS

In seventeenth and eighteenth century furniture, mouldings surrounding the panels of armoires were always an integral part of the stiles and rails. It is only in the nineteenth century

386

that it became general practice to apply mouldings to the edges of panels with glue and small nails. It can easily be determined whether the moulding has been applied, by trying to slip the blade of a pen-knife between the moulding and its adjacent stile or rail. If the blade penetrates, the moulding is applied; if it does not, it means that there is no joint and the moulding is not applied.

11. CORNICES

On most Canadian furniture a moulded cornice would be in three parts which are mitred together and attached to the furniture by long, hand-forged nails. There are a few rare armoires, however, which have a removable cornice like those so often found in France. These were assembled in one piece and fitted the armoires like a crown, neither nails nor screws being needed to hold them in place.

12. PANEL CARVING

There is sometimes reason to doubt the authenticity of lozenges and St Andrew crosses carved on panels of armoires and low buffets. In order to decorate the panels and increase their market value, these designs were sometimes carved on panels which were once plain. The deception is easy to detect, however, as the grooves of the lozenges and St Andrew crosses cut in the old wood will be lighter in tone than the surface of the panel, which is more orange in tone. The deeper one carves into an old wood, the whiter it becomes. If a stain has been added to wax and cleverly applied in new carvings, a touch of alcohol or some similar solvent will expose the freshly carved wood.

Where panels have been decorated with carved floral or fruit designs, woodworkers of the past carved the panel in low relief, and the design was made to stand out from the rest of the panel.

Today, anyone attempting to produce the same type of decoration on a plain panel is obliged to gouge out the design, taking care not to come too close to the edges of the panel because the flat mouldings are nearly flush with the surface. Early woodworkers cut their panels from much thicker wood for such carving so that the design would stand out. When panels of a plain armoire have afterwards been carved, the design is recessed into the panel and does not stand out in relief. In this way it is possible to detect a plain armoire that has had its panels carved at a later period in order to make it more attractive.

13. SIGNS OF AGE

On all traditional furniture of the seventeenth century, signs of wear will be seen on the moulded edges of tables, armoires, doors, the frieze and stretchers of tables, or on the feet of chairs and tables. Naturally these signs of wear are most apparent on the places most exposed to human contact : the spot where hands have opened an armoire door or drawer; the place where generations of people have leaned their elbows on the edge of a table or rested their feet on chair or table stretchers; or the point where the housewife habitually knocked her broom against the bottom rail of an armoire or a buffet.

The grooves and the checks of moulding on the edge of an old table will often be worn smooth with use, but some trace of the original design always remains. Corners, too, are often rounded by constant friction.

If marks of wear are found at regular intervals, or in places where daily contact was not likely, they must immediately be regarded as suspect. They have probably been made with a rasp to simulate age.

After long observation, the true and the false signs of age and wear in traditional furniture become much easier to spot.

14. THE GENUINE METAL FITTINGS

Original brass handles, placed on drawer-fronts of commodes at the time of their construction, are easily recognizable. No trace of an adjacent nail or screw-hole or peg should be visible on the façade of the drawer. If such scars are discovered, they can be taken as the mark of an earlier fitting which has since been replaced. This applies also to key-hole escutcheons, hinged rings and the iron knobs of two-tiered buffets and armoires.

EVEN THE GREATEST EXPERTS...

With all these indications, and long practice, it will be possible for the observant amateur to distinguish the genuine article from the imitation in French Canadian antiques. It must be admitted that anything can be copied, and if enough trouble is taken the forgery can approach perfection. That stage has not yet been reached in Canada.

No matter how skilful the forgery may be, the truth is somewhere waiting to be discovered. In France, I once saw six Louis XV armchairs with caned seats and backs, of which four were authentic and two were perfect reproductions. The resemblance was so exact in every detail that it was impossible to tell them apart. Even the imperfections and irregularities found in all antique armchairs which have been made as a set were there. The Parisian woodworker who had made the two reproductions had used old beech-wood, as in the originals. He had even taken care not to make an exact copy of one of the originals but had introduced subtle variations in the carving. The chairs were evidently alike without being absolutely identical. The only way to detect the reproductions was by weighing them. Although the woodworker had used old beech-wood for the reproductions, it was not as old as the wood of the original chairs. Like man, wood becomes lighter as it ages. And if the woodworker had used a wood as old as that of the original armchairs ? Even the greatest experts...

CONCLUSION

VANDALISM

We have already mentioned elsewhere in this book that vandalism and fires were responsible for the loss of four fifths of the furniture and objets d'art of early Quebec.

Fires were inevitable in a society which used such quantities of wood as fuel to protect itself from the intense cold, but these were mostly due to carelessness in the early days as they are today.

It is less easy to forgive or excuse vandalism, but this is a universal phenomenon. Every country has been affected in some way by vandalism, and the extent can only be conjectured. It is as if each era wished to repudiate those which had preceded it.

French Canada had barely emerged from the pioneer era before the colonists began to get rid of the things which reminded them of their humble past. Vandalism stems from ignorance, from lack of knowledge, or simply from lack of taste. One might conclude that Canadians are irritated and ashamed of the heritage of their forefathers. The image of Quebec as projected in Louis Hémon's novel, " *Maria Chapdelaine* ", is not generally appreciated in Quebec, and there is resentment against being described to the world as a nation of pioneers.

Over the past thirty years, I have witnessed acts of vandalism against which I was powerless. Anyone who protested against the destruction of old houses and furniture, or early churches, was considered foolish and anything which showed signs of age was called worthless, or, in the common language, " *cochonneries* " — the English word " rubbish " conveys only a fraction of the contempt. How many ancient houses, how many enchanting churches built on a human scale, how many old mills have we seen destroyed or allowed to fall into ruin.

If the owner decided to alter them, the results were often just as disastrous. Ugly wings and annexes were added without considering proportion or architectural style. If a church, a hospital, or a house had to be enlarged, the project was undertaken without the slightest regard for the character of the building. It would have been a simple matter to add the space and comforts we consider so essential today while respecting the original architecture.

In Europe many early buildings have been altered without destroying the original lines, especially a number of sixteenth and seventeenth century hospitals.

Many of the most picturesque natural sites of Canada have been spoiled. In Quebec City, for instance, it is difficult to find a clear view of the river, the islands, or the mountains without being aware of the hideous foreground, a confusion of boarded attic windows, shacks built on roof-tops, gigantic bill-boards, factories belching smoke, flat-topped tar-papered sheds, monstrous grain elevators, and oil tanks. And this was once one of the most beautiful vistas in the world.

As for Montreal, where can one see " the Great St Lawrence " ? It is visible only from the top of Mount Royal, and even that view is now despoiled.

How is it that Canadians have lost touch with the magnificent natural beauty of their country ? What is the gift that they seem to have for creating ugliness on every side ? Why have the cities and their suburbs, the towns, the villages, the shores of the great river, and the seaports of Canada been so disfigured ?

Progress is no excuse. I have seen seaports in many other countries where the natural surroundings are jealously preserved, where the sea is always visible, where one can sit at a café table overlooking the water. Take Lisbon or Naples as examples. But I have also seen little fishing villages of great charm in the Gaspé and in the Maritime provinces where heart-breaking changes have taken place from one year to the next. A book could be written on the subject of vandalism, which affects houses and landscapes just as much as it does furniture. It seems to be a sickness common to the whole of North America.

I once witnessed the senseless destruction of a very rare and beautiful armoire without being able to do a thing about it. It had been splintered with an axe just before my arrival and when I asked the reason, I was told that old dry pine made excellent kindling.

On another occasion, I saw a family dancing in a circle around a large bonfire in the farmyard. Through the flames I could still make out poster beds, armoires, chests, and early chairs piled high in a blazing mass. I learned that this family had recently inherited the old stone house nearby with all its contents from an elderly bachelor uncle. They had bought new furniture and were getting rid of the things which they had found in the house and which they considered rubbish. I had known the uncle, and I remembered how he had loved and cared for his early furniture. Many generous offers had been made to buy it but he refused to part with a single piece. That bonfire seemed like a funeral pyre, symbolizing a break with the past ! After it was over, the family invited me to come in and admire the up-to-date chrome tables and chairs, the new easy chairs and chesterfields, and the metal beds finished to resemble rosewood.

There are equally distressing stories about carvings, church panelling, and retables being broken up and used as firewood. I remember a magnificent statue of a patron saint that was left standing in its niche in one of our finest early churches when the heavy stone walls were dynamited to make room for a modern atrocity. The statue was blasted into a thousand pieces, in the midst of the stone and plaster, and all I could do was rescue some of the larger fragments from the debris.

I remember, too, a solid silver sanctuary lamp, signed by François Ranvoyzé, which had been flattened to make a cuspidor. Then there was the splendid primitive wooden calvary which was hacked to pieces one night by a gang of youngsters who had been incited to do so by the very person who should have been its keeper. It had been the work of a pious woodcarver of the past who had donated it to the parish. But the modern parishioners persuaded themselves that the figure of Christ was ugly, and they were ashamed of it. I dread to think what might have happened to the *Dévôt Christ* of Perpignan !

The disfiguring of our most beautiful sites, the destruction of houses, churches, carvings and furniture, the razing of whole blocks to make room for parking lots or skyscrapers — all these things could in the past be put down to ignorance. But there is no excuse for such vandalism today. The destruction of any part of this precious national patrimony should be considered a criminal act, and should be dealt with accordingly by the courts.

TRADITIONS AND AESTHETICS

The early French settlers arrived in Canada at the beginning of the seventeenth century, and French Canadian traditions have evolved over a period of three hundred years.

These pioneers who came to the new world in search of a better life were people of good taste. Their craftsmen were simple people, and their work was designed to appeal to men like themselves. The traditional furniture they left is both functional and decorative, and is the expression of a distinctive folk culture, which is closely related to the folk traditions of the French provinces where the settlers originated. They worked creatively in their new country and added many personal touches. With their own hands they fashioned the furniture most closely associated with daily life : the furniture for storing linen, dishes, or food; furniture on which to eat or to sleep; furniture for sitting by the fire, to sing to the latest baby, or to smoke a pipe.

A mere assemblage of boards could not satisfy them. There was a natural urge to embellish these pieces, giving them a character of their own. The furniture that was used every day had to express joy and harmony, and from the poorest peasant to the wealthiest *seigneur*, from the humblest village *curé* to the bishop himself, things of beauty were of prime importance. Good taste knew no social barrier.

In 1781, Jacques Panet, *curé* of L'Islet, ordered several gold vessels and other articles from François Ranvoyzé and paid for them personally.[1] He followed the progress of the work with intense interest, and made sure that these sacred objects were of excellent quality. When he died, he left them to his church.

There was also the Abbé Pierre Conefroy, a consummate artist and architect, who built the church in Boucherville and designed the churches of St-Roch de l'Achigan, L'Acadie, and several others. Monseigneur Briand, as soon as he arrived in Canada, became a patron of the arts, and ordered his furniture from Canadian craftsmen. The Intendant Jean Talon, asked if he would send " sculptors to carve figures for the prow of a ship being built in Canada, or should the vessel be sent to France without ornaments. "[2] (The ship, 400 tons, was begun in Quebec City in 1671.)

There was an *élite* in those days, it is true, but instinctive good taste was general. What happened during the first decades of the nineteenth century to destroy such strong traditions and cause them to disappear completely ?

The wars between France and England for the possession of the French colony in America certainly caused poverty and misery, and such conditions checked the development and encouragement of arts and crafts. Everyone was mobilized to defend the country, from youths to old men, and the war demanded all their energies until the Treaty of Paris in 1763, when Canada was allowed to breathe freely again. However, in the reconstruction period of peace and prosperity that followed, the architects, masons, carpenters, woodworkers, carvers, and silversmiths worked with a greater will than ever, continuing the traditions of the past.

Furniture-makers finished their work with the exuberant decoration of the *Régence* and Louis XV styles which arrived in New France about the middle of the eighteenth century. After the Conquest, the most prolific period in the history of the craft, Canadian woodworkers delighted in foliated scrolls, shells, spirals and curves. Traditional furniture in French Canada reached its peak of refinement in both technique and design between 1785 and 1820.

I have already mentioned other influences of considerable importance which affected the traditional designs of France. Political refugees, loyal to the British Crown, left their homes in the American colonies following the revolution and settled among the French Canadians in Quebec, Montreal, and other communities. At about the same time, a number of cabinet-makers arrived from England and Scotland.

The established craftsmen were quick to imitate the work of these newcomers, producing furniture in the English and American fashions while retaining the most characteristic features of the French tradition. In this way, they succeeded in developing an interesting mixture of French and English styles.

This mixture of styles is most evident in commodes, armoires and corner cabinets produced

---

(1) Manuscript diary of Jacques Panet, *curé* of L'Islet (quoted by Marius Barbeau).
(2) A P Q, A N C. — c''A3. — Extract from M. Talon's request to Colbert.

during the great period that began around 1785 : commodes in the French traditional style but with touches of the William and Mary period; others showing the influence of Chippendale; and later, armoires and corner cabinets which suggest the work of the Adam brothers; characteristics of English Regency, tables with tapered legs in the Sheraton manner, etc.

From 1820 nearly all the furniture of French Canada lost its traditional French character and fell almost completely under the influence of English and American designs. Traditional furniture in French styles practically ceased to exist, and with the arrival of the industrial revolution it disappeared completely.

I do not wish to lessen the importance and artistic value of English furniture. In England, the Maritime provinces, or the United States, it was the expression of a single culture. French Canadian woodworkers who were influenced by English styles between 1785 and 1820 have left beautiful pieces of craftsmanship in pine, butternut and maple. The attractive pieces became fewer in number, however, and after 1820 a serious decline began, leading to a full break with the tradition and a loss of the aesthetic sense. Only a few woodworker-carvers employed by the church continued the great French tradition until about 1850.

The break did not take place overnight, however. French Canadian woodworkers were well-versed in their trade and continued to produce furniture in the established French tradition. But each year the breach widened a little more, until the gap was too wide to be closed.

The most important causes of this rupture were political and philosophical. When normal communications with France were cut immediately following the Conquest, French Canadians found themselves isolated from the source of their culture.

This isolation became intensified after the French Revolution. Quebec shunned its radical ideology and its dynamic influence. The clergy of French Canada had always had the interests of the country at heart without mixing in French politics, but they clung to the system they had always known and which suited them well — the absolute monarchy. The *émigré* priests expelled by the Revolution strengthened this attitude.

The British also feared the repercussions of the French Revolution, and were as anxious as the church to discourage Canadian contacts with France. When Napoleon took power in France, the quarantine was intensified, and it was only in the twentieth century that any sustained contact with France was established. In my opinion this isolation from the mother country was one of the prime causes of the deterioration of French Canadian design. It was a cultural disaster from which French Canada has not yet recovered.

The thread of precious traditions was broken and it was no longer possible to develop a strong and personal idiom. The exuberance and imagination which characterize so much of the early work of the country might have continued, and might have given direction to an authentic and unmistakable Canadian style today.

This applies not only to furniture, but to silver work, architecture, textiles, wrought iron, carving, and painting. The break was so complete that the heritage fell into total oblivion. Its very existence had been so utterly forgotten that until 1925 no one suspected that there had ever been an original tradition of French Canadian furniture.

In the domain of architecture, the neo-Gothic of England had rapidly taken hold in Canada. In 1824, an architect was imported from New York to draught the plans of the new *Notre-Dame*, Montreal, which was to replace the ancient parish church which stood in the middle of *rue Notre-Dame* at *Place d'Armes*. The old building, the work of Chaussegros de Léry, the King's Engineer-Architect, was demolished except for the bell-tower which remained in use until the completion of the new church towers about 1842. Charles Dickens, who visited Montreal that year, left the following description : " There is a very large Catholic cathedral here recently erected with two tall spires of which one is yet unfinished. In the open space in front of this edifice stands a solitary, grim-looking, square ... tower, which has a quaint and remarkable appearance, and which the wiseacres of the place have consequently determined to pull down immediately."[1]

Supervision of the construction of the church was offered to Thomas Baillairgé, architect, woodworker and carver, but he refused as he had only studied Greek and Roman architecture, which he thought suited Canada, and considered his superficial knowledge of Gothic architecture insufficient for the task.[2]

For more than a century, according to Gérard Morisset, French Canadians had developed " a type of architecture perfectly adapted to the climate, building methods, and the skills of the craftsmen."[3] For this reason, it is not surprising that an experienced craftsman like Thomas Baillairgé found it difficult to make a sudden adjustment to new building techniques which were totally different from those established by French Canadian customs, concepts and needs.

This marks the beginning of the decline of French Canadian architecture. The very distinctive and charming styles of the houses and churches of Quebec, which arouse such admiration today, were soon forgotten. The appalling churches put up since that time demonstrate this decline. Novelty took over, and our *élite* adopted almost anything new as long as it was not of local origin.

With the popularity of neo-Gothic architecture, armoires with narrow Gothic panels, grotesque tables and fantastic armchairs were found even in country homes. The universal plague of Victorian and Louis-Philippe furniture and trimmings darkened Canadian interiors and the most hideous styles of the nineteenth century were indiscriminately mixed. The whole of Canada was disfigured by this outbreak of bad taste.

In Quebec, traditional furniture received its death blow. The lure of ephemeral fashions and the consequent rejection of the past contributed to the loss of a French Canadian identity, and obscured the distinctive character of a whole people.

A reaction was bound to set in.

A few English Canadians, mostly military men, began collecting French Canadian furniture in the late nineteenth century, but the real revival did not begin until 1925. English Canadians and Americans were the first to rediscover Canadian furniture and works of art.

Around 1935, French Canadian lecturers began preaching a return to the small industries and cottage crafts which were being forgotten. This movement to revive handicrafts in French Canada was launched by well-intentioned people who honestly believed that they were giving new life to the traditions of the past. Unfortunately, the movement lacked a real sense of direction, as no serious study of the traditions of the past had been undertaken.

Borrowed indifferently from a variety of foreign sources, the designs developed by this movement were in poor taste, and they became worse after the Second World War when foreign novelties began to be imitated with an appalling lack of discrimination.

Contrary to the opinion of certain people, I believe that in order to innovate, to create, there must be a tradition upon which to draw. This is evident in every European country whose culture developed from folk arts and traditions over a period of many centuries.

This does not mean a step backwards in time or a slavish imitation of the past. But the past must be recognized, respected and assimilated. In this way, tradition is a living thing, continued from the past into the present, to become a modern reality. It is the past which makes it possible for us to revise our values and make a freer choice and clearer estimate of the creative possibilities in the future.

The inferiority complex from which many French Canadians seem to suffer today could easily be overcome if they applied themselves to the task of getting to know more about themselves, their history, culture and traditions. The furniture dealt with in this book is a striking

(1) Dickens, Charles. *American Notes*. New York, 1842, p. 77.
(2) Morisset, Gérard. *L'Architecture en Nouvelle-France*. Quebec, 1949, p. 87.
(3) Idem, p. 56.

demonstration of the existence of a Canadian style, which originated in France but was developed on the shores of the St Lawrence. It is of no importance that this style existed so long ago, but it is of the utmost importance that we should know of its existence as an integral part of Canadian culture, intimately linked with the history and national life of Canada.

In order to recapture justifiable pride in the national culture of Canada, the prejudices and false values that have misled Canadians for so long must be rejected and replaced by a new national enlightenment. This is not limited to French Canada alone.

In Canada's rapidly expanding economy, where traditional values are continually sacrificed to change, English Canadians have for many years been rightly concerned about the absence of a distinctive national identity. Moreover, the overpowering influence exerted by the United States by the means of mass communications — press, cinema, radio, television — has further impeded the shaping of a national image.

Many English Canadians recognize that French Canadians alone have preserved a distinctive character, and this in the midst of the Anglo-Saxon civilization of North America. On the other hand, many French Canadians are disturbed because this character is in danger of being completely submerged by values foreign to their culture.

It is discouraging to travel through the provinces of Canada as I have done for so many years, observing the young people of our towns and villages. Their lack of curiosity and ignorance about their immediate world is soon apparent.

These young people seem to know nothing of the fascinating details of local history, geology, fauna and flora, and apparently are untouched by the beauty of the countryside, historical sites and architecture, and are ignorant of the legends and folklore of their own village or region. It is imperative today to make a thorough and comprehensive study of all phases of the cultural heritage of French Canada and to place the significant results of these surveys — its ethnographic milieu, arts and crafts, natural history and folklore, etc. — at the disposal of parents and teachers. In this way, young people could acquire pride in their country by realizing that their ancestors — simple settlers, *coureurs de bois*, explorers, craftsmen, missionaries or soldiers — had established a civilization to be proud of. If this civilization has disintegrated, the French Canadians have only themselves to blame. But it is never too late to rediscover with enthusiasm a part of their heritage by appreciating " *l'ouvrage bien faite* " of the craftsman of the past.

It would be tragic if this culture, which was once so significant, were to survive merely as a memory.

APPENDIX
FRENCH REGIONAL INFLUENCES AND CANADIAN REGIONAL CHARACTERISTICS

The Index provides under their appropriate headings the names of the places, regions or provinces of France which have in varying degrees influenced traditional Canadian furniture, as well as the names of the places and regions of Canada which gave rise to a number of marked characteristics. The references, scattered throughout the Catalogue Raisonné, relate to certain features of the pieces of furniture illustrated in this study.

The most common French regional influences apparent in Canadian furniture can be traced to the places of origin of the early settlers, soldiers and craftsmen, that is, the provinces of north and west France — Picardy, Normandy, Maine, Orléanais, Anjou, Upper Brittany (in the area of Rennes), the Atlantic coast, the Guérande, the Loire Valley, Touraine, Vendée, Poitou, Aunis, Saintonge, Guyenne, Gascony, Béarn and even Languedoc. Various other influences are obvious; those of Lorraine, Savoy, Dauphiné, Burgundy, Bresse and even some parts of Provence.

The Index will be of great service in elucidating the different Canadian regional characteristics which are expounded in the detailed comments and critical analyses of the Catalogue Raisonné and illustrated in the wide range of photographs.

It is an interesting fact that there are virtually only two areas, Quebec and Montreal, in the Province of Quebec, in which furniture can be clearly distinguished. In Quebec, the furniture is in general lighter, more elegant and less ornamented than the heavier, more baroque furniture of Montreal. The latter is more highly decorated and often exemplifies unfortunate ' gaucheries ' and a mixture of styles. This nouveau riche attitude may have been produced because the area had become the wealthy centre of the fur-traders and the crossroads in New France of the Great Lakes, the West, Illinois and the Mississippi.

The region of Lotbinière, where a wide range of delightful pieces of furniture has been found, remains a curious exception. It may have preserved its craft traditions because it stayed isolated for a longer time than the north shore of the St. Lawrence River which received almost all the road and river traffic between Montreal and Quebec. This would also explain why so many pieces of furniture have been preserved and have escaped the consequences of vandalism.

It is hazardous to generalize about the provenance of furniture, for, as I remarked in the Foreword, a great many objects were removed far from their places of origin. Many pieces produced in the region of Montreal have been found near Quebec and others in the Lower St. Lawrence, even in the Gaspé and New Brunswick. From the end of the eighteenth century until recently French Canadians moved frequently. When they could

no longer earn their living in their own villages, the sons of large families emigrated to new land.

The opening up of the Ottawa valley and of the Eastern townships and, later, of the Saguenay, of Lake St. John and of the Abitibi gave rise to large migrations. In the mid-nineteenth century, many farmers and other workers emigrated to the United States and took some of their furniture with them. In recent years, several objects which have been found in New England substantiate the fact that frequent exchanges took place between the old and the new areas.

I can unhesitatingly confirm, in respect of regional characteristics, that, in the light of my own observations, jointed chairs and armchairs, that is, chairs assembled with tenons and mortises (derived from the chairs of Lorraine), came solely from the Côte de Beaupré, the Isle of Orleans and the immediate region of Quebec. Other types of chairs, such as the ' sabre leg ' (a corruption of the American Directory) are found only in the neighbourhood of Montmagny, Cap Saint-Ignace and Kamouraska; chairs and armchairs ' à la Capucine ' with elm-bark seats woven in basketweave pattern are common in the Montreal region; small contemporary chairs with a ' violon ' seat come from Baie St. Paul, Saint-Urbain and La Malbaie. Equally in La Malbaie are found jointed chairs and armchairs of the Côte de Beaupré and Isle of Orleans type but possessing some English features brought by Scottish settlers after the Conquest. Table-chairs were especially prevalent along the Côte de Beaupré and in Charlevoix County; they were the tables found in the common rooms of almost all the houses of Les Eboulements and the Ile aux Coudres. There are also peasant armchairs typical of the regions of Saint-Joachim and of Saint-Féréol, and others of the Ile aux Coudres and of the Petite Rivière Saint-François. The small chairs inspired by the ' Shakers ' furniture of New England which are widespread in Saint-Hubert, Chambly, Saint-Jean d'Iberville and near the American border must also be noted. The essentially French commodes of the arbalète-fronted type with claw and ball feet (of English, Dutch or Venetian influence) were almost all made in the region of Montreal, whilst the commodes with breakfront drawers and lower rail and cartel carved in openwork (inspired by the commodes in Louis XV style from the district of Grasse in Provence) originated almost exclusively from the regions of Sainte-Geneviève de Pierrefonds, from the Ile Perrot, and from the Ile Jésus, and must have been made, according to my research, either in the workshops of the Liéberts, the Quevillons, the Pépins or by their apprentices.

Finally, I must mention the cradles with heavy curved rockers which are typical of the Lower St. Lawrence, and the armoires and the low buffets, with stiles and rails enclosing small narrow panels, which are especially characteristic of the region of Lotbinière.

LIST OF MASTER-WOODWORKERS, WOODWORKERS AND CARVERS

The following is a list, of necessity incomplete, of the many Master-woodworkers, woodworkers and carvers who lived in French Canada and who plied their trades during the seventeenth, eighteenth and nineteenth centuries. The dates in brackets that follow the name of a craftsman indicate the years of his birth and death or the years during which he was active. In some cases a date indicates the year in which certain objects were made or in which a craftsman was active. It would not have been possible to compile this list without the existence of the early parish account books, the Annals, the Records of Receipts and Expenses of the various religious orders, the Public Archives of Canada, the Judicial Archives of Montreal and Quebec, the Inventory of Works of Art of the Province of Quebec, the works of Marius Barbeau, and Émile Vaillancourt's book, " Une Maîtrise d'Art au Canada ", which lists Louis Quevillon's apprentices.

ACHARD, Charles. 1701 : Montreal, Hôtel-Dieu, Congregation of Notre-Dame.

ACHIM, André. Longueuil, 1819, *baptistery;* 1826, *chandeliers.*

ADAM, Jean. Beaumont, 1699-1700, *altar;* 1705, *confessional.*

AUBRY, Ambroise. Contrecœur, 1818, *pews.*

BAILLAIRGÉ, Jean, (1726-1805). Quebec, Notre-Dame Church, Quebec, *balustrade,* etc. Montmagny, 1790, *pulpit.* Armand-Joseph Chaussat's partner.

BAILLAIRGÉ, François, son of Jean, (1759-1852). Quebec, Notre-Dame Church, Quebec, Baie Saint-Paul, Saint-Joachim, 1815-1825.

BAILLAIRGÉ, Thomas, son of François, (1791-1859). Quebec, Notre-Dame Church, Quebec, Sainte-Anne-de-la-Pocatière, *balustrade, communion rail.* Apprentice to Louis Quevillon.

BAILLAIRGÉ, Pierre-Florent, brother of François, (1761-1812). Quebec, Bon-Pasteur, *altars;* Sainte-Famille, I.O., 1791.

BARET, Jean-Baptiste. 1820 : Saint-Vincent-de-Paul. Apprentice to Louis Quevillon.

BARETTE, Antoine. 1822 : Tanneries des Bélair. Apprentice to Louis Quevillon.

BEAUPRÉ, Sieur. Lanoraie, 1786-1787, *balusters.*

BÉDARD, Jacques. Charlesbourg, 1702.

BELLANGER, Sieur. Saint-Pierre (M), 1755, *pulpit.*

BELLEAU, Sieur. Baie du Febvre, 1787, *candlesticks.*

BELLECOURT, Sieur. Baie du Febvre, 1818, *balusters.*

BELLEMARE, Paul. Yamachiche, 1809-1810, *balustrade.*

BERCIER, Étienne. Beaumont, 1809, *pulpit and churchwarden's pew;* 1848, *armoire.*

BERLINGUET, Louis-Thomas, (1789-1863). Saint-Joachim, 1833; Saint-Rémi-de-Napierville, *altars;* Beauport. Apprentice to Joseph Pépin.

BERLINGUET, Laurent-Flavien. Saint-Rémi-de-Napierville, 1845-1854, *altars.*

BERLINGUET, François-Xavier. Saint-Pierre (I.O.),

1852, *chandeliers.* Son of Louis-Thomas Berlinguet. Apprentice to Thomas Baillairgé.

BERTRAND, Séraphin. L'Acadie, 1831, *chandeliers.*

BIENVENU, Philippe. Kaskakia, Missouri, 1723.

BIRON, Pierre. 1660 : Quebec, Confrérie de Sainte-Anne.

BOISVERT, Pierre. 1821 : Quebec, Confrérie de Sainte-Anne.

BOLVIN, Gilles, (1711-1768). Three Rivers, Lachenaie, Berthier-en-haut, Sainte-Anne-de-la-Pérade, *retable, high altar.*

BOUCHARD, M. 1835 : Notre-Dame Church, Montreal.

BOURGUIGNON, Sieur. 1743 : Lachenaie.

BOUTEILLETTE, Charles. Contrecœur, 1818, *pews.*

BRASSARD, Jean-Baptiste. 1743 : Quebec, Confrérie de Sainte-Anne.

BRIEN (dit Desrochers), Urbain. Varennes, 1816-1818, *pews;* Saint-Grégoire-de-Nicolet, 1812, *altars.*

BRIEN (dit Desrochers), Joseph. 1810 : Varennes; Pointe-aux-Trembles (M).

BUSSIÈRES, Jean. 1756 : Saint-Pierre, I.O.

CAMBAS, Jean-Baptiste, (1735-1784). Saint-Louis, Missouri.

CARTIER, Jean-Baptiste, (1770-1784). Saint-François-du-Lac, *pulpit;* Yamaska, *woodwork.*

CASTONGUAY, Sieur. 1705 : Quebec.

CAVELLIER, Baptiste. Montreal, 1722, *woodwork,* Notre-Dame Church, Montreal.

CHABOILLEZ, Charles. 1699 : Montreal. Charon Brothers School and Hôtel-Dieu, *woodwork and carvings.* Church of the Récollects, 1702.

CHABOT, François. Saint-Pierre, I.O., 1724-1726, *woodwork of the chancel.*

CHALOU, Pierre. 1743 : Quebec, Confrérie de Sainte-Anne.

CHAMPAGNE, Sieur. Saint-Denis-sur-Richelieu, 1772, *altars.*

CHAPELAIN, Louis. Notre-Dame Church, Quebec, *balusters.*

CHARRON, Amable. Saint-Roch-des-Aulnaies, 1811, *retable;* L'Islet, 1816. Apprentice to Quevillon.

CHARTRAND, Vincent. Ile Dupas, 1831, *confessional;* 1836, Sault-au-Récollet, *pulpit.* Apprentice to Louis Quevillon.

CHAUSSAT, Armand-Joseph. 1752 : Quebec, Jean Baillairgé's partner.

CIRIER, Antoine. 1746 : Varennes, Repentigny.

CIRIER, Martin. Longue-Pointe, 1731, *vault;* Pointe-aux-Trembles (M), *pulpit.*

CLÉMENT, Sieur. Ursulines, Quebec, 1751, *tables.*

CLICHE, Sieur. Quebec, Varennes, 1730-1740, *door and lectern;* drew up Claude Filliau's inventory in 1730.

COLLET, Sieur. Saint-Vallier, 1778-1779, *pulpit.*

CONTANT, Marc (Recollect). Saint-Damase, L'Islet, 1800-1802, *pulpit.*

CORBIN, Michel. Berthier-en-Haut, 1802-1803, *balusters.*

COUTURE, Guillaume. Lauzon, 1725, *altars.*

COUTURIER, Sieur. Lachenaie, 1744, *two armoires.*

CRÉPEAU, Basile, (1736-1786). Château-Richer, *candlesticks.*

CRÉQUY, Liénard. 1728.

CUREUX, Michel. 1743 : Quebec, Confrérie de Sainte-Anne.

DAVID, David-Fleury. Sault-au-Récollet, 1816, *retable.*

DAVID, Louis-Basile. Saint-Jean, I.O., 1810, *interiors.* Apprentice to Louis Quevillon; *carvings, gilding.* Kamouraska, 1813.

DENIS, Jacques. 1765, Saint-Louis, Missouri.

DESLAURIERS, Sieur. Notre-Dame Church, Quebec, 1743, *balustrade.*

DESROCHERS, Vital. Saint-Eustache, 1841, *armoire.*

DORÉ, Joseph. 1785, *balustrade;* Les Écureuils, *retable.*

DOYON, Louis. 1820, Notre-Dame Church, Montreal.

DROUIN, Charles. 1839, Quebec, Confrérie de Sainte-Anne.

DUCHAINE, Christophe. 1821, Saint-Vincent-de-Paul. Apprentice to Louis Quevillon.

DUFRESNAY, Louis. Baie Saint-Paul, 1801, *Easter candlestick.*

DUGAL, François. 1842-1843, Terrebonne. Lachenaie, *altar.* Apprentice to Louis Quevillon.

DUGAL, Olivier. 1824, Saint-Mathias. Apprentice to Louis Quevillon.

DUMAS, Jean-Baptiste. Saint-Pierre (M), 1819, *chandelier.*

DUMAS, Jean-Romain. 1820, Saint-Vincent-de-Paul. Apprentice to Quevillon.

DUMONTIER, Sieur. Sainte-Anne-de-Beaupré, 1782-1783, *confessional, armoire.*

DUVERNAY, Sieur. Verchères, 1790, *balusters.*

ÉMOND, Pierre, (1738-1808). Quebec, Notre-Dame Church, Quebec, *buffets, console, tables;* Hôpital-Général, Seminary of Quebec, *armoires, woodwork.*

ÉNOUILLE, Louis. 1743, Quebec, Confrérie de Sainte-Anne.

FAUCHOIS, Michel. 1675, Quebec, Seminary, Cap Tourmente School.

FÉRÉ, Jean-Baptiste. Woodworker-carver, 1797, Sainte-Croix de Lotbinière.

FILLIAU, Claude. 1730, Quebec, *inventory.*

FILLIAU (dit Dubois), François, (1760-1834). Longue-Pointe, *candlesticks.*

FILLION, Joseph. 1743, Quebec, Confrérie de Sainte-Anne.

FINSTERER, Daniel. L'Acadie, 1812, *small armoire.*

FINSTERER, Georges. L'Acadie, 1806, *chandeliers.*

FISET, Louis. 1839, Quebec, Confrérie de Sainte-Anne.

FORTIER, Charles. Saint-Roch-des-Aulnaies, 1787, *churchwarden's pew.*

FORTIN, Gabriel. 1794, Saint-Roch-des-Aulnaies.

FORTIN, Pierre. L'Islet, 1798, *coffer.*

FOURNIER, Claude. 1820, Laprairie. Apprentice to Louis Quevillon.

FOURNIER, Louis. Lachenaie, 1782, *pulpit.*

FOURREUR (dit Champagne), Louis. Lachenaie, 1782-1786, *altar.*

FRANCHÈRE, Jacques. 1779, Quebec (*inventory* Michel Létourneau).

FRÉCHET, Étienne. 1743, Quebec, Confrérie de Sainte-Anne.

GAGNIÉ, Jean. Quebec, Seminary, 1740, *furniture, woodwork, tables.*

GARIÉPY, F. 1660, Quebec, Confrérie de Sainte-Anne.

GAUTHIER, Amable. Saint-Barthélémy, 1823, *altar.* Apprentice to Louis Quevillon.

GAUTHIER, Léon. 1820, Saint-Vincent-de-Paul. Apprentice to Louis Quevillon.

GENNER, Samuel. 1675, Quebec, Seminary, Cap Tourmente School.

GIASSON, Sieur. Montreal, 1712, *pew.*

GIBEAULT, Étienne. 1724, Montreal, Notre-Dame Church, Montreal.

GIRARDIN, Sieur. Saint-Ours, 1761, *pulpit.*

GIRARDIN, Antoine, (1728-1802). Prairie-du-Pont, Illinois.

GIROUX, Sieur. Quebec, 1715, *door,* Hôpital-Général.

GODÉ, Nicolas. Montreal, 1657, *table and coffer.*

GODIN, Jean-François. Quebec, 1739; Cap-Santé, *chandeliers.*

GOGUET, Sieur. Saint-Mathias, 1834, *candlesticks.*

GOSSELIN, Gabriel, (1734-1786). Saint-Laurent, I.O., Saint-François, Sainte-Famille, I.O., *tabernacles,* etc.

GOSSELIN, Jean. Sainte-Anne-de-la-Pocatière, 1785, *churchwarden's pew,* etc.

GOSSELIN, Laurent. Saint-Pierre, I.O., 1778, *balustrade.*

GOURDEAU, Sieur. 1812, Quebec.

GOYET, Joseph. Belœil, 1819-1823, *balusters.*

GRAVEL, Charles. Charlesbourg, 1767, *woodwork.*

GRÉGOIRE, Louis, (1769-1811). Sainte-Marie-de-Beauce, *pews.*

GUAY, J.-B. (senior). 1733, Quebec, Confrérie de Sainte-Anne.

GUERNON (dit Belleville), François. 1754, Pointe-aux-Trembles (M). Saint-Sulpice, 1793, *churchwarden's pew;* Saint-Sulpice, 1774, *pulpit;* 1774, Varennes.

GUIBORD, Charles. 1821, Pointe-aux-Trembles (M). Apprentice to Louis Quevillon.

GUINIÈRE, Louis. 1743, Quebec, Confrérie de Sainte-Anne.

HAGUENIER, Louis, (1719-1755). La Prairie de la Magdelaine, *armoires, doors, altars, balusters,* Kaskakia, Illinois Society.

HAINS, Sieur. 1743, Quebec, Confrérie de Sainte-Anne.

HARDY, Jean-Baptiste. 1768-1772, Varennes, Lachenaie; Yamaska, 1773-1774, *balustrade.*

HARDY, Pierre. Yamachiche, Saint-Antoine-de-Tilly, 1754, *pews;* Varennes, *carvings.*

HAY, Pierre, (1661-1708). Boucherville.

HILAIRE, Sieur. Saint-Eustache, 1790, *churchwarden's pew.*

HUOT, Augustin. 1839, Quebec, Confrérie de Sainte-Anne.

HURTUBISE, Joseph. 1821, Montreal, Côte Saint-Antoine. Apprentice to Louis Quevillon.

JACQUES, Louis. Charlesbourg, 1701, *baptistery, chancel;* Saint-Pierre, I.O., 1720, *pulpit, furniture.*

JACQUIÉ (dit Leblond), Jean. 1677, Montreal; Three Rivers, Ursulines, 1716, *altar.*

JACSON, Antoine. 1770, Quebec, Lachenaie, Saint-Pierre, I.O.; Saint-François (M), 1786, *woodwork.*

JARED, Jean-Baptiste. La Présentation, 1808, *Easter candlestick.*

JOLICŒUR, Sieur. 1848, Lotbinière.

JOURDAIN (dit Labrosse), Guillaume (senior). 1690, Quebec, Seminary and Cap Tourmente School.

JOURDAIN (dit Labrosse), Denis, (1671-1743). Master-woodworker, Montreal, 1729; Varennes, *retable.*

JOURDAIN (dit Labrosse), Paul-Raymond (son of Denis), born 1697. 1746, Montreal, Laprairie; Varennes, 1730-1732, *balustrade and retable.*

JOURDAIN (dit Labrosse), Basile. 1772, Laprairie.

LABELLE, Joseph. 1821, Saint-Charles-sur-Richelieu.

LABERGE, François. Varennes, 1777, *candlesticks.*

LAFLEUR, Sieur. Verchères, 1752, *pulpit.*

LAGARENNE, Sieur. Quebec, Notre-Dame-des-Victoires Church, 1733, *woodwork.*

LAMBERT, Sieur. 1776, Sainte-Geneviève-de-Pierrefonds.

LA PALME, Sieur de. Montreal, 1712, *portal* Notre-Dame Church.

LARCHEVÊQUE, Jean-Baptiste. 1743, Quebec, Confrérie de Sainte-Anne.

LASELLE, Jacques. Montreal, 1717, *justice bench.*

LATOUR, Jacques Le Blond de. 1672-1700, Quebec, Quebec Seminary; Cap Tourmente School, 1690, l'Ange Gardien, *retable.*

LATOUR, Jean. 1677, Montreal.

LAURENCE, Sieur. Saint-Paul-de-Joliette, 1821, *candlesticks.*

LAVOYE, Joseph. L'Acadie, *tabernacle.*

LEBEAU, Sieur. Montreal, 1717, *prie-dieu of the Intendant General.*

LEBLANC, Augustin. Sorel, 1833, *interiors.*

LEBLOND (dit Picard), Michel. 1675, Quebec, Seminary.

LECLAIRE, François. 1820, Saint-Eustache. Apprentice to Louis Quevillon.

LECOURT, Louis. 1818, Terrebonne. Lachenaie, 1825, *pews.* Apprentice to Louis Quevillon.

LEDROIT, François. 1821, Quebec, Confrérie de Sainte-Anne.

LEFEBVRE, Pierre. 1743, Quebec, Confrérie de Sainte-Anne.

LEMELIN, Jean. 1660-1661, Quebec, Confrérie de Sainte-Anne; Notre-Dame Church, Quebec, *retable.*

LEMIEUX, François. L'Islet, 1829, *armchair.*

LENOIR, Antoine. Lachenaie, 1733, *balustrade and prie-dieu.*

LENOIR, Jean. Lachenaie, 1733-1737, *confessional churchwarden's pew.*

LENOIR (dit Letourangeau), Vincent. Montreal, Notre-Dame Church, Montreal, 1694, *armoire* for Louis Hurtebise; 1697, *tables* for the Hôtel-Dieu, Montreal.

LEPAGE, François. Saint-François, I.O., 1797, *chandelier.*

LEPROHON, Alcibiade. 1820, Montreal. Apprentice to Louis Quevillon.

LESCAULT, Louis. 1821, Montreal. Apprentice to Quevillon.

LETOURNEAU, Michel. 1783, Quebec; 1779, *inventory.*

LE VASSEUR (dit Lavigne), Jean, (1622-1686). Master-woodworker, dean of the Confrérie de Sainte-Anne, Quebec.

LE VASSEUR, Pierre, (1629-1686). Master-woodworker, brother of Jean. Quebec.

LE VASSEUR (dit Lavigne), Noël, (1654-1731). Quebec.

LE VASSEUR, Pierre, son of Pierre, Master-woodworker, (1661-1731). Quebec.

LE VASSEUR, Pierre, (1679-1737). Kamouraska.

LE VASSEUR, Noël, Master-carver (1680-1740). Quebec (son of Noël, dit Lavigne). Ursulines, Quebec; Sainte-Famille, I.O.

LE VASSEUR, Pierre, Master-woodworker (1684-1747). Quebec (son of Noël, dit Lavigne).

LE VASSEUR, Pierre Noël, (1690-1770). Master-carver, Quebec (son of Pierre Le Vasseur).

LE VASSEUR (dit Chaverlange), François, (1700-1747). Boucherville, Master-woodworker (son of Pierre Le Vasseur).

LE VASSEUR (dit Borgia), François-Louis. Boucherville, 1707, woodworker (son of Pierre Le Vasseur).

LE VASSEUR, Denis-Joseph. Woodworker, 1712, Three Rivers (son of Pierre Le Vasseur).

LE VASSEUR, François-Noël, Master-carver (1702-1794). Cap Santé, 1770, Saint-François, I.O., 1771.

LE VASSEUR (dit Delort), Jean-Baptiste-Antoine. Master-carver, 1717, died after 1777. Saint-Damase, L'Islet, 1762.

LE VASSEUR, Charles. Master-carver, 1723, Quebec.

LE VASSEUR, René-Michel. Master-woodworker, 1724, Sorel.

LIÉBERT, Philippe, (1732-1804). Vaudreuil, Saint-Cuthbert Church, *altar*, etc.

LORRIN, Honoré. Sainte-Geneviève de Pierrefonds, 1833, *chandeliers*.

LOYER, Guillaume. 1657, Quebec, Confrérie de Sainte-Anne.

LUPIEN (dit Baron), Pierre. 1775, Saint-Louis, Missouri.

LUREKEN, Léonard. 1675, Quebec, Seminary, Cap Tourmente School.

MADOX, Daniel-Joseph. 1730, Montreal.

MALLET, Denis. 1690, Quebec : Seminary, Cap Tourmente School, Saint-Joachim, Jesuits' Church; Montreal.

MALO, Joseph. Montreal, 1819, *armoire*.

MALOUIN, Sieur. Montreal, 1717, *prie-dieu* for the Governor.

MARCHETEAU (dit Desnoyers), Joseph. 1747-1778. Cakokia, Saint-Louis, Missouri.

MARCHETERRE, Sieur. Les Cèdres, 1782, *pulpit*.

MARIER, Charles. Quebec, 1820, *woodwork*.

MAROIS, Prisque. 1839, Quebec, Confrérie de Sainte-Anne.

MAROY, Sieur. Quebec, 1718, Hôpital-Général, *buffet, prie-dieu*.

MARQUETTE, (dit Benoît), Pierre-Salomon. 1824-1831, Belœil, Saint-Roch-l'Achigan. Apprentice to Louis Quevillon.

MARTEL, I. 1839, Quebec, Confrérie de Sainte-Anne.

MARTIN, François. 1820, Saint-Benoît. Apprentice to Louis Quevillon.

MÉNÉCLIER, Louis. 1821, Vaudreuil. Apprentice to Louis Quevillon.

MERCIER, Amable. 1821, Quebec, Confrérie de Sainte-Anne.

MÉTIVIER, Étienne. 1821, Quebec, Confrérie de Sainte-Anne.

MICHON, Jean. Montmagny, 1797, *furniture*.

MILETTE, Alexis. 1830, Yamachiche, Berthier, Louiseville; Seminary, Three Rivers. Apprentice to Louis Quevillon.

MINVILLE, Pierre. 1660, Quebec, Confrérie de Sainte-Anne.

MOISAN, Pierre. 1822, Longue Pointe. Apprentice to Louis Quevillon.

MONDOR, Joachim. 1821, Quebec, Confrérie de Sainte-Anne.

MORIN, Pierre. 1753, Saint-Pierre, I.O.

NADEAU, Joseph. 1758, Saint-Charles de Bellechasse.

NADEAU, Louis. Saint-François, I.O., 1767, *balustrade, chancel*.

NADEAU, Simon. 1791-1801, Saint-François, I.O., *churchwarden's pew*.

NARBONNE, Louis. 1840, Saint-Rémi, Louiseville.

NOBLESSE, Martin. 1699, Montreal, Charon Brothers' School.

NOËL, Joseph. 1820, Quebec, Confrérie de Sainte-Anne.

NORMAND, François. Three Rivers, 1817, Ursulines, *console table;* Batiscan, Bécancourt, 1824-1827, *altars*.

PAGET (dit Carcy), Raymond. 1660, Quebec, Confrérie de Sainte-Anne.

PAQUET, André. 1835, Sainte-Croix de Lotbinière, Deschambault; 1837, Quebec. Apprentice to Thomas Baillairgé.

PARENT, Sieur. Montreal, 1691, *armoire*.

PARENT, Léandre. 1830. Apprentice to Thomas Baillairgé.

PARISEAU, Joseph. Saint-Martin, 1833, *candlesticks*.

PÉPIN, François. 1805, Longue Pointe. Nephew and apprentice to Joseph Pépin.

PÉPIN, Jérôme. 1818, Longue Pointe. Apprentice to Louis Quevillon.

PÉPIN, Joseph. 1801, Saint-Vincent-de-Paul, Boucherville; 1819, Saint-Roch l'Achigan, *console tables;* Les Cèdres, *console table;* 1808-1823, Louis Quevillon's partner.

PÉRÉ (dit Carpentras), Joseph. Woodworker, friend of Charles Chaboillez, Montreal.

PERREAULT, Chrysostome. 1793-1829, Saint-Jean Port Joli; L'Islet, *churchwarden's pew*.

PERRIN, Nicolas. 1800-1823, Sainte-Scholastique. Apprentice to Louis Quevillon.

PERRIN, Pierre. 1800-1823, Sainte-Scholastique. Apprentice to Louis Quevillon.

PETIT, François. 1730, Montreal.

PICHÉ, Joseph. Les Écureuils, 1792, *pulpit*.

POULIOT, Pierre. 1779, Saint-Laurent, I.O.

QUEVILLON, Jean-Baptiste. 1749, Sault-au-Récollet, father of Louis Quevillon.

QUEVILLON, Louis-Amable, (1749-1823). Saint-Vincent-de-Paul, Sault-au-Récollet, Lavaltrie, Notre-Dame Church, Montreal, etc.

QUEVILLON, Pierre. Saint-Vincent-de-Paul. Brother of Louis Quevillon.

RACINE, Pierre. Quebec, 1715, *chairs, armoires, beds.* Hôpital-Général, Quebec.
REICHE, Sieur. Quebec, 1715, *armoires.* Hôpital-Général, Quebec.
ROBERT, François-Xavier. 1820, Verchères. Apprentice to Louis Quevillon.
ROCHON, Antoine. 1820, Sainte-Thérèse de Blainville. Apprentice to Louis Quevillon.
ROLLIN, Paul. 1819-1829, Lachenaie. Louis Quevillon's apprentice and partner.
RONDARD, Sieur. Varennes, 1745, *candlesticks.*
ROUSSEL, Joseph. 1743, Quebec, Confrérie de Sainte-Anne.
ROUSSILLE, F.-Noël. Lachenaie, 1842-1843, *altartable.*
ROY, Joseph. Lachenaie, 1801, *candlesticks.*

SAINT-AMAND, Damase. 1833, Bécancourt.
SAINT-GAUDARD, Sieur. 1705, Quebec.
SAINT-JAMES, René. 1831, Rivière des Prairies. Louis Quevillon's partner. Saint-Mathias, Saint-Eustache, Saint-Sulpice.
SAINT-YVES, Sieur. 1702, Montreal, Notre-Dame Church, Montreal.
SAMSON, Joseph. 1820, Quebec, Confrérie de Sainte-Anne.
SAMSON, Olivier. L'Ange Gardien, 1845, *pulpit.*
SÉGUIN, Pierre. Montreal, Saint-Pierre, 1823-1825, *churchwarden's pew.*
SHINDLER, Jean. 1821, Quebec, Confrérie de Sainte-Anne.

TAPHORIN, Guillaume. 1743, Quebec, Confrérie de Sainte-Anne.
TATTOUX (dit Brindamour), Joseph. 1820, Montreal. Apprentice to Louis Quevillon.
TISON, Jean-Baptiste. 1791-1805, Saint-Louis, Missouri.
TONDREAU, Sieur. L'Islet, 1735-1737, *pulpit.*
TREMPES, Sieur. Berthier-en-Haut, 1788, *pews.*
TURCAULT, Joseph. 1812, Sainte-Jeanne de L'Ile Perrot; 1819, Les Cèdres.

VALADE, François. 1819, Saint-Martin (I.J.). Apprentice to Louis Quevillon.
VALIN, Jean, (1691-1759). Quebec, Saint-Augustin, 1734, *chandeliers and tabernacle.*
VALLIÈRE, Romain. 1839, Quebec, Confrérie de Sainte-Anne.
VAUCOURT, Jacques. 1743, Quebec, Confrérie de Sainte-Anne.
VERDON, Joseph. Canada, 1734; Saint-Louis, Missouri, 1813.
VÉZINA, Charles. Neuville, 1728-30, *balusters, retable;* Les Écureuils; 1732-1740, Saint-Pierre, I.O., *interiors;* Charlesbourg, 1742-1747, *retable;* Saint-Augustin, 1755, *retable;* Saint-Pierre, Ile d'Orléans.
VIAU, Pierre. 1820, Lachenaie. Apprentice to Louis Quevillon.
VIGER, D. 18th c. Saint-Denis-sur-Richelieu, *altars.*
VILLIARD, Germain. 18th c. Quebec, *furniture.*
VINCENT, F. Sainte-Marie de Beauce, 1783, *tabernacle and pulpit.*
VOISEUX, Pierre. Batiscan, 1824, *altar.*

LIST OF ENGLISH AND SCOTTISH WOODWORKERS AND CABINET-MAKERS

A list of woodworkers and cabinet-makers who came from England and Scotland toward the end of the eighteenth century and the beginning of the nineteenth century, whose names and trades are recorded in the directories, almanacs and newspapers of the period.

ASQUITH, John. 1820, Montreal, *Joiner and Cabinetmaker.*
BENNET, James. 1819, Montreal, *Cabinet-maker.*
BLACK, James. 1806, Quebec, *meublier.*
CAHILE, Thomas. 1820, Montreal, *Cabinet-maker.*
CAIN, John. 1820, Montreal, *Cabinet-maker.*
CAMELL, William. 1819 Montreal, *Cabinet-maker.*
COBOURNE, Thomas. 1819, Montreal, *Cabinet-maker.*
CODD, John. 1819, Montreal, *Cabinet-maker.*

COLE, William. 1820, Montreal, *Cabinet-maker.*
DODGE, C. Montreal, *Chair-maker.*
DOW, William. 1790, Quebec, 18, St Peter St. Lower Town, *Cabinet-maker.*
DRUM, William. 1835-1860, Quebec.
EDIE, James. 1792, Quebec, *faiseur de meubles.*
FALL, Benjamin. 1805, Quebec.
FERGUSON, Thomas. 1802, Montreal.
FRASER, William. 1792, Quebec, *faiseur de meubles.*

GRIFFIN, William. 1799, Montreal.
HENDERSON, William. 1810, Montreal, « qui fait toute espèce de meubles dans le dernier goût », *Gazette de Québec*, 14 juin 1810.
HUNTER, David. 1798, Montreal.
MCCUTCHEON, John. 1790, Garden St., Upper Town (*Directory for the City and Suburbs of Quebec*, 1790).
ORKNEY, James. *Cabinet-maker.*

PARK, Samuel. 1799, Montreal, *Cabinet-maker.*
PETRIE, Frederick. 1790, Quebec.
RAY, Joseph. 1810, Montreal.
RHODE, Antoine. 1798, Montreal, *Cabinet-maker.*
SMITH, Samuel. 1798, *meublier* (Dénombrement de la Paroisse, Mgr Plessis).
SWIFT, Tabez. 1808, Montreal, *Cabinet-maker.*
WILSON, Hugh. 1805, Quebec, *ébéniste.*

LIST OF MASTER-LOCKSMITHS AND LOCKSMITHS

A partial list of Master-locksmiths and locksmiths who were likely to have supplied the ironware for early furniture.

AMIOT, Pierre. 1733 : Quebec, *door latches, fische hinges, hinges,* Notre-Dame des Victoires Church.
BEAUPRÉ, Pierre. 1735 : Quebec.
DENIS, Jean. Quebec. (JEAN DENIS stamped on *armoire fische hinges*).
DESLAURIERS, Sieur. 1772 : Château-Richer, *fische hinges.*
FOURREUR (dit Champagne), Pierre. 1744 : Quebec.
GILBERT, Augustin. 1727 : Quebec.
LEBLOND, François. 1744 : Quebec. (LEBLOND stamped on *armoire fische hinges).*
LEMERCIER, Louis. 1688 : Quebec. (1716, *iron fittings for armoires,* Beauport Church).
LETOURNEAU, François. 1783 : Quebec, *inventory : fische hinges for armoires.*

LETOURNEAU, Jean-Paschal. 1783 : Quebec, *fische hinges for armoires.*
LOZEAU, Jean, 1741 : Quebec, Master-locksmith.
MASSÉ, Martin. 1699 : Montreal, Master-locksmith.
MERCIER, François. 1730 : Quebec.
MONTMAIGNIER, Charles. 1710 : Master-locksmith, Sainte-Anne de Beaupré, *five iron fittings, slide-bolts, fische hinges.*
PRUD'HOMME, Pierre. 1690 : Quebec.
QUENET, François. 1727 : journeyman to Augustin Gilbert, locksmith, Quebec.
SÉDILLOT (dit Montreuil), Joseph. 1796 : Rivière Ouelle, *hooks, iron fittings, locks.*
TRUDEAU, Bertrand. 1729 : Varennes.
VOYER, Alexis. 1691. Apprentice to Louis Lemercier.

LIST OF COLLECTORS

The numbers following the names of the collectors refer both to the Catalogue Raisonné and to the illustrations.

403

BRIEF BIBLIOGRAPHY

A list of the most important books and sources of information which I consulted in the preparation of this work. For a more complete bibliography on traditional furniture, refer to the " Manuel de Folklore Français Contemporain " by Arnold de Van Gennep. Paris, Auguste Picard, 1938, tome IV, pp. 892-923.

BARBEAU, Marius. *Au cœur du Québec.* Montréal, Les éd. du Zodiaque, 1934.

BARBEAU, Marius. *Confrérie des menuisiers de Madame Sainte-Anne.* Montréal, Fides, 1946, pp. 72-96 (Les Archives de Folklore, vol. I).

BARBEAU, Marius. *J'ai vu Québec.* Québec, Librairie Garneau, 1957.

BARBEAU, Marius. *I Have Seen Quebec.* Toronto, Macmillan, 1957.

BARBEAU, Marius. *Les Le Vasseur, maîtres-menuisiers, sculpteurs et statuaires.* (Québec circa, 1678-1818). Montréal, Fides, 1948, pp. 35-52 (Les Archives de Folklore, vol. III).

BARBEAU, Marius. *Maîtres artisans de chez-nous.* Montréal, Les éd. du Zodiaque, 1942.

BARBEAU, Marius. *Québec où survit l'ancienne France.* Québec, Librairie Garneau, 1937.

BARBEAU, Marius. *Quebec Where Ancient France Lingers.* Toronto, Macmillan, 1936.

BOISON, J. *L'industrie du meuble.* 4e éd. mise à jour par F. Débat, G. Rouest, L. Malclès. Paris, Dunod, 1949. (Bibliothèque de l'Enseignement Technique).

BOUCHER, Pierre. *Histoire véritable et naturelle des mœurs et productions du pays de la Nouvelle-France.* Paris, Florentin Lambert, 1664.

BOUCHER, Pierre. *The Seventeenth Century from The French of Pierre Boucher.* Translated and edited by Edward Louis Montizambert. Montreal, Desbarats, 1883.

CHAMPLAIN, Samuel de. *Les Voyages de la Nouvelle-France occidentale, dicte Canada, faits par le Sieur de Champlain, Xainctongeois, etc.* Paris, Pierre Le Mur, 1632.

CHAMPLAIN, Samuel de. *The Works of Samuel de Champlain.* Edited by H.P. Biggar, Toronto, The Champlain Society, 1922.

CHARLEVOIX, Pierre-François-Xavier de, S.J. *Histoire et description générale de la Nouvelle-France.* Paris, Giffart, 1744, 3 vol.

CHARLEVOIX, Pierre-François-Xavier de, S.J. *History and General Description of New France.* Translated and edited by Dr John Gilmary Sheae. New York, Francis P. Harper, 1900, 6 vols.

COLLECTION CONNAISSANCE DES ARTS, vol. III : *Le XVIIe siècle français.* Paris, Hachette, 1958.

COLLECTION CONNAISSANCE DES ARTS, vol. I : *Le XVIIIe siècle français.* Paris, Hachette, 1956.

DIDEROT ET D'ALEMBERT. *Encyclopédie ou dictionnaire raisonné des sciences, des arts et des métiers.* Paris, Briasson, 1751.

DREPPERD, Carl W. *Handbook of Antique Chairs.* Garden City, N.Y. Doubleday and Company, 1948.

ÉDITS, ORDONNANCES ROYAUX. *Edits, ordonnances royaux, déclarations et arrêts du Conseil d'État du roi concernant le Canada. Revus et corrigés d'après les pièces originales déposées aux Archives provinciales.* Québec, Fréchette, 1854-1856, 3 vol.

FAUTEUX, Jean-Noël. *Essai sur l'industrie au Canada sous le régime français.* Québec, Proulx, Imprimeur du Roi, 1927.

GAUTHIER, Joseph Stany. *Le mobilier des vieilles provinces françaises.* Paris, Ch. Massin, 1933.

GAUTHIER, Joseph Stany. *La connaissance des meubles régionaux français.* Paris, Ch. Moreau, 1952.

GOSSELIN, Abbé Amédée. *L'instruction au Canada sous le régime français.* Québec, Laflamme et Proulx, 1911.

HAVARD, H. *Dictionnaire de l'ameublement et de la décoration depuis le XIIIe siècle jusqu'à nos jours.* Paris, Quantin [1890], 4 vol.

JAMBON, Dr J. *Les beaux meubles rustiques du vieux pays de Rennes.* Rennes, Librairie Générale Plihon et Hommay, 1927.

JANNEAU, Guillaume. *Les beaux meubles français anciens.* Ch. Moreau, éd., Paris, 1923.

JEANTON, Gabriel. *Le mobilier de la Bresse et du Mâconnais.* Publié sous les auspices de la Société des Amis des Arts et des Sciences de Tournus. Mâcon, Renaudier, 1938.

JÉSUITES. *Le Journal des Jésuites.* Publié par MM. les abbés Laverdière et Casgrain. Québec, Brousseau, 1871.

JUCHEREAU DE SAINT-IGNACE, Mère. *Les annales de l'Hôtel-Dieu de Québec.* [Québec] à l'Hôpital-Dieu de Québec, 1939.

KALM, Peter. *Voyage de Kalm en Amérique.* (Translated from the English of John Reinhold Forster. *Travels into North America).* Montréal, Société Historique de Montréal, 1880. (Mémoires, vol. VII et VIII).

KALM, Peter. *Peter Kalm's Travels in North America.* Revised from the original Swedish and edited by Adolph B. Benson. New York, Wilson-Erickson, 1937, 2 vols.

LA POTHERIE, Bacqueville de. *Histoire de l'Amérique septentrionale.* Paris, Brocas, 1753, 4 vol.

LA TOUR, Bertrand de. *Mémoires sur la vie de M. de Laval.* Cologne, Jean-Frédéric Motiens, 1761.

LEROUX, André-Paul. *Les meubles cauchois,* 3e éd. Fécamp, Les Frères Banse, 1924.

LESCARBOT, Marc. *Histoire de la Nouvelle-France.* 3e éd. Paris, Adrian Perier, 1618.

LESCARBOT, Marc. *The History of New France.* Edited by W.L. Grant and H.P. Biggar. Toronto, The Champlain Society, 1907, 3 vols.

MARIE DE L'INCARNATION. *Lettres de la Vénérable*

Marie de l'Incarnation, première supérieure des Ursulines de la Nouvelle-France. Paris, Louis Billaine, 1681.

MASSICOTTE, E.-Z. *L'ameublement à Montréal aux XVIIᵉ et XVIIIᵉ siècles.* Bulletin des Recherches Historiques. Lévis, vol. XLVIII, février 1942, pp. 33-42; mars, pp. 75-86.

MAUMENÉ, Albert. *Les beaux meubles régionaux des provinces de France.* Paris, Ch. Moreau, 1952.

MAUMENÉ, Albert. *Vie à la campagne.* Paris, Hachette. (Special issues on traditional furniture, 1920-1938).

MORIN, Sœur Marie. *Annales de l'Hôtel-Dieu de Montréal.* Société Historique de Montréal, 1921. (Mémoires, vol. XII).

MORISSET, Gérard. *Coup d'œil sur les arts de la Nouvelle-France.* Québec [l'Auteur], 1941.

MORISSET, Gérard. *L'architecture en Nouvelle-France.* Québec [Charrier et Dugal], 1929. (Collection Champlain).

NUTTING, Wallace. *Furniture Treasury.* New York, The Macmillan Company, 1954.

OGELSBY, Catherine. *French Provincial Decorative Art.* New York-London, Charles Scribners' Sons, 1951.

RIVIÈRE, Georges Henri. *Réflexions sur le mobilier rural traditionnel en France.* In *Art et Industrie,* III, Paris, April 1946, pp. 11-16.

RIVIÈRE, Georges Henri. *Le mobilier traditionnel en France.* Lectures given at the École du Louvre, Paris, 1943. (Manuscript.)

ROY, Antoine. *Le coût et le goût des meubles au Canada sous le régime français.* In le *Cahier des Dix.* Montréal, « Les Dix », 1953, vol. 18, pp. 228-239.

ROY, Antoine. *Les lettres, les sciences et les arts au Canada sous le régime français.* Paris, Jouve, 1930.

SAINT-THOMAS, Mère. *Les Ursulines de Québec, depuis leur établissement jusqu'à nos jours.* Québec [par Mère Saint-Thomas et l'abbé Georges Lemoyne],

Darveau, 1863-1866, 4 vol.

SCHWARZ, M. D., Herbert T. *La commode bombée de la Nouvelle-France.* In *Vie des Arts.* Montréal, nº 21, Noël, 1960, pp. 30-37.

SÉGUIN, Robert-Lionel. *L'équipement de la ferme canadienne aux XVIIᵉ et XVIIIᵉ siècles,* Montréal, Ducharme, 1959.

SPENDLOVE, F. St George. *The Furniture of French Canada.* In *The Connoisseur Year Book.* London, 1954, pp. 61-67.

SPENDLOVE, F. St George. *Collectors' Luck.* Toronto, Ryerson Press, 1960.

TARDIEU, Suzanne. *Meubles régionaux datés.* Paris, Éditions Vincent, Fréal, 1950.

TESSIER, Mgr Albert. *Les forges Saint-Maurice, 1729-1883.* Trois-Rivières, Éd. du Bien Public, 1952.

TRAQUAIR, Ramsay. *The Old Architecture of Quebec.* Toronto, Macmillan, 1947.

VAILLANCOURT, Émile. *Une maîtrise d'art en Canada, 1800-1823.* Montréal, G. Ducharme, 1920.

VAN RAVENSWAAY, Charles. *Creole Arts and Crafts of Upper Louisiana.* In *Missouri Historical Society Bulletin.* St. Louis, Missouri. April 1956. Vol. XII, nº 3, pp. 213-248.

VERLET, Pierre. *L'art du meuble à Paris au XVIIIᵉ siècle.* Paris, Presses Universitaires de France, 1958. (Coll. « Que sais-je? »)

VERLET, Pierre. *Les meubles français du XVIIIᵉ siècle.* I - Menuiserie, Paris, Presses Universitaires de France 1956. (Coll. « L'Œil du Connaisseur »).

VERLET, Pierre. *Les meubles français du XVIIIᵉ siècle.* II - Ebénisterie, Paris, Presses Universitaires de France, 1956. (Coll. « L'Œil du Connaisseur »).

WINCHESTER, Alice. *French Canadian Furniture.* In *Antiques,* New York, May 1944. Vol. XLV, nº 5, pp. 238-241.

WINCHESTER, Alice. *The Armoires of French Canada.* In *Antiques,* New York, June 1944. Vol. XLV, nº 6, pp. 302-305.

ABBREVIATIONS

A A M	*Archives de l'Archevêché de Montréal*	*Archives of the Archbishopric of Montreal.*
A H Q	*Annales de l'Hôtel-Dieu de Québec.*	*Records of the Hôtel-Dieu, Quebec.*
A H M	*Annales de l'Hôtel-Dieu de Montréal.*	*Records of the Hôtel-Dieu, Montreal.*
A H G Q	*Annales de l'Hôpital général de Québec.*	*Records of the Hôpital Général, Quebec.*
A J M	*Archives Judiciaires de Montréal.*	*Judicial Archives of Montreal.*
A J Q	*Archives Judiciaires de Québec.*	*Judicial Archives of Quebec.*
A N C	*Archives Nationales Colonies.*	*National Colonial Archives, France.*
A N D M	*Archives de Notre-Dame de Montréal.*	*Archives of Notre-Dame, Montreal.*
A P C	*Archives Publiques du Canada.*	*Public Archives of Canada.*
A P Q	*Archives de la Province de Québec.*	*Archives of the Province of Quebec.*
A S M	*Archives du Séminaire de Montréal.*	*Archives of the Seminary of Montreal.*
A S Q	*Archives du Séminaire de Québec.*	*Archives of the Seminary of Quebec.*
I O A	*Inventaire des Œuvres d'Art.*	*Inventory of Works of Art of the Province of Quebec.*
R A P Q	*Rapport de l'Archiviste de la Province de Québec.*	*Report of the Archivist of the Province of Quebec.*
B R H	*Bulletin des Recherches Historiques.*	*Bulletin of Historical Research.*

BRIEF LEXICON OF FRENCH CANADIAN TERMS

Armoire de coin : Corner cabinet.

Babiche (an Algonquin word) : Raw-hide leather thong of moose, caribou or deer skin, used for chair seats, snowshoes, etc.

Banc à seaux, banc à siaux : Bucket-bench.

Banc du quêteux : Settle-bed, also used as a spare bed for unexpected visitors (*quêteux*, beggars).

Banc-lit : Settle-bed. It resembles the Breton coffer-bench except that the seat and façade fold outwards to form a sleeping-box.

Bec de corbeau : Betty lamp (U.S.). Wrought-iron oil lamp, that is hooked to a beam.

Bède (from the English or the old French) : Settle-bed.

Ber : Provincial contraction of *berceau* : cradle.

Berce : Rocker or bend of a rocking chair or of a cradle.

Berceuse, berçante : Rocker, rocking chair.

Bœuf Illinois : American bison, buffalo.

Bottes canadiennes : High soft leather boots of the moccasin type, with boot straps but without a separate sole.

Boutonnue (bedspread) : Type of tufted bedspread.

Cabane : Early Canadian cupboard-bed (or closed bed) used by the early settlers.

Cabarouet : Small two-wheel cart with one seat.

Carriole (lit) : Sleigh bed (*Late Empire* style bed).

Catalogne : In the 17th and 18th centuries, a hand-woven woollen bedspread also called *couverte de Normandie*. In the 19th century, bed covers and carpets were woven with either strips of cotton rag or wool. .

Chanteau : Rocker (or bend) of a cradle or a rocking chair (colloquial French Canadian). Resembling in its form the curved sections of the top of a barrel.

Chevreux (chevreuil) : Deer.

Clair de nœuds : Smooth wood, free from knots.

Coin : Corner cabinet.

Coinçon : Corner cabinet (contraction of *écoinçon*).

Côte : Early name for a country road where farmers settled; the first Canadian roads followed the shores of the St Lawrence River. (Cf. *rang*.)

Couvert (couvercle) : Lid.

Couverte (couverture) : Bedcover, bedspread or blanket.

Créendieu : Epithet used in Charlevoix County to signify a God-fearing person.

Crocheté (tapis) : Hooked (rug).

Grand-père (horloge) : Grandfather clock (from the English).

Habitant : Name given to an early settler who remained on his land, as opposed to the *coureur de bois* who preferred the nomadic life of the Indians. It is still in use in French Canada in preference to *paysan*.

Lave-mains : Wash-stand.

Maskobina (an Indian word) : Rowan tree, mountain ash, bearing bitter red berries.

Pièce sur pièce : A type of construction in which rough-hewn logs are fitted one on top of the other.

Pigeonnier (from the English) : Pigeon holes of a desk.

Plaine : Red maple.

Plancher d'haut : The ceiling of the common room (also the floor of the attic).

Planches, sur les : A table made of planks resting on trestles, on which the dead are laid out.

Pointes de gâteaux : In a panel, triangles carved in the form of the cross of St Andrew.

Pruche : Canadian hemlock (tsuga canadensis).

Quenouille (lit de) : Mattress filled with the silks of bulrushes.

Rabat : Settle-bed.

Rang : From the English " range ". Country road lined by farmhouses on one or both sides.

Rassades : Small, vitreous coloured beads, at one time used in trading with the Indians.

Set de chambre : Suite of bedroom furniture.

Traîneau (lit) : Sleigh-bed (*Late Empire* style bed).

Vitrau : Glazed buffet, with one or two tiers.

GLOSSARY

Anse de panier : Semicircular arch of elliptical form.

Arbalète : Cross-bow, crossbow-shaped.

Bahut : A travelling coffer originally with a flat lid; by the end of the 16th century, with an arched or vaulted lid.

Baldaquin : A canopy over the head of the bed.

Baluster : A short upright column or post, slender at the top and bulging below.

Baroque : *a*) A style which appeared in Italy in the sixteenth century and which is a debased variation of the classical styles. *b*) Furniture carved or decorated over its entire surface. *c*) Curious, bizarre.

Bazin : A woven fabric with a warp of thread and a woof of cotton.

Bergère : A large armchair of the Louis XIV-Louis XV period, with upholstered armrests, sides, back and wings.

Cabling, cables : Continuous ornament in the form of twisted rope.

Caissons : Repeated small sunken panels decorated with mouldings.

Campane : In the form of a bell. The upturned *campane* is often found in the centre of the lower rail of commodes.

Caqueteuse : A high-backed armchair with a seat which is wide at the front but narrowing towards the back, used mostly in the sixteenth century.

Cartel : A small ornamental medallion or cartouche

decorated in the *rocaille* style and often executed in openwork.

Cartouche : A framed medallion often surrounded by an ornamentation in the form of a foliated scroll.

Chamfer : A cut bevelled into the square edges or the corners of an upright, a rail or a stretcher.

Chevrons : *a)* Pieces of wood assembled at an acute angle. *b)* Ornament often carved like parallel reeds and meeting at an acute angle.

Console : *a)* A curved projection, swelling at one end; a bracket. *b)* In most cases, a two-legged table attached to the wall.

Countercurve : A curved line, complementary to another curve.

Croisillon : The meeting or crossing of two pieces, found in cross-stretchers, panels, back rails of chairs.

Crosier : *a)* A foliated scroll terminating in the form of a crosier. *b)* An armrest terminating in spiral form.

Dentils : A succession of reliefs in the form of square teeth, separated by equal gaps.

Dents de loup (wolf's teeth) : A serrated edge resembling saw teeth but at a more gentle angle.

Entrelacs : A continuous ornament formed of interlacing curved motifs or interlocking circles.

Faux-palier normand : A Norman dresser without doors in the lower stage, but with open shelves for buckets and pots.

Festoon : Identical and regularly repeated motifs.

Finial : A turned ornament in the form of a flame or a conical spire dowelled in table stretchers and in friezes of the Renaissance-Henri IV-Louis XIII styles.

Fische (hinges) : A type of hinge peculiar to overlapping French armoire doors.

Fluting, fluted : Round grooves or channels, carved into a flat or curved surface.

Foliated scroll : Decoration of flowers and foliage which interlace and run into one another.

Four leaf (Gothic) : Ornament in the form of a *rosace* with four leaves or petals; the Gothic *quartefeuille*.

Fret : A continuous ornament composed of broken lines.

Frieze : *a)* The decoration in relief of an entablature. *b)* The upper rail of a table. *c)* A long and narrow *cartouche* on the upper rail of an armoire.

Gadroons : A series of convex curves resembling pods, joined together in a decorative pattern.

Galette : A concentrical moulding, in a disc pattern.

Garland : A decorative motif representing foliage, flowers or fruit wreathed or entwined with ribbons.

Gouge work : Carving consisting of grooves or an ensemble of grooves.

Grecian scroll : An ornament in the form of the crests of waves.

Groove : A small rounded channel carved into a flat or rounded surface.

Guillochis, guilloché : Ground ornamentation carved in short straight lines or curves which cross one another in a repetitive design.

Linen fold : An ornament of medieval origin, representing a fold of a scroll or of linen.

Mascaron : A carving in the form of a human or stylized

mask, found particularly on the corners of console tables.

Muller (molette) : A small wheel in the form of a grindstone carved with geometric designs, e.g., spokes, sun-rays, incurved rays.

Ormolu : Brass treated to give the appearance of gold.

Os de mouton : An early Louis XIV armchair, with curved uprights and stretchers resembling the shape of sheep's bones.

Ovolo : A continuous ornament in relief in an egg-shaped pattern.

Palmette : Decorative motif, composed of elongated petals or fan-shaped leaves.

Pastille : A continuous decoration in relief in the form of small discs.

Pediment : The arched or triangular upper part of an armoire. A *broken pediment* is in two parts.

Pied de biche : A curved leg ending in a sabot.

Pied de lyre : A pedestal of a table or of a bench, in the form of the base of the instrument.

Pilaster : Decorative part of a façade in the form of a flattened column, or reproducing a column.

Rais de cœur : A repetitive decoration in the form of a heart with branching water leaves and florets.

Reeding : *a)* Cylindrical rods imposed or carved in the grooves of a pilaster or a column. *b)* A decoration of reed-like strips parallel to one another.

Rocaille : An asymmetrical decoration inspired by shells, rocks and plants.

Rococo : *a)* The term generally used in Germany, Austria and Italy to designate *rocaille*. *b)* A pejorative term to describe an exaggeration of *rocaille*. *c)* An object in a ridiculously affected form.

Rococo, Canadian : Term created by Mr Ramsay Traquair in his work, *The Old Architecture of Quebec*, to describe the heavy and overladen *rocaille* of certain Canadian carvers.

Sabot : The foot of a piece of furniture in the shape of a hoof.

Saucisson (sausage) : A cylindrical turning, narrowing at intervals like a string of sausages.

Saw teeth (dents de scie) : A continuous line of projections resembling the teeth of a saw.

Scratch carving : A design engraved on the surface of the wood with a burin.

Scroll : *a)* An ornament resembling a partly unrolled parchment. *b)* A border carved in spiral form.

Sinusoidal : Flowing in a wave-like course; combining opposing curves.

Spiral : A geometric curve with a regularly increasing or decreasing radius.

Stile : An upright in the framework of an armoire, a commode etc., into which the rails are tenoned.

Templet : A paper, cardboard or wooden pattern used as a guide, in certain curved or complicated forms of furniture, for cutting into solid wood.

Tombeau, en (bed) : Eighteenth-century bed with curtains hanging obliquely from the canopy to the foot.

Traite Picarde : A low buffet with three to six doors which was used for storing milk in pails and bowls.

Volute : Curve in the form of a spiral or a crosier.

INDEX

The numbers in Roman characters refer to the pages of the text. The numbers in heavy type relate both to the illustrations and to the Catalogue Raisonné.

410

411